PILLAR
OF SMOKE
AND FIRE

The Legendary True History and Remarkable
Victories of the IDF Artillery Corps

ARIE MIZRACHI

Production by eBookPro Publishing
www.ebook-pro.com

PILLARS OF SMOKE AND FIRE
Arie Mizrachi

Copyright © 2024 Arie Mizrachi

All rights reserved; no parts of this book may be reproduced or transmitted in any form or by any means, electronic or mechanical, including photocopying, recording, taping, or by any information retrieval system, without the permission, in writing, of the author.

Translation from Hebrew: Rechavia Berman
Editing: Evan Gordon

Contact: arie@armaz.co.il
ISBN 9798333707161

To my beloved wife of 57 years, Tamar, nee Zack, who has accompanied me with love and devotion, and the family we have built together – Sagi, Yaron, Ori, and Tom, and our 14 grandchildren, who constitute an ingathering of the diaspora and bring us great joy.

And to my other family, the Artillery Corps family, of which I'm proud to be part, and to which I gave my best years, with all my heart and soul, to this very day.

Throughout the years, in all my roles, as well as in the writing of this book, the fallen warriors of the Artillery Corps have been foremost on my mind. The warm ties with the bereaved families intensified with the falling of 23 fighters of the 405th Battalion in the Yom Kippur War. This book is a monument to the memory of the fallen and an embrace of their families, so dear to my heart.

CONTENTS

A Mandatory Lesson for All Those Engaged
in the Work of National Defense 13

An Autobiography Which Is the Story of a Corps 17

PREFACE 21

FOREWORD 22

ALWAYS A GUNNER 57
    Warrior 58

Kicked Out 60
    Bahad 1, Take 2 61
    "Arie, Get Up!" 62
    In Memory of the Fallen Tamarisk 64
    Cool Cannons on Fire 65

The 402nd 67
    A Clerk Named Tamar 67
    Who Got Sent to the Artillery Corps Back Then 68
    A Major's Good Enough for Them 69
    Gunning and Geography 70
    400 Shots, 2 Hits (in Jordan, to Boot) 72
    A Double Lesson from Yanush 73

The 404th 76
    No Dropouts 76
    Armored Company Commanders' Course 77
    Bahad 1, Take 3 – or "You'll Get Captain" 79
    Pa'il's Special Methods 81
    Who Moved My Searchlight? 83
    Baptism by Fire at Samua 86

FIRST WAR **89**
   Who Are We? *90*
   The Explosive Truck That Killed Carlo *91*
   A Captain in the Desert – Is a Tiger *93*
   Student *95*

REALITY AND VISION **97**
   Repeating a Grade *97*
   Skipping a Grade *98*
   The Egyptian Battery I Didn't Take Out *99*
   Choco Launches *101*
   Operation Drowning Wedge *102*
   Mountain and Mountain Meet *106*
   "Back Bucket" and "Front Bucket" *107*
   The Intercepted Stratocruiser – and the Reprimand I Didn't Deserve ... *110*
   Artillery Corps' Sports Day *112*
   Don't Compromise on Assignments *114*
   A Moment Before Insubordination *115*
   Who Was Yaakov Aknin? *116*
   Love in the Desert *117*
   Bloat and Rot *119*

A Wretched Servant 123
   Gorodish as a Poor Example *128*
   "Follow the Hat" *130*
   Shhhh, the Brigadier's Coming Out *131*

A Missed Opportunity Named Bendigo 134
   Pride in the Sky *134*
   The Artillery That Straightened the Airplane's Wing *136*
   "We Were Attacked by a Concentrated Artillery Fire Strike" ... *140*

The Goal – Command of a Standing Battalion 143
   Establishing a Battalion, Meanwhile *143*
   The Parade Marched On *145*

Lesson Delivered, Courtesy of the Freeloaders.. *148*
"This Is a Corps We Didn't Even Dare Dream Of"................................... *150*

THE YOM KIPPUR WAR **153**

Take the 405th, but... 153
    A Tale of Four Models *155*
    "The 405th Battalion Won't Be Disbanded, There'll Be a War" *158*
    A Gift in the Guise of Revoked Leave *159*
    "Tomorrow Morning Your Battalion Is Deployed in the Golan Heights".....*161*
    With All Due Respect to the Chief Ordnance Officer............................. *162*
    Needless Risk.. *163*
    "You Need an APC for the Command Post" *164*
    The Sky Rains Fire *166*
    We Didn't Grab Dinner in Tiberias *168*

A Non-Digital Commander... 170
    "I Won't Forget Your Calm Voice in the Valley of Tears Battles"........... *170*
    Here, I'm fulfilling My Destiny *173*
    "Prepare 'Danger Fire Missions'" *174*
    On Blindness... *175*
    They Shall Not Pass *177*
    "Thorns" and Thistles *179*
    Gunners on Me!..*180*
    The 7th Brigade, Down to 17 Tanks *182*
    Syrian Armor and Commandos Swoop Down on the Remnants of the 7th... *183*
    Pale Smoke *185*
    How the Name "Valley of Tears" Was Born *188*
    "You're Heroes".. *189*

THE 405TH BATTALION BREAKS THROUGH INTO SYRIA **193**
    Rolling Barrage *194*
    Shrapnel in the Machine Gun Butt... *196*
    "You're Not Arbel 32" *198*
    In memory of Avraham Snir... *199*

The Gunners Take Tel Shams 201
   "Arie, Save Yossi" 201
   "The Artillery Fire Is for the Maneuvering Forces" 203
   Adir Stern Is Left to Die 206
   "The Gunners Did the Job for Us" 207
   Damascus in Our Sights 207
   A Moving Reunion 210

The 405th Battalion – The Valor and the Loss 211
   "Looking at Each Other, Knowing We'll Stay and Fire" 215
   The Battle for Ma'aleh Gamla 220
   Avi Dietschi, Yoel Porat, and Herzl Cohen – Heroes Deserving of Decoration 222

THE ARTILLERY CORPS BEGINS TO TAKE OFF 227
   "The Coats Did All the Work" 228
   "Deployment by Terrain" 231
   "Banishment from Heaven" 232
   Winter on the Golan Heights 234
   "Arie, Where Are You Going?" 236
   From Yanush to Ori Or 237
   Ceasefire – and an End 239
   "We'll Hang It" 241

SHIVTA – CAPITAL OF THE ARTILLERY CORPS 243
   Commanding the Basic Course in Venice 243
   A Live Fire Exercise With... Fire 245
   Fire Discipline Through a Linguistics Lab 248
   What Can Be Learned From the Cavalry's Indian Wars 249
   How I Didn't Get the 282nd Division Artillery 250
   Saving Captain Zuta 251
   On Thin Ice With the Disappointed 253
   A KGB Spy Driving the SPH 254
   "Team Yoel" 255
   Forming a staff 257
   The Crime ("Throw Them Out,") and Punishment (a Hearing With Raful) 259

- *Get 90 or Over, Get a "Regular"* *260*
- *Protecting the Career Military Families* *262*
- *Stopping the Runs* *262*
- *A Test of Leadership* *264*

Bahad-to-Imagination Missile 265

- *"The Adler Effect" Proves Ineffective* *266*
- *An Israeli Doesn't Count as a Jew* *268*
- *Pass the test, Go Home* *269*
- *Shorter is Better* *270*
- *Thanks to the Coffee Anat Spilled* *271*
- *The Twice-Opened Window* *274*
- *Burning IDF Gear* *276*
- *Alone in the Desert* *276*
- *Mayor of Shivta* *277*

Fort Sill – Far More Than an Artillery Course 279

- *What Makes a Housing Complex "Clean"* *279*
- *An Israeli is Not a Jew (Take 2)* *280*
- *Mission: Fundraising* *281*
- *How to Talk an American Traffic Cop Out of Writing You a Ticket* *282*
- *The Family* *283*
- *God Bless America* *284*

SOUTHERN LEBANON IN FLAMES 287

- *"Write It Down, Write It Down"* *288*
- *The Pamphlet Shell* *289*
- *Sometimes You Need Smoke and Mirrors* *290*
- *Yoram Hamizrachi Fans the Flames* *291*
- *Who Destroyed My House?* *292*
- *The Nahariya Cannon* *293*
- *A French-Style Encounter* *294*
- *"Your Slip Is Showing"* *295*
- *FOs as Rangers* *296*
- *The Kukri Knife – and the Sleeping Soldier* *297*

  Sometimes You Need to Dismiss 298
  The Dark Side of "Commander Independence" 299
  Yanush Is Reprimanded for Arms Trading With the Enemy 300
Light Ripples 302
  Taming of the Shrew 302
  "Empty Guns, Huh?!" 303
  We Don't Do Dry Runs 304
  How I didn't Command an Armored Brigade 305
  Chief of Staff Interview 306

CAO IN THE PEACE FOR GALILEE WAR 309
  Telling Yanka'le That Eyal Has Been killed 309
  South Lebanon on Fire 310
  How the "CAO's Target" Went Down in History 312
  "We'll Go In, Lay Down 400, and Come Back" 314
  Haviv Ya Habib 315
  Finding a Coordinate Without a Ruler 316
  Throw Aside Whoever's in the Way. Rush Ahead! 320
  How the Haviv Battalion Was Not Destroyed by Friendly Fire 321
  "You Sent Us to Die" 324
  You're in the Little Mitleh 325
  Salvation Will Come From Neither the Air Nor the Infantry 327
  A Tremendous "Fire Box" Saves the Surrounded Battalion
  at Sultan Yacoub 329

The Art of Posting, Signing, and Growing 333
  How Ofer Nimrodi Didn't Jump From the Balcony 336
  The Boat Method 338
  Nurturing Officers 339
  Promoting Youngsters 341
  That Was Then, This Is Now 343

Four Stories From Lebanon on the Eve of the War 345
  Beirut, Hometown of the Shkuri
  (nee Mizrachi) Family 345

- *Dinner with Bashir* 348
- *"Black Cluster, White Cluster"* 349
- *War Games* 349

A VICTORY, NOT A FAILURE 353
- *"Muster the Entire Corps on Silent Call-Up"* 353
- *Final Field Test* 355
- *Arik Speaks for the Record* 356
- *Nino Levi Is Surprised* 357
- *Me and My "Saifan"* 358
- *Lifting the 411th Battalion* 361
- *Saving the 939th Brigade* 363
- *Genius and Shuach Cross the Uncleared City of Sidon* 365

Thanks to Direct Fire 366
- *"I Shall Insist on Including Gunners in the Front Line"* 368
- *Three Little Tales of Direct Fire* 369
- *Dangot's Battery Cracks a Brigade HQ* 372
- *Ofer Mashraki RIP* 374
- *Pride and Prejudice* 375
- *Shells (Don't) Collide in Mid-Air* 377
- *"Stepping Out for a Sandwich? Toss Twenty Rockets"* 379
- *An FO in a Submarine, an FSO on a Missile Boat, and SPHs in the Hull of a Ship* 380

Soul-Searching 382
- *The Twenty-Minute Window* 383
- *Cluster Bombs at Ein Hilweh* 384
- *How Sharon Was Persuaded Not to Take Beirut With Ground Forces* . 385
- *"Give Me Beirut for Three Days"* 387

The Fire Storm 389
- *"See-Fire"* 390
- *Thanks to Personal Contacts and Barters* 391
- *"We Were Surprised and the Enemy Was Surprised"* 392

    "Non-Combatants" *397*

    What Brought Arafat to His Knees.. *398*

    "Fly in the Phantom
    and Let's See You Identify Targets" *399*

    Caposta Sr. and Caposta Jr. *400*

    What Now?..*401*

Sabra and Shatila: The Disgrace and the Bandwagon 403

Always Speak Your Mind.. 407

Entering Beirut: Thunder Suddenly Rolling From All Directions.......... 408

Ruminations on the Peace For Galilee War 411

    The First Great Fire Concentration – in the Last Great War................... *411*

    How, Who, and Why the Success Turned to Failure............................... *411*

    A Year Off for Reservists... *413*

    How to Prepare for the Next War *414*

GLOSSARY *421*

THANKS... *429*

A MANDATORY LESSON FOR ALL THOSE ENGAGED IN THE WORK OF NATIONAL DEFENSE

Foreword by Lt. Gen. (Ret.) Moshe "Bogie" Yaalon

The first time I came across the slogan "Artillery is the queen of the battlefield" was in Operation Peace for Galilee. I was a major then, deputy commander of Sayeret Matkal, and in command of a force tasked with opening the Wadi Shabaa, the easternmost route in our forces' sector of operations. The route passes at the foot of Mt. Hermon, and was the shortest route to the Beirut-Damascus road. But the route was impassable for regular vehicles or even armored fighting vehicles, and had to be rendered usable by heavy machinery, and the northern end of it was dotted with Syrian commando outposts.

South of these outposts was a desolate, wooded hill, hence the name of this battle: "The Woody Battle." To ensure that the hill wouldn't be taken by the Syrians, a squad from the unit under the command of Ilan was deployed covertly, under the cover of night.

The armored force with the heavy machinery was busy making the route traversable, when at noon Ilan announced on the radio that he had identified Syrian trucks approaching from the north and unloading about a company of commando fighters, who were climbing the hill toward him, in order to capture it.

I organized a force of several squads under my command, and we ran forward to reinforce Ilan. We reached him from the south, after he had already opened fire at the approaching Syrian commandos. We took up positions along the line of his squad, and the Syrian force became sitting ducks for the remainder of the battle, as we had captured the high ground.

I spotted a Syrian tank and two BMP armored personnel carriers moving toward the "Woody" for the north to join the battle. We had

"Dragon" anti-tank missiles with a maximal range of 1,000 meters. The tank and APCs tried to locate us without success, and stopped 1,200 meters away. It was obvious to me that we had to destroy them, but to do so, we had to move the "Dragon" teams to the effective range and therefore to the front slope. This would have exposed them to the Syrian force, and the tank could have hit us once we were revealed.

The FSO, who had been with us since the preparations for the operation, suggested employing artillery with a new type of ammunition, never before used operationally: A cluster shell that releases dozens of armor-piercing bomblets. The ability of these bomblets to pierce the tank's armor stemmed from the fact that these vehicles are well protected from all sides, but not from above.

The precise artillery fire decided the battle. Both APCs were hit and destroyed, and the tank fled. The Syrian commando company was destroyed, with no casualties on our side.

Brig-Gen. (ret) Arie Mizrachi's book describes the development of the Artillery Corps from a wretched servant to the queen of the battlefield, in a personal look back. Beyond the credible first-hand testimony and beyond the fascinating stories, the book teaches us about the past in order to better prepare for the future.

Brig. Gen. Mizrachi, who fought in the Six-Day War, the War of Attrition, the Yom Kippur War, served as the Northern Command's artillery commander when I commanded Sayeret Tzanhanim (the Paratroopers Brigade's Rangers unit), which carried out many operations in Lebanon that were greatly aided by him, and reached the pinnacle of his career as Chief Artillery Officer, preparing and leading the corps in the Peace for Galilee War.

The description of the corps' development, written with a critical eye, includes a detailed chapter about its neglect following the Six-Dar War, out of the assumption that the Air Force would provide close support for the ground troops. This assumption was debunked in the Yom Kippur War, leading to a significant development of the corps, into a powerful Artillery Corps, with impressive capabilities to provide close support to the troops.

In a historical view, the technological development in the world led the generals, preparing for the next war, to face an embarrassment of riches: Which technologies of the plethora on offer, to select in order to develop and integrate into their armies. This is an unprecedented phenomenon in the history of the battlefield, which had been dominated for thousands of years by the same armaments: First the spear, then joined by the sword and shield, until the industrial revolution brought about a quantum leap.

In the age of information and artificial intelligence, it is hard for generals to comprehend the capabilities that technology offers them. Advanced intelligence capabilities allow us today to locate tiny targets, such as a single terrorist on the move, in real time, and to hit it with munitions precise to a radius of a few centimeters, using efficient command and control systems.

The challenge for the commanders is to locate the suitable technologies, invest in their development and turn them into efficient warfare systems; and to integrate them into the army while changing the operational, structural, and organizational perceptions to which we had become accustomed over many years.

In the Peace for Galilee War, the gunners participated in the battle in a manner we had never known, and not only in the "Woody Battle." During the taking of Beirut, I commanded a Sayeret Matkal force, the point position of which consisted of a tank, a Vulcan air defense cannon, and a 155mm SPH. The barrel elevation system of the tank precluded it from firing at the top floors of the tall buildings, from which fire rained down on us. In order to allow us to move from building to building and clear them, the Vulcan would fire at the terrorists on the top floors, and the SPH would drop at least part of the structure by direct fire.

The challenge of detaching from the old and the familiar, and preparing for the next war, requires us to overcome the well-known obstacle of "preparing for the last war." Even today, the Artillery Corps is in a process of development, which is forced by changes in the nature of the threats, fighting against well-armed terror militias, combat in dense urban environments, and of course – amazing technological developments.

The corps has succeeded in adopting technologies, developing and acquiring precision fire means at ever-longer ranges, and utilizing drones – but not relinquishing the statistical, less accurate fire. As one who has experienced the Egyptian statistical artillery fire in the War of Attrition and the Yom Kippur War – it still has a role in the suppression and destruction of the enemy's force.

The development of the Artillery Corps and its effective integration into the Peace for Galilee War shall forever be credited to Brig. Gen. (ret.) Arie Mizrachi, who commanded and oversaw the corps as CAO, leading it from 1980 until after the end of the operation.

His personal story, and particularly his lessons learned in command, as related in the book, are a mandatory lesson for anyone engaged in the work of national defense and in the act of warfare, today and in the future.

Lt. Gen. (ret.) Moshe "Bogie" Yaalon commanded the Sayeret Matkal and Sayeret Tzanhanim commando units, served as GOC Central Command, chief of the Military Intelligence Directorate, the IDF's 17th Chief of General Staff, and as Defense Minister.

AN AUTOBIOGRAPHY WHICH IS THE STORY OF A CORPS

Foreword by Brig. Gen. (res.) Yaakov Zigdon

The Artillery Corps made an acrobatic leap between the end of the Yom Kippur War and the Peace for Galilee War. From 72 modern self-propelled cannons in 1973, it entered the PFG with over 600 such barrels.

Furthermore, beyond the increase in the troop count, the corps entered the war in June of 1982 with a powerful organization, which supported the cannons' exhaustion of fire. It had become an organized, well-practiced, and skilled organization, with division artilleries, comms systems, target acquisition systems, detection and ranging radars, suitable combat techniques, firing computers, and more. And all this happened in under nine years.

The Artillery Corps, which had slogged in the back since the establishment of the state, mostly dragged along, even when provided with self-propelled cannons, now moved to the forefront and became a dominant factor on the battlefield. No commander with the least bit of sense was willing to move toward their mission without artillery support anymore. From a "wretched servant," forced to content itself with scraps, leftovers, and improvisations, artillery became the "queen of the battlefield," without which it is almost impossible to win while keeping the blood toll to an acceptable level.

This book by Arie Mizrachi, Chief Artillery Officer during the PFG War and two and a half years prior, weaves his personal story with a full and detailed account of this leap. The book, perceived at first as autobiographical, surprisingly ends with the conclusion of his term as the corps commander, as though to say, with uncharacteristic modesty: "The story is not mine, but that of the Artillery Corps."

The status of the servant, who received diamond-like beads and thanked her master for them with a lowered gaze, was bestowed upon the Artillery Corps deliberately by the architects of the IDF's force construction, who arrogantly and ignorantly consecrated the tank as the only decisive factor on the battlefield – and the airplane as "flying artillery." This near-exclusive reliance upon these two components led to the disastrous result. The horrific blood toll of the Yom Kippur War brought the decision-makers to their senses twice – Firstly, when they realized the abilities of ground fire, after it was revealed that over one-third of our casualties in the war were caused by Egyptian and Syrian artillery; and the second time, when our forces found it difficult to both charge and defend without preparatory, accompanying, and cover fire. This sobering realization was detected in real-time by the CAO during the Yom Kippur War, Nati Sharoni, who planned and passed a requisition package of hundreds of modern, self-propelled, traversable cannons, with reasonable protection. As a consummate professional, Sharoni wasn't content with the cannons alone, and demanded all the cutting-edge, complementary military equipment enabling the full exploitation of the modern guns.

Sharoni was succeeded by Avraham Bar David, who toiled with infinite diligence and established a magnificent artillery corps. Arie Mizrachi took over from him, and the change bore fruit in the ultimate test of the Peace for Galilee War.

The Artillery Corps entered the Yom Kippur War with 30 battalions, most of them outdated and mismatched. It entered the PFG with over 80 battalions, most of them outfitted with the pride of American industry. And yet building the fighting force, powerful as it may be, is not enough. Mizrachi studied, taught, and developed methods for employing the force with the same daring, initiative, defiance, and operational audacity he inherited from his father, a member of the Watchmen's Union. And so, the offshoots that bloomed in the killing fields of the Valley of Tears in 1973 gave fruit at Sultan Yacoub and the gates of Beirut in 1982.

Schematic force employment, "by the book," does not suffice in complex situations. Such times call for proactive, original, daring, and convention-defying combat leadership. It was unfortunate for the

Syrian 7th Division, which tried to break through the Valley of Tears, that Mizrachi had taken up position on Tel Hermonit as the artillery commander of the containing 7th Brigade. It was fortunate for the IDF's tank battalion, which stumbled into a Syrian compound at Sultan Yacoub nine years later, that Mizrachi set up at Kafr Mishki, as the acting artillery commander of the 446th Corps.

In 1973, despite the Artillery Corps' inherent inferiority, Mizrachi found a way to concentrate a mass of fire to stymie the endless waves of Syrian assaults in the northern Golan Heights. He gathered 21 batteries under his command, almost twice the firepower the Northern Command had had at the war's start. He deployed the fire through his officers throughout the three days of containment, indefatigably, with no preapproval and with offensive initiative. He read the battle well, exploited every opportunity, and exploited the fire capabilities until the Syrian deluge was stopped.

In 1982, when the 362nd armored battalion got trapped at Sultan Yacoub, Mizrachi helped extract it with overwhelming artillery fire, exceeding conventions and fighting doctrines. He broke the traditional chain of command, and at his order: "CAO's target!" – an order not written in any professional scripture, an unprecedented artillery array, including hundreds of cannons and rocket launchers, was deployed from the slopes of Mt. Hermon to the shores of the Mediterranean. Like an orchestra, they furiously spat out thousands of shells and rockets, helping to extract the armored battalion. Thousands of battered and weary gunners, after a week, were filled at once with an electrifying surge of energy and responded as one to the battle cry: "CAO's target!"

It was the supreme test of the artillery system that had been built up since the Yom Kippur War. The Artillery Corps rewarded the great faith placed in it by the IDF with its immense outlay. A corps placing itself front and center, no longer meek of spirit, but proactive at all times and all places, and ready for action long before called upon.

To wit: From a wretched servant to the queen of the battlefield.

Brig. Gen. Yaakov Zigdon planned the extraction of the tank battalion at Sultan Yacoub in the Peace for Galilee War, was a division artillery commander, artillery commander of the Northern Command in Operation Din v'Heshbon, and commander of the IDF's command and staff academy. Author of various studies, and the books "Studies in the Theory of Force Design," and "Totchanin BeShele"g – Sipur Milchama" ("Gunners in the PFG – A War Story," co-authored with Siman Tov Sagi.) Serves as Editor in Chief of "Tamid Totchan."

PREFACE

I chose to write this book myself so that I might, through the milestones of my life, my personal experiences, and my subjective viewpoints, draw a story much greater than myself – the story of the dramatic makeover, whereby the Artillery Corps turned from a wretched servant to the queen of the battlefield.

This is also the reason that the book ends upon the conclusion of my term as Chief Artillery Officer in August of 1983, and my discharge from the IDF. It happened a month before I turned 41, three years and eight months after I was appointed CAO, and 23 years after I had reported to the IDF's intake and induction base, signed off for my uniform, and became Private Arie Mizrachi, military I.D. number 454657.

I am a great believer in genetics and am of the opinion that our family – my wife Tamar, my four children: Sagi, Yaron, Ori, and Tom, our grandchildren, and myself – are living examples of the new "Homo Israelicus," which is a product of the mixture of countries of origin from all over the globe. Our family includes Poles, Ukrainians, Algerians, Yemenites, Georgians, Turks, Russians, Lebanese, and German Jews. All mixed up beyond separation, creating the new Israeli Jew.

The genes we passed on to our children, and the more so, the genes left by our children to our fourteen grandchildren, created an ingathering of the diaspora, contrary to the claims of naysayers and dividers, who act due to political motives, aiming to sow divisions.

I am an optimist, and I have full faith in the State of Israel, the nation state of the Jewish people, formed in my early childhood. It numbered 600,000 Jews back then, and is now twelvefold larger, numbering over seven million of our people.

FOREWORD

From a wretched servant to the queen of the battlefield: The story of the Artillery Corps through the course of my life

The phenomenon of transformation undergone by the status of the IDF's Artillery Corps – from wretched servant to queen of the battlefield – can perhaps be described by terms from the field of organizational sociology, or through the example of Lee Iacocca, who revived the fallen auto manufacturer Chrysler, returning it to success and a position of industry leadership.

There is no precedent or parallel for a case in which a negligible corps, whose leaders for years viewed its apex in terms of technical professionalism and medieval-style hairsplitting, who debated the number of angels that could stand on the head of a pin, became a leading corps.

I have no contempt for professionalism, which was and is an inseparable part of the whole, but it is not the main thing. The incessant delving into meteorology data, the shell's weight, the quality of the propellant, and the precision on the artillery board are indeed most important, and are the foundation of professionalism. However, they have no impact on the battlefield if the barrels are worn out, to the point where their diameter is 159mm rather than 155, so that the shells don't fly to where the launcher intended, or if outdated cannons are mounted on antiquated chassis, which get stuck all the time, or if the fire rate is horribly slow.

Anyone with eyes to see could tell that the Artillery Corps' main problem was defining its core mission. To me, our core mission was clear and unequivocal: To kill the enemy and destroy its weapons and headquarters with each shell or bomb fired, in order to create a situation in which the IDF's maneuvering forces can execute their missions without losses.

The maneuvering forces in the past had very limited trust in the corps' abilities, and the saying "No waiting for the artillery," was carried on all lips. Few were the commanders who realized that the Artillery Corps can create a fist that could turn the tide of the battle. One of the few was Yaakov Aknin, commander of Arik Sharon's division artillery in the Six-Day War, who did so in the Battle of Umm-Qatef, when he created a rolling barrage of fire before the charging forces.

Such commanders were the subject of mockery and whispers back then, but these few, who understood before more senior and celebrated commanders what the role of fire in the battlefield truly is, are the ones whose influence ultimately prevailed. This only happened after the Yom Kippur War, when almost at once the corps became well-equipped and turned into a fighting, proactive, and courageous corps.

Those few came mostly from what was known in the corps as "the front echelon": FOs, FSOs, artillery brigade commanders, division artillery commanders; and the more that curiosity and integration into the maneuvering forces grew, so grew the understanding and realization of the corps' true role. Then, of course, we began wondering how to truly do it – and how to do it in the best manner.

Israel's security brass, at the time the transformation began, included Chief of Staff Motta Gur and Defense Minister Shimon Peres, with Prime Minister Yitzhak Rabin above him, and commanding the Artillery Corps, one of the most important figures to ever rise through its ranks, was Nati Sharoni. They made the most of a golden opportunity to radically change the IDF, and to renounce the dogmas bequeathed – on the one hand by Israel "Talik" Tal ("The tank is everything,") and on the other, by the Air Force commanders through the years, who believed and convinced others that the airplane is the king of kings on the battlefield, only to sorely disappoint in October 1973.

Sharoni, who was supremely prepared for this moment, knew the United States well and spoke fluent English, seized the opportunity and laid a massive, "doesn't hurt to ask" type of shopping bill on the desk of the decision-makers. To his great surprise, and the astonishment of the entire corps, it was approved down to the very last item.

What helped the phoenix rise from the ashes, beyond the amount and quality of purchased equipment, beyond the lessons of the war and the tremendous amounts of experience we acquired in the Yom Kippur War, was a significant reduction in the age of commanders, as well as reinforcing the corps with officers from all over the IDF. The new blood flowing included men from other fields, other life experiences, a global viewpoint, and the ability to locate weaknesses and propose new ideas.

Over the years from 1974 to January 1980, when I was appointed Chief Artillery Officer, I advanced from the rank of major to brigadier general, but that's negligible compared to the fact that the Artillery Corps soared from some 50 outdated battalions, of various types, only half of which took an active part in the Yom Kippur War – and even those were missing equipment, with no advanced auxiliary systems – to a corps numbering 87 battalions, mostly state of the art, equipped with firing computers, radars, laser range finders, sophisticated and airborne observation systems, monstrous artillery rockets, and cutting-edge cluster munitions, many times more lethal than conventional ordnance.

The upgraded equipment and personnel put into the Shivta grinder – a dilapidated Nahal camp, which was later used by the Armored Corps officers' course, and to which Bahad 9, the main Artillery Corps' training base, was moved from Tzrifin. Battalions were built, artillery divisions were created, and a new, updated Artillery Corps fighting doctrine was written. The goal before us was clear and sharply defined: To constitute the IDF's main firepower, to be able to tell the maneuverers: Don't bang your heads against the wall – we'll break the wall before you reach it. The corps was built and grew strong, and was immensely motivated to prove the incredible investment was justified. We succeeded in providing that proof in the Peace for Galilee War, where the Artillery earned its place on the IDF wall of fame. From that moment, everything ran more smoothly, as the maneuvering forces became division commanders and even

IDF Chiefs of Staff. Each of them had excellent personal experience with the Artillery Corps, and so consequently, the precision-guided munitions systems, and many other systems that are still secret, naturally arrived at the Artillery Corps. In my opinion, our Artillery Corps is the best and most advanced artillery corps in the world. Or in other words: From a wretched servant to queen of the battlefield.

I included a glossary at the end of the book, for readers unfamiliar with artillery terms.

Childhood Memories

September 11th

I was born on Rosh Hashanah Eve in the year 5703, by the Jewish reckoning. The Gregorian date was September 11th, 1942. The main headline of "Davar," the newspaper that would accompany my childhood, was "Incessant Stream of Russian Reinforcements to the Stalingrad Area." The sub-headline announced: "93 German divisions shattered and incapacitated." Another item informed that "Desire for Urgent Offensive Dominates America," but the invasion of Normandy was almost two years away.

That same front page featured the greetings of the "administration of the national council of the Knesset of Israel in the Land of Israel" for Rosh Hashanah:

> Brothers and sisters, wherever you may be, in the lands of liberty and in the depths of bondage, Jewish soldiers, men and women, giving their souls courageously and fighting for the freedom of their people and their homeland, receive a true greeting from the Knesset of Israel in the Land of Israel as we approach the new year: 5703 since the creation.

This year, as well, Hitler has raised his foul hand against the burnt embers of the Jews to annihilate and exterminate them, and has failed. The enslaved diasporic Jewry is fighting for its spiritual liberty and national independence, in sanctification of Hashem and the Nation. [...]

The Jewry of the Land of Israel is standing like a solid granite rock on its duty: twenty-six thousand of its finest sons and daughters have thus far pioneered to the fire front, to fight our sworn enemies. To defend the homeland, our country, the Land of Israel. It continues to recruit its finest sons and daughters to the fight against evil, alongside the Allies, until victory comes [...] May this resilient stand of the Jewish population serve as a source of encouragement and hope for the new year, from which you may draw strength to suffer, to fight, and to keep faith [...] in the fulfillment of the calling of the prophets and the vision of Israel for a world of justice, honesty, and peace among nations.

Be strong, brethren, and courageous, and let us live together to see the passing of evil government from the earth, and the flag of liberated Zion shall wave in splendor.

If there is a connection between the day I came into the world and the course of my life, then perhaps it is no coincidence that on my 59th birthday, many in the Western world were disillusioned as they watched the Twin Towers crumbling in New York, realizing what we here learned many years before them, and grasped that there is no choice but to fight for liberty against evil.

The Watchman's[1] Son

The website "Tamid Totchan" ("Always a Gunner"(states that I was born in Kfar Saba. Wikipedia says I was born in Kibbutz Na'an. They're both wrong. The truth is that I was born in the watchman's house, on a high hill in the middle of a giant citrus orchard known as "Thousand Dunams" (a dunam is a unit of area equal to one-quarter of an acre (, near the Arab village of Na'ana, some of whose inhabitants were murderers. The house, which stands to this day, was some four miles from the closest Jewish settlement, Kibbutz Na'an. It was a wonderful place, full of exciting experiences for a little boy.

When I was eighteen months old, we moved to Kfar Saba, which was by then a large moshav ("colony" – see glossary for more on the distinction between settlement types in Israel). We lived in a small structure in "Shlaski Court," which was a square of small, rented apartments surrounding a yard. This, too, should have been a place full of excitement for a little boy, but it seems that life with many people and many children within a closed compound didn't agree with me. I had grown used to being the center of the universe, in limitless expanses, with two dogs, the bulldog, Amotz, and a Canaanite breed whose name escapes me, two Arab nannies, Aisha and Fatma, who came each day from Na'ana, and most of all, within a world of grown-ups, with everyone trying to win my attention, play with me, and make me happy.

---

1 Watchmen were the military elite of the embryonic, renewed Jewish presence in the Land of Israel. "The Watchman" ("HaShomer") association was founded in 1909, becoming the first armed Jewish organization in the country since late antiquity. The organization and its members continued to be influential in the Hebrew population in the following decades, forming the nucleus that founded the Haganah, the main Zionist paramilitary organization under the British Mandate, which upon the foundation of the State of Israel became the IDF. Watchmen were dashing, romantic figures, etched in the popular imagination as mounted on horseback and sporting traditional native garb.

Me as a child, riding a horse in "Thousand Dunams."

The house in "Thousand Dunams" today.

My Parents

My mother, Bella, was born in a traditional Jewish home, one of ten children of Shmuel and Miriam Brik. She grew up in the Krementz district, then in Poland and now part of Ukraine, in the town of Pochaiv (Poczajów in Polish), which is named after a Pravoslav saint, and is centered around a giant monastery, likewise bearing that luminary's name.

Like most Jewish children her age, she received a Zionistic education, and was a member of a pioneering preparatory group, training to make Aliyah to the land of Israel. In 1933, at 23 years of age, she left her parents' house, made Aliyah, and became a pioneer. Her younger sister, Sarah, also made Aliyah with her help, toward the end of the 1930s, becoming one of the founders of Kibbutz Dafna. All other family members, along with the rest of the town's Jews, were led to the slaughter by their Ukrainian neighbors and murdered near the town, after it was captured by the Nazis.

They spoke infrequently of those lost there. On rare occasions, my mother would tell me about her parents, her sisters and brothers, her nephews, and especially Michael, her talented and most beloved brother. My mother refused to even consider a visit to her hometown, and the hatred toward the Ukrainians burned within her until her dying day.

My father, Mordechai, was born in Tiberias to Nathan Shkuri, the son of a wealthy Beirut family, and Batya Ashkenazi, who wound up in Beirut from her birthplace in Poland, becoming my grandfather's third wife. In 1914, when my father was seven, World War 1 broke out, and the family returned to Beirut. There my father learned Hebrew, and when he read the book, Fighters and Dreamers ("Lochamim v'Cholmim,"), his imagination was kindled. The book, written by Yaakov Yaari-Poleskin, describes the lives and deeds of 69 figures from the early days of the Zionist movement to resettle Jews in their ancestral land, from the Baron Rothschild, through the founders of Degania, the first kibbutz, to Trumpeldor, Jabotinsky, and Chaim Weitzmann; but those who captured his heart the most were the members of Hashomer ("The Watchman," the first paramilitary organization of the Zionist movement, established in 1909 to protect the first Zionist colonies from predation and theft by the neighboring Arab villagers.) When he found out that one of the family's neighbors in Beirut, a Jew originally from the Caucasian mountains, had fled to Lebanon after being a watchman in Israel and having killed an Arab in a scuffle, he was even more enthused. At the age of seventeen, he ran away from home, reached the country then known as Palestine, and made a living doing odd jobs. In April of 1928, he found himself in Rishon LeZion, and was offered a position of watchman in the vineyard – at first armed only with a club, with Arabs as the senior watchmen. Only after proving to the farmers that the Arab watchman was also the main thief, did the watchman's duties and weapons pass to my father and his friends.

In 1933, my father joined "Agudat Hashomrim" ("Union of Watchmen,") which was the successor of the original Hashomer, but believed in establishing new settlements alongside the guard duties. This was the elite unit of the times, with legendary watchmen such as Alexander Zaïd, Aryeh Abramson, and Mordechai Yigael. Some were killed in defense of the Hebrew population before the establishment of the state, and were buried – like my parents – in the watchmen's plots at Sheikh Abreik, near modern-day Kiryat Tiv'on.

Not far from my parents, rests Menachem Shmul, who replaced my father as the watchman of "Thousand Dunams" when we moved to Kfar Saba. Shmul was stabbed to death by an Arab from Na'ana, near the train station by the village. Decades later, it was his son Menachem, born ten days after his father's death and named after him, who flew the Lavie, Israel's fighter jet, as a test pilot for Israel's Aeronautics Industries, and one of the designers of the aircraft.

My father had been married to two women and was a father of four by the time he and my mother fell in love. She was a laborer in the orchard, and he a mounted watchman, with all the attendant mannerisms. Watchmen were romantic figures in those days, and their love affairs were grist for the rumor mill. But a love affair between Ashkenazim (Jews from Europe and Western countries) and Mizrahim (Jews from the greater Middle East) was rare, and when my father showed up with my mother to meet her sister, Sarah turned up her nose at the "Frenk" (the derogatory term for Mizrahi Jews) whose hand my mother was holding.

On the rabbi's advice, my father told each of his wives – the one who started a family with him in Haifa and the one who had a family with him in Tel Aviv – that he now had a third wife. Each of the two reacted with fury and demanded a divorce, and thus he was free to marry again.

Meanwhile, when there was no work in the orchards, my mother worked paving roads and doing any job offered to women. After they married, my mother was a full partner in a life of defense and labor. She kept a small homestead farm next to our home in Kfar Saba, with a small cowshed and chicken coop, rows of vegetables, and a few fruit trees, and carried the domestic burden.

To my mother's credit, I don't remember any conflict stemming from my father's previous marriages. I knew my four siblings – Nathan, who died quite young from a serious illness, Zippora, who passed away in 2021, and Yaffa and Ziona, long may they live – and had good relations with all four and their mothers. We are still involved in all of the extended family's festive occasions, as well as the sad and somber ones. I was particularly close to my sister Zippora, who suffered from anemia. I often donated blood to her, and raised further blood donations for her in times of crisis.

My mother raised me as an only child, and was strict about my education and how I was doing at school. However, I enjoyed a free life compared to my "Yekke" friends – this was the mildly derogatory term for Jews from Germany, known for their stiff adherence to timetables and elaborate social mannerisms – who were subject to strict discipline and forced to play the violin for two hours every afternoon, rather than climb trees.

My mother's ability to integrate into the Mizrahi culinary culture – so foreign to her own Eastern European heritage – was astonishing. Her work habits and persistence are an inspiration to me to this day, and her traits and views had much impact on my path in life.

My father, Mordechai, in a British Mandatory Police uniform ("Gaffir"), leading my mother, Bella.

My mother, at "Thousand Dunams."

Tamar

My wife, Tamar, was born in Kibbutz Ashdot Yaakov to Yaakov and Bunia Zack, who made Aliyah from the town of Szumsk in Poland and were among the founders of the kibbutz. Bonya and her sister, Michal, were brought to Mandatory Palestine in the 1930s by Meir Zektzer, also a founder of Ashdot Yaakov, who was their relative. Michal ended up joining Kibbutz Sdot Yam, while Bonya joined Ashdot Yaakov. They were also sole survivors of their family – their parents and siblings all perished in the Holocaust.

Yaakov made Aliyah following his childhood sweetheart Bonya, became one of the main load-bearers of the kibbutz, established a large metalsmithing shop, which employed many laborers from Tiberias, and he served as the kibbutz treasurer during the years of deprivation and food rationing. His entire family perished in the Holocaust, and he remained the last scion. As he and Bonya had three daughters, there is no one left to carry the name of the Zack family, and Tamar deeply regrets this.

The schism in the kibbutz movement in the 1950s – which, ludicrous as it may sound today, centered on the issue of support for the Soviet Union and its "glorious leader," Joseph Stalin – also tore Ashdot Yaakov apart. Tamar and her parents belonged to the faction that remained on the original site, and became known as Ashdot Yaakov Ichud, while their estranged friends moved less than a mile north and established what became known as Ashdot Yaakov Meuchad. She worked in various kibbutz occupations, including waking before dawn to milk the cows. Those years forged her, and her mother's dictum was law to her: Labor is life. Even when she'd come to the kibbutz on a visit – with our children for a holiday, or during wartime – her mother urged her to go out and work. When we married and Tamar left the kibbutz, she left with nothing but the clothes on her back, but Bonya saw nothing wrong with that. "The kibbutz raised you and gave you an education," she said, "Be grateful."

Tamar, the former milkmaid, never gave up a piece of jewelry or a vial of fine perfume, always groomed and dressed to the nines, and never spared herself anything – neither in the spartan kibbutz conditions nor as the embodiment of the biblical "woman of virtue," raising our children as a soldier's wife. The decision not to embark on higher studies was her own, and she saw to the management of the family, the raising of the children, and educating them with the values of honesty, truth, and free thought.

We have been blessed with four children, and through them with fourteen grandchildren, each of whom is an entire separate world.

"Subdued a Giant Sudanese"

"The Watchmen's Union" was founded in the summer of 1933 by a group of watchmen seeking to shoulder an added national mission, so that the realm of physical protection of new settlements wouldn't be the only one they would be "conquering." They sought, concurrently, to establish shepherd villages, based on sheep and cattle husbandry, as well as horses, donkeys, and camels, as befitting the region.

This was a difficult period in the history of the pre-state Jewish population. Lands may have been redeemed by purchase from Arabs, but in many cases, the sellers were wealthy dignitaries who lived in splendor far away. The hard-living peasants, sharecroppers who worked the land as well as shepherds, refused to leave the lands from which they earned a living, and took to attacking Jews and preying on their property.

If all this wasn't enough, shortly before, the British Secretary of State for the Colonies, Baron Pasfield had issued the "Second White Paper," which restricted the purchase of land in Palestine by Jews. The adherents of the militant Muslim nationalist Izz a-Din al-Qassam (after whom the Hamas military wing is named today) increased their attacks and murderous predations, and within this atmosphere, the group of watchmen gathered in Sheikh Abreik, in the home of the Jewish National Fund (aka JNF) oak forests watchman, Alexander Zaid. They decided to establish a professional watchmen's union that, unlike Hashomer, would abstain from all political involvement.

And so it was. "The Watchmen's Union in the Land of Israel" was officially established a year after that founding meeting. It defined itself as a "watch and labor organization," and upon foundation, numbered 74 watchmen scattered throughout the country – and within a few months, doubled in size. Their unofficial leader was Aryeh Abramson, the legendary forest ranger of Jedda (now known as Ramat Yishai), "who spoke four dialects of Arabic," and "whom the Arabs respected after he subdued a giant Sudanese," as his son Zimri described him.

My Father is Sentenced to Prison

The Arab villages of Qusqus and Tab'un were abandoned in the 1920s and their lands, totaling about twelve thousand dunams – or three thousand acres – were purchased from the owner by an American Zionist association named Kehilat Zion. The association purchased the land both out of Zionism and as an investment, but due to the global economic depression that erupted in 1929, its resources grew scant, the territory was neglected, and this triggered a mass incursion of Bedouin shepherds and peasants from Jenin, headed by a Sheikh named Mufalah. Alexander Zaid, who guarded the JNF's lands at nearby Sheikh Abreik and Hartiya, residing in Sheikh Abreik, watched despondently as Arabs were taking over Jewish lands, egged on by the nationalist Arab institutions, and following the massacres and riots of 1929,[2] initiated Hebrew protection of the lands of Qusqus and Tab'un. These were the years of the British Mandate in Palestine, which pretended to protect law and order and to promote the establishment of

---

[2] Although there had been earlier lethal clashes, born of resistance to the growing renewed Jewish presence in mandatory Palestine, the massacres of 1929, most notoriously in Hebron but in other mixed cities as well, were a turning point in the relations of the two communities in the country. Many scholars consider these murderous attacks as the true beginning of the Israeli-Palestinian conflict. In the Hebron massacre, 69 Jews were murdered, almost as many were injured, and one of the oldest Jewish communities in the world was terminated, until Jewish presence in the city was renewed, following the Six-Day War.

a Jewish state, but many in the government loathed the Jewish population and sought to harm it. After a series of lawsuits, which the Arab trespassers lost, the signal was given and a group of watchmen settled on the lands of Qusqus-Tab'un. Among the watchmen who settled in the house of the mukhtar (the village chieftain) was also my father, who had joined the Watchmen's Union with Aryeh Abramson's encouragement, and shared the house with Abramson himself, Yitzhak Hankin, and Yoskeh Dumai. The fight against the invaders heated up after the Jerusalem Mufti, [the notorious] Haj Amin al-Husseini, [later an enthusiastic Nazi collaborator and SS officer,] published a "Fatwa" (religious ruling) prohibiting the sale of land to Jews at any cost. The decision by the Mandate authorities to follow suit, and prohibit the dispossession of sharecroppers from their lands, added fuel to the fire, although that's not what happened at Qusqus-Tab'un. The removal of the trespassers caused clashes on a daily basis. The British police sympathized with the trespassers, the Jewish national institutions were of meek spirit, and the ones who stood their ground were those few, fierce of spirit and instilled with faith in the Zionist vision, the men of "Agudat Hashomrim," who realized that only the combined force of the rifle and the plow would bring redemption to the Jewish people. They were armed with licensed shotguns and unlicensed pistols, supplied by the "Haganah," the main paramilitary organization of the Hebrew population.

On an August day in 1935, the residents of Kibbutz Ginegar decided to plow their fields in the land purchased from the abandoned villages of Qusqus-Tab'un, and realize their ownership of the land. The plowing was scheduled for that night, the tractor came to the field, awaited by the four watchmen. My father was guarding one end of the row, his three friends guarding the other. An Arab mob suddenly appeared, armed with clubs and rifles, and began marching on the plowing tractor. The three guards opened fire from their end, my father opened fire from his end, Abramson ordered Dumai to ride his horse to call for help from Alexander Zaid's house, and my father mounted his horse, meaning to join Abramson and Hankin. The mare was frightened by the shooting and began galloping until it struck the corpse of an Arab and stopped. My father dismounted, emptied his shotgun shells by the dead body, and reloaded. But the fight was over. The Arab attackers had withdrawn after one of them was killed and six wounded.

The tractor driver, who heard nothing due to the engine's racket, kept plowing. Dumai arrived at the police station in Jedda, today's Ramat Yishai, and waited there. Abramson rode my father's mare there as well, alongside Hankin, and my father remained behind to protect the plowing tractor operator. They filed a complaint for the assault, but the policemen who arrived on the scene and found an Arab's body arrested the four watchmen. The self-defense argument in the face of massive numbers was to no avail. The Jewish officer who led the British police investigation determined that the watchmen should be tried for murder, and within a few days, they were indicted. Following a long trial, after the young Hankin took the blame, being the only one among the four who was a bachelor and childless, Abramson, Dumai, and my father were sentenced to two years in prison. Hankin was sentenced to seven years, commuted to five. They were sent to serve their time in Acre Prison, which was a notorious jail, later to house the prisoners of the Hebrew underground militias, who were executed while singing the national anthem, "Hatikva." After a few months, the four were transferred to Atlit prison, which later became Israel's military "Prison 6." Their determined and courageous conduct became a legend of heroism as Kibbutz Alonim was established on most of those lands, and later with the establishment of the modern town of Kiryat Tiv'on.

The group of watchmen who conquered Qusqus and Tab'un.
Standing first from left: Mordechai Mizrachi.

A letter From Jail

It was a custom at the prison that each new inmate is handed over to the care and supervision of Jum'a, the Egyptian sergeant. This specimen, with immense size and the face of a deranged animal, would lead us along with the other prisoners for six kilometers on foot, where he would put us to labor doing unnecessary tasks, solely to break our spirits. Veteran inmates, who had served over two-thirds of their sentence with good behavior, would be appointed as sergeants and help him in his cruel abuse of prisoners. We worked from six in the morning until three in the afternoon, and often witnessed the brutal beatings which the sergeant would disperse most liberally. Luckily we managed, Yosef and I, to befriend him, and this friendship served us in good stead by sparing us the sting of the lash he always carried with him. But we weren't spared the hostility of the prisoner-sergeants, who would curse at us and threaten us with a beating, and also incite the other prisoners against us, as well as the Arabs through whose villages we had to pass on the way to our work.

At the same time, four Jewish settlement mukhtars – from Yavniel, Malhemia, Sejera, and Meskha [(the latter three are now known as Menachemia, Ilaniya, and Kfar Tavor)] – were imprisoned on charges of aiding illegal *Aliyah* (Jewish immigration to Israel). They were beaten viciously, and we couldn't help them. One day, we were visited by the Watchmen's Union coordinator Nathan Fish, who found us mired in mud up to our knees. We told him about the dire straits of the four mukhtars. The coordinator consoled us and promised to do what he could to ease our conditions, and also to look into the situation of the Jewish mukhtars, and indeed, after a while, we were transferred to Camp Atlit. At the Atlit work camp, we were treated more decently. In the first few days, we worked on the road, but then the Arab officer transferred us to work inside the camp. I was appointed cook, and Yosef became a "lampaji," meaning the one who handles the camp's lighting. Here, too, there was no shortage of snitches. A Jew whom I appointed as my assistant in the kitchen informed on me that I was receiving letters from the outside by way of the warden's driver. I was punished. I couldn't hold back my anger and gave the snitch a proper thumping, for which I received nine more days in prison, on top of my two-year sentence. When the bloody events of 1936 began, we were flooded by many Arab criminals from the central prisons, and alongside them, many Jewish prisoners arrived as well, and in the sea of hatred surrounding us, we had to protect our inexperienced Jewish brethren – for their sake and for the honor of the Jewish people. Due to the increase in arrests during these troubled events, the camp was very crowded, and the Jewish living quarters could not be separated from those of the Arabs. We lived, Arabs and Jews, together in the same shack, and so we passed days and months – days of stress and months of suffering – which added up to two years. We finished our prison terms, and were released."

(Mizrachi, Mordechai, "Agudat Hashomrim," pp 272-273)

Shlaski Court

As mentioned above, I was eighteen months old when we left the watchman's house near Na'an and moved to "Shlaski Court" in Kfar Saba, and that life there didn't agree with me. In my frustration, I would leave the closed compound behind me, stray from Tel Chai Street, and head for the open spaces. When asked where I was going, I would reply "to Thousand Dunams."

My father was busy on watch as usual, spending long periods away from home, as well as two years in prison, as I related above. At the end of the War of Independence, he was appointed commander of a large base of watchmen, "Mizrachi Base," which was located in a large estate house between Nir Eliyahu and Qalqilya, a few hundred yards from the Jordanian border. From the high porch of the estate house, it controlled Qalqilya and the area's orchards by line of sight and fire alike.

An Arab named Musalah was in charge of the food supply, the cleaning, and the workers on the base, and looked after all the wants and needs of the forty watchmen at Mizrachi base. Rawda, his younger sister, was my best friend – a cute blond girl whose beauty was only marred by her perpetually bleary eyes, probably the result of a neglected inflammatory condition. Falah was our "domestic help," and my Polish mother gave him a nickname: Feivel. To me, Falah was the ideal partner for all manner of mischief, and he showed me warm love as though he were my elder brother. I did not view the Arabs as an enemy, and felt no animosity, hatred, or alienation toward them. Relations with them were natural. They have become complicated – for all of us – over the years.

After the end of the War of Independence, we viewed the "Little Triangle" – The area bounded by Tira, Taybeh, and Jaljulya, annexed to Israel in the Rhodes ceasefire agreement – as a semi-separate Arab entity. Like all Israeli Arabs at the time, they lived under martial law, which limited the hours during which they were allowed to be outside their settlements and the hours they were allowed outside their homes. My father was considered a respected man there, and when I would go with him and with the military governor, Zvi Alpeleg, to dinner or a wedding at one of the villages, they would treat us to the finest cuts of meat, and shoot in the air with all manner of firearms, in a traditional sign of celebratory respect. I didn't view it as a lordly mannerism. It seemed completely natural to me. That was how I was brought up. Over the years, as I formed insights regarding our place in this land, I understood that what is now called a binational state must be prevented. I hold the same opinion to this day, and favor a Jewish and democratic state with a Jewish majority, precisely as the Declaration of Independence says. A state that has a place for Arab citizens with equal rights – and insofar as possible, equal duties as well, with national service in lieu of military service. When I was a child, the term "Palestinians" didn't exist. The Palestinian entity should be an independent state neighboring Israel, and Jews wishing to live there should receive Palestinian citizenship – as a mirror image of the Arabs living in Israel.

The Only Slap of My Life

My father allowed me to operate and shoot all the weapons at the Mizrachi Base. One day, when we were already living in a home of our own, I was entertaining my friend Yitzhak'aleh Matzkin in my room, demonstrating the process of shooting my father's double-barrel shotgun. I opened the breach, loaded a boar-hunting bullet in each chamber, switched the safety on, and said: "You see, when the safety is on, the rifle won't shoot."

To illustrate my words, I pulled the trigger. An immense explosion sounded, and everything filled up with smoke.

Luckily for me, my mother's electric baking oven stood in my room, with a peep hole to check if your pastry was ready, and the bullets miraculously hit the peep hole like a bullseye. My parents were alarmed at the explosion, my father stormed into the room, and for the first and last time in my life, gave me a ringing slap in the face. I fled outside to the corner of the yard with my cheek flaming and stinging, but the shame burned worse than the pain. It taught me for the rest of my life how to handle weapons and what safety truly means, not as just another subject to learn and memorize by rote. What you learn on your flesh remains etched forever.

Mizrachi Base

The men of Mizrachi Base protected the orchards between Nabi Yamin, the burial site of the biblical Benjamin, according to tradition, and the newly established Kibbutz Eyal. They had plenty to do, for gangs of thieves, mostly from Qalqilya, used to raid the orchards to steal equipment and fruit, and they didn't blanch at violence. This base, which was a sort of civilian force in governmental service in the state's early years, had a semi-military status. The watchmen were equipped with Czech rifles, English rifles, Sten submachine guns, Tommy guns, and there was even a German MG34 machine gun, "maglad" in the IDF's lingo. Almost all were military veterans of the War of Independence, and some were former French Foreign Legionnaires. The kibbutzim Eyal and Nir Eliyahu, also newly established, were a spitting distance from the border. Ramat Hakovesh, which was a bit further away, and the moshav of Neve Yamin had been established next to the Arab town of Qalqilya. Often skirmishes broke out not only with infiltrators and thieves, but also with the Jordanian legion troops. In other words, the base protected not only the orchards, but also served as a defensive bulwark and provided fire support to an IDF base, also erected near the tomb of Benjamin. This base served a unit of minority Druze and Circassian troops, under the command of Ismayil Kabalan, who was one of the first minority volunteers to Israel's security services, and the first Druze officer in the IDF. They belonged to the Frontier Corps, which later on became today's Border Police. Many years later, while on business in Lima, I happened to meet the Israeli Ambassador to Peru, Walid Mansour, a resident of Isfiya and a retired IDF colonel. As we waxed nostalgic, we discovered that Walid's father had served, after Israel's establishment, at that same base near Nabi Yamin. I remembered him well from his visits to our home and our visits to the base.

The IDF used Mizrachi Base as a fire base to cover patrols along the border and raids into Jordan. Legend has it that one of these nighttime incidents was witnessed by Moshe Dayan, then head of the IDF Ops Division and about to be appointed Chief of Staff. When the MG was fired from the porch overlooking Qalqilya, Dayan listened to the rhythm of the gunfire and said, "That's Shmulik Tzamri from Moshav Avichail shooting." He wasn't wrong. Tzamri, who had been a soldier in Dayan's "commando battalion" in the War of Independence, was indeed the machine gun operator.

ENCOUNTERS WITH COUSINS
Father Rafiq and Son Tariq

The relations with our Arab neighbors were good, as I mentioned, although my mother never forgave the fact that her childhood friend Yitzhak Goldberg was murdered during the Great Arab Revolt (1936-1939) by gang members, while standing his watch. I even saw signs of hatred in her demeanor when Tariq Abd al-Hai, later Tira's first mayor, would come to our house. Tariq was the son of Rafiq Sheikh Nagib, the head of the gang my mother blamed for the murder. The son, Tariq, was blessed with many gifts and rare eloquence. After earning a degree at Bar-Ilan University, he became a teacher at the local high school, was a central activist for "Al-Jabha" ("The Front,") which was the most extreme and nationalist party among Israel's Arabs – and yet was a Shin Bet informant. His meetings with his handlers were often held in our home, like meetings with other informants, and often shouts of "Kazab!" ("Liar!") could be heard from the closed room.

Years later, when I was awarded the rank of captain, Tariq told my proud father: "It's all thanks to his *Bolish* mother," – Being a native Arabic speaker, he had no "P" – "you're an Arab like us." Several years after that, Tariq told me a story that sounded fictitious, from the time my father had watched over the orchards of Wadi Falik (Poleg Stream), east and south of Netanya. However, I'm convinced that the incident did indeed occur, simply because Tariq had no reason to lie. "If my father, Rafiq Sheikh Nagib, hadn't saved your father from certain death," he told me, "You wouldn't be here today." Seven watchmen, Tariq told me, went to sleep in the "Baikeh" – a combination of a well house and a packaging space for the oranges, the main export of the days – in Gan Ephraim, near Qalansuwa and Kafr Miske, from where many attacks were launched against Kibbutz Ramat Hakovesh. Gang members arrived, captured the watchmen, with their mounts and weapons, and the gang leaders gathered in Nablus to discuss their fate. Or to be precise, not to discuss the fate of the captives, but the manner of their execution.

When they all finished speaking, Rafiq Sheikh Nagib stood up, and explained why the watchmen must not be killed, and so it was. Rafiq's influence was so great, that the abductors returned the horses and weapons to the watchmen and sent them on their way. It should be noted that the watchmen were almost the sole channel of communication with the Arabs in those days. They spoke fluent Arabic, gathered intelligence for the Haganah, and often pre-empted murderous attacks brewing among the gangs.

"The Arabs Are Conquering Kfar Saba!"

In the War of Independence, my father would sometimes bring collaborators from the Jordanian army to our home in the middle of the night. They would stay in our house for a few days, and the "Shai" people – the Haganah intelligence service – would come in the middle of the night, often headed by Rechavia Vardi (later a senior Mossad figure and Israel's Coordinator of Government Activities in the Territories aka "COGAT") and sometimes with Ariel Sharon, the latter who would in time become Israel's prime minister. They would interrogate the collaborators and send them back to Jordan, laden with dinar bills. My father would escort them to the border, and I recall two of them in particular. One was a Major in the Jordanian Legion, who built me a "tayara" (Arabic for "kite"), went out to the field with me, and taught me to fly it. The other was a dignified Arab with an immense mustache, named Abu Hussein. We lived on Ha'emek Street then which was the easternmost street in Kfar Saba, facing the Arab village of Kafr Saba. Abu Hussein went out into the yard one morning to make coals for his hookah, and across the fence, our neighbor, Sarah Yudilevitch, also came out to her own yard. She saw in front of her an Arab dressed in the traditional garb and headdress, in the middle of the War of Independence, and began shouting: "Arabs! The Arabs are conquering Kfar Saba!"

Friend Turned Terrorist

My father was skilled at forging ties with both the Arab neighbors and the grouchy, sour-faced Jewish farmers – and it wasn't easy. The farmers looked disapprovingly at anyone on the public payroll, including watchmen, but they had a special regard for my father, for he always managed to track down the thieves. Following negotiations, he would return the stolen item to its owner – be it a cow, a herd of sheep, a load of produce, or irrigation pipes.

On the other side, one of the Arab families with whom friendly relations existed, was the Abu Sneina family, which we called the "Sabri" family, after the paterfamilias. This was a big family, which prior to the War of Independence lived in the village of Jalil – today on the border of Herzliya and Kibbutz Glil-Yam. During the Mandate era, the family collaborated with the Haganah, and as their village was destroyed in the war, the Abu Sneina family received 97 dunams between Neve Yamin and the border in compensation. The Israel Land Authority retained a part of each plot, to ensure that the lands wouldn't be sold without the state's consent.

Ibrahim, Sabri's son who was my age, was my friend in games and adventures such as horse riding, shooting .22 rifles, and pigeon hunting. Therefore it was a painful blow for me to hear, two decades later, that Ibrahim and his brother, Abd al-Karim, had laid an explosive device in Tel Aviv's central bus station, killing one person and wounding 60 others. They were caught and sentenced to life in prison, but were released in 1985 in the Gibril prisoner exchange deal, among 1,151 prisoners who went free in exchange for 3 IDF soldiers. Long before that, both brothers attended my wedding. During my university studies, I availed myself of their help, and I felt betrayed when I learned of the heinous act they'd committed. In time, after their release from prison, Ibrahim asked us to come for lunch. I agreed reluctantly, following pleas from my sister Yaffa, who was on good terms with them, but I projected what I felt: Anger and disappointment. Ibrahim and his brother tried to provide a twisted explanation. At first they said they had committed the act for money, then they gave another explanation: Their cousin, later to become Qalqilya's first mayor under Israel after the Six-Day War, and who had married their sister, was threatened by Fatah militants, and they did what they did to prevent harm to their sister and her family. I feel that Ibrahim was dragged along by Abd al-Karim, who was an extreme nationalist, and didn't hesitate to voice his extremist views in our living room even before the terror attack. We never thought that he would cross the bright red line separating opinion from an act of terror, and far less did we imagine that Ibrahim would be party to such a contemptible crime.

The Needless Death of Sharif Mansour

Sharif Mansour was the eldest son of Hassan Abdallah, head of the second strongest gang in Tira. His eyes, like those of his father, were kind, unlike those of Rafiq Sheikh Nagib, whose blue-green eyes seemed to me like the eyes of an assassin. The Mansour family was considered more prestigious, even though it would be Tariq Abd al-Hai, as I mentioned above, who would become Tira's first mayor.

I met Sharif by chance, after my father left me a small piece of land near Qalqilya. He worked it out of a sense of need to create facts on the ground and be present in all corners of the land, and I received permission from Ramat Hakovesh to use their water for my small plot. I decided to sow it with wheat, and Sharif, who knew who I was, offered to plow it for me. This was the start of a friendship that lasted many years, replete with mutual visits. But this family came to a bitter end. The youngest son, Ihab, began to study at the Technion in Haifa, and on a visit home, he went with two of his friends to rob a bank in Jaljulya. They were caught, and Ihab was sentenced to long years in prison for armed robbery.

If that weren't enough, Ghassan, Sharif's eldest son, a talented guy and an energetic entrepreneur, also fell into bad company. Two friends of his committed murder in broad daylight in Tira, and fled into the Mansour family's walled courtyard. Ghassan sheltered the murderers and refused to hand them over to the friends of the victim. The two were arrested by the police, but the victim's family and friends were not content with that, and revenge followed swiftly. Sharif Mansour, an honest person, exemplary family man, and soulmate, was murdered in broad daylight while sitting in a café in Tira. The enormous funeral was attended by a huge crowd; and the Egyptian Ambassador to Israel, family friend Muhammad Bassiouni, eulogized Sharif. At the widow Samira's request, I spoke with Ghassan, to dissuade him from entering the maelstrom of vengeance. The mother's pressure, along with the pleas of many friends, me included, was ultimately successful, and the family chose to relocate far from Tira, and to start a new life in Canada. My contacts with them were severed.

The Destructive Seed of Racism

From my father, I inherited the ability to develop friendly, and even close relationships with Arabs, and at the same time to remember that we are on opposite sides of the critical dispute over control of the land and the character of the country. I never felt hatred toward an Arab for being an Arab, I never shied away from contact with Arabs, and I never feared encounters and ties – not as a child nor as an adult, neither as a soldier nor as a civilian – not in Israel, not in Lebanon, not in Jordan, and not in Judea, Samaria, and Gaza. I am convinced that the fight for the land of Israel was decided in favor of the Jews the moment the first pioneers made landfall on the shores of Israel (then Ottoman-ruled Palestine) some 150 years ago. Despite my personal and family history, and despite my connection and crossing of paths with Arabs in Israel and beyond over the years, I fear that the fact that generations of Israelis have been born, brought up, and served as soldiers in a reality in which we occupy, arrest, invade homes, stand at checkpoints, and sustain murderous attacks, has bred condescension and hatred toward Arabs in general and Palestinians in particular. Here lies the destructive seed of extremism and racism, and the situation will only become further entangled should it result in a binational state. I have said before, and will not tire of restating: We must formulate a solution in which there is a clear and solid Jewish majority in the State of Israel, so that it can continue to be a Jewish and democratic state, and not abandon its foundational Zionistic and moral values.

Captain Kassis

And to end this chapter, a short leap into the future, to the time I served as the ops officer of Artillery Brigade 209.

A commander's time watching night drills includes long periods of idleness, and it is at such moments that the stories begin to come up. One night we stood on a hill overlooking the artillery barrels spread below us, and two of those present began to tell of their travels around the world. The Chief Artillery Officer, Aryeh Levi, spoke about his experiences from the advanced artillery course he took at Fort Sill, Oklahoma. The Deputy unit commander, Moshe Levi, told how he and Eli Doron, who had created the 405th Battalion as a state-of-the-art M-109 battalion, one of German extraction and the other of Polish, were sent in 1965 under false identities to the artillery school in Fez, Morocco, to instruct the local artillery corps, which was in its infancy. I mustered the courage to admit that I had never left Israel's borders. Aryeh Levi took this as a challenge, and said: "I'm arranging a trip for you." As I was 27 years of age, with academic studies under my belt, and most of the literature in Middle Eastern studies were in English, it was assumed that I spoke the language. Two weeks later, I was summoned to the offices of the United Jewish Appeal in Jerusalem, and I was tested. The sole question on the "test" was: "How is your English?" To which I replied: "Very good." This sufficed to send me on a speaking tour in California, moving my home base of operations for two weeks from Refidim, in the barren Sinai Desert, to Beverly Hills, Los Angeles. For the first time in my life, I flew on a civilian aircraft. Until then, I had only jumped for a plane in a parachuting course, or flown in military Pipers and Dornier Do 27s (a German-made aircraft, renamed "Dror" by the Israeli Air Force) under threat of Egyptian surface-to-air missiles during the War of Attrition, and here I was in the front of the plane, sitting in first class on a huge Boeing 747 en route to New York, receiving exceptionally attentive treatment and maximum comfort. My cousin, Shaul, was a customs officer at Lod Airport (as Ben Gurion International was then known, the man himself being still alive at the time) – and all the stewards, stewardesses, and even the pilots wanted to get on his good side. The pampering continued after we landed, as well. A guy wearing a limo driver's cap was waiting for me at JFK with a large sign reading "Mizrachi, Major," and took me to a swanky Manhattan hotel, to meet Cy Lesser, the 'big man' at the United Jewish Appeal.

I had never stayed in a hotel before this, and Cy Lesser explained to me that I needed only to peruse the menu, and order whatever I wanted. He armed me with some spending money, explained that I was to fly the next day to Los Angeles, and promised that a limo driver would take me from the airport to the "Beverly Hilton."

I went up to the room, glanced at the room service menu, and the only thing I recognized was "steak." The words "New York strip" also appeared, but I paid no intention to it. I never imagined that a table would be brought up to my room, and upon it a massive, blood-dripping steak, of a thickness I had never seen in my life.

The next time I flew to the U.S., in late 1974, my wife Tamar and my children Sagi and Yaron were along with me. This time it was a year-long journey, to attend the advanced artillery course at the U.S. Army's artillery school at Fort Sill, Oklahoma. This time we sat in the back of a Boeing 707, near the lavatory. It was a sixteen-hour flight, with a stop in Amsterdam, with a five- and a seven-year-old with energy to burn, running around the plane. This time no one awaited me. Tamar and I – with a suitcase in each hand and a child hanging from each of our shoulders – had to search the terminal for the connection flight to Washington D.C., to receive instructions from the attaché's office. The Holiday Inn in D.C. also looked nothing like the Beverly Hilton, and when we finally managed to put the suitcases on the floor and the kids to bed, all Tamar asked was: "So this is the America you raved so much about...?"

Fort Sill is located in southern Oklahoma, not far from the Texas border. I was a Lt. colonel. All the other 250 cadets were captains, or majors at most, but almost all were about my age, 32 or even older, and we connected quickly. There I met Rasu Govinda, who would be Chief Artillery Officer in the Singapore Army, concurrent with my own term, Luis Bustamente from Peru, and also a Lebanese captain my own age named As'ad Kassis. Despite being representatives of enemy militaries that had clashed in the past and would do so in the future, we found a common language. My father had grown up in Beirut, and some of his family arrived in Israel ten years after independence, following the severe clashes between Muslims and Christians in 1958, and I had heard many stories about Beirut. Captain Kassis and I forged a friendship mixed with competition, as we battled for first place in the course overall, and the score of each test. One time he would get the better of me, and the next time it would be my turn. This friendship reached such a height that when, on a trip to D.C., we met foreign cadets from other military schools, including officers from Jordan, Saudi Arabia, and other Arab countries. During lunch, Kassis got up from the "Arab" table, sat next to me, and said loudly: "These dogs want me to boycott you. This is my answer." The course went on, and during one conversation, Kassis told me that he admired Israel for the war we wage against the Palestinian terrorists, who were ruining Lebanon, and viewed us as allies and partners. He also told me that when listening to our comms while stationed on the Lebanon-Israel border, he hears his name – "Rasis." I had to curb his enthusiasm and explain that "rasis" is shrapnel in Hebrew. "I love you guys," he said, "even though right before I came here, you guys fired a 175mm cannon at the ops center of an armored battalion in Tyre, and one of the four officers killed was my cousin. That hurt me very much, but that's war. I have nothing against you." I froze, for I was involved in the incident. On the eve of my departure for the U.S., the Israeli naval commando unit ("Shayetet 13") conducted a raid on a terrorist outpost near Tyre, and as I was available, I commanded the artillery support for the operation. I sat off the Tyre shoreline, on the missile boat the commando fighters left for shore. A battery of 175mm M-107 self-propelled guns was deployed at Rosh Hanikra, on the border, and as always, the desire to shoot the guns burned within me. I heard on the radio that the fighters under the command of Yedidiah Ya'ari (in time he would become the commander of the Israeli Navy and director-general of Rafael Advanced Defense Systems) had landed, and that combat had begun, and I knew that one of the specified targets of the mission was the HQ of the Tyre armored battalion, which we feared would be deployed to help the terrorists. I took advantage of the fact that there was an artillery forward observer with the landing force. He was a green 2nd lieutenant, and the dialogue between us went thus:

"Can't you hear tanks?"

- No.

"Listen carefully," I said. A few seconds went by before the FO understood that I didn't actually hear anything either, and gave the code word anyway to fire artillery at the Tyre armored camp. Five shells were fired in total. The first projectile hit the bullseye, destroyed the ops center, and killed four officers. One of these, I learned at Fort Sill, was the ops officer, As'ad Kassis's cousin. And to me – the dissonance is the heart of the story.

I said nothing to Kassis about my part in that shooting, but the incident touched my heart – the more so since toward the end of the course, his grades slipped, and a constant worry clouded his face. When I asked what happened, he replied: "The dogs burned my house and I have nowhere to return to." Captain Kassis flew to Paris with his wife and children once the course ended. The Palestinian terrorists had driven him from his homeland. They settled in France, but he never overcame the pain, and died of a broken heart.

I'll Be a General

Katznelson High School in Kfar Saba was renowned nationwide. The cream of Kfar Saba's youth studied there, including those of the surrounding moshavim – Gan Haim, Tzofit, and Neve Yamin, and even boys from Ra'anana, from Magdiel, and Ramataim, now part of the city of Hod Hasharon.

Classes were small. My class in the liberal arts major, for example, consisted of seventeen students. The teachers were mostly veteran educators with a love for the calling – although there were exceptions, such as the English teacher who tried her best, but was simply devoid of any teaching skills, the confused math teacher, and Zechariah, the Arabic teacher, who preferred to entertain us with fantastical tales.

It was an opinionated and energetic class. We located and exploited the weaknesses of certain teachers, but knew how to derive the best out of the really good ones – history teacher Eliezer Bergman, physics teacher Lotta Hass, PE teacher Yariv Oren, and poet Aryeh Sivan, the literature teacher, with whom I forged ties of affection. Sivan was the type of teacher who only gave the time of day to the students he liked. Sivan poured his attention into his pets' Hebrew, their reading habits, and instilling a craving for knowledge – while the others might as well have been air to him. For me, he was an excellent teacher, and I thoroughly enjoyed his classes – particularly when I managed to not only display familiarity with an obscure expression from ancient Jewish literature, but also to explain its meaning in plain modern Hebrew. He knew how to instill in us a love for the Hebrew language, the study of its origins and its plethora of expressions and proverbs, encouraging me to probe the mysteries of the world. Sivan was also noted for his weakness for pretty girls, and drew ridicule for his habit of only calling willowy beauties to the blackboard, chief among them Tamar Dinner, the class belle.

Then there was Murad, the Arabic teacher who swept into our lives following the termination of Zechariah, the storyteller.

Murad entered the classroom on a cold winter's day, wearing a shirt with the sleeves rolled up. We ignored his presence until he opened his mouth. The first words that came out were "open the windows," uttered in an intimidating voice, without the trace of a smile. He had the gait of a prizefighter, impressive biceps, and the chest of a wrestler. All the heroes became subdued, and silence ensued in the classroom. At long last, we began to learn Arabic.

The greatest of all was Gedalyahu Lachman, the school principal. Lachman survived the Holocaust, and upon his release from the British detention camp in Cyprus, he found work as a teacher in the Jordan Valley, and lived with his family in Kibbutz Ashdot Yaakov, the one where my wife Tamar was born and raised. As a principal, he was notoriously strict. The students feared him, and he ruled the staff with an iron fist as well. He determined who would study and who would teach at the school, rejecting many. We, the happy few who passed the screening, he called "grade school geniuses," for the glowing report cards we had received, mostly through teachers' affections. At the end of junior year, Lachman ran another screening test, advancing to the senior year only those he was certain would succeed in the matriculation exams. He did so in order to meet the goal he had set for himself: First place in the country in matriculation scores. Two students, each for their own justified reason, were left out of our class. Only after three months, with much pressure, and successful admission tests, were they returned from exile.

As a history teacher, Lachman was positively gifted. His fascinating stories merged with my interest in events of the past, and the knowledge I had acquired through the books I read as a child: Tolstoy's "Peter the First," "Genghis Khan," Peniakoff's "Popski's Private Army," "Ivan the Terrible," Remarque's "The Road Back," "All Quiet on the Western Front," and "The Army Behind Barbed Wire," by Edwin Erich Dwinger, about the experiences of soldiers from the Central Alliance countries, as well as Germans and Austrians who had been captured by the Russians. These, and many other books, gave me knowledge and created a common language between myself and Lachman. He knew how to imbue the dry facts with a soul, to deduce from them the processes currently taking place around us, and to teach us how to use historical examples in life.

One day in homeroom class, close to the end of high school, Lachman asked us what we wanted to do with our lives, and what our aspirations for the future were. My friend Baruch Amrami replied: "A veterinarian," because they had a large dairy farm in the middle of Kfar Saba, but became a lawyer. My friend Micha Vidra said, "a diplomat," but became a successful businessman, and has been living in New York for many years. When my turn came, I said firmly: "I'll be a general." And indeed, I was fortunate enough to become a general in the IDF, Chief Artillery Officer, during the corps' ultimate test, the First Lebanon War (which I will go to my grave calling by its proper name: The Peace for Galilee War.) I didn't say, "I want to be." I said: "I will be." And when I was appointed Chief Artillery Officer, reporting directly to the Chief of Staff, (the Commander-in-Chief of the IDF), they held a reception for me at the Kfar Saba city council. Legendary Mayor Ze'ev Gellar invited Lachman to the special meeting, and the revered educator told those present the General story. To this day, I recall and use little anecdotes Lachman revealed to us, which added vitality to the history lessons. For instance, the skills of Napoleon Bonaparte, originally an artillery officer, who could write two letters simultaneously – each with a different hand, and could dictate two letters at once to two separate aides. This may explain some of his astonishing abilities – not only in leading the Grande Armée on its many conquests, but also in formulating the Napoleon Code, which consolidated the rights of French citizens, in giving rights to the Jews, and in the planning of Paris, the fairest city in the world.

ALWAYS A GUNNER

When I was drafted into the IDF, on August 14th, 1960, a month before I turned eighteen, I sought to attain the rank of officer as quickly as possible, and didn't care too much where or why. In our bougie social circle, formed after we had left the socialist youth movement in which we spent most of our teens,[3] there was a guy named Shuli Dannai, who was a year older than us. He had finished an artillery officers' course, and explained to me that the shortest route to an officer's rank was in the artillery – especially for those recruited in August, who as high school graduates were marked as potential officers.

At the initial screening at the intake and sorting base (aka "Bakum" in the acronym-heavy dialect known as IDF Hebrew), I was found fit for the prestigious pilots' course. I was very glad to be chosen, although I hadn't been to the aerial military prep, nor built model planes and plywood gliders, as other hopefuls had done. But my Air Force career was brief. The medical exams they gave us at flight school turned up a minor vision defect. I had managed to hide it until then, but the meticulous testing at the Tel Nof base revealed the flaw, and I was sent packing back to the Bakum.

This time, I didn't wait for anyone to decide for me, and said that I wanted to go to artillery. The sorting officers jumped at the opportunity. They usually had to send the artillery recruits who would rather be anywhere else – in stark contrast to today, when many recruits vie for each spot in the corps.

They loaded us on a truck and dropped us off in Tzrifin, at the 403rd Battalion's base. This was a battalion of relatively new French towed 155mm guns, 1950 model. And there, at the 403rd Battalion in August

---

[3] "HaNoar HaOved VeHaLomed" the main socialist youth movement – akin to the boy scouts but with political indoctrination mixed in. Literally: "The Working and Learning Youth."

of 1960, is where my long journey as a gunner began – all the way from a rookie who didn't know a thing to Chief Artillery Officer, who would be a main fulcrum and leader in a historical turnaround.

Warrior

From an early age, as I mentioned, I was exposed to firearms. As a child, before the War of Independence, I picked up my cap gun one day, added an even younger toddler, and we began marching toward the checkpoint at the eastern entrance to Kfar Saba. My father was actually in charge of this checkpoint, and when I was asked: "Isn't it dangerous?" I said: "No! I have a gun!"

Later on, my father bought me a .22 rifle, and on that I learned the rules of firearm handling, and of course how to shoot. In addition, I was in charge of caring for the "Jift," my father's double-barreled hunting shotgun, and of course his FN pistol, and so as a child I was already trained in dismantling, cleaning, and assembling firearms.

The infantry boot camp at the 403rd Battalion suited me. I felt like a fish in the water at the firing ranges, and as a child of the open ranges, I did well in the field training in Nitzanim as well. I loved the camouflage and infiltration drills, I loved the bilateral (platoon vs. platoon) practices, and not only did I not suffer; I even enjoyed the long hikes on foot, let alone the fire drills. All these were intended to train us as infantry troops. This was a necessary starting point for the course I had laid out for myself.

To this day, I remember my platoon commander from those days, Uzi Salant, and the squad commander Moshe Dolev, who made the exhausting boot camp interesting and helped me flourish. Much later, as Chief Artillery Officer, I appointed Salant to command the 218th Artillery Brigade as a Colonel, after he excelled as a reserve battalion commander and spent much time at it, despite his high-profile civilian job as director of the Leumit Healthcare Fund (one of the HMOs in Israel). Dolev, the squad commander, already held the patent and was a cofounder of the massively successful "Rav Bariach," which the reader might know better as RB-DOORS.

The artillery training, which came after the infantry training, was less exciting, and included digging trenches for towed 155mm Howitzer guns. It was grueling manual labor, with shovels and picks, added to the operation of the gun itself, including quick deployment and packing, in a large twelve-man crew.

From there, I continued for a short training program at Camp Shivta, undertaking a squad commander course as part of the squad commander school, and from there to the preparatory course for the officers' school. I flourished there as well, and I clearly remember the squad commander, Beno, the platoon commander, Shai Huldai, as well as the long runs, the command exercises, and the fire drills.

The recruiting committee, for a military unit so secret, its name was banned from mentioning, summoned me to appear before it one day. [To spare the reader any undue suspense, it was the highly regarded Sayeret Matkal commando unit, later to become world-famous in rescuing the Entebbe hostages and many other daring operations, some still classified.] I didn't ask to be transferred to "The Unit," and as soon as the interview began, I realized that I was summoned due to my last name, on the belief that I was born in an Arab country and that I spoke the language fluently. I spoke some Arabic since childhood, but far from native tongue proficiency, and they passed on my services. I felt no disappointment. My goal – and the road to it – were clear.

KICKED OUT

The IDF officers' school, aka Bahad 1 ("Bahad" is a Hebrew acronym for "Basis Hadracha," i.e. "Instruction Camp") was located after the establishment of the state at Camp 80, moving to Camp Sirkin before relocating, in 1968, to the outskirts of Mitzpe Ramon. I underwent the basic officers' course[4] at Sirkin, right after completing the squad commanders' course and officers' prep. I had become a soldier a mere few months prior to that, and had yet to command as much as a squad, not including exercises in boot camp and the squad commanders' course. I didn't think it was a problem, or that it would bother me, but I entered the officers' course on the wrong foot. I was a good soldier, in excellent shape, and yet suffered from a lack of confidence. I didn't feel myself sufficiently ready, and this impacted my reactions.

In one case, I clashed with my squad leader, Kotik, and on one of the hikes, I kept repeating as I marched, "Kotik ben zona" ("Kotik is a son of a bitch"). This got on the nerves of Eitan Barak, the other platoon's instructor, and he grabbed me at the end of the hike and led me straight to a disciplinary hearing with Haka, the base commander.

As expected, Haka bounced me from the course. I was sent to serve as the squad commander for rookies at the 404th Battalion, at infantry training held on the training grounds at Beit Govrin. My company commander was Shlomo Gudelevich (nee "Gal,") who won a medal of courage ("Itur Ha'oz") for his performance as an FO in the Paratrooper Rangers unit at the Battle of Qalqilya, when he rained artillery fire on the enemy and prevented the Jordanians from surrounding Dovik

---

4   In the IDF, all prospective officers, from all corps, first undergo a "basic officers' course" which is based on infantry training. Upon graduating this course, one is qualified to command an infantry platoon, and only continues to a corps-specialization course – learning to command tanks, or artillery units, or a naval unit – as the case may be.

Tamari, and later on, became a senior Mossad figure. The deputy company commander was Aldo Zohar, my friend to this day, who also left the IDF with the rank of Brigadier General. My platoon commander was Oded Kaplan from Kfar Saba, another true friend, whose father owned "Kaplan Photo" in our hometown.

The deputy battalion commander, Nati Sharoni, gave me the intake interview. This was a positive first encounter that led to a deep friendship, and mutual appreciation. The first thing I told him was: "I want to join the next class at Bahad 1." Nati looked at me and said: "You'll go to Bahad 1, but in the meantime, you'll be a rookies' squad commander." I enjoyed a supportive environment, was afforded the option to put initiatives into action and show leadership, and in late 1961, I left for the officers' course again.

Bahad 1, Take 2

The second time I arrived at Bahad 1, I was sure of myself. I connected with two cadets from the naval commando Shayetet 13 unit, Gadi Sheffi and Shaul Ziv. We remained friends after the course ended, and collaborated later on, in various operations. Toward the end of the course, I was almost certain of being awarded "most excellent cadet," but on the very last night, I had a disciplinary charge levelled against me, and to my great disappointment, Defense Minister David Ben Gurion pinned the platoon commander's insignia on the lapel of Yossi Peled, later the Northern Command General.

We had done a raid exercise on Nabi Rubin that night. I was in the point team under a cadet named Yossi Ne'eman, who relied on me for navigating, and upon returning to Sirkin, I was slotted in the first watch at the gate. I clearly remember that I bayoneted my rifle and leaned on the bayonet, hoping to keep from falling asleep, but I was dead tired.

The second my eyes closed, a rotating platoon instructor from another company came to the gate. He came up stealthily, in sneakers, and shone his flashlight on my closed eyes. I didn't even feel the stab of the naked bayonet in my armpit from the fatigue, but the beam of light straight onto my eyes woke me up. Suddenly I saw a skinny major standing in front of me, with a face like the Grim Reaper. I felt my heart drop. Kicked out again? I pointed at the bayonet, still stuck in my armpit, but the major, overjoyed at catching a cadet in misconduct, turned a deaf ear to my pleas. And what would become of me?

My platoon instructor, Reuven Leshem, a paratrooper from Kibbutz Afikim who was killed in the Six-Day War, insisted that I be awarded "most excellent cadet" anyway, but the ranks above him decided to give me a D in discipline, dropping my general score to a B. I missed meeting Ben Gurion face to face, and only got to do so when my artillery battery protected him and his wife, Paula, at their cabin in Kibbutz Sde Boker, where an officer would accompany him on his morning walks.

One morning, he was accompanied by a younger officer, who told me that he thought the former Prime Minister was senile. When I asked why, he said that when the float of the water cistern on the hill had been lifted, the water overflowed, and Ben Gurion kept repeating: "The water is overflowing." This seemed odd to the young officer. I explained to him that Ben Gurion made every effort to settle the Negev and bring water to it – first with the Yarkon-Negev line, and then with the "National Carrier" project – and that needless waste of water, after the immense effort of bringing it there, was almost criminal in my view as well.

But let me return to the next step of the officers' course: Artillery Corps Specialization (henceforth: Artillery Officers' Course) at Bahad ("Instructional Base") 9, in the Camp Tzrifin compound.

"Arie, Get Up!"

I loved geometry even back in high school. I was no stranger to calculations, logarithms, and measurements, and at the artillery officers' course, I excelled again at artillery studies. But the main part was field training and navigation: Nighttime navigation by car, ranging, deploying, choosing, and defending positions. Happily for me, I stood out here as well.

The platoon commander of the other company was Captain Yaakov Erez, an imposing man with a thick mustache, who spoke sharply and decisively, using unusual expressions – like a Holocaust survivor on one hand and a tough, opinionated officer on the other. One night we were stationed at the observation post (OP) at Khirbet Maahaz, in fire zone 309 C-D, with the firing unit, which was meant to train us to shoot a battery of 25-pound guns.

Night ranging was conducted in those days with enormous artillery searchlights, 60" in diameter, which projected light over long distances, weather permitting. All the cadets sat on the hill with binoculars, a compass, a map, and a flashlight, and suddenly Yanka'leh Erez says: "The next ranging is a distant target – a target range of eleven kilometers. I'll give you the target's coordinates. You have to locate it, range, and drop fire for effect."

Ranging at such a long distance was rare even in the daytime, let alone the night. Ranging was almost always done up to seven kilometers, and even ranging at that distance was considered difficult in terms of identifying the impact of the small bore shell, about half the size of the 155mm shell, with little explosives. If the projectile fell in a depression, you had to wait for smoke to rise, and if there was wind blowing, the smoke showed up far from the impact site. All my friends cringed, kept their heads down, and hid behind the person next to them. Erez pointed the flashlight at us, the same way John Travolta and Samuel L. Jackson chose whom to shoot in "Pulp Fiction," counted us off one by one with his finger, and said: "Arie, get up!"

Nobody had taught us how to perform such a mission. We had never tried to find coordinates in the dark, at a distance almost impossible to sweep even with an artillery searchlight. But the commander gave me a task, and I had to carry it out. I racked my brain and came up with an idea: I'll get the azimuth from our location from the map, meaning from the OP to the target, I'll hold the compass in my hand, also at azimuth to the target, I'll relay the coordinates of the target to the searchlight, to point the beam at it, and then I'll order to move it sideways slowly, until the searchlight beam intersects with the azimuth from the compass – and that's the target.

And indeed, it worked. I identified the target, ordered the searchlight operator to use a wide beam, saw the explosion through the binoculars, and from there it was short work to range and drop fire for effect, which was only one shell.

When Erez asked: "Any comments?" silence ensued. Most of the guys were catching z's. Even the most alert didn't quite follow what I did, and were afraid to show it. Erez, who in the Yom Kippur War would be the commander of the 209th Brigade, the artillery brigade of the Sinai Division, smiled. "Excellent," he told me. "One of the best ranging displays I've ever seen."

In Memory of the Fallen Tamarisk

Another time we took the command car for a nighttime navigation with aerial photographs, in the area between the kibbutzim Dorot and Ruhama, and Khirbet Ma'ahaz. The instructor Samiko, Shmuel Meir, later a colonel in the corps, tasked me with the navigation. The destination was Khirbet Ma'ahaz and the interim target was Tel Najila, which means "the hill of grass," although it was better known for the lone tamarisk that rose from its top.

The night was starry. From time to time, Samiko would stop me and ask where we were. I put my finger somewhere on the aerial photo, knowing he too has no idea where we were, and he always said "OK." I drove by Azimuth, and at some point, I decided to stop the car, lie on the ground, and seek out the lone tamarisk. I identified the tree against the star-strewn night sky. We climbed the hill, and the navigation from there to Khirbet Ma'ahaz was easy. The lone tamarisk, by the way, is sadly gone. It was felled by a fierce storm in the winter of 2020.

Ahead of the end of the basic course for Artillery Corps officers, the most excellent cadet title once again eluded me. The dominant Erez won out over my platoon instructor, Aryeh Jacobson, and Amos Tor from the other platoon was chosen for the honor.

Cool Cannons on Fire

My first posting as an officer was as commander of a platoon of rookies at the 403rd Battalion, the same battalion at which I myself underwent basic training – this time in the area between Gimzo and Kfar Daniel. Aldo was the company commander, Oded Kaplan the deputy company commander, and I felt that I was back in my natural element. I loved the material I taught, loved to lead drills, displayed leadership, and brought many new ideas to the table.

After one class, I went back to artillery in a new role: The first Executive Officer (XO) of the first self-propelled M-50 battery – three self-propelled 155mm guns on a Sherman tank chassis. This was a first-of-its-kind project by the ordnance corps, in which towed French cannons were mounted on WW2 tanks, and these were the first cannons to come off the ordnance corps' restoration and the maintenance center's production line. In time, the SPH guns would form the main firepower of the corps, and would play an important role in the War of Attrition and the Yom Kippur War. Our battalion commander was Chaim Yarkoni, formerly the commander of the 404th, who came to teach the 403rd the ways of the self-propelled gun. The battery commander was Oded Kaplan.

The crew commanders were picked with extreme care: Davdul and Rami the kibbutzniks – a rare breed in the artillery, and excellent crew commanders, and also Chai and Tzahal, likewise outstanding crew commanders, who were killed in the Six-Day War. The tank mechanic was Haggai Shalom, later the head of the IDF's technology and logistics division, with the rank of a Major-General, and later a successful businessman, and Amram Eitan, in time head of the planning division at the IDF's planning directorate, with the rank of Brigadier General, who would introduce the innovative TQM management system to the IDF. I recruited him many years later, in 2005, at IMI Systems, to manage to Turkish tank project – the largest project in the history of Israel's defense industries up to that time, at a scope of 700 million dollars.

At the end of a preliminary practice run at Tzrifin, we went down for training at the "Ovdat Rectangle," and it seemed like the operational aspect was running smooth. We deployed, fired, and hit our targets, practicing movements and positionings, using the radio to communicate with crews, hasty deployments, and the like. But then the problems began: The gasoline tank of the "Continental" engine in the tank sat above the engine, under the deck. The engine exhaust pipes released their smoke and heat near there, and as a result the fuel heated, the exhaust pipe began spitting fire, and if that wasn't enough, the SPH looked like a flame-spitting monster in the dark. It too had caught fire.

The exercise was halted after two SPH guns had caught fire. When we got back to Tzrifin, I was summoned by battalion commander Yarkoni, who told me: "If you sign up for the career military, you'll be appointed the commander of the first self-propelled M-50 battery."

It was an offer I couldn't refuse, and I jumped at it. I had just been promoted to 1st Lieutenant, and I'd already been a battery commander. A huge shortcut to realizing the dream.

But I was too quick to rejoice, and after I signed, in March 1963, they pulled a fast one on me, reminiscent of what Laban the Aramean did to the biblical patriarch Jacob. Instead of the Rachel I was promised, I was sent to Leah. The real deal turned out to be: Work the 402nd for a year, with its antique 25-pounder towed guns (which were used by Montgomery in Al-Alamein, 20 years prior) – and then you'll get a battery in the 404th, the pride of the corps.

THE 402ND
A Clerk Named Tamar

I considered withdrawing my commitment to the career military, and consoled myself with the only advantage I saw in the 402nd Battalion: Its home base was in Jalameh, near Haifa, and not in God knows where. In retrospect, this turned out to be a minor advantage. Far more importantly, I won one of the great prizes in my life there, in meeting the clerk, Tamar Zack. She had just arrived at the battalion, a gorgeous, willowy blond with magnificent blue eyes, and my soul cleaved onto hers to this very day.

The click happened at the impromptu parties held by the young officers and the girls in the battalion, in the elongated cabin that served as the officers' and ladies' quarters, and we grew tighter over dates in Haifa. It was love at first sight. Due to the fact that Tamar suffered from backaches in her first military role as a parachute folder, she was sent to us – leading her to break up with her paratrooper boyfriend.

By the way, Tamar arrived as a clerk in the battalion adjutancy. The position of company clerk didn't exist in the Artillery Corps, just as a battery commander didn't have a personal jeep, despite it being a post comparable to a company commander in the armored or infantry branches. I'll speak more at length of the disparaging treatment of the corps, but at the moment I'm romancing Tamar.

To leave the base in the evening, we were dependent on the goodwill of the deputy battalion commander, who was an older captain, or on our relations with the veteran sergeant-major, who was in charge of vehicles. Luckily for us, they favored our relationship and played along.

Who Got Sent to the Artillery Corps Back Then

The one who informed me of the disappointing trick being pulled on me was the Deputy Artillery Corps Commander, Manos Kol (Kolodny.)

He explained that there was an urgent need for battery commanders at the 402nd Battalion. Since these were, as mentioned above, 25-pounder cannons, WW2 veterans, this was a free-fall from the new SPH to the oldest possible towed guns. To add insult to injury, they sent me first to be a company commander to the raw recruits slated to man the planned battery. Infantry training again, this time in the area between Elyakim and Givat Ada, this time with the class of May, no more high school graduates, who accept anything and carry out all orders without too much backchat. Being recruited in May meant recruits who had dropped out of school prior (sometimes well before) to their 12th year of schooling, and that meant a more challenging population. The year was 1963. I had become closely acquainted with the recruits, most of whom were excellent people – you only needed to know how to spark their motivation and desire to serve, despite their problems at home, and often deprivation too. I spent long hours visiting families and bringing back AWOL soldiers with the welfare NCO, as they called the "Tash," or "Service conditions" NCOs back then. [Since military service is mandatory in Israel, and not composed strictly of professionals, and since military service, especially back then, was essential for many fields of employment and for social advancement, my approach was not to give up on people, and leave as many as possible in service – to man the batteries, to prevent good people from becoming derelict, and to create good citizens for the State of Israel.]

The atmosphere in the battalion was excellent. I was only 21, and the other officers were likewise young – some ROTC types were my age, and some a year younger. All were educated at similar institutions, brought up on the same values, and all were hardworking. We were blessed with a young and highly energetic battalion commander, Maj. Moshe Peled (Eisengeller), who was attentive to every initiative and a full participant in the battalion's social life. The battery soldiers – including my own battery – like most recruits to the Artillery Corps, a low-prestige posting in those days, came mostly from struggling homes, many of them on welfare. Many soldiers went on month-long work furloughs, to help provide for their families, and my role brought me in touch with what is now termed "Second Israel." Poverty, difficulties in earning a living wage, partial and poor education, and on the other hand good people, torn between their desire to serve in the IDF, to advance and feel a common bond with society at large, and commitment to their families.

A Major's Good Enough for Them

I mentioned the profile of soldier they used to send to the artillery back then, and mentioned our excellent battalion commander, Moshe Peled, and perhaps this is the place to mention that in the Artillery Corps, unlike in the Infantry and Armored Corps, the standard rank of a battalion commander in those days was Major, rather than Lt. Colonel as was customary in the other branches of service, while the rank of the deputy commander of a battalion was Captain, rather than Major. How and why was this distinction/discrimination created? My theory, based only on my own feverish conjecture and which no man has yet confirmed by research, holds that this procedure was cemented following the War of Independence. The Artillery Corps, in its initial days, drew a concentration of the "separatists" – the members of the Irgun and Lehi underground movements, who joined the IDF upon its establishment, but maintained their independence of besieged Jerusalem during the war. They were mostly right-wing, and politically opposed to the ruling labor movement, headed by Mapai. The high command of the IDF back then was mostly staffed by Members of the ruling party, Mapai. And following the Altalena incident, (in which the Etzel ["Irgun"] paramilitary movement refused to yield a shipment of weapons to the fledgling IDF, leading to a deadly firefight), concern arose that promoting former Etzel and Lehi members to high ranks would allow them to effect a coup or declare a revolt. Ben-Gurion, who ruled autocratically over the security establishment and was a political man through and through, ordered (allegedly, as his modus operandi was to deliver orders only verbally when mixing military and political considerations) to divert the "separatists" to the unglamorous Artillery Corps, and not to forward charging units such as the Infantry and Armored Corps, and at the same time to reduce standard ranks in the artillery, so that fewer officers who are not "our kind of people" would choose to sign on for a career in the military, following their mandatory service. Add to this the condescending attitude of the former Palmach fighters, graduates of the socialist youth movements, then at the zenith of their power, and the former Haganah figures, the leading security establishment, toward the weirdos who had served in the British military, or the Holocaust survivors, who were "ancients" (i.e., in their forties) – and you get the inferior status of the Artillery Corps, baked in right from the IDF's birth.

When I proposed this little theory to former IDF Chief of Staff (and former Armored Corps man) Haim Laskov, when he served as the IDF's soldiers' complaints ombudsman, and I hosted him as commander of Shivta Base, he rejected the theory vehemently. This only convinced me further that I was on to something.

This discriminatory standard, by the way, remained in effect for years in the 402nd and 334th Battalions. During Laskov's term as Chief of Staff, the standard was brought in line with that of the Infantry and Armored Corps only in the two other artillery battalions in existence back then – the 403rd and 404th. Over the years, the standards were equalized to those of the rest of the IDF, and recently the Chief Artillery Officer at the time of this writing, Brig. Gen. Neri Horowitz, decided to also standardize some of the unique terminology, so that a "battery" is now a company, and a "division artillery" is now a firing brigade.

Gunning and Geography

Even as a battery commander, I didn't always walk the path paved before me and often did things my own way. Thus, for example, when my battery, the 3rd, was scheduled to go on training in the south of the country, I decided that the soldiers and officers wouldn't ride in the WW2 "Six" trucks, which towed the ancient guns. Instead, I announced that we would do a "series of deployments and 'country knowledge,'"[5] in order to familiarize ourselves with the route and locate deployment areas, especially along the Green Line – then the border of Israeli-held territory, before the Six-Day War. Peled, the battalion commander, was, as mentioned above, open to innovation and gave his blessing to the initiative. The battery troopers, for their part, were pleased to be spared a slow, annoying ride with the guns.

The series became a unique hallmark and the pride of the company, so I revived the idea of combining gunnery and knowledge of the country when I commanded the corps' officers' course, leaving Shivta for a series of navigation and surveying intended to familiarize ourselves with the Negev – Israel's large, desert in the southern half of the country. Even before then, just before the Yom Kippur War, as commander of the advanced branch at Bahad 9 (the IDF's artillery school) I initiated a deployment series like that on the way from the base in Tzrifin to a firing range in the Sinai Peninsula, and as commander of Shivta, I initiated and hosted the IDF's annual country knowledge quiz. This required me to convince the senior brass of the Education Corps of the importance in schlepping to Shivta, which wasn't easy, but they couldn't withstand the pressure I applied.

In addition, my battery, with its antiquated cannons, was often called to fire honor shots at Lod Airport (now Ben Gurion International). Israel was flooded at the time with visiting foreign leaders, mostly presidents and kings from Africa and Asia, which according to protocol, are entitled to a 21-gun salute as they descend the aircraft ramp, and the 25-pounders were the only IDF guns equipped with honor salute shots.

---

5 "Yediat Ha'aretz," literally "knowledge of the country," is a uniquely Israeli concept, combining geography, history, and national identity. It was developed in order to turn the theoretical "love of Zion," espoused by Zionist activists in Europe, coming to an ancestral country they knew little of, into a true native relationship with the land.

400 Shots, 2 Hits (in Jordan, to Boot)

But all that was marginal. We trained most of the time, and were often called to support Golani brigade battalions, mostly in the Elyakim firing zone. One time we even "succeeded," at dawn, to 'slide' a projectile directly into a home in Dalyat al-Carmel – the projectile, fired at a flat trajectory at a target in the firing zone, kept on flying and entered the home of a Prisons Service officer. The police suspected the explosion to have been caused by a hand grenade, as a criminal attack of retaliation or warning, but the shrapnel proved that it was our ordnance.

One of the battery's duties was to provide fire support to Bahad 9 in live fire ranging drills in the Ma'ahaz fire zone, where Route 6 and Route 40 now merge, north of Beit Kama. The battery would deploy, and the basic course cadets would fire at various targets, throughout the day and night. It was a monotonous, boring duty, that lasted for several days.

One morning, I decided that the XO, Avraham Ben-Shlush (my deputy), could carry on with his excellent work, and I would go on reconnaissance in the field. The forward fire control vehicle was a Fargo 4X4 pickup, ancient but reliable. I took it and left Ben-Shlush in the fire control tent. The artillery board, containing the details of the position and targets, was set on an easel with a radio beside it. As I needed a map, I took the only map in the tent. The target's coordinates, I told myself, are already written on the board anyway.

Happy and carefree, I left on my adventure, but upon returning, I found everything in uproar. The firing had been halted, and the commander of the officers' course, Yaakov Livni, was forced to rush to the fire control tent after the battery had fired at the village of Beit Mirsim, on the Jordanian side of the border. (Recently, in an archeological tour of Jewish settlements from Old Testament times, archeologist Sa'ar Ganor told us that many of the village residents are antiquities thieves, and that this has been their trade for many generations.)

At first, one shell was fired. As it was not observed where it was supposed to hit, the observation personnel gave the order: "Repeat," based on procedure that assumes that an unobserved projectile landed in a deep valley or ravine. The second shot fell in the same spot in the village – and again went unobserved. Luckily for us, no one was hurt by the impact. However, UN officers were rushed to the site, and an international incident was about to break out. Ben-Shlush had meanwhile, innocently wiped the artillery board clean, but a major who was a stickler for procedure and detail, was appointed to investigate the incident, and somehow noticed that the nearly erased coordinates were reversed: North was erroneously noted as east, and vice versa. The mystery was solved, the armistice committee was dispersed, matters with Jordan were smoothed over, and the incident was averted.

I took full responsibility and was put on a disciplinary court-martial procedure adjudicated by the commander of Bahad 9, Colonel Asher Blicher, but I got off lightly with a warning.

However, the 402nd earned a dubious nickname that evening – "400 shots, 2 hits (in Jordan, to boot.)" That blame, and the enduring bit of shame, is entirely on my shoulders.

A Double Lesson from Yanush

The Artillery Corps' doctrine, and that of the IDF as a whole up until the Yom Kippur War, were modeled after the British example. This meant that at wartime, the Artillery Corps is divided into two parts: The firing echelon, which includes the gun batteries with all their auxiliary support, ordnance, and logistics, whose duty it is to produce fire, and a forward echelon, which plans the fire along with the maneuvering forces, observes, ranges, and operates the firing echelon on all levels.

Accordingly, the division of tasks within artillery battalions was clear: The battalion commander becomes a brigade's artillery commander, emphasis on the word commander, and he commands all the cannons supporting the brigade with fire. The battery commanders become classic fire support officers (FSOs), present with the maneuvering battalion, and the lower officers are posted with the maneuvering companies as forward observation officers, or FOs for short.

Those who remained behind to command the firing echelons were the deputy battalion commander and his aides – the reconnaissance and surveying officer and the fire direction officer at the battalion level, along with the ordnance and logistics officers, and the medical officer. The comms officer, intelligence officer, and the ops officer manned the fire support command center alongside the battalion commander. The 402nd Battalion was joinable to the Golani Brigade, while the 334th was a full part of that brigade. As such, I was FSO at Golani's 51st Battalion, while the fire support commander and the other FSOs were from the 334th.

I took part in some battalion-level planning groups and several fire exercises, headed by the 51st Battalion's commander, Tzvika Levanon, and according to battle procedures, as an FSO, I was alongside the maneuvering battalion's commander in the brigade command group, meaning one level above the company commanders.

It was the same at the brigade level, where the fire support commander took part along with the brigade commander in all planning and all command groups in the division, and the orders went down to the battalion commanders. This procedure gave the forward echelon officers a broader perspective, a better understanding of the battlefield at the planning stage, and helped them in battle during operations and wars.

I first saw Yanush when he was commander of Company S of the 52nd Battalion in 1964, at a battalion-wide exercise held at the Northern Command's fire zone in Elyakim. He came as a captain with his armored company to take part in the 51st Battalion's exercise, and was considered the leading light of the generation, especially by the infantrymen, who greatly appreciated the artillery and armored firepower.

Yanush took part in the battalion's planning group for that exercise, and displayed creative tactical thinking. This happened, for instance, when battalion commander Levanon determined that the SS-11 anti-tank company, which had just been attached to the battalion, should travel at the end of the convoy. Yanush stood up, and explained at length why he needed the anti-tank missiles, how they should be utilized, and how they could be full partners to the battalion in battle.

He proposed to deploy them on the wings, to surprise the "enemy's" tanks, and turn the SS-11 into an integral part in armored combat.

Levanon accepted his comments. Infantry commanders were more open than armored commanders to changes, and Yanush was an odd duck in the Armored Corps milieu. In any case, I received a triple lesson: How to utilize anti-tank missiles well, and mostly how to explain my position, as well as why it's a good idea to listen.

THE 404TH

No Dropouts

After a bit over a year at the 402nd, I transferred to the battalion I sought, the 404th, the pinnacle of the Artillery Corps, but I was once again tasked to command a company of rookies, class of August '64 – this time in Nitzanim.

I was appointed commander of the "Boaz" battery, and for the second time, began commanding a company of Infantry rookies. This time, after we had all read "Battle Cry," by Leon Uris, which has just been translated into Hebrew, we decided to turn the Infantry rookies entrusted to us into marines, and used every stupid example in the book.

In many cases, the squad commanders were overzealous, and without my knowledge, committed acts I would not have approved. But I was company commander. Responsibility rested with me when the squad commanders made the rookies run with buckets on their heads or in sleeping bags. Sheer abuse, which fell right into the lap of Talik (Israel Tal), later a famous general, and then commander of the Armored Corps. He leapt at the opportunity, and decided to make an example for the entire IDF out of us. Of course, there wasn't a single armored platoon where rookies or *"youngies"* were treated any better, but it was easy to make a cautionary tale at the expense of the gunners.

We all stood court-martialed – from myself to the last squad leader – at the Armored Corps' court in Castina Base, with Talik's dictate, to make scapegoats out of us, hovering above. The prosecutor, Captain Rahamim Levi, fought to spare us a conviction anyway, and we were close to acquittal – but Talik received constant updates from the court president. He called in Yaakov Kedmi (then a major at the JAG unit and in time to become a Supreme Court Justice) to take over the prosecution, and managed to get a conviction. The worst sentence was my demotion from 1st to 2nd lieutenant. All the others got off easy.

On the courthouse lawn, after sentencing, Kedmi stopped me. "Arie, file an appeal right away," he said. "You don't deserve this punishment." And as Talik was abroad, the appeal was heard by Herzl Shafir, his deputy. Shafir, an enlightened and open-minded man, repealed the verdict, and therefore my sentence as well. The conviction was stricken from my disciplinary record, which remained clean and unblemished. I don't know how Talik reacted when he came back from abroad. What's clear is that Shafir wasn't among his worshipers, nor did he treat the man like a god.

Like a paratrooper whose chute won't open, and he's sent up to jump again, after a year of trial that ended in nothing, I was once again appointed commander of a rookie company. The man behind this development was the deputy commander of the 404th battalion, Michael Carmeli (aka "Mondi"), with the support of the battalion commander, Yehoshua Behar.

This time I had learned my lesson. No more punishment for the rookies, but instead – red, black, and white points, with the stick and carrot involving weekend leave passes. The rookies of the class of August '65 slept six hours a night, and were free of humiliating initiation practices. We took them out on long voyages and advanced field skills practice. We trained them in all weapons, and held elaborate fire exercises. I put a premium on physical fitness and marksmanship, and pushed all of the recruits to earn the gold physical fitness and gold marksmanship medals, and no settling for silver or bronze. The goal we set ourselves was, once again: No dropouts. Bring all our rookies to the finish line – and so it was.

Armored Company Commanders' Course

The three other battery commanders in the 404th – Carlo Segev, Avraham Bar-David, and Mondi Carmeli (before he was appointed deputy battalion commander) – were more veteran than me, all three were graduates of the armored company commanders' course, and after hearing their stories, I aspired to take the same course. In addition to all I would gain there, I said to myself, it would put the stamp on my belonging to the armored forces. I am, after all, a battery commander in the 404th Battalion, which belongs to the Armored Corps, and I wear the green/black diagonally striped tag of the armored forces.

In late 1965, I arrived at the course on the recommendation of my battalion commander, Yehoshua Behar, who had meanwhile been appointed the artillery instructor at the course. I found friends from Bahad 1 alongside me, including the future Northern Command General, Yossi Peled, and two men awarded the medal of distinguished service, Elyashiv Shimshi and Uzi Lancner (nee Levtzur), and we had reservists, mostly kibbutzniks, including Ilan Yagoda from Megiddo, Yosef Sarig, son of the famous Palmach fighter, Sergei (nee Nachum) Sarig of Beit Hashita, Sassi from Glil-Yam, comms officers like Israel Zamir, in time CEO of Tadiran, Talik's adjutant, Kuti Sharabi, and also Gavriel "Gavrush " Rappaport, who was a reservist, a kibbutznik, and also a legendary Palmach fighter, one of the heroes of the battles for Burma Road (the road through which supplies and reinforcements were brought to Jerusalem under siege in Israel's War of Independence.) The course commander was the future Brig. Gen. Uri Bar-On.

The course suited me to a tee. I loved the movement and command over a tank, and quickly adapted to a tank fighter's orientation – both in daytime motion and nighttime navigation. The company commander's role in the exercises was reserved to tank crew members, and I filled other roles. In the concluding exercise, which was a bilateral exercise between two armored companies, I was given the role of commander of a reconnaissance platoon in Yagoda's company. The opposing recon platoon commander in the "enemy" company was recon legend Gavrush, and my mission was to locate the enemy forces, identify its movements and report to Yagoda. As I knew the ground well – the Halutza sand dunes in the vicinity of Revivim, Mashabei Sade, Tze'elim, and Halutza – and as I had acquired a hunter's vision in my youth, the kind that picks up the tiniest movement, I quickly identified Gavrush and his jeeps and discovered the location and direction of the entire "enemy" company. I reported on the company comms network continuously, until Yagoda was forced to plead for some quiet.

After defeating the enemy comprehensively, we sat down for a summary discussion in the field. Talik was present at the exercise and spoke first. He referred to the recon 'toon commander with the most amazing superlatives, such as "I have never seen such recon action," heaped some more praise, and then asked who the recon 'toon commander was. I raised my hand, and Talik grimaced instantly. He was sure it was a tank crewmember, probably one of his pet company commanders, but lo and behold, it turned out to be a gunner – and not just any gunner, but the one who cheated the gallows Talik had personally built for him, at the Armored Corps' court in Castina.

I critique myself fiercely and in detail. I look into every utterance and action to see what I did right or wrong. This time I was breathing mountaintop air and felt great. Everything was really in fine order. The perfect execution resulted in a victory in the training exercise, and I even registered a little personal triumph over Talik.

Bahad 1, Take 3 – or "You'll Get Captain"

At the end of the course, the Deputy Chief Artillery Officer, still Manos Kol, called me for a placement interview. After two or three oft-repeated phrases, he said: "You're going to be a 'toon instructor at Bahad 1."

I tried to decline. I had been a career soldier for three years now, and what he was proposing was a detour from the path I had set myself. I wanted to be with my men at the battery, but he wouldn't budge. "We have to give Bahad 1 a 'toon instructor, as a corps (today the corps has to assign a company commander), and it has to be a captain, a company commanders' course graduate."

"I'm not a captain," I said.

Kol didn't bat an eyelid. "That's fine," he grinned. "You'll get captain."

My viewpoint changed. This was a shortcut, reducing the required time served between rank promotions, and would turn my loss into a gain.

Bahad 1 was still located in Camp Sirkin back then, and was a completely different world than Talik's armored forces world, from which I had just arrived. I was deeply impressed right from the start by the long, thorough preparation and the number of red boots (denoting paratroopers and other elite units) and the lapel merit wings affixed to various colored backgrounds on the instructors' chests, and I felt a sort of weakness. How would I compete with all these heroes?

Once people opened their mouths, I realized that just like everywhere else in the world, wisdom lies between the ears, not on the feet, or the chest, or the shoulders. I fitted in just fine in a joint ops division course for armored corps, artillery, engineering, intelligence, naval commandos, and Sayeret Matkal. Company commander Moshe Yosef appreciated me, and I was undoubtedly the leading platoon instructor in the class.

This was a fascinating stop along my career. The man who impressed me in particular, and whom I was deeply fond of, was Meir Pa'il, the commander of the officers' school – a great man, whose talk on leadership lasted for eight hours without a single cadet falling asleep, for each minute was more riveting than the last. Pa'il, for his part, took a liking to me as well. Our friendship lasted afterward as well, and he was godfather to my firstborn son, Sagi, who was born on Independence Day in 1968.

Among other things, I instituted a system in my platoon of expulsion by the cadets, which was part of Pa'il's overall vision: developing commanders with broad vision, openness, and leadership, which manifests in recognition of their leadership by those around them. It was a sort of "active sociometric test," in which the platoon decided who is and isn't worthy of being an officer, for the cadets know better than anyone who their fellows really are. One cadet was indeed kicked out like that, and rightly so. At the pace of events in the course, there was no time for scheming and politics. The truth was revealed on its own, and usually the cadets' decision matched those of the staff.

I enjoyed every minute – from the basic exercises to the concluding series in the south, where I played a mechanized infantry company commander, charging at the head of the company, riding a half-track armored vehicle and shooting a Browning M1919 machine gun.

This period gave me experience, and also insights for the future. First – to always maintain openness to any idea or initiative. Second – I could fit into any framework in the IDF, not as a simple gunner, but as a professional and a leader. The friendship formed between me and the three squad leaders working with me, Reuven, whose last name I have sadly forgotten, Danny Gramaty, and Avishai Vilner from Yifat, who was killed in the Yom Kippur War, and my deputy Shmulik Zohar, continued for many years.

Pa'il's Special Methods

The "Camelot and the Knights of the Round Table" period, when anyone's opinion was equal – whether cadet or instructor – ended in heartbreak, when Pa'il was deposed from command of Bahad 1 in front of the entire staff, at a stormy meeting with the then Chief-of-Staff Yitzhak Rabin. I was torn there between two men whom I highly appreciated, almost worshiped.

Pa'il's command and leadership style was unique and innovative, but it wasn't always suited to the environment. The military is a tough, orderly, hierarchical organization, and there is operational importance in following orders. Pa'il loved, encouraged, cooperated, and supported those who got him and followed his spirit with all his might, but those who resisted or displayed obtuseness and narrow-mindedness were ignored. This was a system of self-discipline, where everyone had the right to voice their own opinion, and eventually act on it too. But what didn't always work even in the kibbutzim surely wasn't suited to the military.

The man who initiated the firing was Talik. Again Talik. He sought to increase the power of the armored forces, which he commanded, at the expense of any other branch. Even Bahad 1 seemed unimportant to him (even though he himself had commanded it for two years). The armored officers' course, which as actually the corps specialization course, was a perfectly sufficient officers' course in his view, and he saw the preliminary training at Bahad 1 as unnecessary – especially considering it was an infantry course, and who needs the Infantry? Tanks and armored troops are all you need.

In practice, some of the Armored Corps cadets were of poor quality, but when we put up some of them for dismissal, right in the first stage, a repeal order came straight from the Chief of Staff, Rabin, who was greatly influenced by Talik and ordered to leave them in the course. This undermined the authority of the instructors and that of the school commander, at whose office dismissal hearings were held. This created an intolerable situation in the platoon as well. The other cadets knew that there were rejects among them who enjoy immunity, aren't appointed for duties, and constitute a sort of dead weight.

For lack of a better choice we decided, in consultation with Pa'il, to bypass Talik. The idea was to put the ones who weren't worthy on the three stages of dismissal – the platoon instructor, the company instructor, and the school commander – at night. That way, the Armored Corps men wouldn't be able to do what their command had ordered them to do: inform their higher-ups that they were up for dismissal, so that the move could be blocked.

At dawn, all the Armored Corps' rejects were put on a truck and sent packing to Castina, to the Armored Corps' headquarters. A few days later, Rabin and the head of the IDF ops division, Ezer Weizmann, arrived for a talk with all the Bahad 1 instructors. The hall was packed to the hilt, and it was clear that the object was to teach Pa'il a lesson. We just didn't know how far Rabin would go. Pa'il, after all, was his buddy from the Palmach.

The talk was long and eye-opening. Instructors of all ranks voiced their opinions. Yaakov Even didn't voice his own opinions, but simply read an article out of the "Book of the Palmach." The title was "Quality vs. Quantity," and Rabin beamed broadly, as he happened to be the essay's author. He repeatedly explained that the military is an organization whose object is to fight and defeat the enemy, and therefore discipline must be upheld, and orders obeyed. You can argue, but once an order is given you must carry it out, for these are matters of life and death.

Meir'ke Pa'il was deposed. This also happened to be my own final chord at Bahad 1 – until I attended the graduation ceremony of one of the courses as Chief Artillery Officer, and then when two of my sons graduated the officers' course. I came from the start for only a single three-month course, and in late 1966, I went back to the 404th Battalion.

Who Moved My Searchlight?

FSO of the 82nd Armored Battalion. That was the operational assignment awaiting me upon return to the 404th, along with command of the "Boaz" battery. This was a battalion of Centurion tanks. The battalion commander was Binyamin Oshri, the Ops officer was Ilan Yekuel, and the company commanders – Shammai Kaplan, Ori Or (later the Northern Command General), and Gideon Avidor, later a brigadier general. I fitted in with them excellently, and quickly learned that the finest company commander among them, beyond a shadow of a doubt, was Shammai Kaplan.

On the professional level, I came to understand through the many exercises what it truly means to be an FSO in a tank battalion. The brigade commander was Herzl Shafir, and his deputy was Shlomo "Cheech" Lahat, in time a major-general and then the Mayor of Tel Aviv. Shafir, who always showed up with the brigade Women's Corps officer by his side, initiated battalion-wide exercises for the 7th Armored Brigade, in which we would ride half-tracks, do long nighttime maneuvers of 20 or 30 km, encounter, attack, and take over objectives.

Beyond all that, I gladly served as FSO in the exercises of two other battalions in our brigade – the 52nd and the 46th – because there was nobody else to do it, and mostly because it was convenient for my battalion commander in the 404th, Tzvika Shpitzer (nee Shafir) who was the artillery commander for the 7th Armored Brigade. He viewed me as a pro.

This way, I also came to know the battalion commanders and their skills – Gideon Altshuler, commander of the 52nd, Gideon Gordon, commander of the 46th, Maxi, aka Mordechai Avigad, commander of the 9th, and of course Oshri, commander of the 82nd, who was without question the best of them all. Sadly, he sustained a severe head wound at the Jordan River headwaters in the "Battle for Water" – a series of clashes between 1964 and 1967 over control of the sources of the Jordan River's waters.

Herzl Shafir delivered the commander briefings in person, and I was greatly surprised that he gave any mind to the role of artillery fire and the roles of the FO and the battalion FSO in encounter battles. In this, as well, he was exceptional in the armored forces landscape: A commander who believes in combining all components, rather than placing all his hopes on the tank alone.

An FO or FSO should be an initiator in an encounter, he said. From the moment the force encounters the enemy and begins preparation for attack, the FO or FSO needs to range fire and prepare a quick firing plan, not ask for permission and wait for approval.

The battalion commander, Shafir said, has no attention span for anything other than ordering the companies as to who retreats, who covers, who flanks, and who charges. Once the FSO is ready, they have to tell the tank battalion commander, "Ready." The bat-com will give his blessing, and leave the authority to deploy fire to the FSO, pursuant to the attack plan being relayed on the radio.

I was also sometimes assigned as FSO in the Golani and Paratrooper Brigade battalion-wide fire exercises. This happened mostly when some battalion's regular FSO wasn't available for some reason, and an experienced FSO was needed to take his place. This is how I came to be at a fire exercise held by Golani's 12th Battalion, under the command of Musa Klein, who was later killed at the Tel Faher battle in the Six-Day War, winning the Medal of Distinguished Service posthumously, after having won the medal of courage in the Sinai War of 1956. It was a nighttime exercise. I aimed the battery and the artillery searchlights at my disposal by the last light of the day, and then a long hike on foot commenced. When we approached the destinations, I commanded the artillery batteries to fire control projectiles and put the searchlights "on" – but the beams shone in a completely different direction. While making French fires and coffee – standard operating procedure for searchlight crews during the long wait for the order – someone must have knocked them off-target. When I was done venting my fury, I aimed the searchlights again, on the march. I had a hard time spotting the targets, but despite this, managed to land the fire on time and on target, precisely according to plan. The Chief Artillery Officer, Israel Ben-Amitai, was watching the exercise and praised me – or at least so claims my good friend David Maimon, who was a logistics officer in the corps' HQ at the time.

At a fire exercise with the 50th Paratroopers' Battalion, I operated alongside battalion commander Chaim Nadel, deputy battalion commander Moshe Yosef, Ops officer Benda and company commanders Dan Shomron, later Chief of Staff, Amos Yaron, later military attaché at the Israeli embassy to the U.S. and Director-General of the Defense Ministry, and Yos'ke Ravon.

Shomron stood head and shoulders above the rest, and I was surprised when he began to ask questions and interrogate me on each and every stage of my work. I wasn't used to interest, and certainly not to in-depth details, and replied with a touch of impatience when he queried me on professional aspects. I thought they were none of his business, but he wouldn't let go before ascertaining every detail and understanding fully what we were supposed to do, including safety ranges, firing rates, munition types, what happens in case of malfunction, and so on. And just as Oshri chose Shammai Kaplan, his star company commander, when he had to decide which company would join the 82nd Battalion, with Nadel it was always Dan Shomron who led and navigated the 50th, and always successfully.

As part of the exercise, we left on a long hike from hill 272, somewhere between Shivta and Ketziot, and the plan was carried out without a hitch. Despite Shomron's thorough debriefing ticking me off, it dawned on me that I should explain myself more in depth. That way I could discover problems I hadn't identified previously and which, if not for Shomron's queries, could have caused malfunctions.

Baptism by Fire at Samua

My first baptism by fire, more as a combat trooper and less as a gunner, was the battle of Samua. It was the first battle I had taken part in, after dozens of exercises and training sessions. I had taken part before that in the planning of night raids with the 202nd Battalion, under the command of Ephraim "Pihotke" Hiram, and also a long-range incursion into Sinai, but all those operations had been called off at the last moment.

The Samua action was the last large-scale military operation prior to the Six-Day War. A raid in broad daylight by the Paratroopers Brigade and armored troops, commanded by Rafael "Raful" Eitan, (later Chief of Staff), after three paratroopers from the 890th Battalion had been killed in a terrorist attack and the terrorists' tracks led to the village, south of Hebron – concurrent with a raid by the 7th Brigade on two villages in the Jordan Valley. The operation was called "Shredder," and was held on November 13th, 1966, and I was appointed as FSO to the 35th Rangers, under Giora Haikeh, later a division commander and a brigadier general. I arrived for mustering at Camp Nathan, on the outskirts of Beersheba, with a half-track from the 404th, with a comms operator and a driver, both armed with Uzis. The first person I bumped into was my old friend Amos Gotlieb (nee Kotzer.) We were born on the same day, our fathers had been good friends since the battle for Arab Kafr Saba in the Independence War and often visited each other – me at Amos's home in Kfar Shmaryahu, and he at mine.

"What are you riding?" he asked.

I replied: "A half-track."

"Alone?" he asked.

"Yes."

Amos was Haikeh's deputy at the time. "I'm not going to let you get killed," he said, assigning me an entire platoon, including a platoon commander from the Rangers unit, armed with machine guns and other goodies. This allowed him to mobilize an additional platoon, and take care of a childhood friend at the same time.

We were supposed to take up the western cordon and moved at the head of the force, with Haikeh riding in the same Centurion tank as

Yehuda Bachar, the Armored Corps company commander. But they had erred in navigation, and we found ourselves in a wadi, with Jordanian soldiers dismounting from a truck and coming down toward us to stop us. Bachar showered them with fire and a Jordanian jeep mounted with an M-40 106mm recoilless rifle, which was also firing at the column, received its rations and went up in flames.

The sight of dead Jordanian soldiers was chilling. They had just dismounted the truck, in their green uniforms, and now they lay lifeless. On the other hand, the alternative was us lying there dead. Arabs in civvies joined in the fire at us. The platoon commander trained the machine gun on them and silenced them too.

We kept moving toward the village. To the left, we saw the Sherman tank company, under the command of future Major-General Yaakov Lapidot, firing barrages of fourteen shells at a time at the Jordanian military base located in the Rujum al-Madfa police station. There was no occasion to employ the artillery, although my battery – "Boaz" – was deployed and aimed at the planned targets, and we had – truth be told – an intense desire to join in the fun and fire.

Fifteen Jordanian soldiers were killed at Samua, dozens were wounded, and dozens of homes were demolished in the village and neighboring villages. Our forces lost one man – Yoav Shacham, commander of the 202nd Battalion. Ten soldiers were wounded. The action received aerial support, incidentally, after eight Jordanian Hunter aircraft threatened to attack us, and were forced to flee.

FIRST WAR

From a bird's-eye view, pun intended, Israel's Air Force decided the Six-Day War and defeated the armies of Egypt and Syria within the first three hours of the war, when it completely annihilated their air forces. The ones to ride on the coattails of this success were Talik and the armored corps, which exploited the open skies, stormed all the way to the Suez Canal, and conquered the Sinai Peninsula. The book "The Tanks of Tammuz" put the final stamp on Gorodish and Talik's status as public idols.

Elation swept over the Israeli public with the conquest of the Western Wall in Jerusalem and the return to "ancestral homesteads," after weeks of nerve-racking waiting, digging trenches in city centers, piling sandbags at the entrances to residential buildings, and fear of another Holocaust.

Alongside all this, I personally felt disappointed and frustrated. On the eve of the war, I was scheduled to be appointed to a post that would fit me like a glove – FSO at the 79th Armored Battalion. I took part in the group planning and ordering for the 7th Armored Brigade, and I have no doubt that I could have deployed effective fire and prevented a few incidents of the battalion banging its head against the wall – including the Giradi Battle between Rafah and Al-Arish, and the ranger unit's battles under Ori Or in Rafah – with preparatory and accompanying fire. The 7th Brigade and the Steel Division had enough artillery, and the missions could have been carried out with fewer losses and perhaps no losses, but the man slated to replace me sustained a leg wound, and the 79th Battalion went to war without an Artillery Officer.

And why replace me at all? Two days before D-day, Tzvika Shpitzer, my battalion commander at the 404th and also the 7th Brigade's artillery commander, decided to leave me at the battalion as recon and survey officer. The Southern Command had decided that the 404th, which in planning was scheduled to join with the 7th Brigade, would move south to the Kunteila route with the 8th Brigade. The object was to create a deception and secure the flank, as the American M7 "Priest" self-propelled Howitzer cannons had better mobility and reliability, and could withstand the long trip. The 647th Battalion, with French AMX 105mm guns, under Aryeh Zinger, was sent instead of the 404th with the 7th Brigade to northern Sinai – the main penetration sector.

I was very upset. Finally a war, after the long wait and professionalization as an FSO, and they send me back, to the firing echelon, and to a negligible sector to boot. Shpitzer noticed my disappointment. "You're right," he said. "But we're headed toward war. There has to be another experienced officer at the battalion, to help Carlo Segev, the deputy battalion commander, in case of trouble."

He had no idea how prophetic his words would prove to be.

On June 5th, at 08:00, we left on the long journey, with Aryeh Biro, commander of the 129th Battalion. The radio sent out a broadcast: "Red Sheet" – this was the codeword for war – "The nation of Israel is going to war. Move, move, out." Our objectives were Kunteila, Nakhal, and from there as ordered. We assisted Biro's battalion with fire in taking Kunteila, and took Egyptian counter-battery fire. I moved with the battalion's recon group immediately following the forward charging forces, behind Aryeh Keren's mech-infantry battalion, to be able to build positions. The short range of the Priest guns, 11 km in total, forced me to move dozens of kilometers ahead of the battalion, to locate positions and steer the batteries to them.

Who Are We?

A few kilometers before Nakhal, I stopped to wait for the battalion. Thirsty and famished Egyptian soldiers, some barefoot, some wounded and in pain, were also trying to make their way to the Canal. Defeated, frightened, and unarmed, they walked with lifeless eyes and begged for water.

One of the battalions' aid stations passed by such a group of soldiers. The medic and the paramedic dismounted from their vehicle, bound the wounds of the injured, gave them water to drink, and continued on their way. The exhausted Egyptians sat on the side of the road and couldn't have imagined this was their end. Two recon jeeps appeared suddenly out of nowhere, stopped by them, and opened machine gun fire. Within a minute, sitting all the while in their jeep, they roared on ahead.

Before my very eyes, I saw that the Israeli people are divided into two kinds: One that heals and aids the forlorn and beleaguered, even be they enemy soldiers, and the other cruel and murderous, capable of butchering subdued soldiers in chilling cold blood, in the very style of those horrible images from dark times in our own annals.

I had many missions and tasks in those days, and pushed the incident deep into the back of my mind. From time to time, to this day, those sights float up into my consciousness, stirring an inner debate within me, whether we truly deserve the title "Light Among the Nations." I am no anthropologist, nor a psychologist, but I have often seen in my life, and have encountered even as a child, a pathological hatred of Arabs. I too have caused the death of people, and I hope they were all soldiers. I did so in battle, whereas there, on the road outside Nakhal, there were unarmed shadows of men on hand, and elite soldiers, my own countrymen, on the other.

The Explosive Truck That Killed Carlo

At dawn, I received instructions to report to the commander of the 520th Armored Brigade at the missile base at the Mitleh Pass. Even back then, the Egyptians were armed with first-model SA-2 surface-to-air missiles, ready for combat in well-sided trenches, with a fire-control center.

This was the fourth day of the war. I reported with my two jeeps and my half-track, waited patiently, and eventually four recon jeeps arrived, followed by a brigadier's half-track – four pole-mounted headlights and flags.

The half-track stopped, and I approached and saluted. "Who are you, young man?" the brigadier asked, in a typical armored corps' tone.

"RSO of the 404th, reporting at your command," I replied, by the book.

"Very nice. And who am I?"

I knew it was the deputy brigadier, promoted only yesterday to brigadier, and replied: "Jacky Even, Brigadier of the 520th."

Even had been promoted from deputy to brigadier after his brigadier, Elhanan Sela, had been deposed for procrastination and lack of progress. Even was pleased to see that word had gotten around, and said: "Full marks, young man. Full marks."

Jacky Even was considered the armored corps' wunderkind at the time. He had been sent to Germany at the head of a delegation of officers to intake the Patton tanks, and founded the 79th Battalion. I knew the battalion and its personnel well from exercises I had performed as the battalion's regular FSO, and Even was always pleased. He wasn't as vain and cruel as Gorodish, and although the armored corps' arrogance clung to him, he maintained his humanity.

He ordered me to arrive at the "Madonna," a post at the end of the Mitleh, on the banks of the Suez Canal, to deploy the 404th there and be ready to fire. Then he added: "I've issued a clear order to the entire brigade – no looting!"

I drove quickly to the "Madonna," located positions, prepared and surveyed by the battery recon officers, and went with the battalion's sergeant-major, Haim Maimon, who was part of the recon group, to receive the battalion, headed by deputy battalion commander Carlo. The column arrived late at night. I boarded the deputy commander's half-track and to my surprise, saw before me not Carlo but my old acquaintance Itzik Nir, who was deputy commander of the 403rd Battalion when I was starting out as XO and commander of the first self-propelled battery.

"Where's Carlo?" I asked.

"Go, go, lead the way," he replied in a dull, heavy voice.

"But where's Carlo?"

Maimon, who had meanwhile gathered intelligence, took me aside. "Carlo was killed," he said.

I put the battalion in positions, and turned to figure out what happened. It turned out that Carlo had gathered the troops during their stop at the Mitleh, and instructed them clearly: No looting, and no touching any Egyptian belongings. Anyone caught will be severely punished! And then, along with HQ company commander Amos Haviv and vehicle officer Hananiah Azriel, Carlo went looking for large Egyptian trucks, to load the ammunition arriving from Israel onto huge trucks. He climbed onto a truck, opened the door, and a massive explosion shook the site. The truck was rigged with a large amount of explosives, and the three of them were killed on the spot. Carlo was recognized by a tuft of grey hair that adorned his flowing mane, the trademark of the tall and handsome Carlo.

A Captain in the Desert – Is a Tiger

There was no time to mourn. Itzik Nir went back to his post as ops officer of the artillery brigade of the Yaffe Division. I remained the senior officer in the battalion, and suddenly Yaakov Erez showed up, my instructor from the basic course at the officers' school. He commanded an armored force sent to take Ras Sudar, and without much chitchat, told me: "You are appointed deputy commander of the 404th, effective immediately."

"I'm a Captain," I said. Deputy battalion commander posts were reserved for veteran majors, and I knew that there was a long waiting list.

"A captain in the desert – is a tiger," he replied. It hurt, because I was replacing a fallen comrade, but I was flattered to be chosen.

The first order I received was to hit targets across the Canal, shortly after the cease-fire, and the Egyptians did not stand by idly. We immediately took counter-battery fire, and Mordechai Bagleibter, one of the gunners of my battery, "Boaz," the son of Holocaust survivors from Beit Eliezer, was killed. I tried to find out who could be scoping us from the other side, which was flat, and four kilometers away I identified a tall comms tower with soldiers on it. They looked like

FOs. I aimed one of the self-propelled guns, it hit the base of the tower, and the FOs fell to the ground like autumn leaves.

Concurrently, two Egyptian Mig jets attacked us, hitting Battery B – but this time with no casualties. While there was a battalion of anti-aircraft guns deployed next to us, their deputy battalion commander, who commanded the post, folded under the pressure and ran as soon as the counter-battery fire started falling, abandoning us to the mercy of the aircraft. My rage knew no bounds. I ran with my AK47 to shoot him, but the AA commander, who wasn't present during the deputy fleeing the battlefield, had meanwhile returned and calmed me down.

I continued to actively seek engagement, as per the core value of the IDF, and visited my friend and classmate at Bahad 1, Uzi Lancner, the commander of the armored company at the wharf outposts and the village of Al-Ayash, at the southern end of the Canal, across from Port Tawfiq. Gorodish had just initiated an action meant to demarcate Israeli sovereignty by flags posted on buoys in the middle of the Canal. Recruited for the operation were Shayetet 13 naval commando fighters on a rubber speedboat, as well as a company of SS-11 anti-tank missiles, commanded by classmates of mine from the basic officers' course, Alex Lapidot and Shaul Noy. The Egyptians were not enthused by Gorodish's initiative and dropped heavy artillery fire. I took cover behind a building with an officer, who had navy field stripes, crouching next to me. I looked at him, astonished. It was my good friend from Bahad 1, Gadi Sheffi.

"Arie," he said, "How can you live in this reality, having artillery fired at you all the time and continue functioning? We at the Shayetet are shitting our pants from the shells falling around us. It's frightening to death. You don't see the enemy, and don't know when a shell will drop on you." I replied: "Gadi, get used to it, that's how it is with us. We stopped minding it long ago. Put me underwater in the dark, to fight one on one, and I'll probably feel the way you do here."

The series of incidents was in fact one big incident. It led to a series of battles which indicated the War of Attrition, even as far back as the end of the Six-Day War, although it officially began only later.

The trigger was the decision by Gorodish to set the armistice line in the middle of the Canal, so it wouldn't stay in the Egyptians' hands as it had until the war. The Egyptians levelled fire on the naval commando troopers, and we responded with cannon fire for cover as well as heavy fire on Port Tawfiq. Concurrently, to ease the pressure on Lancner and Sheffi, we received an order to torch the refineries in Suez City. They went up in flames in short order. The counter-battery fire which rained on us scored a direct hit on one of the self-propelled guns. The shell hit the Priest steel hull and did not penetrate, but one of the troopers inside the self-propelled gun was hurt by parts that went flying from the impact.

Student

Before the war, I had signed on for the career military, aiming to begin academic studies at the military's expense in October '67. I signed for twelve years – yes, twelve years – which included the two and a half years of study. I had been a replacement deputy battalion commander, and supposedly I could have insisted on a permanent posting, but at the meek Artillery Corps that would entail a struggle, and I wasn't sure that Shpitzer would back me up. He was a good and pleasant man, but I didn't view him as being built for twisting arms.

Aryeh Beckinstein, who was six years older than me, replaced me as deputy commander of the 404th Battalion, and I would later replace him as commander of the 405th. Meanwhile, as a student, I was appointed as the deputy commander of the 827th Battalion – a reserve battalion of Priest guns – and spent about half a year there, in operational duty, training, and being in battles during the War of Attrition along the Suez Canal, the Jordan Valley and the Beit She'an Valley for this time period, at the expense of school.

REALITY AND VISION

Repeating a Grade

The day I finished my studies and got to Sinai, to the War of Attrition, and the harsh conditions in which the Artillery Corps was fighting – even back then, the vision of combined arms had begun to coalesce, and consequently, what the Artillery Corps should look like in the future. Vision is a big and imposing word, but a reality like the one I encountered – the wretchedness of the Artillery Corps, an enormous Egyptian advantage, and a lack of regard by the IDF to all of these – caused me, and other people in the corps, to see how and what needed to be done. This harsh reality gave birth to the vision, and nurtured it, but before all that could even get traction, there were some bumps right at the outset.

My assignment interview with the corps commander, Baruch Baruchin, could have been a comedy skit, straight out of a Marx Brothers or Three Stooges act. The miscommunication between me on one hand, and Baruchin and his aide, adjutant Micha Krauthammer (Keret) on the other, was funny more than anything else. To paraphrase an expression, I spoke of apples and they of oranges.

For four years, I filled a long list of posts – battery commander, armored company commanders' course instructor at the officers' school, FSO, RSO, and carried out all the company commander roles, including FSO of armored and infantry battalions which I'd entered on a moment's notice, in the field and in combat, into the role of battalion XO of the 404th Battalion. I accrued quite a bit of combat experience in the Six-Day War and the fire exchanges that followed, and I was a fully commissioned XO of a reserve battalion in three different theaters during the War of Attrition. I was considered – if I may – a very good, even excellent officer. And after all this, I am told by these two clueless mates that I have to go down to the Sinai, and go back to a battery commander's posting.

Why? Because they were short on battery commanders in the Sinai.

"And when will I be deputy commander of a standing battalion?" I asked. Baruchin looked at the long list Keret handed him. "You're seventh in line," he said, specifying who the six in front of me were. Cautious time estimate – two years. Anything to do with qualifications? Purely coincidental. Everyone waits their turn, just like at the drive-thru. No matter if you're good, talented, experienced, or well-regarded – you wait your turn. Seniority is all that matters. I began to entertain sinful thoughts. I realized that no logical argument would break through the wall of obtuseness, and perhaps I should keep quiet and reconsider my future. And so, in the last half year of my undergraduate studies, I began studying for a master's degree as well. It began with the head of the faculty, Prof. Shimon Shamir, who told me: "You must continue."

"And what about tuition fees?" I asked.

"I got you covered," he replied. "Change your direction in the IDF, transfer to MID,[6] and do a direct track toward a Ph.D. with me."

I told Shamir that I would think of his offer and get back to him, and to myself I thought: Let's see what happens. The option exists, and there's another possible path of action.

Skipping a Grade

I went down from Tzrifin to Refidim in a Dodge WC command car, with a group of young cadets who had just completed the basic officers' course, and reported to the division artillery commander Nati Sharoni. The same Sharoni who sent me to Bahad 1 for the second time. The same Sharoni who posted me at the Nukheila observation post, across from Tel Dan, when he commanded the 403rd Battalion. I was a young battery commander at the time, and was sent to reinforce the sector in case of skirmishes.

---

[6] The IDF's Military Intelligence Directorate. "AMAN" in Hebrew.

I entered the office full of confidence that I'd find a sympathetic ear. An admired officer, Israeli-born, who speaks my language. And indeed, we didn't waste time on protocol and courtesies, especially since midway through the conversation, there was a power outage in the base.

"What do you want?" he asked, after I described the bizarre interview and offer.

I said: "Deputy battalion commander and the rank of major."

"In two months precisely, you'll be a deputy bat-com and a major," Sharoni replied.

"And what about the Groucho Marx act?"

"Was Yechezkel at the interview?" he asked.

"No," I replied, "who's Yechezkel?"

Lieutenant Yechezkel Daskal was the Artillery Corps' staffing officer.

"Pretend that interview never happened," Sharoni said. "I'll take care of it with Yechezkel."

And indeed, two months later, I was promoted to major, and appointed deputy commander of the 402nd Battalion.

The Egyptian Battery I Didn't Take Out

Meanwhile, Sharoni intended to appoint me as the battalion's ops officer. This was a key role, as the ops officer sat at the brigade's HQ in Tasa (where the HQs of the 14th and 401st Brigades were located.) The ops officer coordinated all the artillery units and artillery fire, was right by the brigadier's side, and took part in all the command groups. Furthermore, since the battalion commander spent most of his time with the battalion, the fire control was also entrusted to the ops officer.

I settled at Tasa and once in a while hopped over to Refidim, where they would fly me in a Dornier aircraft with an air reconnaissance man and a pair of 20X120 binoculars to range targets. In addition, in order to familiarize myself with the terrain closely and thoroughly, I often visited the outposts, in all sectors, even when it required travel along the most dangerous route, the route to "Tempo" – the northernmost stronghold along the Suez Canal line, and the one worst battered by Egyptian artillery. "Tempo," later renamed "Limousine," was located five kilometers from Port Said, and the route to it was completely exposed to the Egyptians' line of sight and right in the line of fire. Its unofficial moniker was "3,000," after the 3,000 Egyptian artillery shells it was once bombarded with in a single day.

IDF brass explained at the time that budget shortages prevented the acquisition of advanced cannons. Yehuda Naot, commander of the 209th Division Artillery, the artillery unit of the Sinai Division, who had been detained by the British in Eritrea and had become an outstanding gunner, volunteered to operate pieces captured in the Six-Day War. Even when the twisted idea of employing tanks as artillery was proposed – an utterly unfeasible idea, technologically speaking, which required the complete inversion of the laws of ballistics, Naot decided to carry out the order and employ "Stalin" tanks at Tempo by indirect aim, like artillery (contrary to the nature of the tank, which is designed to operate by direct aim). Their guns obeyed the laws of ballistics, and the results of their barrage were quite poor, with a scatter of 2-3 km from the targets.

On one flight, I ranged an Egyptian 122mm artillery battery, which was located in Shalufa. The battery assigned for the mission was one of the batteries of the 402nd Battalion, and in fact was only two barrels, because the procedure was that a four-barreled battery operates with only two barrels, while the other two are undergoing maintenance. The SPH barrels had been worn out over the War of Attrition, and their diameter had long since forgotten that it had once been 155mm. The firing was done with large propellant charges, in order to achieve maximum range and to try to evade the Egyptian counter-battery fire. If that weren't enough, there were also many malfunctions with the old turretless Sherman tanks upon which the cannons were mounted.

The Egyptian batteries were always deployed in a circle, and despite my rich experience as an FSO, I only managed to hit the center of the circle with the seventeenth shell. The shells – or rather, the gaping barrels – simply didn't respond to the ranging orders. When I finally hit the target, I ordered fire for effect. These were twenty shots, fired from both barrels at a "Sinai pace" – a languid fire rate, in the Bedouin spirit that had infected us. I expected great things, but not another shell hit the target. They all "wandered" around at a radius (or "mean point of impact," as gunners say) of 500 meters and more.

Upon landing, I immediately reported to Amos Baram, deputy commander of the division artillery, for an investigation of the incident. He was apparently not used to immediate reports, and seemed surprised at my even wanting to discuss it, and then concentrated on attempts to console me.

"Arie," he asked me, "Did the shells cross the Canal westward?"
I replied: "Yes."

"Excellent," Baram said, telling me how he once went up for aerial observation, and a shell he ranged hit 50 meters from one of our trucks, moving along the Canal – on our side, of course – and there was a serious risk of the vehicle catching fire. It was nice to know that I wasn't alone, but misery shared isn't really misery halved. I was tasked with accurate strikes, and I felt like I took a hit myself.

Choco Launches

The War of Attrition in the Sinai, which cost hundreds of fatalities and many more hundreds wounded, was a trench war in the style of "All Quiet on the Western Front," and "The Road Back" – Erich Maria Remarque's novels about WW1. From my visits to the fortifications and my stays in them, I recall mostly the fear in the eyes of the soldiers, aged eighteen to twenty, and the terrible stench that assailed your senses upon entry.

There was also a phenomenon there known as "choco launches." At the entrance to each fortification stood a large icebox with squeezable bags of chocolate milk. When someone would take a bag and let the lid slam shut, it sounded like an artillery shell launching from the other side and everyone would hit the deck.

But the most dangerous weapon was the Egyptians' 60mm mortars. They made a very faint sound upon launch, their travel time was short, and those caught outside the bunker didn't have time to take cover. This caused many casualties.

On one of my excursions to the Canal, journalist Ron Ben Yishai caught a ride with me, and we ran into a massive Egyptian bombardment on the way. Even the bravest men in face-to-face combat panic during an artillery bombardment, which turns your insides into jelly and makes you want to bury your head in the sand, just to flee the terrible noise, and the red-hot shrapnel threatening to tear you to shreds, but Ben Yishai is a brave and experienced individual, and to his credit, he showed no sign of fear.

It was hard to identify the source of the fire from the other side of the Canal. It was a flat region, we didn't have good visibility, and some of the targets we fired at without ranging, in a method far as east from west than anything I was raised on and taught as a gunner. It was called "scatter-scout," and what we did was to fire despite not knowing for certain where we'll hit, relying on statistics and luck. It was unavoidable, and the professional justification was that even if a 155mm shell hits 200 meters from you in open terrain, it will splatter you on the ground.

Operation Drowning Wedge

In mid-May of 1970, we were informed of a secret operation about to be launched – "Operation Wedge," under the command of the Commander of the Armored Corps, the legendary Avraham "Bren" Adan himself. The task was assigned to the "White Bear" unit, a battalion-size unit, established by Yoel Gorodish-Gonen, brother of the famous Gorodish. "White Bear" specialized in amphibious operations, and was equipped with captured Soviet amphibious vehicles – PT-76 tanks and BTR-50 armored personnel carriers.

The unit's commander at the time was Yosse'le Yudovitch, a native of Kibbutz Kfar Menachem, and a good friend from the armored company commanders' course. The basic idea was to carry out an amphibious raid at Timsah Lake – from our promontory fortification to the Egyptian promontory fortification across the water, by surprise of course.

The operation was scheduled for Saturday night, May 23rd. We gathered a significant artillery force, and as ops officer, I was responsible for its deployment and employment. The impromptu artillery command group was given by the division's artillery commander Nati Sharoni to the few unit commanders who received targets from him. They didn't know exactly what was going to happen, due to the secrecy of the operation and the executing unit.

I desperately needed an experienced officer to sit in the FO's position in the promontory fortification, range the targets, observe the fire, and be able to drop a bombardment on the sources of enemy fire. But there were no FOs available. The Egyptian fire had increased toward the end of the War of Attrition, the number of casualties was increasing, and nearly each day brought another operation. Beyond these factors, due to the secrecy of the operation, I had only begun searching that Saturday. The only officers remaining in the batteries were the ones needed for their operations, and people were not quick to volunteer for such a mission. It was rare for an FO to stay alive for long, and this time it was an operation that couldn't be discussed anyway.

For lack of choice, I chose the FO myself. The chosen one was David Eisen, assistant ops officer in his official role, and beyond that, an experienced, veteran officer, an excellent FO, brave, intelligent, and blessed with a sense of humor, whose charm had all the women serving in the brigade HQ swooning, and who armored battalion commanders requested for every mission. Eisen was well versed in the intricacies of the War of Attrition, greatly helped me settle into my role and understand what was going on, and became a friend and partner. I asked him to go down to the promontory and do the ranging and cover fire missions.

He went pale. I had never seen him like this. "Arie," he said to me, "I have a bad feeling. I'm getting discharged in a few days, and somehow I've managed to stay alive. I can't go down to the Canal."

It was clear that the man was truly distressed, but it was only the two of us – and I had seniority. I had to remain with the brigadier, because our battalion commander was on weekend leave.

Eisen was a friend, and the dilemma was hard. I said: "No choice, you have to go down," and I gave him my pistol. I had hoped that the simple gesture would give him some meager solace.

Eisen went down to the promontory, and was killed on Saturday afternoon along with the commander of the 79th Battalion and three other troopers. A 120mm mortar bomb hit the mess hall, which was "protected" by corrugated tin and some sandbags. I had felt bad with the decision to begin with, and now felt pangs of guilt along with the sorrow and pain.

But there is no time for emotions in war. There was a mission to carry out. I decided to fill the late David Eisen's place myself. Deputy ops NCOs would remain at the brigade HQ in Tasa and keep in contact with me.

There were, of course, no drivers to be had, and the only vehicle I could take was the new battalion commander's jeep, all shiny and accessorized by Maimon, the legendary HQ company commander. Antennae, headlights, coolers, and in short – all a battalion commander could ever want. A joke at the time claimed that a bat-com coming home for the weekend will first of all call the base, to make sure his jeep is OK.

I got in the jeep and zoomed down to the promontory fortification on my own. A few dozen meters from the front gate, those damn mortar bombs began dropping all around me. I kept on driving, until one of them hit the hood. The jeep caught fire and I, by sheer luck, managed to jump out in a fish leap Yariv Oren had taught us in high school, and ran into the fortification. There too, no one, except the commander, knew a thing about the amphibious raid about to be launched right under their noses in a few hours.

I hurried to the FO's post, at the front of the fortification, facing the Egyptians. A narrow slit allowed me to view the Egyptian outpost and its surroundings through binoculars, but my position was under fire. The Egyptians, knowing that there was a dangerous troublemaker here, aimed an anti-tank gun at the slit, and each time they saw movement, they fired. Luckily for me, they didn't manage to slip one through the slit.

The number of barrels at my disposal seemed large at that moment, but these were only the guns of about 5-6 batteries, some belonging to a reserve battalion which had been deployed along another sector of the Canal, and had been called in for reinforcement. Fire was directed per battery, because that was the deployment in the Sinai. An enormous area to cover and a limited number of gun barrels dictated it, in order to achieve full artillery coverage of the entire sector. The ranging took longer than usual, due to the smoke and dust raised by each Egyptian hit on the FO post, obscuring my view of the targets.

Darkness slowly fell. The operating force – enclosed in six tanks and seven half-tracks – went down into the water, but very quickly stopped. Traversability experts from the Navy's Unit 707 had checked the soil several days earlier. They had reached the conclusion that the amphibious vehicles could cross Timsah (or "Crocodile") Lake, which is actually a swamp, and reach the large Egyptian outpost on the opposing promontory. In practice, in the moment of truth, reality turned out to be the complete opposite: The tanks and half-tracks sunk instantly into the morass. The drivers began attempting to self-extricate, and were quickly joined by tanks from the 79th Battalion, trying to tow them back to solid ground. But the Egyptians realized what was happening and launched a heavy artillery barrage, accompanied by light bombs. As luck would have it, they failed to pinpoint the vehicles trying to retreat, but the inaccurate projectiles still caused many casualties.

"Operation Wedge" had turned from a game-changing raid to a rescue operation. I fired for effect with everything at my disposal to silence the artillery on the other side, until the tanks managed to pull the raiding force out unharmed. Even then, most of the troops on the promontory fortification didn't understand why they were being bombarded more heavily than usual.

The next morning, I caught a ride and got back to Tasa. I was informed that I would be appointed deputy commander of the 402nd Battalion within two weeks. This would be the last time I would be a deputy. I'm made to lead.

Mountain and Mountain Meet

The battalion commander under whom I came to serve as deputy was Meir Doron, commander of my gunnery course in basic training. He was considered an excellent bat-com, and the battalion's men loved him and viewed him not only as a commander, but a leader as well.

I am also a leader by nature, I came with extensive combat experience in the War of Attrition, and I was – again, if I may – quite highly thought of by the battery commanders and other officers. Naturally, a covert conflict developed between myself and Doron, who was a good and pleasant man, and who didn't shove his leadership down my throat or pull rank. However, I did notice an interesting phenomenon: Whenever a senior officer came to visit, such as the Artillery Corps commander, the division artillery commander, or the division or brigade commander, Doron would send me on a mission to one of the batteries, to visit the FO at the "Tempo" outpost, or to do all kinds of administrative assignments in Refidim. I said nothing. There was no doubt of my status in the battalion, and I didn't think it worthwhile to fight over these keep-away tricks.

I kept fulfilling my duties in the best possible way, and so thought Doron as well, until it came to the welfare of my soldiers, and then I didn't hold back. The battalion HQ sat near Pelusium, along with the fire support HQ. The northern sector of the line was held by a paratroopers' reserve brigade, and Doron, who in the past had been the artillery officer of the 35th Brigade, which is the standing paratroopers' brigade, and also the commander of the 332nd Battalion, that brigade's mortar battalion, had close ties with the commanders of the paratroopers' brigade.

One Friday, I let a round of troops out for leave, after three grueling weeks of deployments, firing, and experiencing exhaustion in a hot, barren summer. To my surprise, Doron called me suddenly and said: "They asked me to give the paratroopers our buses. We'll let the troops out for leave later."

I had bitter experience with such promises. Rami Dotan, the HQ company commander at the 9th Battalion, told me the same tale when I was a battery commander, took the transports intended for my battery, and stuck us between Shivta and Ketziot for another three days. I said: No way, no how. Our troops will go on leave now. The paratroopers' reservists are getting discharged today, and aren't coming back.

Doron sent the deputy commander of the paratroopers' brigade over, and he threatened me with the saying from the Sages, which has become a favorite in the IDF: "Mountain and mountain do not meet, but man and man meet." I heard him out, and sent him packing.

"Back Bucket" and "Front Bucket"

Yanka'le Aknin, who had replaced Nati Sharoni as division artillery commander, quickly noticed my talents. It is also not impossible that Meir Doron also warmly recommended me for promotion. Either way, in early 1971, Aknin decided to appoint me as staff ops officer (equivalent to an "S3" in the US armed forces) of the standing division artillery in the Sinai.

The 209th was the only standing division artillery in the entire corps, and commanded most of the corps' manpower with three full battalions – the 402nd, 403rd, and 404th. The 55th, which was an IDF artillery HQ battalion on paper, was in fact provided for by the division artillery, and was subject to it operationally, as its permanent camp sat at the entrance to Blockade Route, near Refidim. Four of the other six battalions, save for the 334th in the north and the 405th in the center, just recently converted to the latest model self-propelled M-109 cannons, also arrived for operational tours of duty under command of the division artillery.

There was a new Artillery Corps doctrine being developed at the time, particularly under Moshe Levi as deputy commander of the division artillery. Levi, meticulous, painstaking, and professional to the core, focused his efforts on turning the slogan coined Aryeh Levi (the Chief Artillery Officer who replaced Baruchin) – "First shot on target" – into reality. Moshe Levi (no relation) availed himself of the corps' doctrine and research departments, and as a dominant personality, managed to overcome Aknin's distaste for the Chief Artillery

Officer and his entire HQ, and the fact that he relished any opportunity to butt heads with them and flout their instructions.

Aknin and Moshe Levi began formulating a doctrine whose objective is "deployment of artillery as a fist to turn the battle's fulcrum" – despite the shortage of guns and their advanced age, and despite the lacking and outdated support equipment.

To become a fist, we had to develop the ability to range with a single gun, and to add the three battalions of the division artillery to what we then termed a "pesel" target, a division-sized target. Thus the "back bucket" and "front bucket" system was developed. This meant a shared measurements grid for the firing echelon and the maneuvering forces. Such a grid allowed us to range one gun in the "back bucket" space – a trapezoid about a mile long, where all the firing guns of the same type are located – and by the ranging of a single gun, to fire the other guns at a target-filled space in the "front bucket" – also a trapezoid, about a mile long, in the direction we were firing at. All this was done so that the other data, and particularly weather data such as wind direction and air density, would also be included in the correction.

We are talking about a time before GPS, and to launch an object weighing over 40kg over a distance of dozens of kilometers, and actually hit your target, it was necessary for the gun's coordinates and the target's coordinates to be precise. One option was to tap into the official national survey grid, noted on the ground by "trig" (triangulation) points, and to use survey and direction tools connected to the trig.

None of this was possible in enemy territory, and then the target measurements had to be added to those of the gun. The method invented was connection by fire, which meant the precise ranging of a target in the middle of the target sector. Such a target is called a "registration target," and the correction is achieved through the ranging applied to all targets in the "front bucket" sector.

The presence of many Technion graduates and other ROTC types among the senior division artillery ranks gave the division's professional level a boost. The new methods were developed, studied, practiced, and improved over time by talented, knowledgeable officers.

They found these topics fascinating, and enjoyed an intellectual challenge no less than the practical one.

The Sinai division artillery became the leader in the Artillery Corps' fighting doctrine, and that was where ideas were tried out after being developed by the corps' doctrine department and research branch. There was never a problem of ammunition for practice, and under Aknin, we often practiced and used live fire in every fire exercise by maneuvering forces. Aknin enjoyed great prestige in the Sinai Division, never hesitated to voice his opinions on any matter at commanders' meetings, and enjoyed great respect both from division commander Dan Laner and Southern Command General Arik Sharon, as well as from his fellow armored brigade commanders.

Aryeh Levi, who was an excellent Chief Artillery Officer, was appointed by Dado, David Elazar, then deputy to Chief of Staff Haim Bar-Lev. Dado had been Levi's commander in the Armored Corps and at the Northern Command, and thought very highly of him. This helped him advance the corps in terms of weapon systems, although the Air Force and Armored Corps (both Bar-Lev and Dado's alma mater) were still prioritized. But external appreciation and backing alone are not enough. Aryeh Levi was blessed with leadership ability, used the stick-and-carrot method exceptionally well, and was highly esteemed within the corps as well, where he effected a revolution in the corps' fighting doctrine as mentioned above, attempting through creativity to overcome the enormous lack of hardware, and particularly advanced equipment.

To me, the appointment as S3 of the standing division artillery was a serious leap forward. I was part of the division HQ, spoke at command groups and at planning approval sessions in front of the division commander and the regional command general, and felt like a fish in water.

Aknin, who was a command and staff (C&S) school instructor before receiving command of the division artillery, apparently saw who he was dealing with, and decided to give me an expedited C&S course in the best tradition of "toss him in the water to teach him how to swim." At a certain point, he decided to handle the division artillery's operative plans, which were derived from those of the division and the regional command. These were mostly megalomaniacal offensive schemes that started with a crossing of the Suez Canal, continued with entering Cairo, and in general became the symbol of the hubris of the times. Aknin had me shred the plans, the artillery divisional appendices, the commands for the division artillery and the entire corps firepower in Sinai, and write it all from scratch.

With great patience, he sat with me, taught me, polished, and also overruled and demanded rewrites, until he was pleased. Along the way, I had become quite the expert, and what I learned there stuck with me. First, in terms of the "how": The ability to impart messages in a clear and simple way, understandable by all and executable, was one of my guiding principles in all future postings, and I became an expert around the corps on command groups. Second, in terms of "what" – translating the order into performance in the field.

Battalion exercises, division artillery exercises, maneuvering brigade and division-wide exercises followed each other at a dizzying pace. Our main occupation was fire exercises, alongside command of the batteries deployed throughout the sector.

The Intercepted Stratocruiser – and the Reprimand I Didn't Deserve

As the War of Attrition ended, after the Egyptians violated the agreement and drew air defense (AD) batteries close to the Canal, the Israeli Air Force struggled to execute intelligence missions using fighter jets, which came under Egyptian fire. So they began taking intelligence aerial photos using a long-range camera mounted on a Boeing 377 Stratocruiser. Concurrently, the Egyptians too tried to go on photographic excursions in the Sinai. In late 1971, two Sukhoi 7 aircraft were forced to flee under AD fire, and on September 11, 1971, a Sukhoi doing low-altitude reconnaissance photography was shot down over the Suez Canal. Egyptian President Anwar Sadat announced that he is willing to sacrifice a million people for independence and liberation, and that Israel should be prepared to sacrifice a million people too.

On Friday, September 17th, 1971, a Stratocruiser was sent on a diagonal photography excursion east of the Canal, to collect information on the location of Egyptian AD batteries drawn near the Canal. The atmosphere along the sector was tense due to the interception of the Sukhoi six days prior, and phantom fighter jets accompanied the Stratocruiser.

The aircraft posed a large, slow target, and after 14:00, as it flew north of the Great Bitter Lake, two SA-2 missiles were fired at it from a planned ambush. One missile hit the wing, the other exploded right beside the fuselage, and the plane went into a tailspin. The pilot, who had lost control of the plane, ordered the crew members to abandon the plane with him, but only one managed to parachute and save himself, sustaining light injuries. The plane crashed, and the remaining seven crew members in it perished.

Aknin was on leave, and I couldn't reach him on the phone. His deputy, Avraham Bar-David, had also gone on weekend leave. I was the commander on call, and I decided in consultation with the division to deploy the entire division artillery, the 55th Battalion included, in a forward deployment according to plans, in case of trouble.

It's quite complicated, on a moment's notice, to move two battalions stationed in Refidim and another two deployed along the line – let alone on a Friday night, with most of the commanders on leave and some of the guns deep in maintenance. Beyond this, we had to coordinate the rapid deployment with the other forces moving toward the Canal, and to verify that the deployment spaces and positions are ready and clear of enemy threats. The situation was murky in more than one regard: Night began to fall, and the fear of renewed enemy fire was breathing down our necks. We had to be ready to fire in record time.

The traffic routes became jammed in a heartbeat. Transporting the ammunition also became a problem, and above all, we needed to quickly and accurately plan the artillery deployment, set the targets, plan the fire, update orders, and make adjustments to the situation – all on the move and under pressure from the division HQ.

The transport was done quickly and efficiently. We deployed and were ready to fire long ahead of schedule, arriving so far ahead of the maneuvering forces that I was commended by the division commander, Dan Laner. But the drama in the skies intensified. At the break of dawn on Saturday morning, our Phantoms attacked Egyptian surface-to-air missile batteries west of the Canal with Shrike missiles. The Americans had used these missiles in Vietnam, and the attack failed because the Russians had taught the Egyptian radar operators, working with the AA missile batteries, to turn their machines off. The Shrike, which homes in on a radar signal, had nothing to home in on.

We were prepared to fire back on Friday night, waiting in full readiness for an Israeli government decision to open fire, with me in effective command of all artillery forces in the Sinai. Eventually, the government decided to contain the incident and forego retaliation, especially since the Air Force failed to destroy the surface-to-air batteries. The incident led to the accelerated planning of Operation Bendigo, which I will get to later.

At some point, we got in touch with Aknin. He flew in on Saturday, received all the explanations from me, and learned that the operation was carried out in full without him. Despite this, he said to me, in a reproachful tone: "Next time, don't do anything without my instructions."

This was the only reprimand I received from Aknin in three full years of cooperation, and even that one I didn't deserve. But Yanke'le is an intelligent man, who always knew to sift the grain from the straw. Deep inside he knew I did the right thing – not sticking to my pay grade, but precisely as expected from a responsible commander with initiative, and as he himself would have done.

Artillery Corps' Sports Day

Aryeh Levi, one of the smartest Chief Artillery Officers I knew, decided in the summer of 1972 to hold a corps' sports day, and decided to have it at the 209th Division Artillery, and not at Bahad 9 as usual. The organizing of it was tasked to me. The whole HQ enlisted to the prestigious assignment, and working harder than all was the ops team – the ops officer Tzvika Hershtik, a chemical engineer and later on one of the developers of "Copaxone," the drug that turned Teva into an empire, my aide Noam David, and his future wife and the ops division clerk at the time, Naomi Tverski.

As Levi somehow managed to interest the national press in our tug of war games, hoping to raise the prestige of the corps in the public's eyes, we had to give the battalions code names and not use their actual numbers. The 405th was titled Namer ("Tiger,") the 403rd was Eyal ("Ram,") the 55th was "Dragon," the 402nd was "Reshef" ("Flare") and the 404th was "Shfifon" ("Viper,"). As odd as it may sound – those code names have stuck to this very day.

On the other hand, I was forced into the middle of power struggles between the corps' head honchos. I already mentioned that Aknin, the division artillery commander, didn't care one bit for Levi or the entire corps' HQ, because the majority of the corps' standing force was under his command. He was the one that decided officers' assignments, approving or rejecting the corps' commander's recommendations at his sole discretion. In the matter of the sports day, too, he ignored all directives from above and spent no time on it at all. I tried to navigate as best I could, with an emphasis on perfect execution of the mission.

The event was very successful – apart from one small malfunction. The mayors of the sponsor cities and the people from the Committee for the Soldier didn't receive their drinks on time, and they were sweating in the Sinai summer. Levi himself alerted me to the situation, I summoned the adjutancy officer, and the cold drinks were delivered. Problem solved.

At the end of the day, in his summary speech, the Chief Artillery Officer said: "I wish to mention the man who worked and toiled and executed a perfect sports day, and who deserves special thanks: Arie Mizrahi." Not a word did he say about the division artillery commander, Aknin.

Years later, while I was serving as Director-General of the Housing and Construction Ministry, and working on the completion of two schools in Eilat within three months, to make sure they opened on time for the school year, I received a "special thanks" in Mayor Rafi Hochman's ribbon-cutting speech. Seeing the annoyance in the eyes of my minister, Binyamin "Fouad" Ben Eliezer (whom Hochman neglected to similarly honor), was a flashback to that sports day in the desert.

Back to 1972, there is no doubt that my performance regarding that sports day helped me win appointments as the establishing bat-com of the 412th, and later as bat-com of the 405th.

Don't Compromise on Assignments

Aknin and I understood each other at a glance or a nod. I learned a lot from him and was 100% loyal to him, although as an independent and proactive commander by nature, there was some difficulty involved. Aknin, and later Yanush, were my idea of the model commander, and I followed them through hell and high water.

We held long conversations during our long drives through the expanses of the Sinai – both of us in a jeep, with me driving between outposts or battalions, or in experiments we conducted with the "Hatchet" – a 203mm (8") gun intended to penetrate fortifications, and with the observation tank Aknin invented – a tank with a giant crane, which lifted a steel basket holding an FO high up in the air, to overcome the dirt mounds erected by the Egyptians along the Canal, which blocked the flat desert landscape and hindered our ground-level observations.

In one of these talks, Aknin asked me what the most important thing is in commanding a unit. I said: Leadership, professionalism, and handling people.

"Try harder," he said.

I thought hard, and couldn't come up with a smart enough answer.

"Assignments," Aknin said.

"Assignments are a matter for adjutants," I said.

"No! Assignments are a matter for the commander alone! You have to know to put the right man in the right place, because only then will you be sure that assignments will be carried out properly. Never compromise on this," he said, "and if you don't have the right person, better leave the post vacant. It's much worse to assign someone who doesn't get you, won't carry out orders in your spirit, and won't see your ideas through."

This short lesson has accompanied me since then everywhere – in the IDF, at the Housing and Construction Ministry, the IMI, and companies I launched. Each time I deviated from this sacred principle and compromised – I failed.

A Moment Before Insubordination

One of the issues that constituted a constant bone of contention with the Chief Artillery Officer's HQ was the matter of FOs. Ahead of IDF operations, we were almost always required to send FOs to reinforce the Northern Command (most of the time) or sometimes the Central Command, and the matter often devolved into power and ego struggles, beyond reasonable disputes due to a shortage of officers on hand to meet the division artillery's own needs. The CAO HQ used to utilize the ops division at the IDF HQ's ops division, through the division's own ops, in order to force us to comply, and this was a sensitive move in terms of corps politics.

On a Friday in 1972, while I was commander on call at the division artillery, an order came to send FOs to the Northern Command, effective immediately. Now of course you don't do that without approval from the division artillery commander, especially in light of my experience with the Stratocruiser affair, but contact with Aknin was lost again.

Pressure from the north intensified, but the phone call I received wasn't from Aknin, but rather from the Southern Command's Chief Artillery Officer, Yaakov Erez, the man who appointed me deputy batcom in 1967. He said to me, and I quote: "Arie, for your sake and that of your military career, carry out the order and send the FOs."

I had no hesitation, despite Erez's "friendly" approach. "I'm not doing it without approval," I answered him.

The clock kept ticking. The matter came to a boil in the form of a direct order from the Ops Division and the Southern Command, and I persisted in my intransigence, risking the charge of insubordination. Just before I was about to lose control of the situation, I received a call. Aknin, the savior, was on the other side of the line. "Send the FOs," he said. It turned out that he knew about the demand, and realized that given our relationship, he couldn't hang me out to dry.

"How did you know to call just at the critical moment?" I asked.

"The art of command," he replied.

Who Was Yaakov Aknin?

Yanka'le Aknin's last role in the IDF was commander of the Command and Staff School, and as a civilian, Ariel Sharon recruited him as Director-General of the Israel Land Administration immediately following his discharge. He passed away in the summer of 2022, and I decided to dedicate a chapter in his memory, to describe who he was, and where he drew his inspiration as a bold warrior. He told me this story in one of our long drives together in the expanses of the Sinai desert.

Aknin was Jerusalem-born, a scion of an old and distinguished family, of the city's centuries-old Sephardi nobility, and was a member of the Etzel (aka "Irgun") underground resistance movement, that fought against the British Mandate, and later in the War of Independence. He quickly stood out in leadership and courage, and was a mere lad of seventeen when he commanded the famous operation in which Etzel blew up a barrel of explosives at the Jaffa Gate of Jerusalem's old city, in retaliation for a series of anti-Jewish terror attacks, killing dozens of Arabs.

According to the plan, Aknin and his comrades were supposed to back up with a pickup truck toward a packed café. Two fighters were supposed to open submachine gunfire at the café, and Aknin was tasked with sitting at the back of the pickup's flatbed, wait for the moment when the Arabs rushed in panic from the café, and then light the fuse and roll the explosive barrel from the flatbed.

Everything went according to plan. The shooters fired, the Arabs fled, and the fuse was lit, but the moment Aknin rolled the barrel, the driver panicked, released the clutch, and the vehicle flew forward. Aknin flew out of the pickup along with the barrel, with the lit fuse drawing nearer to the explosive charge.

Luckily for him, another fighter sitting in the back of the pickup managed to grab him by the collar and pull him back onto the pickup truck, which sped away.

Aknin, as commander of the 214th Division Artillery in Ariel Sharon's division in the Six-Day War, was the one who created the rolling barrage at the battle of Umm-Qatef, which has been recognized as a classic combination of land-based fire with infantry and armored troops, and landing paratroopers from choppers in the rear of the compound. He advanced the artillery, then of short range, in broad daylight, bringing the artillery firepower to an optimum. Or as Sharon put it: "The ground shook."

In the Yom Kippur War, as well, Aknin commanded the 214th Division Artillery within Ariel Sharon's division, proving his mettle in the fearsome concentration of fire he created during the crossing of the Suez Canal. He was the man who coined the phrase that became my guiding light: "Creation of an artillery fist to shift the fulcrum of the battle."

Love in the Desert

The establishment of the 209th Division Artillery's reconnaissance company was one of the most challenging, enriching, and enjoyable missions I have ever been tasked with, and perhaps tasked myself with, as an ops officer. The satisfaction was doubled and tripled when, immediately following, I established recon companies in the other division artilleries as well, and was tasked with their training.

The idea was conceived by Chief Artillery Officer Aryeh Levy, and execution was tasked to me, as mentioned above. I began by recruiting newly discharged elite unit troopers, as recon companies were by definition reserve units. The art of reconnaissance was familiar to these men, and they needed training only in artillery-specific skills, such as leading battalions for deployment, preliminary recon for designated positions, to ascertain deployment and leapfrog options, defending position by perimeter patrols, locating suitable locations to station support equipment to survey the artillery space, leading munitions and logistics convoys, evading counter-battery fire in unarmored jeeps, establishing a recon perimeter, observation at the post for defense, warning of advancing enemies, and more. Concurrently, we had to refresh the battalions on recon and surveying doctrines, and learn how to combine them with the newly established recon companies.

We formulated a short, focused training program. It was led by Yossi Blich, a prominent officer in the division artillery's intelligence department, and among the elite unit commanders recruited to the division artillery I can't help but mention Yigal Erlich, in time Israel's Chief Scientist, Amnon Shiloni, who established Israeli radio's pop music outlet, "Channel Gimel," and Yossi Ozrad, the prolific TV executive, who commanded the division artillery recon companies. I particularly recall Shiloni, who commanded the 212th Division Artillery's recon company in the Golan Heights in the Yom Kippur War, and greatly helped the blocking and penetration maneuvers led by the division under the command of Raful (Rafael Eitan, later IDF Chief of Staff) by leading the artillery ammunition trucks right to the firing positions, which were under enemy counter-battery fire, commando raids, and tank attacks.

The training included familiarity with the expanse between Refidim and the Canal, and knowledge of the deployment and observation posts marked in various operational plans. I threw myself into this mission and enjoyed every moment.

First, I enjoyed the art of driving on sand dunes. As I recalled from repeated reading of "Popski's Private Army," it described in precise detail how to ascend the top of a dune, explaining that if you stop too soon, you'll get dug in – whereas if you stop too late, you have a good chance of toppling into the downward slope on the other side. Beyond this, I discovered incredible places, including secluded palm-filled oases in the hidden deeps of the desert.

Each recon company underwent a series of training exercises, so that whenever I grew weary of the tasks of an ops officer, I gladly joined daylight or nighttime navigations, returning to the stories of Lawrence of Arabia.

All this helped me impress Moshe Peled, my bat-com at the 402nd, (the battalion at which I took my first steps as a battery commander when he replaced Aknin as commander of the division artillery. The 405th Battalion had just arrived for operational deployment on the Canal. I sent them on a nighttime navigation and movement to the destination along the "Artillery Corps' Route" – the route of traffic and deployment paved in the sandstone especially for the Artillery Corps' units, some ten kilometers from the Canal – and Peled and I decided to await them there without informing them.

That night was particularly dark. I drove the jeep very fast with no headlights, and Peled didn't say a word and had no comment. When I stopped and turned the headlights on to shine precisely on the little sign reading "G-19," hung on a pole, all he said was: "Nice."

Bloat and Rot

Aknin's departure marked the end of an era for me as well. I remained for a short while alongside Peled, and did all I could to acquaint him with the atmosphere in the division artillery, and the magnitude of commander of the standing division artillery. Although Peled was my senior and the more veteran of the two of us, for three years, I had simply breathed, ate, and lived this division artillery, which was – as I mentioned above – the beating heart and soul of the corps.

During these years, the vision regarding the role of artillery fire in ground combat, how to create combined arms – and the revolution the Artillery Corps needed to undergo to get there to be able to fulfill its role properly – began to coalesce within me. All this took place against the backdrop of the harsh reality as a marginal corps in the

War of Attrition, in which the IDF placed all its hopes on the "flying artillery" of the Air Force, and the all-powerful Armored Corps.

In command groups and operational planning, the senior brass kept talking in terms of "we'll blow the Arabs away," should they try to cross the Canal. Memories ran to the burnt Egyptian convoys, smoking vehicles, and the stench of corpses. A sense of arrogance dictated the tone. Gorodish spawned plenty of 'mini-me's' who adopted the same approach.

Reliance on the Air Force and the "Jewish tank" as a response to any threat against the new empire led to mental stagnation and imperial trappings. The HQs adopted Egyptian military culture, lounging on armchairs captured in battle, wasting time in interminable meetings about insignificant details. The Sinai Division commander had fresh breakfast rolls, cheese, and yogurt flown in daily from his favorite Tel Aviv restaurant. Contractors showered these men with whisky and delicacies, while ordinary soldiers in the outposts reexperienced WW1. In the batteries, the gunners leapfrogged, took counter-battery fire, and returned fire despite enemy shelling, the heat, the flies, and the sandstorms that invaded every pore in the skin and crevice in the body.

When I returned from academic studies, I was shocked. I couldn't understand how the small, alert, high-quality professional military from before the Six-Day War had become a giant, bloated monster, with a rash of headquarters on the one hand and combat troops in real danger of death on the other.

Studies on the IDF wounded from the War of Attrition and the Yom Kippur War, found that half of them were wounded by enemy artillery. And indeed, the combat troops along the Canal, as well as the battalion, company, and platoon commanders, were not arrogant. They saw friends – many friends – killed and wounded, and they understood full well the importance of artillery fire. The combat troops, the tank crews, and infantrymen in the outposts and the fortifications, viewed us as brothers-in-arms and sought our aid. They saw the lack of equipment and means, but also saw the bravery, the fighting spirit, the creativity, and the devotion.

The dangers of surface-to-air missiles and the 9M14 "Sagger" anti-tank missiles, which began appearing both along the Canal and in the Golan Heights, created further dissonance regarding the Armored Corps and Air Force commanders, who insisted on continuing to rest on the laurels of '67, and dreamt of realizing plans such as "Desert Cat" and "Man of Valor," in which the armored columns were to cross the Canal and charge on to Cairo.

The absurd cried out to heaven. We, the gunners, creative, knowing what was needed, poor and hungry; in sharp contrast to the air and armored people, fat and content, feeding on past glory, unable to help the men at the outposts, but refusing to let anyone move their cheese. This supercilious attitude bred the conception that led to the intelligence and diplomatic failure of October 1973. There is only one word for it: Hubris.

The truth must be told that we too fell prey to that same sin: When Yanush came back from meeting the Northern Command general at noon on Yom Kippur, informing us that all-out war with Egypt and Syria would break out at six in the evening, we said: "No rush. They're just Arabs." Rot spreads, and that's what happens when rot sets in. This lesson is true today as well: We must not be complacent. We must eradicate any sign of petrification, and lance every boil, significantly cut back on headquarters, and direct the lion's share of the resources to strengthening the executing arms. They are the ones who should receive the most attention and resources – not only in lip service, but in actual practice, in budgets and quality personnel. See the special English edition chapter on the 2023 war at the end of the book.

I was exposed to the rot in the phenomenon of the "rear unit" as well. Officers with the rank of captain and up enjoyed a privilege: A driver with a "white" car, designated as a "rear unit." The Artillery Corps had such a rear unit at Camp Tzrifin, in imitation of the Armored Corps, and each officer in the Sinai, from captain and up, had a driver, tasked with serving their family – driving their kids to school, the wife shopping and to cafés, and so on. Nobody in the public said a word or as much as a peep. The adoration of the heroes of the Six-Day War was still immense, and when a general walked into a restaurant with his friends, nobody dreamed of presenting them with a bill. The royal mannerisms of the IDF generals seemed natural, and when satirical playwright Hanoch Levin dared shout that the emperor had no clothes, in his seminal play "Queen of the Bathtub," the play was vehemently chased off the stage.

Throughout the Sinai, another phenomenon grew. It started on a small scale before the Six-Day War and exploded exponentially thereafter, in a sort of imitation of the armored warfare heroes of WW2 – Rommel, Guderian, Patton, and Montgomery: The trailer car fad. Every senior officer, from bat-com up, had a trailer. After June of '67, this was usually a trailer captured in war, converted and detailed for the brass's use with a shower, a kitchenette, and a comfy bed.

I, too, received a trailer as deputy bat-com of the 402nd. Moshe Levi inherited it from Amos Baram, and left it for me in Pelusium. I won't lie, it was certainly comfortable, providing me with both privacy and pride. Here, I too have a trailer – a status symbol. The rot was so deep that no one noticed the downward spiral.

A WRETCHED SERVANT

Asher Blicher, commander of Bahad 9 in the mid-sixties, was the very model of the character of the artillery battery commander in S. Yizhar's seminal novel about the War of Independence, "Days of Ziklag." And if the direct inspiration wasn't Blicher himself, a good officer and typical "Yekke" (Jew of German origin), then it was another officer of the same make and model.

The officers of the "Artillery Service," as the corps was known in its early years, were mostly British army veterans, or new immigrants who were versed in the art of artillery from the Russian or Polish armies. They were Zionists and patriots, but struggled to fit into the IDF dominated by ex-Haganah and Palmach personnel. I also mentioned above my own theory, that Ben Gurion decided to concentrate the former Etzel and Lehi members who sought a military career in the corps, people like Eliyahu Lenkin, who had commanded the Altalena and would become a bat-com in the corps, Zvi "Cactus" Barzel and Israel Ben-Amitai, who had been incarcerated by the British in Eritrea and would go on to be Chief Artillery Officer of the Southern Command and of the entire IDF, respectively, during the Six-Day War, and others as well.

This is what Yizhar wrote about the artillery officers:

"The knocking of a jeep stood out and grated now in the air round the hill. When the dust settled there strode towards us the tall figure of Tsviko, the Platoon Commander, and behind him Kobchik the driver, secretly sniggering without getting down from his seat, and also two others unknown, getting down with great care. – 'Meet the gunners!' Tsviko said to Gidi, and from his way of disregarding a snigger you could tell that he had brought some strange birds with him this time – and, moreover, one of the two extended his arm and came over to clasp Gidi's hands and said: 'How do you do?' – wreathed with a polite smile – something which caused Gidi to raise his eyebrows high, with unconcealed puzzlement, and it immediately transpired that the other was simply a German Jew with all due respect, an old man of forty or so, and moreover, with sunglasses and a Panama hat, which he raised to reveal hedgehog-like hair close-cropped and very gray; but he was all vim and vigor.

And when all the good-mannered formalities were completed, when that leader of the gunners turned to go – and he could be forgiven anything on account of his big guns – there was revealed behind his back, bowing and scraping all that time, with heels joined, and extreme courtesy, another German Jew, younger than the previous one, albeit more serious and formal than he, as though it were the British army here, or God knows what, fully equipped with field glasses, maps, and a pistol. So much so that Gidi, totally confused, went up to him, extended his hand, and hailed him with a perplexed 'Greetings,' while he rubbed his wooly nape with his left hand, and the other responded by favoring him with a smile that revealed his teeth, bowing benignly with a rubicund face, and it was very pleasant indeed.

Then they decamped and went off to the lower part of the hill among the thistles to see the view, and there joined them each from his own direction, as their role demanded, Jakusz on the one side and Buma on the other, and in such an important gathering they stood to reconnoiter, and Tsviko the PC lit a cigarette, so as to gather the strength to make a speech and to say: 'Okay, Gidi will explain everything to you.'

And while Gidi waved his hands in every direction, and poured out his lecture, adding to each sentence what he had forgotten in the previous one – the chief gunner uttered various foreign expressions, peering through his field glasses, which the one behind him offered him respectfully, and called each cardinal point by its name, North, Northeast, and the light range of hills two thousandths to the left, and eight o'clock from the target, and the original objective and the zero line, and various other clever remarks, which more than anyone else were fully understood by that other man, the one standing behind, a terribly serious, terribly knowledgeable, terribly red-faced man, who also stood up terribly straight when he was addressed. Then he too took with permission the field glasses and uttered for his own part: the control ridge, a forward lookout officer, a reduction of the shells, and also: shrapnel shells, a battery, a detachment, range-finding, reporting, lines of communication, high explosives, armor-piercing, and other such wonderful things."[7]

IDF commanders, perhaps inspired by Defense Minister Ben-Gurion, did not have great faith in the abilities of the Artillery Corps, and restricted it both in material and human resources, as well as in rank and status. An example of this was Meir Pa'il's attitude toward the place of the artillery when he was head of the fighting doctrine department at the IDF's instruction department.

As a battery commander at the 402nd Battalion, I was part of the control group at a large-scale exercise in the Negev. Our role was to critique the performance of the artillery, and at the end of the exercise, I witnessed an argument between my bat-com, Moshe Peled, and Pa'il. It centered around the number of people intended to participate in the divisional command group. Pa'il claimed that there were too many people in the command groups, and the fire support commanders were put on the chopping block. Following the British model, adopted by the IDF, they were artillery bat-coms. Even if Pa'il's argument was a professional one, the way he expressed it was in a mocking fashion. "You gunners," he said, "All you think about is respect," pronouncing the word derisively in Yiddish.

Pa'il was the one who studied, exposed, and published the Deir Yassin massacre,[8] and consequently became the target of unhinged attacks by some Etzel and Lehi veterans. So I think his position stemmed from hostility toward the "splitters," many of whom filled the officer ranks of the corps. Despite this, the friendship formed

---

[7] S, Yizhar: Days of Ziklag. Translation: Nicholas de-Lange, with Yaacob Dweck and Oliver Geffen.

[8] On April 9, 1948, a joint force of Etzel and Lehi fighters attacked the village of Deir Yassin, on the outskirts of Jerusalem, and massacred some 110 villagers, including women and children.

between Pa'il and myself, when I was a platoon instructor under him at Bahad 1, was true and sincere, and our appreciation was mutual.

I also encountered a reserved and even condescending attitude by Major-General Dan Laner, the Palmach veteran who in the War of Independence had commanded a battalion in the battles for Mishmar Haemek, and whom I met when he was the chief commander of the IDF forces in the Sinai.

During one of the exercises, the control shots diverged from the target, because the weather conditions had changed since the end of the ranging. I was with the new commander of the division artillery, Peled, and Laner arrived in a jeep, stopped beside us, and yelled: "Shit!" As if this wasn't enough, he circled around again in his jeep, yelled "Shit!" again, and vanished. Nobody was hurt, the exercise was just getting started, and the divergence was corrected immediately, but the "shit" stain remained.

And a final anecdote, starring someone far better known, and bringing us back to my theory of the Artillery Corps as the ruling party's dumping ground for supporters of the opposition: During the waiting period before the Six-Day War, newly installed Defense Minister Moshe Dayan visited the Southern Command one day. When "Cactus" showed him the artillery pieces, Dayan winked at him with his one remaining eye, and asked if the cannons could be swiveled backward. Cactus innocently asked why, and Dayan replied: "Toward the Knesset in Jerusalem…" A joke, but one based on the underlying tension and concern about the obedience of the "splitters."

It should be noted that Ben-Gurion did not content himself with exiling former Etzel and Lehi personnel to the Artillery Corps, but appointed Shmuel Admon from Kibbutz Alonim as the first corps commander – another former distinguished British Artillery NCO, loyal to the Ben-Gurion party, who was a friend of my father at the Watchmen's Union. Admon, who was an excellent officer, was not selected solely due to leadership and professional skills. He was sent to keep an eye on the former splitters, and make sure they didn't "split" again. His son, Itay Admon, served under my command in the 405th Battalion, and was the artillery commander at the 226th Paratroopers Brigade when it captured Sidon in the Peace for Galilee War.

After all these, and assuming my theory is true, there is one thing that Ben-Gurion and all the former Palmachniks in the IDF's senior command didn't take into account – the fact that the former underground fighters were tough men, warriors who had survived detention in camps in Africa, a bloody clash with the Haganah in the "Sezon,"[9] and an unyielding struggle against the British, and survival ran deep in their blood. They practiced forbearance, withdrew into the corps' shell, and did the best they could with the means and tools at their disposal.

The same went for new immigrants who integrated into the corps, mostly Holocaust survivors, or people who had experienced antisemitism in the Red Army and the Polish Anders' Army. They too learned the hard way how to fit in – in Israel in general and the Artillery Corps in particular – and knew how to make the best with whatever was put at their disposal.

These men, the founding fathers of the Artillery Corps, laid the foundation for the corps and prepared the ground for a generation that followed, devoid of any sense of inferiority. A generation of young officers, full of energy and knowledge, who refused to bow their heads before soldiers with different berets and tags, and refused to content themselves with the scraps of the other branches. A generation that proved itself in battle, and knew how to turn the artillery into the queen of the battle.

---

9   The "Saison" (from French: Season, as in "Open [hunting] season") was a period in the history of the pre-state Jewish population in Mandatory Palestine, between Dec. 1944 and Feb 1945, during which the majoritarian Jewish paramilitary organization, the Haganah, took active hostile measures against the more radical underground movements, Etzel and Lehi, in order to force the smaller groups to stop attacking the occupying British forces while the WW2 effort against the Nazis was still ongoing. These measures included delivering Etzel and Lehi personnel to the British authorities, as well as cases of abduction, followed by detention and interrogation under harsh conditions. This period, along with the Altalena affair mentioned above, created deep pools of bitterness among the supporters of Etzel and Lehi toward the ruling party, Mapai, which was headed by Haganah leaders, and toward the prevailing order of the early state period.

Gorodish as a Poor Example

The first time I ran into Gorodish, Shmuel Gonen as he was known to the population registry, was on the day of my wedding, November 23rd, 1965. He was a lieutenant colonel back then, and I was a lieutenant, an experienced FSO, a veteran battery commander, and a professional recon and survey officer, and we were both taking part in a division-wide comms and movement exercise.

The trainee was Yeshayahu "Shaikeh" Gavish, head of instruction and later Southern Command general, who in the Six-Day War commanded the three divisions that conquered the Sinai Peninsula. Playing against him were two armored brigades. The 14th Brigade's command post was commanded by deputy brigadier Chaim Dimm. The 7th Brigade's command post was commanded by Deputy Brigadier Gorodish. He had just returned from an advanced armored warfare course at Fort Knox, wearing a tank crewman's overall and a shoulder holster like American tank fighters wore, with an ivory-grip pistol.

I was sent by the bat-com, Tzvika Shpitzer, who was also the fire support commander for the 7th Brigade, to take his place in the exercise, so I was under Gorodish. The exercise took place in the Tze'elim area, and we sat under camouflage nets, with the command post half-tracks creating a courtyard. Gorodish, of course, had a trailer, and only once in a while would he deign to come down and talk to us mortals. On one of those rare occasions, we were forced as extras into an absurd and infuriating scene.

"Intel officer, come here," he ordered his intelligence officer, Major Y, whose name I shall omit out of respect. Y. came running, with the expression of someone desperate to please his superior. Gorodish gave him an empty soft drink bottle, and told him: "Run." After ten or fifteen meters he yelled "Stop!" Y. stopped, and Gorodish barked: "Put the bottle down." Y. put the bottle down and luckily managed to step aside before Gorodish drew his pistol and shattered the bottle with a shot, in a scene that looked like something out of a Tarantino film, or "The Good, The Bad, and The Ugly."

That day I was supposed to leave Tze'elim in a jeep, to reach Ashdot Ya'akov, 300 km away, for my wedding with my beloved Tamar (and the nuptials of three other couples, held concurrently.) The roads then were a far cry from today. The last part of the journey, from Beit She'an in the north, ascended the Kaukab al-Hawa ("Star of the Winds") ridge, in order to go down into the Jordan Valley, and it was already late afternoon.

After the demonstration with Y., I was afraid to approach Gorodish and ask him for permission to leave for such a marginal event compared to a divisional exercise, but still, it was my wedding.

Necessity overcame trepidation. I explained the matter to Gorodish, and he surprised me and said: "A wedding? Excellent! Mazal tov to you. We need lots of Jewish children."

A weight lifted from my heart. I quickly got into the jeep, before anything changed, and sped north. I arrived at the kibbutz an hour before the Chupa ceremony, had time to kiss Tamar and fell into a deep slumber. Luckily, she woke me up after half an hour, sent me to shower, gave me the black trousers and white shirt – and straight off to the Chupa I went.

Tamar and I on our wedding day.

"Follow the Hat"

On Independence Day of 5726 (1966), the IDF held its annual parade in Haifa, and I was sent in the first self-propelled cannon to lead the 404th Battalion's column. The entire armored column was commanded by the Brigadier of the 7th, Cheech, and his deputy, Gorodish. They gathered us for a briefing, and immediately made it clear precisely who's boss. A Lt. Col. from the Signal Corps, who stood up and asked a question out of turn, was tossed out of the shed in a split second. To those, like me, who were astonished, not belonging to the 7th Brigade and not accustomed to such behavior, the two emperors explained: "What is permissible for Jupiter, is forbidden to the ox and the donkey." All this ... a year prior to the Six-Day War, after which it all ***really*** went to their heads.

After this, during the prolonged pre-war waiting period, I often participated in command groups in the 7th Brigade, as the FSO for the 79th Armored Battalion, and Gorodish's command groups were bizarre events. He was already the brigadier by then, and still competed with his deputy, Baruch "Pinko" Harel, and the ops officer Yossi Ben-Hannan, to see which of them was wilder and most incorrigible.

Thus, for example, when Gorodish wanted to indicate a point on the map hanging on the large map board, he wouldn't get up from his comfortable cloth armchair, but instead would draw his dagger and hurl it. If the dagger missed, Pinko would unsheathe his own dagger and throw it. Then came Ben-Hanan's turn, for none of them were great marksmen.

This was the atmosphere, and into one of these meetings entered the brigade's intel officer, Aryeh Zinger, a paratrooper who was my squad leader at Officer's School. Zinger is a calm person, who did as he pleased, and at the same time was the complete antithesis to Gorodish and his cohorts. He stood up to present the intelligence updates, and not only was he wearing red paratrooper boots, which were like a waving red cloth before the armored corps' bulls, he also wore a broad-brimmed hat, which was allowed in the IDF but against the internal regulations of the 7th Brigade, and was banned on order from none other than the Brigadier himself.

Gorodish, seething with rage, didn't even let Zinger open his mouth. "Give me the hat," he said, tossed it out of the war room shed, and told Zinger, a redhead who had to protect himself from the sun, "Follow the hat out of here and don't come back."

Shhhh, the Brigadier's Coming Out

At the end of the Six-Day War, the 7th Armored Brigade's command settled in the Egyptian military HQ at Bir Gafgafa, which was renamed in Hebrew as Refidim, which is the biblical name, controlling the entire peninsula from there. I arrived at Refidim one morning as deputy bat-com of the 404th, for a meeting with my bat-com Shpitzer, who sat at the brigade HQ as the fire support commander. I attempted to enter the elongated HQ building, when a guard with his weapon cocked quickly intercepted me.

"What's going on?" I asked.

"The Brigadier is coming out," the guard responded, in whispered awe.

On the huge parade ground in front of the HQ stood a straight row of vehicles, including a recon jeep with all the paraphernalia of command, a brigadier's half-track with its headlights, antennae, flags, a Patton tank, an M-113 APC captured from Jordan, a brand new white jeep, still emblazoned with UN insignia, and finally a black American Chevy Impala, taken as war spoils in the Gaza Strip. All had a driver who was seated, keeping the engine running, and this ritual was repeated each and every morning.

A moment later, the Brigadier emerged from the HQ, a short greatcoat thrown sloppily over his shoulders and "Zamama" – the legendary camp commander, preceding him and cleaning the path, like some slapstick skit. Gorodish picked the vehicle that struck his fancy – that morning it was the jeep – and all the other drivers turned their engines off and sighed in relief. All they had to do for the rest of the day was shine their machines ahead of a repeat ceremony the next day. Just like a scene out of the motion picture "Patton." And indeed, The American Patton and the German Guderian were the role models of our armored corps' commanders.

These are but a few of the many examples of Gorodish's pathological behavior. He and other officers were convinced that they were gods, but Gorodish definitely brought the madness to heights previously unheard of. The few officers who warned against the phenomenon were pushed out of the corps, while Talik, Gorodish's master, held the bulldog's leash and played along. This was how those two pushed Avigdor "Yanush" Ben-Gal, in time Northern Command General, who was then the ops officer of the 7th Armored Brigade, out of the way. According to Yanush, he fell out with Gorodish after the latter tried to force himself on a secretary, and due to the accumulation of semi-psychotic behavior by the idolized brigadier. Most turned a blind eye and ignored their conscience, to preserve their military careers.

The end is well known. Terrorizing your underlings is not enough. You need skills and you need leadership, which is based on professionalism, but mostly on the faith of the troops in their commander. Lofty talk such as "We looked death in the eye, and he lowered his gaze" doesn't get the job done. Nor does a shiny, looted UN jeep. Refusing to deploy artillery, refusing to deploy infantry, and refusing to deploy combat engineers to clear landmines took a heavy blood toll on the 7th Armored Brigade Rangers' unit in the battle of Rafah in the Six-Day War, especially after it turned out that the Egyptian forces had received orders to retreat, and despite Gorodish later depicting the incident as a heroic battle. Six years later, Gorodish's poor performance early in the Yom Kippur War would lead to former Chief of Staff Haim Bar-Lev being "dropped" in command on top of him.

My own command style was diametrically different, but more important, is what was happening in the Artillery Corps in those days. While the Air Force and Armored Corps were mired in the past, we were searching incessantly how to revolutionize a corps with outdated equipment and primitive support means. We came up with original methods, developed creative solutions, and practiced hitherto unknown modes of operation.

Everyone pitched in to the mission, headed by Nati Sharoni, Yaakov Aknin, and Aryeh Levi. The fact that Levi was the darling of newly appointed Chief of Staff David Elazar, since Dado had been Northern Command General and Levi was the command artillery chief, now gave him a foothold in the hallways of the IDF HQ. Some of the innovations we introduced seeped through Levi to the IDF HQ, and some of them had already manifested in the Yom Kippur War.

A MISSED OPPORTUNITY NAMED BENDIGO

The Air Force, as mentioned above, was the Israeli public's "rock star" since June 5th, 1967, after it determined the outcome of the Six-Day War within three hours. Years passed until the realization dawned that air power isn't everything. It is interesting to note that this realization spread in the Air Force itself, and did not disseminate among the rest of the IDF. On the other hand, the attitude promoted by Major-General Israel Tal, "Talik," who ruled that artillery is unnecessary, as the "flying artillery" can support the armored columns alone, was based on detachment from reality and indicated a flawed understanding of the modern battlefield, which requires full integration of all branches. But Talik, who had worked on the development of the Merkava tank in the early 1970s, and was a dominant figure in the IDF and in political circles as well, persisted: Armored force alone will triumph on the ground, with the Air Force providing cover fire.

The blue-clad airmen delighted in this determination, which augured significant budget increases, while the upcoming fire support missions for our forces – the "Scratch" ("Srita") order – were vague.

Pride in the Sky

In today's age of combined arms, there is no need to direct pilots, but only to enter a target or a destination, and the command and control system passes it on to the attacking aircraft. In the early 1970s, the direction of the aircraft at the brigade and battalion level was tasked to the Artillery Corps, and an infantry officer and a pilot were integrated for this purpose into the instructional crew of the advanced branch at Bahad 9, which is the equivalent of an artillery officer company commander and battalion commander course. All the corps' officers – from the basic officers' course to the most senior brass – studied the subject, and practiced it dozens of times. The dry runs came to a climax in a practice run with a pilot in a light aircraft. The Air Force, for its part, treated the matter derisively. Worst of all were David Ivri, in time Air Force Commander, and Giora Rom, in time deputy commander, who would blame the gunners for the Air Force's failure in the Yom Kippur War. Rom was quoted as saying that to rely on the Artillery Corps to direct aircraft is like painting automobile headlights blue to black out city streets. Or in plain language: The primitive corps upon which the Air Force relied was the cause of its failure. But let us return to the pre-war days and to the truth, which was the opposite. We were prepared and trained, while the Air Force pilots were not – with a capital N. Since the Six-Day War, all they did was watch films on air battles, destroying airports, and aiding ground troops. Coordination with flight directors from the Artillery Corps was the lowest thing on their priority list, and we never got to do a live fire, wet drill with aircraft on targets.

Only in the midst of the War of Attrition, when the Air Force and the IDF HQ realized that the serious problem of Egyptian and Syrian surface-to-air missiles was endangering our air control, did they begin seeking solutions, especially since the American Shrike missiles, which were supposed to home in on the Egyptian battery radars, failed miserably. Only then were other methods adopted, such as "slingshot" attacks or "swipe" flights (two forms of low-altitude flight followed by sharp upward soars near the target), to suppress the missile batteries.

Concurrently, 175mm cannons were purchased at the expense of the Air Force budget. They were intended to blaze pathways for the airplanes, so that they could attack the surface-to-air batteries. By October '73, guns for four battalions arrived in Israel – the 55th, the 647th, the 329th, and the 412th. I was appointed establishing bat-com of the 412th, which I will elaborate on later on.

The Artillery That Straightened the Airplane's Wing

The main reason I am elaborating on this chapter is the importance of Operation Bendigo as a trailblazing undertaking, an operation solely based on artillery, for the strategic aim of supporting the Air Force in overcoming an acute problem. This, as mentioned above, was the problem of surface-to-air missiles, which threatened Israel's main strategic edge – control of the skies and the ability to transfer the fighting to the enemy's territory.

The planning effort, creativity, and originality that characterized the operation's preparation, alongside dotting every tiny "i" and crossing every fine-print "t," and the full one-to-one live fire exercise – all these made Bendigo an artillery operation ahead of its time. It received full cooperation from the Air Force, full attention, and proper budget allocations. Fifty years have gone by since, and I'm still proud of it.

In July of 1969, in the midst of the War of Attrition in the Sinai, Ezer Weizmann, then head of the IDF Operations Division, visited the Canal, and happened upon one of the horrible artillery bombardments that were our daily lot in life. He returned to IDF HQ shocked by the combat conditions and the intolerable numerical inferiority of our troops (36-gun barrels compared to 1,000 on the Egyptian side), and ordered his successor as Air force Commander, Moti Hod,[10] to solve the problem.

The Air Force did indeed train its full force on the problem. Within a mere few weeks, the outdated SA-2 batteries were pulverized, Egyptian artillery was severely battered, the Egyptian army's bases were heavily bombarded, as were Egyptian cities along the Canal. Egyptian President Gamal Abd al-Nasser rushed to Moscow and begged for help.

---

10 Major-General Mordechai "Moti" Hod (1926-2003) was the seventh commander of the Israeli Air Force, serving from April 1966-May 1973. Despite being the commander of the Air Force during its greatest hour in the Six-Day War, he was greatly overshadowed in the public's imagination – as well as history's verdict, it can now be said – by his predecessor, Ezer Weizmann, who is widely acknowledged as the architect of both the Air Force itself, and the precise plan to demolish the enemy's air forces at the start of the war.

The Russians quickly reinforced their allies with improved SA-2 missiles, state-of-the-art SA-3 missiles, and added a few self-propelled SA-6 batteries to boot. These were manned by Russian crews due to the urgency. Alongside the missiles, the Russians sent innovative electronic devices to disrupt the operation of our aircraft – also operated by Russian crews.

In the summer of 1970 Phantom jets began falling at an alarming rate, and the Air Force practically lost the ability to fly by the Canal. Ezer Weizmann coined the term "Electronic Summer." Israel was forced to the negotiating table, and in August 1970, a ceasefire was declared. As compensation for its consent, Israel received Shrike missiles, and the four 175mm artillery battalions I mentioned above.

The Egyptians, for their part, didn't abide by the conditions of the ceasefire, and immediately began advancing their new missiles toward the Canal. Using three missile brigades – 54 batteries in total – they managed to create a hermetic seal, preventing the IDF from deploying the Air Force. For some reason, the response of Israel's government was feeble. The Egyptians worked and worked, and fire was not resumed.

On September 17th, 1971, after the Stratocruiser was shot down and the Shrike missiles fired at the intercepting battery missed their mark again, the wakeup call finally sounded. IDF HQ resolved to silence the surface-to-air missiles in a combined operation, in which the artillery would open clean, missile-free lanes of attack for the Air Force's planes, allowing them to destroy the enemy batteries. The mission was assigned to the Southern Command, which assigned it to the 209th Division Artillery, which Aknin commanded, and I was his ops officer. The operation was codenamed "Bendigo," and we got planning it right away. Participating in the planning on the Air Force side were Lt. Col. Oded Marom, head of the AF Ops Division, and his aide, Major Menachem Sharon. I was there on behalf of the ground forces, and everything was shrouded under darkness, with "Bendigo" classified "top secret."

The main idea required simplicity in the use of artillery, a clear schedule, and yet a sophistication in designating the attack lanes, in the deployment of the batteries, and in the deceptive measures designed to disrupt the radars of the surface-to-air batteries. The new 175mm cannons reached a range of 32.8 km, the captured Russian 130mm guns had a range of 27 km, and the standing artillery's M-50 guns were assigned to fire artillery chaff, designed to mislead the radars and defend the longer-range batteries, by firing at Egyptian batteries that threatened them.

During the planning, more of the new 175mm guns arrived in Israel from the American emergency depots, and two more battalions were established – the 647th and the 329th. The 209th Division Artillery was supposed to do all the preparations, such as building munitions piles, preparing positions and surveying them, as well as practicing the system.

Since we had been in the Sinai, the division artillery had the ability to send out reserve units for preliminary scouting and lead them to the positions when the need arose. The problem we faced was how to range. The attempt to place an artillery officer in a two-seater Skyhawk for ranging failed. The six Skyhawks assigned to the mission were to take off as usual with its pilot and navigator, and a ranging system was devised whereby the pilot denoted the impact point of the projectile, and the distance from the target, with a "clock on the target." For example: 3 o'clock, 500 meters. We, in the forward command post at the division artillery HQ, were supposed to translate this report into an artillery correction in gunners' lingo, and pass it on to the battery.

To avoid confusion, we determined which plane would target which surface-to-air battery, and a battery of ours was assigned to that trio. So a given surface-to-air battery was targeted by a specific pilot, and a specific 175mm or 130mm battery. After strenuous work, we passed on orderly commands to the battalions. There were still few privy to the secret, and in the units themselves, people knew only what any gunner knew ahead of any operational activity:

Deploy, fire, range, and fire for effect.

In the first article of the detailed order, the "intent" article, I wrote:

The 209th Division Artillery will immobilize the surface-to-air missile bases in the Suez Canal sector and the Port Said sector, at a range of 30 km from the Canal line.

I learned much from the close encounter with the Air Force officers, and was greatly impressed by their serious attitude toward the matter, the surgical attention to each and every detail, and at the same time, I was impressed by the compartmentalization as well. Everyone knew what they needed to, and no more. At the end of the project we carried out a skeleton exercise with live fire. The coordination was done through the 209th Division Artillery's forward command post, which received data, relayed fire commands, translated the ranging, and ordered fire for effect.

To make the practice realistic, we drew a 1:1 simulation of missile batteries in the "blockade" in the fire zone, near Refidim, and these simulated the position relative to the Suez Canal and to other batteries for the pilot, on a true scale. We marked the fake surface-to-air batteries with black diesel fuel, their fire direction centers were built of sandbags and a simulated trailer, and the missiles were barrels we soldered together and tilted to resemble missiles ready to launch.

The Chief of Staff, Haim Bar-Lev, watched the live fire exercise throughout, retaining a sphynx-like silence. Talik complained that we prepared refreshments for the guests, saying that we look like French officers who only have food on the brain. The exercise was highly successful and achieved its objectives. One of the lessons we drew from it was to distribute ground-to-air radios to the batteries, so that the ranging and the fire for effect could be done directly, without the command room playing middleman.

But the awaited "Bendigo" order never came down – even when the skies grew dark, and it was clear that war was going to break out in October 1973. The surface-to-air missiles were spared the harsh blow they could have taken, and our Air Force's aircraft were shot down at a murderous rate. Or as Ezer Weizmann put it: "The missile bent the airplane's wing."

Why? First, the schedule for execution required advance notice of 48-72 hours, and entailed calling up some 3,000 Artillery Corps reservists. Beyond that, the new Air Force commander, Benny Peled, never heard or knew about "Bendigo," and the ones who did know – Peled's deputy, Ivri, and the head of the Ops Division, Giora Forman, didn't do so. Ivri was ill, and Forman was at loggerheads with Peled. As I related above, in a desperate attempt to salvage the Air Force's lost honor, Giora Rom and other senior airmen tried to blame the artillery, and tarnish us with the blame of not providing fire support to the ground forces. These were low-level apologetics, beneath the dignity of the blue stars.

The bottom line is that an important operation, properly planned and well-practiced, which embodied true cooperation with the Air Force and maximal combined arms – was not carried out. Small comfort can perhaps be found in the fact that the planning and practicing of "Bendigo" bore fruit not long thereafter, in the second part of the Yom Kippur War, and also nine years later, in the First Lebanon War, when we destroyed SA-6 surface-to-air missile batteries.

"We Were Attacked by a Concentrated Artillery Fire Strike"

According to a study conducted by ret. Brig. Gen Meir Finkel, which was published in 2022 in "Yesodot," the periodical of the IDF's history department, and according to the studies of Benny Arbel, who writes often about the Artillery Corps, the meticulous planning and strenuous training of "Bendigo" had, as aforementioned, a blessed effect in the second part of the Yom Kippur War. Our artillery, using ranging by Skyhawk pilots trained for "Bendigo," destroyed eleven surface-to-air batteries – five on the eastern bank of the Canal, on October 14th, and six on the western bank, a week later. The man who initiated the operation was Haim Bar-Lev, appointed commander of the southern front, over Gorodish's head. Bar-Lev, who had been present at the "Bendigo" exercise, may not have said a word throughout the demonstration, but he was the type that doesn't lose a drop of knowledge, once acquired. The brilliant planning, endless training, and perfect execution resulted in the artillery "straightening the airplane's wing," as Benny Arbel put it, guaranteeing the Air Force almost full freedom of action in the second part of the war on the Egyptian front. Arbel, in his study, cited the book written by Egyptian War Minister, Fariq al-Awal Muhammad Fawzi, who wrote as follows:

> With the launch of the offensive, these batteries were attacked in a concentrated artillery barrage by the enemy's 175mm long-range cannons, which struck these five batteries.
>
> The Second and Third Armies could not defend the positions of these missile-defense battalions on the eastern bank [of the Suez Canal], and the air force was also unable to lend any assistance whatsoever.

The study also cited a book by Abdul Munim Wassel, commander of the Egyptian Third Army, who recalled:

> "The offensive of the 3rd Armored Brigade began in unencouraging fashion, for according to the plan to secure it, the offensive was supposed to be preceded by an airstrike. This did not take place, as no contact was established with the surface-to-air battalions transferred to the eastern bank of the Canal before dawn on October 14th, in order to secure the air raids and prevent them from coming under attack.
>
> When contact was finally established, the surface-to-air battalions couldn't operate, as the enemy employed its long-range artillery against them. The enemy fire restricted their operations, as some of the antennae necessary to direct the missiles were damaged. Thus the brigade was left with no air cover and no air protection.[11]"

In the book *Inside the Kremlin During the Yom Kippur War*, the author, historian Victor Israelian, tells that Soviet Premiere, Alexei Kosygin, returned from Cairo "with his tail between his legs," after Sadat rejected his demand to reach a ceasefire. U.S. Secretary of State, Henry Kissinger, arrived in Moscow on the evening of October 20th, and failed to reach any agreements with his hosts. But the next morning, Soviet leader Leonid Brezhnev convinced Egyptian president Sadat to agree to a truce. According to Israelian, it is unclear if Brezhnev told Sadat

---

11 Wassel, Abdul Munim: *The war battles on the Egyptian Front*, (Cairo 2002)

about Kissinger's visit, but Hafiz Ismail, the Egyptian president's aide and adviser, informed the U.S. Secretary of State that Sadat had agreed to a ceasefire. In other words, by October 21st, Kissinger knew it as well. The destruction of eleven surface-to-air missiles may explain why Sadat, who but a day prior still persisted in obstinate refusal, was suddenly willing to hold his fire, devoid of aerial protection and with the Israeli Air Force free to operate.

A missile damaged by a 175mm battery.

THE GOAL – COMMAND OF A STANDING BATTALION

Toward the end of my term as ops officer of the 209th Division Artillery, in late 1972, I was summoned to an interview with the Chief Artillery Officer. The division artillery commander, Moshe Peled, was good friends with the corps commander, Aryeh Levi, and before we parted, he told me, "Any battalion in Sinai you want – I'll see to it that you'll get to command it right away." The height of my ambition was to command a standing battalion. Baruchin's waiting list was a thing of the past, and you could now advance based on skills, and not just age and tenure.

Levy must have received a glowing report about me from Peled, listened patiently, and said, "Arie, you'll be Chief Artillery Officer someday." Then, after tossing this dramatic prediction, disarming me of all my arguments, he added, "By autumn, you'll command a standing battalion. Meanwhile, you'll be the establishing commander of a new reserve battalion of 175mm guns, the 412th, and you'll be an instructor at the advanced branch at Bahad 9."

Levy picked the term 'autumn' in order to avoid committing to a clear-cut date, but he gave his word, and I threw myself headlong into both missions.

Establishing a Battalion, Meanwhile

The 412th Battalion's initial training took place in January 1973 at the "Blockade" fire zone in the Sinai. The training plan I formulated left minimal time for training at the encampment, focusing instead on field training. The troops were veterans of the 55th Battalion, which hosted the initial training, in addition to people who served in administrative roles during their compulsory service – people I knew, whose abilities I was familiar with, and of whose experience I wished to avail myself. Those whom I knew to be excellent, creative, proactive, hardworking, and trustworthy– were recruited. And indeed, I managed to put together an extraordinary team. My deputy bat-com was Israel Bar-Lev, an airborne mortar trooper with red boots, an architect by trade, who didn't quite understand where he found himself. The self-propelled cannon was alien to him, but we found a common language. It became clear that we were on the same page when he offered to paint the battalion's banner at home, with the aid of his skillful wife, likewise a gifted architect.

My objective was to train the battalion for the next war on one hand, and on the other, to decisively beat the 55th Battalion, the standing battalion whose men were sent as training opponents for us, in all metrics of the final exam: Speed of deployment, precision of first shot, rate of fire for effect, and all other metrics.

The principle of competition holds true in all aspects of life, and the way to coalesce a new unit and challenge it is to instill an ethos of achievement: The setting of almost unattainable goals, and demanding achievements and victories. In so doing, I set an almost unachievable goal. The 55th Battalion, which had run and operated the establishment of the other 175mm battalions after receiving initial training in the U.S., had recorded some highly impressive achievements. To compete and outdo it was something that bordered on wild fantasy. Happily for me, the officers of the new battalion were infected by my enthusiasm and ardor, to no small degree thanks to the lesson I had received from Yaakov Aknin, and had long since internalized, regarding the overwhelming importance of assigning the right people to the right positions. Moshe Eisenberg, who came from the 405th Battalion to be a battery commander, Aharon Abramowitz, who I imported from the 55th as an XO, Sami Malama, the HQ company commander from the 402nd Battalion, Ami Shiloh from the 55th who I appointed as battery commander, Hezi Nagar, the XO of the Nahal battery at the 55th, Oded Gruber the FDO, and many others.

The pinnacle of the training session was the final exercise, in which I decided to practice a long-distance night movement, without lights, at high speed. We moved at top speed, and the malfunctions quickly began:

As was customary in 175mm battalions, some of the crew members of the M-548 tracked ammunition carrier sat in the cabin, as there was no room for them all on the self-propelled gun. One carrier stopped suddenly, and the long barrel of the self-propelled gun following it butted the carrier's "rails" which transported the ammunition. The rails shot forward, and only thanks to a heavy dose of blind luck, passed between two crew members, hurting no one.

We kept moving at breakneck speed. The barrel of one of the self-propelled guns "ate sand" while moving from one streambed to another, and the team leader was unaware of it, due to the darkness and the speed. When I gave the order for a hasty deployment, the SPG stopped and got onto the shovel – the elongated platform, which digs into the rear of the SPG and helps the cannon remain stable despite the immense recoil caused by the firing – and when the projectile was fired, the barrel exploded due to the sand filling it, and split open at the end like a sort of lily.

I didn't halt the exercise despite both malfunctions. Investigations and accounting could wait. The exercise ended successfully. We broke the 55th's hasty deployment record, and it was clear to me that the 412th was ready for war.

I should add that standard operating procedure is not to cover the barrel while moving toward snap deployments, so that the barrel won't have to be lowered in order to remove the cover. Movement should be done in a fire-ready state. The phenomenon of barrels "eating sand" had happened in the past, but somehow this bit of lore was not passed on to me, and I was forced to learn it the hard way.

The Parade Marched On

The other job Aryeh Levi tasked me with, as I mentioned, was instruction at the advanced branch, under the command of Oded Boneh. Boneh, it seemed to me, didn't quite understand where I had come from to disturb the branch's routine with all types of outlandish ideas. At Bahad 9, time stood still.

I realized that there was no place for initiative and effort, and along with Yaakov Reshef, my brother from another mother till the day he passed, we had already decided to buy white clothes and play tennis, like British officers used to in the old, Mandate-era tennis court at Bahad 9. But a moment before we retired to a life of sporting leisure in the guise of professional military service, I was suddenly tasked with another assignment: Staff ops officer of the corps' column in the IDF's Independence Day Parade in Jerusalem. The very same parade that marched in pomp and vanity, a mere half year before the resounding slap in the face on Yom Kippur.

Eli Eshet (Krost) was the one who gave me the assignment. I remembered him from my youth, after he came one Saturday from his home in Herzliya to the home of the Sabri family, riding a horse. As commander of Bahad 9, Eshet was appointed in charge of the Artillery Corps' column, which was part of the armored forces column, commanded by Yanush Ben-Gal. According to the plan, our column was supposed to include a battalion of M-50 155mm cannons, a battalion of heavy 160mm mortars on Sherman chassis from Bahad 9, a battalion of 175mm SPH guns, a battalion of 203mm SPHs based on the 55th Battalion, a battalion of M-109 guns (the 405th), and a battalion of 240mm rocket launchers mounted on twelve trucks. Seventy-two pieces in all. It was determined that each battalion would be preceded by the bat-com on a half-track, and the Artillery Corps' column command would lead the way in three M-113 armored personnel carriers, with Eshet in the lead APC.

A large camp was erected at the staging area, near the Atarot airport. As was my custom, I wrote a proper order, and delivered command groups at Tzrifin to all the commanders. There I specified everything – from the order of travel and the manner of travel, through the preliminary training, the painting of the pieces taking part in the parade in the same color, continuing with a uniform and well-coordinated appearance of all the pieces, and finally the complex logistics of transporting over 80 pieces to the staging area, setting up there, and training.

After touring the area, I chose a segment of the old road connecting Jerusalem and the Jordan Valley as a training site. The road was partly ruined. King Hussein had a new road paved to replace it, opened in great pomp and ceremony just before the Six-Day War. We marked the road according to the markings of the relevant streets in Jerusalem, and were also occupied with preparations for the "prettiest encampment" contest. I had a mind to forego this contest, but ultimately decided to give it a go anyway. My friend Shlomo Cohen, the adjutant of the 7th Armored Brigade in 1973 and during the parade as well, reminded me shortly before the time of this writing that we actually won first place in that contest. During all this hard work, we didn't miss the opportunity to dine at Jerusalem's excellent "Minaret" restaurant – where we paid our bills in full, from our hard-earned cash. The generals' custom of eating for free was foreign to us.

As the whole thing was laid entirely upon the ad-hoc staff I had put together, I was busy day and night with organizing, orders, solving problems of every sort and type, as well as reviewing and undertaking intense training of the drivers and commanders. The final nights were dedicated to rehearsals in the streets of Jerusalem – first skeleton rehearsals and traversability tests for each and every vehicle, followed by full general rehearsals.

And suddenly, who shows up at the training ground but the overall commander of the armored forces column, Brigadier of the 7th, Yanush Ben-Gal. I received him, and he was very businesslike, and asked to drive every vehicle scheduled to participate in the parade. We gave him a crash course on the M-109 and the 175mm, he also drove the other pieces, and in all of them made an effort to stick to the white lines which marked the way for the drivers.

Once again, I witnessed the creative and wise commander I had met way back when, at the fire exercise with Golani's 51st Battalion, when he was a tank company commander and I an FSO. Yanush went into each and every detail, cut himself no slack and cut none to others. He conducted himself as a commander whose word is final, but before that, he was willing to listen. Most of all: he didn't act like some callous Roman emperor.

A guest of another type entirely was Paul Page, aka Leopold, the handsome and dominant character from "Schindler's List," whose personal story inspired the book and the film. When I was in the U.S.

on a fundraising mission for the United Jewish Appeal, Page hosted me for an entire day at his home – from the country club, through lunch, to dinner with friends at his home. He remained as mercurial as depicted in the film – incessantly moving, talking, doing, initiating, and he also volunteered to host me on weekends when I wasn't hiking in the Sequoia National Park, or travelling to Las Vegas.

Page and his wife had come to Israel for Independence Day, and among other places – to my joy – wound up in our gathering area. I hosted them lavishly, inasmuch as I could in uniform, with a ride in all the war machines, and a dinner a-la the Thousand Arabian Nights. Later on, Paul and his wife would tell me that this was the highlight of that visit to Israel.

When Independence Day arrived, the parade marched most successfully. The elation of the entire people and the senior leadership was sky-high. Who could challenge us after such a show of might in the streets of the eternal, unified capital.

Lesson Delivered, Courtesy of the Freeloaders

The next step in the variety of roles I filled over my years in uniform was command of the advanced branch at Bahad 9, where the various corps' specializations take place – from training for FDO (fire-direction officer) and RSO (recon and surveying officer), through training for more senior positions, such as RSO for an entire division artillery, and deputy division artillery commander, up to training for senior firing echelon positions. I planned an advanced course in the style of the armored company commanders' course, where cadets are treated like kings, and all they have to do is train and meet their assignments. As I had previously conducted a shooting camp for all the corps' battalions at Khirbet Ma'ahaz, and one battalion after another came there to practice live fire ranging, I decided to avail myself of the excellent staff that helped me there – my deputy Yaakov Reshef, Yigal Barzilai, Ze'ev Amit, and others.

One irregular incident occurred at that firing camp, on a night when I went to sleep in Beersheba. I was late to return in the morning, and a ruckus broke out in my absence: A 6X6 truck, that was supposed to pick up the reserve officers from the rendezvous point on the road and drive them to the encampment, was late to arrive. The reserve bat-com, A., who didn't like to wait, came into camp with his civilian car, showering Reshef with a torrent of screams, spiced with invective about all the "freeloading career military guys," who "sit on their asses all day," and "have no respect for reservists' time." The more A. poured on the bile, Reshef – who was nicknamed Herschel'e, after the trickster of Yiddish lore, and was known for his cool demeanor – replied in his calm, unemotional fashion. A's rage flamed, his face went bright red, and he was close to exploding.

I arrived and straightened matters, and we began the training session. I too received his invective, but decided to forebear. Meanwhile, we taught and practiced all types of ranging – all with live fire, of course – and then we reached the pinnacle: Ranging in motion. Somehow, I had managed to get my hands on two Sherman M-51 tanks, and asked who wanted to go first to demonstrate.

Silence ensued. I said: "Bat-com, perhaps you should come up."

A., a legendary commander, couldn't decline the challenge. He got into the tank and took up the radio operator-loader position,[12] while I, from the tank commander's position, gave orders to the driver. The first thing I did was turn the turret around, to make A. lose his bearings, and when he finally identified the target, I gave him five seconds at the observation post, for after all, we were "under fire from enemy tanks." He began ranging, I ascended with the tank just as the projectile was falling, gave him a few seconds to identify the impact site, and slid back down, precisely as per the procedure of ranging in motion from a tank.

A.'s orientation skills failed him, and he struggled to range as the turret didn't remain with the barrel forward at all times, but turned by 90 and even 180 degrees while rising to an observation post. He asked for a break. I explained the rules of ranging and orientation to him, leading him step by step until he made it. Call it "Taming of the Shrew" – the soft and easy way.

---

[12] Unlike in the U.S. Armed Forces, IDF tank crews number only four, and the radio operator is also the one loading the shells for the gunner to fire.

When we did a summary meeting, after the nighttime exercises had concluded as well, A. praised the training, the professionalism, the logistics, the food, and the conveniences, and said not a word against the career military personnel. We shook hands, and remained friends.

This wasn't the only time I had encountered dismissive and/or hostile attitudes by reservists toward the career military. Many of them, especially senior reserve officers, were the cream of Israeli society – prominent industrialists, senior bankers, famous lawyers, and few of them were the type to hide their lights under a bushel. They viewed a career in the military as a dishonor, a sort of lifesaver for people who couldn't cut it in civilian life. Few said so out loud, but many evinced it wordlessly.

This phenomenon vanished at once following the Yom Kippur War, when the company commanders, the bat-coms, and the brigadiers, at the head of their conscript troops, defended the State of Israel with their bodies until the reserves arrived.

"This Is a Corps We Didn't Even Dare Dream Of"

As usual, in the planning of the advanced course as well, which featured standing and reserve officers marked for senior positions, I sought to go out in the field and not sit around in classrooms. In this spirit, the curriculum included two weeks of study on-base at most, and then we left Tzrifin, mounted on ACs (Ammunitions Carriers, M325 Command Cars) on a series of navigations and surveying all the way from Tzrifin to the "Blockade" fire zone in the Sinai. There I planned to "drop in" on the 403rd Battalion, commanded by Rami Ziv, and train the cadets in fire, with each battery representing a battalion, and the senior position – FDO, RSO, deputy bat-com – manned by the cadets. For the finale, I planned a division artillery-scale live fire exercise, with the cadets filling the senior positions in the division artillery HQ as well.

Herschel'e arranged rather luxurious logistics. Each cadet's gear was packed in a security box with their name printed on it in large block letters, and when we reached our night camps en route south, awaiting us at each stop were tightly erected tents and field bunks with foam mattresses and sleeping bags. Dinners were always rich, and a lit tent awaited us for summary meetings, drawing lessons, and debriefing. In short, VIP treatment unheard of in the Artillery Corps until then.

The course ended very successfully, especially the navigation and surveying series, as well as the live fire exercises. It gave the cadets a true sense of the missions and a clear understanding of what we expected of the firing echelons in the next war – including concentrating division artillery-level fire. However, this being the Jewish people, there was no shortage of comic moments as well.

One of these began not so comically, when Herschel'e, who worked night and day, collapsed one evening and passed out from exhaustion. One of the cadets, Ran Federman, found an original way to solve the situation: he pulled out a bottle of whisky, and revived Herschel'e with a few good swigs poured into his numb lips.

Speaking of whisky: The instructions of the IDF's Instruction Department, which applied to Bahad 9, then required the wearing of steel helmets even when on administrative rides in command cars. The head of the Instruction Department at the time was none other than our old acquaintance Gorodish, who tried to impose the super-strict regulations of the 7th Armored Brigade on the entire IDF, but reservists weren't about to snap to attention at every whim.

On one ride, I noticed two cadets in the command car ahead of me – Ran Federman from the previous anecdote, and Yaakov Mirimchik, a 6'6 giant nicknamed "Chick," who in civilian life was the Hadera fire chief – without steel helmets. I passed them and raised a finger, a well-known signal that they were "fined" a bottle of whisky for the graduation party – but they made no response. I raised another finger. Two bottles. Again, I was completely ignored. Out of options, I pulled them over on the side.

"What's with you two?" I asked.

"You know what, Arie," Federman said, "take a whole crate of whisky and leave us alone with the steel helmets."

And the rest is told in the somewhat hazy annals of the graduation party.

A third story happened when a senior officer from the corps came to visit the fire zone at the Blockade. He summoned an admin jeep to await him at Refidim air base, and came to us in the field wearing overalls, wrapped in a camouflage-hued scarf made of parachute cloth, in the middle of summer.

We climbed up a hill which overlooked the division's artillery deployment, and found the RSO taking measurements and passing on data. It was Dr. Ilya Leibowitz, today Prof. Emeritus, a renowned astronomy expert, one of the founders of the Mitzpe Ramon observatory, and son of Prof. Yeshayahu Leibowitz (incidentally, Leibowitz's grandson, Prof. Yoram Yovel, was an artillery officer as well, serving in the Peace for Galilee War among others.) The senior officer asked Ilya what the strategic reason was that caused him to place the theodolite – the device that facilitated the pointing of all the guns of the division artillery in the precise same direction – on that particular hill.

Ilya looked bemusedly at the man, who looked like a visitor from one of the distant planets he studied, and replied indifferently: "This is where my command car broke down."

The state of the Bahad 9 fleet of vehicles was always in shambles, and a designated maintenance squad was set aside to make sure that the command cars assigned to the course kept going even in the harsh field conditions. Obviously that wasn't the reason Ilya had chosen that hill, but it was a prime opportunity to raise an irksome problem.

At the course summary, attended by new Chief Artillery Officer, Nati Sharoni, the cadets stood up one by one, lavishing praises on the course, on the curriculum, on the navigation and surveying series, and particularly on the crown jewel – the live fire exercise in the Sinai. One cadet stood up and said: "This is not the corps we knew. This is something else, which we never even dared dream of."

Sharoni, as a new Chief Artillery Officer, tried as hard as he could to hear some negative critique, but came up empty. He, too, was forced to admit that a singularly successful course had concluded.

THE YOM KIPPUR WAR

The Golan Heights are in flames. Thirty thousand shells are fired from one thousand Syrian barrels, landing on each and every IDF site – outposts, bases, junctions, and the few artillery batteries. All battered by fire. Mig and Sukhoi airplanes swoop down from above, passing low, precisely over us. We jump in the vehicles and exit the "Sa'ar" base, which is alongside Nafah. No shock and no fear, just accepting reality.

When you're a commander, people look up to you, await your every word. On October 6th, 1973, our mission was clear. There was no fear – and no shred of hesitation.

Thus opened the Yom Kippur War, THE war, whose effects are felt across Israeli society to this day. THE war which also changed my own life, and following which the artillery vision, which I had formulated for over three years, since finishing my academic studies and landing in the heart of darkness of the War of Attrition, became a reality.

TAKE THE 405TH, BUT...

My entry interview as bat-com of the 405th was held with Nati Sharoni on August 22nd, 1973. "You're getting an American battalion, with the most advanced SPH in the world," he told me, "but morale in the battalion is poor. You need to get the men on a track of confidence in their abilities, raise morale, and considerably improve operational performance. It won't be easy, because next April the battalion is scheduled to be disbanded and become a reserve battalion."

And why? First of all, because according to the announcements proclaimed by the leadership, there won't be another war for ten years. Complacency spread through all walks of life. Israel convinced itself it was an empire, a mighty military power with strategic depth of occupied territories, and the best air force in the world. In this spirit, the government decided to shorten the mandatory military service, and consequently to disband standing units and turn them into reserve units. Beyond this, as Sharoni explained to me, the 405th Battalion was slated for disbanding and conversion to a reserve unit, as there was no intention of purchasing any more M-109 SPHs. The corps had 23 barrels, the 24th dismantled for instruction at Bahad 20, the Ordnance Corps' school, and the reserve array had no shortage of artillery troopers.

"And what will happen with me?" I asked.

"When the 405th becomes a reserve battalion," Sharoni said, "You'll get the 55th, which is also a standing battalion with advanced American guns." I was very familiar with the 55th Battalion's main weapon – a 175mm SPG with a replaceable 203mm barrel, which turns an M-107 "Lance" into an M-110 "Hatchet" – the gun I ran bunker-busting experiments within the Sinai. Sharoni didn't confide in me about his traumatic meeting with Talik, when he was appointed Chief Artillery Officer. Talik was by then head of the IDF's Ops Division, deputy Chief of Staff, and the man in charge of building the IDF's force. The meeting was held several weeks prior to my interview. Ahead of his appointment as CAO, Sharoni asked why to disband the 405th, and the deputy Chief of Staff replied: "I have 120 105mm barrels in an armored brigade. I don't need the added twelve barrels of 155mm."

Sharp as a surgeon's scalpel. The thesis was clear and simple: Only armor and only tanks. No need for infantry, engineers, and artillery, save to serve the tanks.

"And what of fire power?" Sharoni pushed.

"For that," Talik replied, "we have the best air force in the world, a "flying artillery" that will destroy the enemy's artillery and thwart any attempt to assail or harm the empire." He didn't actually use the word 'empire,' but his words were the epitome of the dissonance between our self-confidence in the artillery, our faith in our strength, the methods we developed and perfected, and the training we had undergone, with a clear vision and understanding of our place and our role in the complex, multi-armed machine named the IDF – and the approach of the IDF brass to the Artillery

Corps as some primordial, negligible niche. And to prove it – even the 175mm guns were purchased with air force funds, to suppress the missile batteries endangering our aircraft.

Talik's strident ruling made it clear to Sharoni that the days of artillery acquisitions were over, and into this almost hostile reality, he invited me to step in. He knew that I wasn't made of stuff that breaks or folds. I looked forward like a horse with blinders on. I saw only the mission and my vision, ignoring all surrounding and background noises. I was appointed bat-com of a standing battalion, and I knew what I had to do and how to prepare my troops for war. The war nobody was seeing even on the edge of the horizon.

The vision burned within me, and even if I wasn't aware of the whole of it myself, I knew exactly what needed to be done in the battalion and in the Artillery Corps. I wasn't even deterred by the weird situation in which I found myself – a major replacing a veteran Lt. Colonel, six years older than me, with my deputy bat-com also my senior by a year. I knew of the deterioration of a once glorious battalion, commanded for years by a series of quality personnel, none of whom remained. A battalion with a decorated tradition, established by Mondi Carmeli in 1969 as a battalion of long-barreled 122mm guns captured in battle, which were converted to 155mm M-109 guns at Fort Sill by Eli Doron, A battalion which fought in the War of Attrition, and which was codenamed "Tiger" for a reason. And despite all my lofty thoughts of vision, I took my introductory scene at the battalion with a grin.

A Tale of Four Models

I stopped my Carmel[13] jalopy at the entrance to the battalion camp near Bilu Junction, outside Rehovot. A rope was stretched across the

---

13   Carmel (sometimes also known as "Susita,") was an Israeli car model manufactured by Autocars Ltd., notable for its fiberglass chassis, used to save on the cost of purchasing and transporting heavy metals. These cars were of dubious mechanical reliability, poorer comfort, and the fiberglass chassis was liable to be chewed through by camels if left unattended to in the desert.

entry path, and a long-haired fellow, with a stubbly beard, naked torso, and sandals stood attached to it.

"Who are you?" he asked tiredly, as though wondering who comes at high noon to disturb his peace.

"The bat-com," I replied.

The fellow was unimpressed. Without another word, he used his toe to move the rope from the post, allowing the Carmel through. I looked left and right. Every patch of ground was covered with weeds, and everything screamed neglect and filth. Uri Manos, the deputy bat-com, who awaited me, was exhausted following a year in the post and a grueling training session at the Ovdat rectangle to top it off. And here comes Arie Mizrahi to wake sleeping bears.

I understood what was happening and recalled my encounter with Yossi Peled, when he was bat-com of the 195th in El-Qantara on the northern bank of the Suez Canal. I had arrived to visit him as deputy commander of a reserve battalion, and Peled told me how he had imposed discipline in his battalion during the War of Attrition. The idea had caught my fancy at the time, and I recalled it now.

I summoned an officer's meeting for 20:00. Prior to that I called Avi Dietschy, the battalion sergeant-major, and Yoel Porat, the adjutant – two excellent men, who yearned for leadership. I ordered them to secretly prepare four soldiers – two as sergeants, one in dress uniform and the other in work fatigues, and two with officers' insignia, again one in dress uniform and the other in fatigues. All four, I said, must be clean-shaven, immaculately groomed, dressed to the nines, with shoes you could use as mirrors, a tightly stretched beret on their heads, or a standard work hat.

In the evening, I examined the four models volunteered by Dietschy for the demonstration, commenting on the height of the sergeant stripes on the shoulders and the lacing of the shoes, until the four were perfectly decked out. They were asked to wait in the next room behind a closed door.

At 20:00:00, I entered the bat-com's office, where all were awaiting my arrival. I saw a nice young bunch, looking like they just emerged from the jungles of Vietnam. Most egregious of all was Avraham Snir, commander of battery C, with a wild mop of hair and his shirt open down to the navel. I ignored it, and began speaking of professional matters. I explained at length what I expected operationally, what achievements they needed to reach, what they needed to do to be ready quickly, and so on.

The attendants asked (a few) questions, I answered each one, and when the meeting seemed to be over, I ordered the battalion sergeant-major to bring in the four models. "Take a good look at these four," I said. "They will remain here until you study each detail. The day after tomorrow, in the morning, there will be a bat-com's review. Anyone not looking like this will hit the brig for 28 days, and their battery commander for 35 days. The review will include quarters, surroundings, SPHs, supplies, outfitting, and munitions bunkers. Let's get to work."

Dudi Haramati, commander of the "Boaz" battery, the senior battery commander in the battalion and since then a soulmate, told me that they sat together afterward – the three battery commanders and Herzl Cohen the ops officer – and discussed whether to obey or tell me to go to hell. Most radical among them was Snir, a former Nahal[14] trooper, who failed to comprehend the need to cut one's hair, or to button up one's shirt in the scorching August and September weather.

Following a long debate, they decided to obey anyway. This was a first injection into their awareness, and from theirs to their underlings: There's a leader in the battalion, he knows what he wants – and he doesn't hesitate to enforce his wishes.

---

14 Nahal (acronym: Pioneering Fighting Youth) is an IDF brigade whose troopers combine infantry military service with "pioneering" work of establishing new settlements and manning the borders. Traditionally, they spend a year as a "settlement nucleus" at an existing kibbutz or moshav prior to beginning boot camp and regular military service. "Nahlawis," as the brigade's troops are affectionately known, are traditionally considered the most "free-spirited" of the Infantry units.

"The 405th Battalion Won't Be Disbanded, There'll Be a War"

All of the above took place in late September 1973, two weeks before the Yom Kippur War, because before that, since receiving the official appointment, I went on a divisional exercise of the 146th Division, as brigade artillery commander for the 288th Recon Battalion, under Tzvika Dahab. After the exercise, I ostensibly joined the 405th Battalion vacation at the Goldmintz House sanatorium in Netanya, but in practice, I only showed up for the farewell party for Aryeh Beckinstein, the bat-com I was replacing.

The ten days of penitence, between Rosh Hashanah and Yom Kippur, began on Wednesday, Rosh Hashanah Eve. The battalion was scheduled to go on a long holiday leave. The buses had already arrived and all the soldiers and commanders gathered for a bat-com's talk in the open space in front of the base gate. At last, I saw soldiers. This was an army. Everyone stood in order, in spotless dress uniforms, berets on their heads, rank insignia properly placed. It seemed that they were even pleased with the change, and not just with the impending leave.

During the talk, doubts began to surface, and troopers spoke freely about the elephant in the room: Why are they disbanding an artillery battalion equipped with the best and most advanced SPHs in the world? We didn't know back then that even today, in 2024, many militaries, including the IDF, would operate 6,000 such guns, but we knew that it did a hell of a job.

As bat-com, I had to answer. I deliberated inwardly about what to say, when suddenly a voice from heaven sounded, speaking from my mouth. "The 405th Battalion will not be disbanded," I said. "There will be a war."

The faces before me were struck with surprise. However, my decisive answer marked a target, and that was precisely what this battalion was lacking, causing it to dither for too many months.

As I was speaking, deputy bat-com Manos approached me and whispered "Leaves are canceled throughout the IDF. The buses are leaving and we're all staying for the holiday and weekend."

A Gift in the Guise of Revoked Leave

The four days of canceled leave provided the exact amount of time I needed to know the troops better and practice outfitting and dismantling the self-propelled guns again and again – until everyone met the demanding schedules I set. As we were in real alert, we trained and worked over the holiday as well. This allowed me to also bring the officers closer together and to connect with them socially as well. Happily for me, my skills in being the life of the party back at the bougie salon get-togethers of my youth in Kfar Saba came in very handy. All this also allowed me to better understand the relationships among the group of officers. This would be manifested as soon as the morning of October 6th, when I would order Yossi Koren to leave the battery he was commanding – but not to serve as FSO, but rather to be the battalion's Fire Direction Officer (FDO.) As I expected and anticipated, he did so professionally and confidently in the moment of truth and trial.

During these get-to-know talks, I found an attentive ear in Dudi Haramati, and realized that I could consult with him thanks to his inherent emotional intelligence. I recognized Snir as a bold warrior, whom I could count on in battle as a proactive thinker outside the box, which is why I assigned him as FSO of the 77th Battalion, which was the shock battalion of the 7th Armored Brigade, under a veteran, experienced bat-com named Avigdor Kahalani – soon to emerge as one of the leading heroes of this terrible war. I kept Herzl Cohen by my side as fire HQ ops officer. I was also impressed by the coolness under pressure of Alex Redlus, the intel officer – an inveterate hedonist, who knew how to keep things in proportion. I had met Uri Manos, my veteran deputy bat-com, when I was a squad leader in the 404th Battalion. He was a tall officer – the very model of an Israeli "Sabra," handsome, with an impressive head of hair, or perhaps sort of like S. Yizhar's "Tzviko." During the War of Attrition in the Sinai, when he was a battery commander in the 403rd and I was fire ops officer at Tasa, we held long talks into the night, because he would sleep with the field phone by his side, and would awaken at the slightest rustle.

Yoel Shaked, the adjutant, was someone I took a liking to because he wasn't an adjutancy officer at core. He came up as a commando fighter in the Haruv Ranger unit, was wounded in one of the operations and couldn't go back to a combat posting. Avi Dietschy, the battalion sergeant-major, was also not your typical artillery sergeant-major, but a calm, quiet guy, relatively young, free of the mannerisms of veteran sergeant majors.

In short, it was a battalion with a good, even excellent human infrastructure. It just needed a serious shakeup, to remind the men that they were soldiers, and more than this: that they were warriors, and that they were part of the IDF.

One of the first rules of leadership is to use group dynamics to make the people under you accept your authority. To this end, I had to identify the "influencers" among the officers and crew commanders, and enlist their support and cooperation. I knew that I was on the right track.

On Sunday, as the holiday ended, I felt far more confident. These four days filled me with confidence, and I felt capable of taking on any mission assigned to us. I knew the men with me, and knew I had people I could count on. We didn't know – I and all those around me – that we were only six days before the most brutal and difficult war in Israel's history, if only due to the number of casualties – 2,685 dead – in a very short time, sixteen days, out of a population of 2.6 million Jews in Israel.

In the War of Independence, we had lost 6,000 troops, a full percent of the Jewish population in the land of Israel. But that war lasted for two years. The surprise and shock that seized the people of Israel on Yom Kippur doubled the blow.

"Tomorrow Morning Your Battalion Is Deployed in the Golan Heights"

On Sunday morning, Sept. 30th, I received instructions from the Chief Artillery Officer of the Central Command, Mondi Carmeli, and his ops officer Eliyahu "Uppo" Barak, to leave the battalion's battery C. on alert, send the "Boaz" battery for an educational series in Jerusalem, and let battery A. go on a "regular" (one week) leave. In short, back to normal. The next day at 16:00, there was a ceremony scheduled, marking the succession of the Central Command General post, with Rehavam "Gandhi" Ze'evi leaving to be replaced by Yonah Efrat.

In the course of his farewell tour from the command's units and New Year's toast ceremonies, Gandhi came to our battalion as well and gifted me a book with a personal inscription, which I have kept to this day. It was written by Col. Richard Meinertzhagen, of whom I had read in Lowell Thomas's book "With Allenby in Palestine." Meinertzhagen, a British nobleman who was Allenby's intelligence officer and initiated the deception operation that led to the taking of Beersheba by the ANZAC cavalry, became an ardent Zionist. This despite the fact that as a youth – like all the British upper class – he held precious little respect for Jews, and was even antisemitic to some degree. In his book, he explains that what turned him into a Zionist was the profound difference between the Jewish settlements in the country – clean, orderly colonies, with advanced agriculture and hardworking, honest, and welcoming people – as opposed to the country's Arabs, who in his words were "greedy."

"Pillage and rapine," he wrote, "were their chief occupations, and they do not build or initiate developments, throw the trash in the public domain, while their corrupt and pleasure-seeking effendis live in Lebanon and the Gulf countries, making a fortune off the toil of the serfs working their lands, and spending their money on amusements and gambling [sic]."

The 405th Battalion was unique in the fact that it reported directly to the command general. There was an artillery command officer beneath the command general, but no division or division artillery.

Formally, we belonged to the 213th Reserve Division Artillery, itself part of the 146th Division, but we had no true affiliation with it, as it was a reserve division artillery, commanded by a reservist, Danny Avidar. Gandhi, too, in his farewell from the battalion, repeated the shopworn mantra "there won't be a war for ten years," when asked about the battalion's dismantling. As commander of a battalion directly under the command HQ, I arrived for the first time at Fort Kfir, outside Jerusalem, and en route to the replacement ceremony, got to see Gandhi's famous pair of pet lions[15] with my own eyes. Megalomaniacal trappings of officers were not limited to the Armored Corps back then. Many others contracted the illness, including a Palmach veteran like Gandhi.

Mondi approached me. Before I could realize what was happening, he said: "Your battalion needs to be deployed in the Golan Heights by tomorrow morning,"

With All Due Respect to the Chief Ordnance Officer

By evening I was back at Bilu. The endless practice I imposed on the battalion proved itself, and despite all difficulties, we brought the outfitted SPHs up to the Golan Heights, including the guns and gear of battery A, whose troops had left on regular leave just the day before, and we properly executed night movements on trailers and deployed.

In accordance with the instructions of the Northern Command's Chief Artillery Officer, we deployed in battle day formation, rather than concentrate the entire battalion as a single fist in the southern Golan Heights: Battery C. deployed next to Tel Hermonit, to the west, the "Boaz" battery at the foot of Tel Fares, in a fortified position adjacent to the mound from the west, and the A battery – with the deputy bat-com and the battalion aid station – at Shaaba-

---

[15] The symbol of the Central Command is a lion (after the tribe of Judah, whose symbol is a lion), and Ze'evi decided that stone relief lions were insufficient, so he had two live specimens shipped from Africa, and kept them in a cage on the base.

nia, about two kilometers southwest of Tel Fares. Entering into positions allowed me to run dry drills and familiarize myself with the territory through observations from the mounds. The area was foreign to me. I was a man of the Sinai desert, where I knew every sand dune.

Then I made a tour of the batteries. "Boaz" settled in positions lined with what we called "Gabionis" – iron-wire cages filled with rocks (basalt, in this case, invented by an Italian engineer named Gabioni.)

Dudi the battery commander said: "We'll fire at targets in a wide lateral movement," meaning targets located up to 90 degrees on each side of the guns. To my astonishment, I saw the SPHs beginning to maneuver back and forth, like turretless M-50s, backing up on "shovels" and bragging about how little time it took.

I asked: "Why don't you swivel the turret? After all, you have a turret that can turn 360 degrees."

"IDF Chief Ordnance Officer orders require getting on shovels in any aiming of over fifteen degrees to either side," replied our battalion ordnance officer, Nehemiah Arody.

"Do you see the COO anywhere around?" I asked.

"No."

"From now on," I said, "we aim barrels in all directions, in all batteries, only by swiveling the turret."

In the moments of truth, when we had to fire at targets to the side of the batteries, and at times even behind them, my order would save much precious time.

Needless Risk

Unfortunately, I had only a short time to train the battalion in different scenarios and prepare it for war. I did so with the 412th, which indeed performed splendidly in battle, but I didn't have time to train the 405th in infantry combat, which includes professional use of the personal weapon, taking positions, eye and ear observations, charging on foot, and most importantly: Direct fire.

On Yom Kippur Eve, Bar-David appointed me artillery commander of the 7th Armored Brigade, commanded by Avigdor Ben-Gal. Concurrently, I received orders to leapfrog the Boaz battery eastward, to Juhader, so it would deploy about a mile from the engagement line, because a battery from Bahad 9 was supposed to enter the fortified position at Tel Fares.

It seemed odd, but I couldn't reach Bar-David, and meanwhile had arrived at Tel Fares. I participated in "Kol Nidrei," the prayer that opens the holy day of Yom Kippur, and then we leapfrogged the battery to Juhader.

In between I called Yanush. He told me to come the next day to the brigade HQ, near Nafah. Only in the morning did I manage to reach Bar-David on the phone as well. I asked permission to have "Boaz" deploy along with battery A. at Shaabania, some two km west of Juhader, so that it wouldn't be right on the engagement line, thus sparing itself needles risk. He refused, with an explanation about a Syrian 122 mm battery, which needs to be within range.

I was surprised at his insistence. We stood there with eleven batteries against 157 Syrian artillery batteries, and "Boaz" has to worry about this particular 122mm battery, and for that purpose to be within spitting distance of the Syrians. Dudi the battery commander and Uri the deputy bat-com listened in on the conversation, and they too realized that "Boaz" was exposed to needless danger, and an order is an order.

"You Need an APC for the Command Post"

To the best of my understanding, the Northern Command knew what was coming later that day as early as Yom Kippur morning. It is likely no coincidence that that the command intel officer, Haggai Mann, was reprimanded by the head of MID, Eli Zeira, for "creating panic" – and for allegedly inciting the Command General, Yitzhak "Haka" Hofi. The knowledge of what was to come was probably the reason that the Northern Command was reinforced by the 7th Armored Brigade, by the 405th Battalion, by two batteries from the 55th Battalion, and by the Bahad 9 Battalion.

I assigned the battery commanders as FSOs with the armored battalions – Snir, as mentioned above, with Avigdor Kahalani and the 77th Battalion, and Haramati with Haim Barak, the new bat-com of the 82nd. I did so because the company commanders of the battalion were Harmati's classmates at military boarding school, and the bat-com Barak was still a major, and not as experienced. Snir and Haramati took with them FOs from the battery – Haramati took Yirmi Tene, from Kibbutz Ma'anit, and Snir chose Amir Kalmar from Pardes Hannah. To the 75th Armored Battalion, under Yos Eldar, I assigned Baruch Benbenishti, who had become a commander of a battery of Priest guns in the 822nd Battalion in his reserve posting, and Dror Yekutieli from battery A as his FO. With the 71st Battalion, under Meshulam Rattas, I assigned Itzik Weiss, an instructor at the corps' platoon commanders' course.

The brigade command group was set for 12:00. The FSOs were scheduled to participate in it, and then to receive the detailed fire support order prepared by Herzl, the ops officer. But only at 12:00 did Yanush return from a meeting with Haka, which was held in the command bunker of Tzvika Barazani (nee Bar), the freshly appointed commander of the 820th Regional Brigade, and huddled together with the Northern Command HQ, and the HQs of the 188th and 820th Brigades.

"Tonight at six, war will begin with Egypt and Syria," Yanush said. Well, I said to myself, six in the evening, there's time. I didn't feel like I was hit by a thunderbolt, nor did those around me look or behave so. We were busy – each with their preparations and responsibilities. Despite the feeling that had stuck with me since Rosh Hashanah, the realization that Egypt and Syria were capable of such a move had yet to penetrate. And if so – the air force would pulverize them and we would sweep them away, like in the Six-Day War.

It sounds odd in retrospect, but that was the atmosphere. That was the infamous "conception," and it set in, to a degree, even among its doubters.

"In what vehicle are you moving with the command formation?" Yanush suddenly asked me.

"In a half-track," I replied. That was the Maintenance Corps' standard for the command vehicles of bat-coms and their deputies, despite the fact that as an "American" battalion, the XOs had APCs.

"You need an APC as a command vehicle," he said, ordering his deputy, Jacky Hizkiya, to transfer a ranger's APC to me, with a ranger as driver. It's not that the artillery commander's level of traveling comfort stood foremost in his mind, but that he wanted his artillery commander available, moving in battle with him and keeping his pace. This raised the questions of why, in contrast to the 7th Brigade, its sister standing armored brigade, the 188th, went to war without an artillery support commander and without a brigade-level artillery HQ.

I ordered Uri Manos to get all the troops in battle gear, break their fast and eat battle rations. But there was plenty of time till six in the evening. No rush.

The Sky Rains Fire

A moment before I entered the brigade-level command group, pushed back to 14:00, the sky began raining fire, and an immense barrage of shells fell down on us. The camp filled with casualties, and then enemy aircraft opened fire on us as well. Our own air force didn't try to chase them away, as it was busy trying to penetrate Syrian airspace, but that didn't go too well either. Every Phantom or Skyhawk that crossed the border was met by the trails of dozens of Syrian surface-to-air missiles, which gave chase. In too many cases, we saw a fireball after a few seconds, and in the rare, best cases, a parachute or two opening.

We rushed to the vehicles, but when I tried to get on the ramp and get into my new APC, I found myself blocked by Jacky Hizkiya. His own APC had fled the scene without him, and he commandeered mine.

"Deputy Brigadier," I said, amidst the almighty mayhem surrounding us, "that's my APC."

Hizkiya glanced back and said: "Was."

We returned to the miserable half-track we came in. We tried to commandeer a deserted APC, only to discover that it was deserted because it was inoperable. Outside the camp, once the command formation got set to move, Hizkiya found his own APC and we got into ours. At that point, two developments took place, starting with an argument on the radio between Itzik Ben-Shoham, Brigadier of the 188th, and Yanush. Haka had flown back to the "pit" – the IDF's command room in Tel Aviv – prior to the outbreak of the war, and remaining in Nafah were Uri Simchoni, ops officer of the Northern Command, and the staff of the 188th. Ben-Shoham fancied himself the "commander of the Golan" in the absence of the Command General, and ordered Yanush (who, as the reader may recall, held the exact same rank and post of armored brigade commander) to mobilize the battalions of the 7th Brigade. Angry exchanges crackled on the radio, with Yanush announcing "You're not my commander and don't tell me what to do," and Ben-Shoham replying with "I'm ordering you!" like that would impress Yanush, the more senior, more veteran, more experienced commander, who thought little of his counterpart.

Simchoni settled the dispute with instructions to move the 7th as a concentrated brigade against the northern Syrian effort, centered on the Quneitra Gap, and to do a castling move: switch the 74th Battalion to Yanush's command, instead of the 82nd, which was at Sindiana in the southern Golan Heights, and to set the sector line separating the two brigades south of Quneitra.

We rushed north, with the dispute still raging in the background. Haim Barak, bat-com of the 82nd, didn't reply to Ben-Shoham until Yanush gave him a direct order to do so, under pressure from Simchoni. Concurrently, Raful arrived at Nafah with the 36th Division's HQ, and squeezed with them into the crowded bunker, which by now held four separate HQ staffs, while he waited to be officially appointed commander of the Golan Heights.

The second development stemmed from Bar-David apparently realizing the error in the too-forward deployment of the "Boaz" and Bahad 9 batteries, and passed the hot potato to Benny Arad, commander of the 212th Division Artillery, the artillery unit of Raful's division. Arad, too, refrained from making a decision, passing the buck on to Raful. A live-action demonstration of the Artillery Corps at its most dependent: Rather than make decisions, you roll them upward or sideways.

"The front line fortifications have tank crews and infantry troops," Raful decided. "Let the gunners stay where they are too," and so two artillery batteries would be destroyed.

Itzik Ben-Shoham, brigadier of the 188th, left the Nafah bunker early in the evening with a single APC, loaded with officers, without an artillery support commander. He may have shown courage, but caused a six-battery artillery force – two from the 405th, two from Bahad 9, and two from the 55th – which covered the entire Heights by range, to be unable to cover his brigade and unable to assist it with fire.

Furthermore, an artillery support commander in the command post would have naturally been updated on developments along the front line, and thus would have known about the breakthrough of the Syrian armored division, and would have been able to warn the 405th and Bahad 9 batteries. This did not happen, and blood-curdling accounts of eye-witnesses, which are available on YouTube and elsewhere, give a glimpse into a chaotic state of affairs, hysteria, and a situation out of control.

We Didn't Grab Dinner in Tiberias

We moved toward the brigade's position, along a sector stretching from Quneitra in the south to Mt. Hermon in the north. Yanush also received under his command the 71st Battalion, from the Armored Corps' school, commanded by Meshulam Rattas, alongside the 74th, under Yair Nafshi, and the two organic battalions of his own brigade – the 77th, and the 75th mech. Infantry brigade, under Yossi "Yoss" Englander, a friend from back in the Sinai.

Mid-drive, I realized that my intel officer, Alex Redlus, was not with us. I looked back, and saw the mobile brigade command post– three tanks commanded by Noni Baruchin (the brigade's ops officer, and son of former Chief Artillery Officer, Baruch Baruchin), and three APCs commanded by the brigadier, the intel officer, and the artillery commander. Behind all this I saw Redlus's jeep.

I asked him on the radio why he wasn't with us. He replied with his typical indifference: "I know the Heights. This is a battle day, and it'll end by nightfall. We'll be the only ones in the brigade HQ with a jeep, and we'll go down to Tiberias for dinner."

A few minutes later, a shell hit Redlus's jeep, wounding him in both arms. I turned the APC around and performed a flanking maneuver to pick him up. He remained with us – in bandages – till the end of the war, replacing Herzl Cohen as ops officer (after Herzl volunteered as FSO of Golani's 51st Battalion in the taking of Mt. Hermon on the last day of the war, and was killed in battle) and served throughout the post-war attrition period as ops officer of the 7th Brigade's artillery support staff.

A NON-DIGITAL COMMANDER

"I Won't Forget Your Calm Voice in the Valley of Tears Battles"

Giora Lavi, a trooper in the 334th Battalion, told as follows at a reunion of the battalion's fighters through the years, at the "Gunner's House" in Zichron Yaacov: "To this day, I recall the voice of Arie Mizrachi on the radio, ranging and deploying the battalion in the hard battle at the Valley of Tears." Troopers from various battalions have also told me: "I won't forget your calm voice in the midst of the containment battles." I was particularly moved by my classmate at the basic officers' course, Moshe (Maurice) Ben-Shaul. I hadn't met him since the course, and at that reunion, he told me: "Arie, when I heard your voice on the radio, I got my self-confidence back, and I realized we'd win the war. As a reservist who had just kissed his family goodbye, leaving his warm home for the unknown, it was important to me to know that we had a calm commander, and one who is a friend to boot."

Ben-Ami Cohen, commander of the Bahad 9 Battalion, later told of the battalion's experiences on October 9th, also speaking of the calmness and effectiveness of the firing commands and the relaying of the firing results. He also wrote of it in an essay titled "Born to War Alone," in a booklet titled "The Yom Kippur War at 30," published by the IDF's Maarachot periodical, where he told:

Immediately after reaching the position, I turned one of the radios to the 7th Brigade's ops channel A. I listened to the battle management, the commands and notices passed on this important channel. I noted all the coordinates we received in the fire orders from Lt. Col. Arie Mizrachi, the 7th's artillery commander, on an impromptu situation map.

That's how I followed the development of the battle. At first, we fired at targets at ranges of up to 7.5 km. I noticed that the range to the targets we were engaging with fire, had gradually shortened to five km. The more the demands for fire increased, the more the distance to the targets we were firing at decreased. Soon we were firing at targets at a range of three km. The sounds of the battle – the tank guns and the engines of the tank maneuvering and changing positions – were close, right past the ridge before our position. In addition to the Syrian tanks approaching very close to our position, Syrian helicopters landed by us, discharging commando troops. In addition, we were attacked by Syrian fighter jets on low altitude swoops, which greatly hindered concentration and control.

All these goings-on impacted the ability to keep commanding the position. It took great concentration to function effectively and alertly, and much self-control was required to project confidence and leadership, as the battalion troops studied us, the commanders, with hawk eyes, and were greatly impacted by our behavior. The commanders were required to locate the most urgent problems, focus on them, and continue operating the battalion in producing support fire for the tanks on the engagement line, which was essential to decide the battle.

There was no need to urge us on to further efforts. Everyone in the battalion felt that these were fateful hours to decide the battle for the Golan Heights and the entire country. We knew that every shell fired impacts the outcome of the battle.

Arie Mizrachi was calm throughout the fire direction. All morning long, I listened to his fire commands. He was decisive and matter-of-fact, clear and consistent. He phrased the orders in a manner where we could understand it immediately, without wasting time on needless clarifications and explanations. His transmissions didn't indicate the great stress he was under. From time to time, amidst the furor of war, he informed us of direct artillery hits on Syrian tanks. Arie gave us, the gunners in the rear, a sense of being important partners in deciding the battle.

Mizrachi planned the engagement of the targets so that an artillery ambush was created in the middle of the valley, and that's where he directed the Katyusha battalion. The horrific roar of the Katyushas launching, bursting almost simultaneously from all launching pads, was impressive and frightening. There is no doubt that this fire strike, landed under Mizrachi's management on the Syrian force, was one of the important factors in deciding the defensive battle at the Valley *of Tears.*

At the height of battle, some two hours after demanding ammunition, two civilian semi-trailers, commanded by Maj. Alexander Berger, entered the front of the position. At the time, the position was down to 20 shells for two batteries, meaning a 2.5 shell average per gun. Had the ammunition trucks arrived a few minutes later, we would have been left without ammunition and unable to assist.

Despite the great danger, we brought the ammunition-laden trucks into the center of the gun positions, with crates and sacks of excess propellants. With no order given, all those present at the position – cooks, medics, drivers, officers, and anyone who could – got to dismantling the bales in which the explosives were packed by hatchet. There was no time for the "refill" procedure. Immediately upon unloading the crates we passed the ammunition straight to the crews and into the gun barrels for firing. The fire never stopped for a moment.

During the frenetic activity of unloading the ammunition crates, I noticed military photographer Avraham Vered. He laid his cameras on an empty ammunition crate, and set to help move the heavy ordnance from the truck to the guns. The immediate danger to life and limb was most palpable, and the need to help outweighed the capturing of these unique moments.

At a certain stage, the distance between the spearhead of the Syrian tank force and our position was so short, that I considered ordering "Prepare for tanks" – an order requiring to prepare the cumbersome field guns for direct fire, meaning adjusting the telescopic sights for direct fire, and position the guns for direct, rather than indirect fire. Due to the artillery commander's fire demands, and the more import-

ant and urgent need for support fire on the targets, I postponed giving the order minute after minute, until it turned out that during those very moments, the Syrian attack had been stopped. Following our Katyusha fire, the Syrians broke and began retreating eastward. Each time we received another fire order, it turned out that the range to the targets had increased. There was no more need for direct fire.

When the firing ranges grew, Mizrachi informed us on the radio that the enemy had broken and was beginning to retreat. We continued our fire at maximum rate, until firing ranges reached eight kilometers. From the orders we received, we realized that the defensive battle had ended successfully. We had managed to stop the enemy's offensive, and inflicted immense casualties upon it. The Syrians had retreated behind the borderline. Most of their forces had been destroyed, and were scattered all over the Valley of Tears[16].

Here, I'm fulfilling My Destiny

Indeed, from the moment the war broke out I was focused on my purpose, and in the heart of the inferno and chaos, a serenity descended upon me. I understood precisely what I was supposed to do, after all the years preceding the hour of this ultimate test. Everything I learned, practiced, taught, picked up in endless FSO drills, the Samua operation, the Six-Day War, the War of Attrition in the Sinai, in the Jordan Valley, and the Beit She'an Valley – as the ops officer of the 209th Division Artillery, as commander of the advanced branch, in specializing on the 175mm SPG when I established the 412th Battalion, in training the corps' troops of the firing echelon, in diligent study of all aspect of the corps, and intimate acquaintance with all the secrets of the craft – all this experience of many years, the books I had read about the world wars, about famous battles, and personal experiences of soldiers around the world, even what I learned from my father's stories – everything was distilled within me and was focused on this

---

[16] Ben-Ami Cohen, ("Born to War Alone"), Maarchot, Issue 391, Oct. 2003, pp 24-33.

fateful time of trial. *Here, I'm fulfilling my purpose.* I slid into my role as though I were an old hand at do-or-die wars, and as though I had been born and raised in the Golan Heights.

I was as well acquainted with the brass of the 7th Armored Brigade, as I was with the battalion troops. I knew my officers, commanders, and artillery battalion troopers well, from long years of sweat in all roles, in several battalions, and in advanced courses and ranging camps. I knew precisely what to do, and felt no shred of hesitation whatsoever.

"Prepare 'Danger Fire Missions'"

In the late afternoon hours of Yom Kippur, Yanush convened a sort of short planning group, which was translated into orders on the radio:

-- Yair Nafshi will be responsible, with the 74th Battalion, for the southern flank of the brigade's sector – from Quneitra to outpost 107, which controlled the Quneitra-Damascus road, through the Booster Ridge, which crosses the area known as the "Quneitra Gap," behind which the Bahad 9 batteries were deployed – Yos Eldar, with his mech. infantry battalion plus tank companies from the 77th Battalion, was put in charge of our ramps in the central sector – from Tel Hermonit eastward – Meshulam Rattas with the 71st Battalion took the northern ramps to Buq'ata, where the Golani Brigade was supposed to take charge.

The topography, as can be seen, dictated deployment mostly toward the Quneitra Gap, a flat area allowing for continuous tank maneuvers across a broad sector. The constructed area of the city of Quneitra did not allow for this. The area north of the Hermonit was demarcated on the Syrian side by Tel Dahur and the village of Dahur Taranga, and became more mountainous, rocky, and thick with vegetation, so it also did not allow for continuous tank movement. It was clear that the Syrian armored offensive would be concentrated on the plains between the Booster Ridge and Tel Dahur, later to be immortalized as "The Valley of Tears."

"You," Yanush said to me, "will prepare 'danger fire missions'" – this meant pre-ranging critical defensive targets, mostly along access routes to our outposts, and the crossings over the anti-tank trench, so that measured blasts of fire could be deployed toward there, on pre-arranged code words – if and when the enemy should reach such a point.

There was a lot of sense in this instruction, as the Syrian tanks began penetrating through bottlenecks – the crossings over the anti-tank trench, dug by the IDF to prevent the movement of Syrian tanks – but the horses had already fled the barn. Too many enemy tanks had already broken through to the flat area and even ascended our tank ramps.

On Blindness

Night fell. Utter darkness ensued, and Eldar's force desperately needed light. The Syrian tanks were equipped with infra-red night vision gear – for the drivers, the gunners, and the commanders, and they moved in the darkness as though zooming ahead in broad daylight. In contrast, our tanks weren't equipped with night vision means. They had 52mm mortars with short-range battlefield illumination, Xenon searchlights (which were mounted on the tanks as nightfall approached), and small commander searchlights for very short distances.

If all this weren't enough, it turned out that Yanush's explicit warning about war at six in the evening never reached Nafshi. He kept operating like he was in a daytime battle, and didn't take the 52mm mortars and the cumbersome Xenon searchlights, as did the 7th Armored Brigade's tanks, and those of the 71st Battalion from the Armored Corps' school.

The Syrian infantry accompanying the tanks got within RPG range of our tanks, and at the end of the battle, I found dozens of RPG shells on our ramps, which reminded me of my father's shotgun shells. Their location attested clearly to the depth of the Syrian penetration, and Kahalani's story about the Syrian tank that snuck into his row of tanks only proves further that this was a battle of the seeing versus the blind.

Two excellent artillery officers took up positions with a Golani Brigade squad on Tel Hermonit – Yossi Dagan, who was a battery commander in the 334th Battalion, and Nachum Davidovitch, who functioned in various operations as FO with the Sayeret Matkal commando unit. They were my eyes, since the FSOs and the FOs couldn't see much. With them was also Asher Sadan, assistant intel officer at the 820th Brigade, the line brigade under Zvi Bar. As the regional brigade's fire support HQ, the 334th's support HQ under Aryeh Shacham was supposed to control the fire throughout the Golan Heights, including Mt. Hermon, from the bunker packed with four HQs at Nafah, but it was mostly occupied with desperate attempts to support the engagement line outposts with fire. This was considered the artillery's main purpose in those hours.

Upon reaching the sector, I didn't hesitate and immediately added Dagan and his fire units to the "Hermon" radio channel – the 7th Brigade's fire direction channel. This was my channel, and my code name was "Arbel 1." Dagan, as he related in the documentary "Esh-Ness,"[17] was glad that someone was finally giving him orders and clearly defining his mission. He began illuminating over the anti-tank bridges with the 334th Battalion's 155mm guns, doing so in "diamond lighting": He fired a volley of four battlefield illumination shells, creating a square of parachuting bombs, which illuminated the area delineated between them, allowing us to range on the one hand, and for targets to be identified for our tanks on the other.

The battlefield illumination shells were only partially effective, as the wind carried the illuminators hanging from the parachutes far off-target. I tried another method – phosphorous bombs, which blinded the Syrian night vision devices, and set the desiccated late-summer shrubbery of the Golan on fire.

None of this stopped them – and at that point, we still didn't know

---

17   "Esh Ness," Directed by Rami Kedar, Produced in 2016. First aired on Kann – Israel's Public Broadcasting Corporation – on Oct. 3, 2018; available at https://www.kan.org.il/content/kan/kan-11/p-444781/107111/

that these tanks didn't belong to the Syrian armored division, but to infantry division armored brigades. We also didn't know that the enemy's main effort was concentrated in the southern Golan Heights, where their 1st Armored Division, equipped with T-62 tanks, had broken through. This was the division that mortally damaged our two batteries, reached Qatzabieh, destroyed the 405th Battalion's ammunition convoy, and chased Battery A. all the way to the Gamla Junction.

Brigade 46, belonging to the 12th division, was part of the Syrian effort. It destroyed the "Boaz" battery, and Brigade 61 chased battery A down from the Heights.

They Shall Not Pass

Our mission was "They shall not pass," not in imitation of Gandalf, then only beginning to acquire popularity, but after the French battle cry at Verdun, in the First World War: No *pasarán*. But the Syrian tanks penetrated into our territory and the battlefield illumination shells were about to run out. Eldar addressed me by name on the radio: "Arie, light." I knew he was begging for his life. I called the 334th Battalion's battery A directly, and ordered the XO Shlomo Nahon and the recon officer Eliezer Hemeli to look around the SPHs for battlefield illumination shells that may have been left in the evening and perhaps went unnoticed in the furor of battle. They found some wayward shells, which were quickly fired. I was again unable to help, but then Syrian planes suddenly appeared in the sky above us, as though in answer to my prayers. They illuminated the battlefield in a white and greenish light for a few moments, and then pitch black again, with us blind in the dark.

At 02:00, the Syrian offensive stopped suddenly – not due to the (limited) abilities of the IDF tanks and artillery, but because the enemy had decided to withdraw for a night's rest. Tremendous luck for us. I had a short while left till first light, and I planned to try to intercept the Syrian tank columns that would continue moving at the crack of dawn, despite the sun being in my eyes, and leave the ones that had already broken in for our tanks to handle.

The scant artillery at my disposal allowed me to focus on only one task, and not to amuse myself with diversions. Luckily for me, everything I'd learned over the years was concentrated into an essence, like a beam of sunlight, piercing through the heavy clouds, allowing me to see precisely what I wished to see. My decision was clear: Stop the Syrian tanks, streaming down from Ufana and Khan Arnabeh, before they reach the anti-tank trench.

From the start, Yanush let me do what I knew and as I saw fit, and didn't interfere, as other brigadiers did to their artillery commanders. This was the start of a true friendship, which continued till the day he died.

The man who helped me locate and range the plethora of Syrian vehicles flooding westward was the ultimate FSO, Yair Nafshi, the experienced veteran bat-com of the 74th, who knew the sector better than he knew his own hand. Yossi Dagan and Nachum Davidovitch, who sat atop Tel Hermonit despite the incessant fire raining down on them, got the drift, ranged the Syrian convoy, prepared artillery ambushes along the routes, directed the fire from the Tel, and hit their marks as well.

The bridge over the anti-tank trench in the Valley of Tears, which was hit by the fire of the 334th Battalion's 155mm battery.

The Syrians had laid four bridges across the trench. One bridge was destroyed by Yossi Dagan, who ranged the 334th Battalion's 155mm battery. A shell hit a Syrian ammunition truck as it was crossing the bridge and it exploded, taking the bridge with it. Another bridge was destroyed when a Syrian bulldozer tried to cross and fell into the trench along with the bridge. The Syrians had two bridges left. We tried to concentrate our fire on them in order to prevent the passage.

"Thorns" and Thistles

"'Thorns are coming your way," came the update from Gideon Etzion, the ops officer of the command artillery HQ, in the midst of the battle. Finally, after a full day of full air control by the Syrian Air Force, during which Mig and Sukhoi aircraft came to see how we were doing and how they could make it worse, our own aircraft started coming to aid us.

I had studied, taught, and was well-versed in the craft of directing aircraft to targets, often practicing map leading and ground leading, by which the pilot is guided to the target by map, and then by eye contact. The problem was that almost always, as I mentioned above, we did so with ourselves. The Air Force didn't view us as a worthy partner, didn't train with us; so in practice, no coordination had been established between the Air Force and the ground forces, and there was no understanding of our needs.

I turned on the #24 ground-to-air radio, which was installed in the APC, and tried to contact the thorns – but there was nothing except silence. Despite this, Yanush then gave a large Syrian tank concentration in the Valley of Tears as a target. I noted it as a target for Etzion, to pass on to his Air Force counterpart. I received a "TOT" – time on target, and heard airplanes humming in the distance.

In accordance with procedure, I opened a red smoke grenade, which was the agreed sign to mark our forces' line. Two Skyhawks did indeed show up, but they discharged their bombs almost right on us, and as a grand finale, rocketed one of our own tanks, north-east of the Hermonit.

"Get them off me," I heard Yanush yell, as though I were the staff of God in the hands of Moses.

They got lost even without me, though, and that was the last we saw of the Israeli Air Force until the end of the war. Rumor has it that they participated in the breakthrough into Syrian territory on the fifth day, but I neither saw nor heard them.

Gunners on Me!

The desperate battle to stop the Syrians from breaking into the country continued. The IDF continued to draft reserves, but on the morning of Monday, October 8th, we got the news that the southern Golan Heights had fallen in the hands of the enemy. My concern was, of course, for my two batteries there, and although it seemed unconnected, I remained focused on the urgent tasks.

The Bnot Yaakov and Arik bridges were under threat by the invading Syrian tanks, and were pre-rigged for demolition, and the reserve artillery battalions were therefore directed to the Gonen route, ascending the Heights through the Waset Junction. The 212th Division Artillery was still getting organized and was bumbling around in the dark. I began gathering the new units, ascending the Golan Heights one by one, under my command, switching them to my channel.

The first inkling in my mind about this immense potential was the 412th Battalion, which was now deployed by the emergency supplies depot fence. At first, I didn't know which battalion it was. Someone named "Herzl," (the battalion's radio call sign) came on my channel. I asked who he was, what kind of fire unit it was, and what he was capable of, in order to use the new force in the most effective manner., and the reply came: "Herzl Mizrachi."

This was enough for me to recognize the cadence of speech – Oded Regev (Gruber), the battalion's FDO. I gave him a target on the anti-tank trench crossings, ordered "fire" – and fire rained down on the Syrians.

The war fell on the people of Israel like thunder out of a blue sky. Reservists ran to the emergency depots, were equipped and outfitted, and went into the unknown. The rumors running around on the home front were dark and bitter, the number of casualties in the first days was really tremendous, the Egyptians had crossed the Suez Canal, part of the Golan Heights had been captured, and the feeling was one of confusion and chaos.

Under such conditions, people seek an authoritative voice, who knows what's going on, instills confidence, and displays leadership; the voice of someone who is positioned forward with the armored forces, and has the situation under control. To the reserve units, this was a lifeline. The transition from the warm bed and comforting bathroom light to nighttime maneuvering in the dark, with no sleep, into the unknown was traumatic.

Each reserve battalion received targets, deployed in accordance with range, and began firing. Most of the men were veterans of the Six-Day War, who had acquired further experience during the War of Attrition, and were armed with richer experience than the standing army conscripts. Their integration was instant, and soon they began following the orders accurately and nimbly.

There was a hodgepodge of artillery pieces: A battalion of 155mm towed guns and self-propelled M-50s, a battalion of long-range (27km) 130mm guns, captured in the Six-Day War, with ammunition manufactured by Israeli Military Industries[18] which malfunctioned often, two 105mm Priest battalions, and the surprise piece de resistance – the "Shekem" – a battalion of war-captured 240mm rockets, which emerged precisely at the moment the battle turned, on Tuesday, October 9.

The doctrine we developed at the 209th Division Artillery, which we taught in the advanced course, and of which I have already made

---

18   IMI, which I later headed as a civilian.

mention of – was that of a common measurements grid, back and front bucket, and sharing data between units with the same kind of weapons – all this didn't work, and we had to range for each unit separately. What small advantage we had lay in the fact that we had a defined area, and we had the ability to apply data from the same unit to different targets. In many cases, we fired at the same targets multiple times over during the four days of the containment battle.

The 7th Brigade, Down to 17 Tanks

On Sunday and Monday, we continued at the same pace, with another artillery fire unit added every now and then, and more and more tanks were being concurrently hit and dwindling in numbers.

The painful tidings on the loss of the Boaz battery and the number of casualties invaded my consciousness at every free moment. The remnants of the battery gathered at the Command Artillery HQ, at Camp "Yusuf" in Rosh Pina. I ordered them up the Heights immediately, to reinforce the remaining batteries. Their crews were falling from their feet after dozens of hours of opening ammunition crates, carrying hundreds of 90-lb shells, and standing strong against counter-battery fire, spiced with air strikes and commando raids, with no sleep and precious little food.

Despite this, the fact that the men of Boaz were back in action helped them overcome trauma. Returning to full activity is now recognized as the best medicine, and in many cases may neutralize the impact of the blow. None of this was what motivated me at the time, but you can call it a blessed side-effect.

The Boaz battery's fourth SPH, which was concealed in a way that the Syrian tanks couldn't fire low enough to hit it, survived with minor damage. It was quickly fixed and along with crew 2, joined battery A, which was fighting with five SPHs.

On Monday, the IDF managed to regain control of part of the southern Golan Heights. The 7th Armored Brigade, after three straight days and nights of stubborn combat, would remain that night with only seventeen operating tanks, out of around 100 it went to war with. The attempt to reinforce them with a reserve company of Sherman tanks – "tweezers" as we called them on the radio – was useless. The Shermans were nicknamed "Ronsons," after the popular lighter, since they went up in flames upon impact, and Yanush moved them back.

They Syrians knew the number of our troops and anticipated our movements, having captured our code maps back on Saturday afternoon, when they took Mt. Hermon. They listened in on our channels, blocked them, and cursed us in Arabic. In the maelstrom of battle, we didn't always maintain radio security. Assad realized that the only sector where he could still tip the balance, and break through toward the Hula Valley and Rosh Pina, was the narrow sector held by the battered 7th Brigade. The tanks remaining in it were withdrawn to a rearward position, and were in "refill" in military parlance – rearming, refueling, and undergoing necessary maintenance. Some of the crew members may have had the time to grab a bite as well.

Syrian Armor and Commandos Swoop Down on the Remnants of the 7th

At dawn on Tuesday, October 9th, two Syrian commando assaults were carried out in preparation for a breakthrough. Eight choppers packed with troops passed over our heads westward, aiming to destroy our artillery batteries and raid headquarters, mainly in the Nafah area.

The bitter reality of the previous days was supposed to make it clear to us that our air force, the national savior, had vanished, and yet we still lived under the impression of the Six-Day War. We couldn't imagine that Syrian helicopters – planes were one thing, but helicopters?! – would penetrate our space and fly over us in broad daylight. Even I, the veteran hunter, who had taken over the APC's machine gun from the very first, fired furiously any time an enemy plane appeared in the sky, and even took credit for downing a Sukhoi 7 (as did anyone else around at the time, of course) – even I didn't fire at the choppers that passed over us that morning. We were all shocked.

Despite this, the incident ended very badly for the Syrians. One chopper was shot down west of Tel Avital by a gunner in the 822nd "Priests" battalion, a reservist named Rafael Sarusi, firing a .50 Browning Machine Gun (and as alluded above, as usual in such cases, there were other soldiers in the 822nd who claimed credit for the downing.) Three other choppers were shot down by Israeli Mirage aircraft, which appeared from the rear in a low-altitude sortie, and four other choppers limped back to Syria. As they passed over us, Uri Segal, a platoon commander in the "Tiger" company, raised the gun barrel and fired a high explosive squash-head shell, hitting the chopper and setting it ablaze. The commando troopers discharged by the chopper earlier near Nafah were taken out by Shai Avital and his Sayeret Matkal crew, in hand-to-hand combat.

Two Syrian commando battalions were preparing concurrently to take the Hermonit. Yossi Dagan, who noticed the preparations and saw the red flags demarcating the staging area for the offensive, didn't hesitate and trained the two, sorely depleted self-propelled heavy mortar batteries remaining in the 334th Battalion, after one such mortar flipped over and crashed, and another was disabled by a double intake accident, which claimed the lives of five troopers. The remaining six barrels began firing at a tremendous rate, scattering the enemy commandos to the winds.

The same day, the remaining Syrian forces attacked the 7th Brigade's Rangers unit, in a hard-fought battle that took place west of the Hermonit, between Buq'ata and the Elrom Junction, virtually annihilating the 7th Brigade's recon company. The main Syrian effort was focused on an all-out assault against what remained of the 7th Brigade, and we received reports from the observation post on the Hermonit about a large number of tanks concentrated east of the anti-tank trench. Reporting these developments from the Booster Ridge was Shmulik Yachin, a deputy company commander with the 74th Battalion, whose father, Yitzhak Yachin, was at one time the bat-com of the 404th.

The Syrian assault opened with heavy artillery fire – on Tel Hermonit, on the tank ramps, and on the Booster Ridge. The two bat-coms were in the rear at the time – Nafshi at Quneitra Base and Kahalani in "refill." Snir, the FSO, whose tank was disabled, got on another tank and kept fighting, but was also by Kahalani's side on the rear slope.

Toward 08:00, all the brigade's forces reported murderous Syrian artillery fire. Everyone went backwards, as told by Ilan Sahar, the brigade's intel officer, in the study of the 7th Brigade's containment battles. The Syrian tanks crossed the anti-tank trenches and advanced like a Greek phalanx, with grinding artillery advancing before them. They meant to gather as many tanks as possible across the anti-tank trench, with the Assad Force – 100 state-of-the-art T-62 tanks, commanded by the president's brother, Rifat, alongside some 70 infantry division tanks.

Pale Smoke

It was a critical moment. Few of our tanks were in position, the sun was in our eyes, Syrian artillery – "Dante's inferno" in Yanush's term – came down incessantly. Yanush didn't lose his cool. "I want hail," he told me on the radio from the next APC, emphasizing his words with hand gestures. And indeed, a hailstorm of steel and fire came down on the Valley of Tears.

The artillery force at my disposal by that point constituted six battalions, eighteen batteries total, and they all fired on targets. Joining in the orchestra were all the units who ascended the Golan Heights via the Gonen route and gathered on my radio channel, the "Hermon" channel. My APC crew, Herzl, Alex, and myself, passed on the orders to the various units, some of which still operated in a battalion command framework. Others, like my own battery C., batteries from the 55th and from the 412th Battalions, found themselves at this point operating as separate units. Like much of the equipment, the Artillery Corps' radios were outdated, short-range devices, and difficulties in transmitting orders, receiving them, and in ranging targets ensued. We were tired and bleary-eyed, and to boot, in our crew, Alex was wounded, but the adrenaline was pounding due to the magnitude of the moment, and the batteries were firing at breakneck speed, first along the anti-tank trench, and then, when the Syrian tanks advanced, we shortened the ranges and fired at targets that kept advancing nearer all the time.

Ben-Ami Cohen, from whose article "Born to War Alone" I have already quoted, describes in it the firing of the two batteries under his command, deployed behind Tel Mahfi. He described how the targets drew closer, ranges shortened, shell trajectories became flatter and flatter – and he had already decided to prepare the SPHs for direct fire. This was the point at which I diverted the Bahad 9 batteries and battery C. to fire on our ramps, as I realized that the Syrian T-62 tanks were flanking our ramps and climbing onto our positions.

Noah Timianker was a platoon commander in the 77th Battalion at the time. Over 40 years later, when we met at a memorial, I told him that I had fired at the ramps. "Oh, you're the one who shot at me," he said, and in an interview that he gave to Yair Keadan, he told of those dramatic moments, during which he thought that it was the Syrians firing at him. The aerial photos displayed by Timianker in the interview clearly show that the shells' smoke was pale, meaning Israeli-American munitions, and not dark grey, like that emitted by Syrian-Russian ordnance.

At this critical moment, with Ben-Ami Cohen about to switch to direct fire and me already firing with the Bahad 9 and 405th Battalion's 155mm guns, certain of their precision in the type of surgical fire required when firing at our own forces' ramps, I suddenly heard on the radio: "Shekem at your service." *Shekem* is the IDF term for the military canteen service, and the reader will understand my perplexity at having a branch of the military known mostly for stale chocolate-coated wafers bursting in on my battlefield channel. "Get the hell off my channel," I yelled. But the voice on the other side persisted. "I'm a fire unit," he said. Very good, I said to myself. Another hand on deck.

I ordered: "Code 425, 20 per barrel, maximum rate – fire! No time to range. The valley is thick with Syrian tanks."

But the mysterious weirdo replied: "I can't. I'm firing differently."

The speaker was Uri Kolski, the Artillery Corps' chief research officer, and a reserve bat-com on secondary commission. Out of nowhere, he placed twelve trucks, each carrying twelve 240mm rocket launchers which were captured in the Six-Day War, at my disposal. An immense, and unexpected firepower.

I ordered again: "Code 425 fire," and 144 rockets dropped on the Syrians and shook the Valley of Tears.

The "Shekem" battalion of 240mm rocket launchers, firing on the Valley of Tears.

Brig. Gen. Asher Sadan was assistant intel officer of the 820th Line Brigade, staying with artillery officers Dagan and Davidovich on Tel Hermonit until the Tel was abandoned, at 09:30-09:45 on October 9th. Here below is a short segment from a conversation we had about that battle, which was held on January 26th, 2023:

Asher: "On Tuesday morning, I saw T-62 tanks advancing toward us, meaning to climb up and take the embankment. I saw that a battle was beginning both from the direction of outpost 107 and from outpost 105. They took artillery barrages, and only in hindsight did I realize that these were rocket launchers. I remember that at some point the entire valley was filled with a tremendous amount of fire. I didn't know these were Katyushas, but I saw a horrifying barrage all at once, boom-boom-boom-boom. It was near the village of Al-Hamra."

"Yes. I remember it because it was extraordinarily effective. I had known the Syrians to fire hundreds of shells, and suddenly, for the first time, you see it in the other direction, coming down on them, raising a hell of a lot of smoke and dust."

The advancing Syrians were stopped. According to Sadan, the monstrous fire of seven artillery battalions astonished them. The paralysis that beset them gave pause for our tanks, now no longer under Syrian fire, to organize and get back in positions.

How the Name " Valley of Tears" Was Born

Between 09:30 and 09:45, Kahalani managed to ascend the ramps of the Hermonit with four or six tanks from the 77th Battalion (the number varied each time Kahalani told the story.) They joined him only after Kahalani waved flags, shot at the tanks with his machine gun, and scolded his men that the Syrians were braver than them.

Nafshi, who had already ascended the Booster Ridge, asked for a battery to hit a concentration of vehicles and antennae, which looked like a headquarters to him. I assigned a battery to him, and as a crack FSO, he ranged himself, fired, hit the HQ of the 7th Syrian Armored Division, and killed its commander, Amid Omar al-Abrash.

According to information that only reached me some ten years ago, our sigint unit, (then called "848" and now world-famous as "8200," the training grounds for myriads of successful hi-tech startups), picked up the transmissions of the two Syrian bat-coms who had penetrated into the Valley of Tears, back to their brigadier. "We can't go on," they said. "The Israeli artillery is killing us."

"Then hold your positions," he replied.

"The crews are leaving the tanks and running away," said the bat-coms. Their reply attested to the confusion that ensued among their battalions following the artillery fire that rained down on them. And indeed, quite a few Syrian tanks were captured whole, by the time the dust had settled on the Battle of the Valley of Tears, some with their engines still running.

The titanic battle went on until almost 12:00 pm. At some point, Kahalani and Nafshi recognized that the Syrians' strength was faltering. They bravely conducted a fire fight at short range with the Syrian tanks whose crews were still moving and firing. Shortly before the battle was decided, the "Morning Exercise" force showed up too. Yossi Ban-Hanan had returned from his honeymoon in Nepal, collected 11 tanks from the remnants of the 188th Brigade, and stormed up the booster just in time to take part in the final chord, and take a light wound as well.

In my estimate, 3,000-4,000 shells and artillery rockets were fired from the start of the battle till it ended at noon. Only then did I employ the "Canteen" rockets on the anti-tank trench crossings, against the retreating Syrians. Afterward, I went up with the brigade's command post to the Booster Ridge. A strange silence enveloped us, descending upon the Valley of Tears. Smoke still rose from hundreds of burnt tanks. Once in a while, ammunition caught fire. A tank exploded suddenly. Haggai Regev, the brigade's staff ops officer, who was with us in Yanush's command APC, was a yeshiva student as a youth, and would serve years later as Yitzhak Rabin's military secretary, with the rank of brigadier general, was the one who coined the name that became an ethos: "Emek Habacha" – " Valley of Tears."[19]

"You're Heroes"

In all the theaters of the Yom Kippur War – from the Sinai to the Golan Heights – the only place the enemy didn't manage to break through the lines was the northern Golan Heights – the sector entrusted to the 7th Brigade. The nonpareil field general, Yanush,

---

19 See Psalms 84:6.

conducted a heroic and professional battle there, eliminating the last attempt to sever the "Finger of Galilee" from the State of Israel.

While we watched silently over the smoking valley, Raful arrived on the scene, with his Australian hat trying to shade his redhead face, his nose peeling, and his hand bandaged, sans two fingers lost to a mishap at his home woodworking shop on the eve of the war. He gazed at the smoking valley with us, and uncharacteristically said: "You're heroes – I hadn't seen such bravery even in the San Simon and Katamon battles in '48."

Raful, as may be recalled, had been wounded in that very battle as a squad leader, holding a last grenade to blow himself up along with the wounded, until the battle was won.

In the same breath, he added: "Why aren't you charging after the Syrians and exploiting the success into their territory?" There was no telling him that we hadn't slept since Saturday, and had nothing to charge with.

It is hard for me today to describe what went through my mind in those fateful hours. Happily, I was focused and sharp, and managed to function with maximum efficiency, attentive to Kahalani and Nafshi's channels, attentive to the 7th Brigade's channel, and employing a hail of heavy artillery on the "Hermon" channel. All of this, with the Boaz battery and its fallen soldiers in the back of my mind. The heavy blow it had sustained disabled a full third of the 405th Battalion's firepower. Battery A, having been left without ammunition mid-combat, deployed at the foothills of Ma'aleh Gamla, at the quarry by the junction. It refilled with the ammunition waiting there for it and managed – along with a force from Golani's 51st Battalion, under deputy batcom Zion Ziv, and the 4th Brigade's 39th Battalion, under Yoav Vaspi – to stop the Syrian forces trying to come down to the Sea of Galilee. Vaspi would be killed days later in battle near Tel Ghasnia.

The cliché "fighting for home" was a painful reality for me during those four days and nights. My wife, Tamar, and my two toddler sons, five-year-old Sagi and three-year-old Yaron, were in Ashdot Yaakov Ichud, along with Tamar's parents and extended family – a half-hour's drive by tank from Ma'aleh Gamla, and a bit over an hour from the Valley of Tears.

In general, "defending my home" is not an abstract term or a cliché for me. It is a grim, cruel, poignant reality, which impacts your conduct even when focused on the mission.

Yanush awarding me the rank of Lt. Col., following the battle for the Valley of Tears.

THE 405ᵀᴴ BATTALION BREAKS THROUGH INTO SYRIA

"Battery C. of the 405th Battalion entered Syria first," thus with his overt Polish diction, did Israel Kigel tell of his part in the Yom Kippur War in the documentary film, "Esh-Ness."

And indeed, great honor is owed to the 405th and to battery C, the battery under the late Avraham Snir, Kahalani's FSO, and Kigel the XO who fought like a lion, holding off a commando raid, fired at short range, tank ranges, brought the ammunition from the semi-trailers to the SPHs, maintained a high morale, and made sure to project victory. "Kigel, as usual, all happy, smiling, giving orders," as described by Issachar Bruck, one of the survivors of "Boaz" who went straight back up the Heights and joined with Kigel's force. And most important of all: 2nd. Lt. Israel Kigel brought all his troops safely home from war.

In Tel Shiban, near the Waset Junction, we held the divisional command group for the fighting ahead on Wednesday morning. The fact that we had driven the invading forces from the Valley of Tears had not ended the war. Raful wanted to break through into Syria as early as that afternoon. Yanush, knowing that the 7th Brigade wasn't ready yet, hesitated whether to say so, for he assumed that Raful might tell him straight away: "You're a coward." So he preferred to use Amir Drori, Golani's brigadier. "Look," said Drori to Raful, "We're infantry. I have no problem to gear up and start walking. But the tank crews and the artillery units need time to arm, fuel, recon their positions, set movement routes, and observe the penetration routes. They need time."

With visible reluctance, Raful said: "Fine, tomorrow at 10:00." And indeed, on Thursday morning – not at 10:00 but rather at 11:00 – we penetrated into Syria.

Command group ahead of the breakthrough into Syria – seated (left to right): Yanush Ben-Gal, Amir Drori, and Yoni Netanyahu. I'm standing behind Yanush.

Rolling Barrage

The breakthrough effort fell on the shoulders of the 7th Brigade, which was significantly reinforced. Laner's Division, the 210th Reserve Division, was supposed to break through along the "America" route (the Quneitra-Damascus road), but ran into many difficulties and was forced to halt immediately upon the start of the breakthrough. Raful, who insisted on a separate route for the 36th Division, actually for the 7th Brigade, received permission from Haka to break through north of Laner. The Golani troops were supposed to take Tel Dahur and Dahur Taranja, and the 7th Brigade, with its four battalions, would take Tel Ahmar and Jubta al-Hashab.

The eleven artillery battalions that had gathered for the penetration began a massive artillery softening in the early morning hours. We were told that the Air Force would participate too. That's even what the official history says, but I didn't see a single Israeli plane. If there were any, they operated in "slingshot" mode, in which bombs are cast from afar and with compromised accuracy.

Around 09:00, the mobile brigade command post ascended Tel Hermonit to overlook the penetration routes, when suddenly a horrific tempest of whistles and the most awful noise sounded. My comrades in the command post and everyone around thought that it was Syrian fire, and hit the ground, with some quick enough to dive into dugouts. "Calm down," I said, "The 'Canteen' battalion deployed at the foot of the Hermonit is firing a 144-rocket barrage."

At the brigade command group the night before, I explained the artillery plan: Ben-Ami Cohen and Arnon Ben-Ami will range the penetration targets at dawn. Before each penetrating battalion, we would create a rolling barrage with 160mm mortars, and the targets of the attacking forces would be struck with the 155mm cannons.

The Bahad 9 Battalion, in which the 405th's battery C was included as the point battery, would enter Syrian territory first, deploy close to traffic routes and be ready to move after the penetrating tank battalion, in order to gain range for the next stage. I also announced that the FSOs with the penetrating battalions would be Avraham Snir with the 77th Battalion, and reservist Elhanan Korach, commander of a battery of Priests with the 822nd Battalion, Yossi Ben Hanan's ad-hoc battalion. Ben-Hanan had already appointed himself brigadier of the 188th in place of Itzik Ben-Shoham, who was killed on the first day, announcing that he was "Kodkod Toffee." Herzl Cohen and Alex Redlus detailed the plan for the FSOs and FOs at the firing units' command group, and I stood up after them and told the FSOs and FOs: "You've been through a hard war in the containment phase. If any of you feel that they don't have enough energy and strength to continue to the next phase, which will be difficult and bloody, raise your hand and I'll release you."

One of the FSOs raised his hand. I released him back to his reserve battalion. Now I had a hole to plug. I recalled that just before the command group, I noticed Arnon Ben-Ami wearing overalls, his trademark when he was an officer in the 334th Battalion. "I have just flown in from the United States," said Ben-Ami, who had made a name for himself in the War of Attrition, "Give me a job."

"You're Yair Nafshi's FSO with the 74th Battalion," I told him now, coming out of the command group, and since then Ben-Ami and Nafshi had become bosom buddies, to this very day. Their first encounter opened with Arnon saying to Nafshi: "I want a platoon commander's tank. I can best employ the artillery with a tank commander who knows what's happening, and can take me to the best vantage point." Nafshi, surprised at the guy trying to deplete his force by a tank and platoon commander, replied: "Declined." Ben-Ami, in response, said calmly: "No tank – no artillery." Nafshi, taken aback yet again, conceded. He did not regret it.

Exiting the side tent of the artillery commander's APC, where the command group was held, I noticed a soldier on the ground, in a sort of crouching position. It was Shmulik Reshef, deputy bat-com of the 334th, who had fallen asleep mid-command, racked with fatigue. The five exhausting days of combat, with no sleep and six dead, a self-propelled heavy mortar that blew up in a double-intake accident, and another that flipped over, all caused him to sink into depression. I woke him up and told him that we were winning. That was enough for him to get back to his battalion and keep doing his duty.

Shrapnel in the Machine Gun Butt

We began at 11:00, as mentioned above, to enter Syrian territory. The 160mm mortars set a rolling barrage – a moving screen of fire. The targets were occupied with continuous fire at a murderous rate. Prewar terminology such as "harassment," and "sustaining immobilization," which mean saving on ammunition while moving toward the targets, being content with forcing the enemy to keep his head down – all went out the window. My order was explicit: We fire at the highest rate possible, all the time, until the enemy is destroyed and the target is taken.

As we passed the border line, Syrian danger fire missions were set off. A piece of shrapnel missed my head by a hair's breadth and embedded into the wooden butt of the machine gun next to me, as I was also functioning as a combat trooper. I took a severe blow, but survived.

A danger fire mission is a particularly important location, which is pre-ranged and given an employment code. If the enemy reaches that location and endangers that outpost, junction, bridge, or such, the pre-ranged artillery fires at it. When Ben-Hanan crossed the fence, Syrian danger fire was unleashed at him as well. "Twenty-seven, hold your fire, you're shooting at me," he yelled at me on the radio. I saw the shells exploding and the grey smoke, typical of Russian ordnance, and didn't even bother to answer. I also, of course, did not halt the vital artillery fire.

The penetration went like a hot knife through butter, but also like a knife in the heart. Elhanan Korach, a battery commander in the 822nd Reserve Battalion, and a classmate of mine at the basic officers' course, whom I assigned as Ben-Hanan's FSO, was killed by Syrian commandos. They climbed on his tank, which was next to Ben-Hanan's, and shot him from behind.

With all the sorrow, there is no room for regret and pangs of conscience in battle. I was immersed in the mission and focused on blazing the path for the advancing tanks. By nightfall, we'd reached the Halas camps, and overlooked Tel Shams at last light. Kahalani came within contact range of Mazra'at Beit Jann. At night, we went into night camp, arranged in columns, so that the supply and fuel trucks could drive between the columns of tanks according to the Armored Corps' drills, just like in practice.

I fell asleep on the lowered ramp of the APC, but as usual, my ears remained attentive and the radios were on. Around 02:00, I suddenly heard Raful on the channel commanding Yanush to move, take up positions, and attack. Amir Drori was ordered to cover from the flank, and orders were handed out to all sorts of new units, as though a new Grande Armée was going to war.

Yanush was sleeping, just the same as myself, on the ramp of the brigadier's APC. I rushed to him and woke him up. He listened to the orders and called Raful on the field phone – a wireless telephone device of the time, installed in HQs of units from brigade size and up.

"What's all this?" he asked?

"Confusing the enemy," Raful replied, and we went back to sleep for the few hours left till dawn.

"You're Not Arbel 32"

On Friday the 7th, the Armored Brigade split into initiating two efforts. The main effort – capturing Mazraat Beit Jann in order to open the route to the Syrian army camps at Kenaker, and from there to Damascus – was led by Avigdor Kahalani and Amos Katz with two full armored battalions; and a secondary effort, south of there – to capture Tel Shams, which controls the Quneitra-Damascus route – was led by Yair Nafshi. I called on the radio for "Arbel 32," the commander of battery C and Kahalani's FSO, Avraham Snir, to coordinate the attack to which most of the artillery units had been assigned. A different voice answered me from the other end. I assumed that it was the tank commander, and that Snir had gone to measure the azimuth, as the steel mass of a tank disrupts the functioning of a compass.

"Arbel 32 here," said the unfamiliar voice.

"You're not Arbel 32," I said, and noticed Haggai Regev approaching me. "Snir was killed," he said. Kahalani, it turned out, being a sensitive friend, had asked: "Don't tell Arie."

Snir's death was a traumatic event for the fighters of the 77th Battalion, although they had already lost many comrades by then. Platoon commander, Noah Timianker, whose platoon included Snir's tank, told later that while they were overlooking Mazraat Beit Jann, and Snir stood between the tanks and ranged the targets, a Mig 17 swooped in from behind them and dropped two bombs. One fell between Kahalani's tank and Snir's. Kahalani, with the help of ops officer Gidi Peled, who had noticed the enemy aircraft at the last moment, managed to dive into the tank. Snir was hurled out of his tank along with the tank commander, Yehoshua Stranzi, and was killed. His body remained intact.

Stranzi was paralyzed. Everyone was certain he wouldn't survive, but he recovered and returned to full function. He constitutes a living testament of the event, and he documented it in the film "Esh-Ness." Other soldiers were killed and wounded in this attack as well, and according to Timianker, the battalion was thrown off-kilter, and it took time for its men to recover.

The man who answered me on the radio was Yehuda Geffen, a reservist who arrived in the Golan Heights, and being acquainted with Ben-Ami Cohen, was attached with no defined role to the Bahad 9 Battalion. When Eitan Kauli, deputy bat-com of the 77th, reached the position at Tel al-Ahmar, where the battalion was deployed, and sought an FSO to replace Snir, none volunteered, save Geffen. Within an hour he got a tank, began ranging targets at Mazraat Beit Jann, prevented Kahalani's battalion from firing at Amos Katz's, and continued as FSO throughout the remainder of the war.

The fact that Kauli ran, in the midst of battle, to find a replacement for Snir, testifies more strongly than a thousand witnesses as to the recognition of the importance of artillery fire – a recognition that formed during the containment and the penetration phases, and increased to the level of an existential need.

In memory of Avraham Snir

On Saturday, a week after the war broke out, I made my first call to Tamar, who had meanwhile returned with Sagi and Yaron to our Kfar Saba home. I asked her to go console the Snir family. The next day, she asked my driver to take her in my "Carmel" jalopy to Moshav Nir Galim. But upon arriving at the center of the moshav, she saw no mourning notices and noticed no unusual activity. She realized that the Snir family had yet to receive the bitter tidings, and returned as she came.

After the war, we developed close ties with the Snir family. A huge basalt boulder which I brought from the site where Avraham had fallen, was placed at the center of the "Avraham Garden" in the moshav, and we used to visit them each year during the autumn holidays. We would park the car outside the religious moshav, recite with them "Let the year and its banes end, may a year and its blessings begin," and gorged on the incredible Hungarian delicacies cooked by Rachel, Avraham's mother.

His father, Shevach, and his brother, Yossi, helped me establish the "Netzach Latotchan" ("Gunners' Eternal Memory") when I was appointed Chief Artillery Officer, and through this organization, contact was renewed with the families of all the corps' fallen since the War of Independence. The handling of anything to do with the fallen was transferred to the corps' casualties officer and the CAO's adjutancy, reaching families no one had contacted since their loved ones had been killed. Among other things, we organized bar-mitzvahs for the corps' orphans and other events, which are held to this day, in addition to a benefit celebrating the corps' wounded, and the inviting of the corps' bereaved families to any gathering of a battalion and larger, as well as participation and assistance to events initiated by the families.

Even before then, I had instituted a procedure at the 405th Battalion, which I later turned into a CAO's order, and which since has become an IDF-wide procedure: On the IDF Memorial day (which is celebrated in Israel the day before Independence Day), each fallen warrior's grave is attended by a trooper holding the same role unit as the fallen soldier. The trooper receives an advance briefing, and speaks with the family. Young soldiers are often embarrassed, and are hesitant to approach the bereaved parents, siblings, or orphans. But the families are already familiar with the drill, and make it easy for the soldiers to overcome the natural reticence.

After my discharge, my son Yaron, commander of battery C in the 405th Battalion, took my place at the Nir Galim cemetery. He had been there more than once as a child, but this time he came on Memorial Day to represent the battery and the battalion.

THE GUNNERS TAKE TEL SHAMS

Tel Shams stands like a sort of castle, a tall hill, dug out and fortified, controlling the Quneitra road to Damascus, stuck like a dagger in the bowels of the lands south of Mazraat Beit Jann, and overlooking the bases at Kenaker. Nafshi's force of tanks moved toward this hill on the morning of Friday, October 12 on the road, not yet in charge formation.

The brigade command post overlooked both efforts from a vantage point allowing for control of both, and while we were focused on Kahalani and Katz, meaning the main northern effort to take Mazraat Beit Jann, I saw a cloud of red dots landing on Nafshi's columns of tanks. I knew that what seemed like red fireflies was actually an amalgam of Malyutka anti-tank rocket (what we called "Saggers") tail imprints, and immediately issued a "phosphorous blast" order, employing the 334th Battalion's 155mm battery.

The battery responded quickly, I heard the launches, but saw no impacts – until I looked to the right and saw the phosphorous shells exploding there. An error of 1,600ths, which constitutes 90 degrees (the circle is divided in artillery into 6,400ths, for maximum accuracy.) Nafshi extracted backward by the skin of his teeth, with casualties and losses, and it was decided to forego the taking of Tel Shams for the time being.

"Arie, Save Yossi"

In the afternoon, Yossi Ben-Hanan showed up at the command post. In consultation with Ilan Sahar, the brigade's excellent intel officer, they proposed that Ben-Hanan maneuver through the Lega area through a sort of trail which Ilan had located through the endless basalt rocky landscape, following a prolonged study of aerial photos. The idea was for Ben-Hanan to strike at Tel Shams from the rear, which is to say from the northeast, rather than frontally.

Staff ops officer Haggai Regev and I didn't like the plan. We said that moving through Laja would create a dust cloud, and the force would be spotted from afar. In addition, we said, the fearsome Malyutka unit had not been destroyed, nor had we located its position, the direction of movement is into the sun, and the entire plan was drawn up hastily. Ben-Hanan, Yanush's protégé, talked him into approving the plan. I proposed that Herzl Cohen, my ops officer join Ben-Hanan in place of Elhanan Korach, the FSO who was killed. Ben-Hanan replied that there was no need, as he was going with only six tanks, and if need be, he would range and employ fire himself with the portable "25" radio in the turret basket.

A few moments later, he had already headed out toward Tel Shams, at the head of six tanks gathered from various units. This was an inorganic force, lacking prior acquaintance. The tank movement was supposed to be a surprise, as the basalt Laja is ostensibly not traversable. But as I feared, they raised a dust cloud, the Syrians noticed the movement, waited patiently, and only when the six tanks arrived at the foot of the embankment did they launch an immense volley of Malyutkas.

All the tanks were hit. Four of them retreated quickly, but the commander's tank and the tank next to him were very badly damaged. Ben-Hanan, with a leg wound, jumped out of the tank and extracted himself. He didn't forget to take the radio with him, and began crying out: "Yanush, my buddy, Yanush, save me."

Yanush, pale as snow, racked by guilt and anxiety after Raful forbade him to carry out the attack, told me, "Arie, save Yossi." I quickly activated the Bahad 9 Battalion, including the 405th's battery C, driven by a desire to avenge their commander, Snir. I tried to create a ring of fire around Ben-Hanan and the men with him, to prevent the Syrians from taking them captive. They listened in on our networks, realized that a bat-com, a Lt. Col., was about to fall into their hands, and tried to reach him.

I stood by Yanush. He asked Ben-Hanan for fire corrections, to draw it closer around him. Yossi replied with corrections according to the cardinal winds – west 200, south 100 – and Herzl, the "unneeded FSO," translated it into fire orders for Ben-Ami Cohen, commander of the Bahad 9 Battalion.

The guns fired at maximum rate. Mt. Hermon was still in Syrian hands, and our forces were exposed to their FOs. Battery B, with Nissim Hajaj and Avner Rosenberg, from the Bahad 9 Battalion, took a direct hit. Hajaj reported "counter-battery fire in the position," and asked for permission to leapfrog to an alternate position. But in extracting a damaged unit, with the wounded and the dead, we don't leapfrog, and we maintain continuous fire. And this time there was a Lt. Col. in danger of being captured. I ordered them to keep firing, as did Ben-Ami Cohen.

What happened there, I shall relate from his point of view, as described by him in Maarachot, vol. 391 (Oct. 2003), 30 years after the war:

"The Artillery Fire Is for the Maneuvering Forces"

Around six in the evening, I received an order from Arie Mizrachi to open fire on Tel Shams immediately, and aid with cannon fire in the extraction of Yossi Ben-Hanan, who was badly wounded and left lying at the foot of the embankment, unable to self-extract. The order on the radio specified his full name.

Yossi to me was more than commander of an aided force. I instructed alongside him at the armored corps' company commanders' course, at the time when Yanush commanded the course, and we had a whole year of shared activities and experiences. In addition, we were taught at the corps that providing fire for extraction of our forces would always take precedence over other fire support missions.

We quickly completed the preparations for hasty firing, and opened fire according to the fire orders we got from Mizrachi. The battalion fired at full fire rate at Tel Shams.

I assume that, on some ad-hoc observation post on the eastern slopes of Mt. Hermon, or from the Hermon outpost itself, a Syrian FO was watching us. The FO was apparently a talented young officer, who immediately understood the opportunity that presented itself to him, to hit an active artillery position. He initiated the fire request and called in his headquarters to receive an assigned fire unit. I can only imagine that he reported on the radio that this is an Israeli target very much taking a shot at –an Israeli artillery battalion in the midst of firing. Had the FO held a more senior rank, he likely would have received more than a single barrel and four shells. As it was, with the Syrian array in collapse and the IDF moving along the routes toward Damascus, the Syrian artillery commander gave the FO a minuscule amount of fire means – similar to what was at my own disposal the day the war broke out – the bare minimum.

Two or three minutes after the Syrian FO gave the fire order, the first shell fell on the ground. From his vantage point commanding the entire area, with no dead spots, he located the impact site of the shell with no difficulty. As he'd learned in ranging lessons, he gave a correcting order in order to complete an enclosure on my battery B. This was the proper ranging actions, intended to ensure that the target he was firing upon was located between two controlled impact sites, and that the distance between these was known both by the FO and the firing battery.

From my half-track, I saw the falling of the first shell clearly. I hoped it was an errant shell, which had just happened to fall right in front of battery B. I also feared that soon another shell would fall behind the battery – one that would confirm that we were being ranged. At this point, I didn't have enough cause to stop the fire support of the extraction. So I ordered battery B. 'Prepare to move without halting fire,' adding: The SPH drivers must be in the cabin with the engines running. Anyone who can, take cover by the guns. Do not stop firing. The Syrian FO's correction fire was accurate. The second shell hit near the fire direction center and precisely "closed" on battery B. I'm sure that the Syrian FO was well pleased, and instantly ordered to bisect the enclosure on the next shot – meaning to fire the next shell to the center of the space between the two points defining the enclosure. Both of us, on both ends of the battlefront – the Syrian FO on the one side and me, the position commander, on the other – understood the reading of the *ranging. It was clear that the next shell would hit near battery B's guns. I suppose that our professional conclusions were similar as well, but there was a difference in our operational situations: The Syrian was attacking my position, and therefore did not deliberate regarding the next fire order, which he quickly issued. I had various misgivings: Should I consider only the interest of defending the position, or also my obligation to aid, at almost any cost, in the success of extracting the wounded? Do I have the right to abandon the ranger unit extracting Ben-Hanan, and halt the fire support just as it was fighting for Tel Shams? Would it be justified to halt the fire because I feared that artillery shells would fall close to the gun positions? What impact would the halting of the support fire have on the extraction mission?*

My response had to be immediate. I knew that I had less than a minute till the next shell hit, and that I had no time to present the problem to Arie Mizrachi, and receive his permission to halt the support fire and leapfrog the battery.

In incident analysis exercises, priority in similar cases is always given to the supported unit. But it's easier to reach this conclusion in the lecture hall, with the cost of an incorrect decision being an instructor's comment and at worst a low grade. In the field, things are different. There is no one to discuss the dilemma with, the responsibility is all yours – and it's life or death on the line. At such a moment, you're the loneliest person in the world.

I decided to postpone battery B's leapfrogging, and continue firing. Perhaps it was numbness, perhaps I had grown inured to danger. Apparently, what won out was our responsibility, the gunners, to provide effective supporting fire to the supported unit. I was more concerned with the results of the battle at Tel Shams – somewhat due to personal acquaintance, but mostly due to the principle I was taught and taught others, that the artillery fire belongs to the maneuvering unit. The fire units are a means to create the support fire in the place and the time that the supported unit needs it. To stop artillery support fire in the middle of battle requires a stronger reason than fear of fire on the position.

The third and fourth shells that hit the positions of battery B caused severe damage. One shell fell right between crews 3 and 4, mortally wounding all the gunners taking cover next to the side of the SPHs. The SPHs acted quickly, driving quickly out of the position. The guns remained undamaged.

Six gunners were killed and eight wounded. Spare propellant bags lying around the position ignited, starting a fire. The SPHs scattered in all directions through what only hours prior was a protected Syrian space, with minefields and possible Syrian commando presence. Complete darkness fell on the black, rocky soil of the Syrian Golan Heights.

Adir Stern Is Left to Die

The Sayeret Matkal force, under Yoni Netanyahu with Shai Avital and Mookie Betzer alongside him, managed to reach Ben-Hanan and extract him, but Netanyahu and his men, who were under the impression that no one else was left alive, left Ben-Hanan's tank driver, Adir Stern, behind, while he still may have been wounded in his cabin, with another man apparently left wounded in the other tank. They brought Ben-Hanan to the command post on a stretcher, and a chopper landed nearby us to evacuate him, but the pilots suddenly received instructions from their controller to take off without Ben-Hanan for other rescue missions. Yanush ordered them to stay. They tried to say that they had to get up in the air to make radio contact, but Yanush, a man you didn't want to play games with, cocked his AK47. The pilots took the hint and waited till Ben-Hanan was loaded on the chopper. Two fighters remained behind and died in the field. There is no telling whether they died before the Syrians reached them, or afterward.

"The Gunners Did the Job for Us"

The fact that the Syrians remained seated on Tel Shams and in control of the Quneitra-Damascus road halted the momentum of the assault toward the Kanekar camps and Damascus beyond, and on Saturday, Raful decided to take the embankment in a nighttime battle, with the 317th Reserve Paratroopers' Brigade, commanded by Chaim Nadal. Arnon Ben-Ami unleashed two "Canteen" volleys of rockets – almost 300 rockets in two continuous volleys. Around another 3,000 shells were fired by the 827th and 822nd Priest Battalions, at a rapid-fire rate, with varied munitions including high-explosives, phosphorous, and air burst.

Elisha Shalem, bat-com of the 567th, which entered Tel Shams that night virtually unopposed, with a single man wounded, admitted freely and fully: The gunners did the job for us.

Damascus in Our Sights

On Saturday, the seventh day of fighting, as we were in success exploitation mode, 35 km from Damascus, Moshe Dayan ordered the Northern Command to fire on Damascus with the long-range 175mm guns. The object was to tell Hafez al-Assad, in the language he understands: *The IDF is within artillery range of Damascus. These are not just airplanes. These are the ground forces knocking on your door.*

When firing from a high spot to a low one, the range of the 175mm guns can be extended from 32.5km to 35km, and the target chosen at Command HQ was Al-Maza Airport in Damascus. The battalion chosen for the mission was the 412th, the battalion I had established just before the war, and which remained the apple of my eye. We, the 7th Armored Brigade, were responsible to lead the two SPGs and with them an M548 track-mounted ammunition carrier, up to the 71st Battalion's line of engagement, near Mazraat Beit Jann, which was the most forward line held by our forces.

The force, led by battery XO Aharon Abramowitz and deputy bat-com Israel Bar-Lev, fired twenty shells as planned – ten from each barrel. The strikes were accurate, not just on the runways, but hitting parked aircraft as well. Israeli war prisoners were held at the time at Al-Maza Prison, near the airport, among them the two survivors of the Boaz battery who had fallen prisoner, Tzachi Avinoam and David Abaki. Abaki reported upon his return that he received twenty slaps from the Syrian prison guard – one for each shell exploding in the airport, which were heard loud and clear in the prison.

The firing achieved its purpose, and Assad turned to Egyptian President Anwar Sadat, threatening to pull out of the fighting if Assad didn't do something to ease the pressure on him. Sadat obliged, attacked on the eastern bank of the Suez Canal, shifted tanks east without the AD umbrella, and that's how the October 14th shift on the southern front began: Some 200 Egyptian tanks were destroyed, and the way for a crossing was paved.

The next night, October 14, another volley of fire was planned – this time on Damascus itself: The presidential palace, the Syrian military's HQ, and the Air Force HQ. We marked the targets on the aerial photos, and I drew a large safety circle around the Jewish quarter. Then we took luminescent direction rods from the Bahad 9 Battalion, and decided that this was what the Sayeret Matkal troopers would use to mark the route for the 412th Battalion's guns – this time under the command of bat-com Aldo Zohar, and battery commander Ami Shiloh.

The operation generated much excitement, for this time the target was the heart of Damascus, a direct hit on the snake's head. The force had already begun moving silently, with no headlights, but Dayan got cold feet, feared the reaction of Big Brother, U.S. Secretary of State Henry Kissinger, and called the operation off.

On the strength of our great achievements, chiefly the taking of the enclave within Syrian territory by the 7th Armored Brigade, we were not discouraged by the cancelation and began planning the next phase – advancing on Damascus. I can attest to myself that throughout the war, I was confident of our victory and confident in myself, projecting optimism and a fighting spirit to those around me and the many fire units I employed. The target now was the Kanekar camps, but meanwhile, an armored brigade of the Third Iraqi Division had arrived, attacking Laner's division. While it was defeated through the effective use of artillery fire by Moshe Levi, commander of the 282nd Division Artillery, the Northern Command and IDF HQ realized that our strength was spent and would not suffice for an offensive effort against the Syrian division defending Damascus.

Parenthetically, it should be noted that the Air Force had disappointed yet again. There was no air defense fire along the path of the Iraqi forces, and our aircraft took no aerial photos. The only action offered by Air Force Commander Benny Peled was to land a commando force which would stop the mass of Iraqi tanks with bazookas. A failed attempt at this scheme was carried out by Shaul Mofaz (later on IDF Chief of Staff and Israel's Defense Minister), and the troops were extracted with great difficulty, by the same squadron commander who rescued the airborne 105mm "Tiger" battery from Jabel Ataka – Yuval Efrat, who was awarded the medal of distinguished service for that action in the Sinai.

There is no doubt that the 412th Battalion's firing on Damascus on the night of October 13th, and the launching of Operation Bendigo in the second part of the war in Sinai were unique artillery operations, which led to strategic shifts on both fronts and in the war in general. The firing on Damascus aroused Hafez al-Assad's concrete fear that IDF ground forces were knocking on his door. He threatened Sadat with a separate ceasefire and drove the Egyptian president to move the Egyptian armored forces to the east bank of the Canal, where it was destroyed – leading to the change in the balance of power, which allowed the IDF to cross the Canal on October 15th. The fact that the Egyptian surface-to-air missiles were destroyed in Operation Bendigo between October 14th and 22nd, led Sadat to sue for a ceasefire, with our Air Force operating unhindered and pulverizing the Egyptian 3rd Army.

A Moving Reunion

The 405th Battalion reunited as two batteries under my command on October 14th. Battery A, under Yossi Koren, came from the southern Golan Heights, consisting of five SPH guns, as mentioned above, and joined Kigel's battery C, which was with me the whole time. Around that time, Yona Efrat, Central Command General, came for a visit in the Syrian enclave we had captured, along with his artillery command officer, Mondi Carmeli, his chief of staff Moishe "And A Half" Levi (later IDF Chief of Staff), and the command staff ops officer, Matan Vilnai.

The Central Command had effectively been left out of the war, and its command was frustrated. Efrat, who had heard from Yanush about the wonders worked by the artillery forces, asked me: "What do you want?"

I replied: "Only one thing: Send me four SPHs to replace the Boaz battery's guns," but I only received them after the war had officially ended. They arrived during the fighting in the enclave, during the attrition period, and all the veteran SPHs were replaced by new ones, with a long-range barrel reaching distances of 18km, rather than the 14.5km reached by the short barrels.

While we were fighting, we received a visit from Nati Sharoni, the Chief Artillery Officer, and Musa Peled, commander of the adjacent 146th Division, who complimented me on the fire support we'd provided him in the taking of Tel Masshara, in an act that could be termed good neighborly relations. The long-range artillery was capable of hitting any target in the area, and I didn't skimp on shells when Danny Avidar, Musa Peled's division artillery commander, contacted me asking for help.

THE 405TH BATTALION – THE VALOR AND THE LOSS

On the 40th anniversary of the Yom Kippur War, "Always A Gunner," the Artillery Corps association's periodical, published an article I had written about the battles waged by the 405th Battalion on the Golan Heights in October 1973, and my experiences there – both as a bat-com and as the 7th Armored Brigade's artillery commander. Below are the main points, with requisite omissions, so as not to repeat events already described:

> To this day, I blame myself for not ordering Uri, the deputy bat-com, to leapfrog the Boaz battery to a more rearward position at Shaabania, despite the argument with Bar-David, the artillery command officer. It is possible that in the heat of battle, no one would have noticed that I had disobeyed a direct order, but at noon on Saturday, Yom Kippur, when Yanush announced that all-out war would begin at 18:00, battle hadn't broken out yet. When the war did erupt, I was entirely focused on the mission of stopping the Syrians.
>
> Batteries A and Boaz began firing about half an hour after the Syrians' opening barrage, when a flood of requests for fire and assistance had poured in, mostly from the Infantry outposts.
>
> Yossi Koren, who was also the battalion's fire direction officer, and the XOs, who are essentially position commanders, Nissim Sarousi (RIP) with Boaz and Adi Shuman with battery A, trying to fulfill all requests for fire, in the midst of counter-battery fire raining down upon and all around them.
>
> The fire was directed forward until Saturday night. We didn't fire sideways or backward for the simple reason that the 188th Armored Brigade, in charge of the southern Golan Heights sector, didn't have an artillery liaison in the form of an artillery com-

mander. There was an FSO with the 53rd Battalion – Yigal Sapir – but he was wounded when his tank was hit, thereby depriving the brigade of the option of receiving artillery support.

The Boaz battery fired some 1,000 shells throughout the fighting, from four self-propelled cannons, with the target data being received from the British "Face" computer. The computer was mounted on a Land Rover jeep, which originally came with the firing computer and was right next to the elevated command APC, from which Koren directed both batteries' fire.

The 405th's first casualty was ammunition truck driver, Shabtai Matzri, from Even Yehuda, the son of an old-school Yemeni Jewish family, salt of the earth. Shabtai was hit by shrapnel that slipped under his flack vest. The battalion medic, Dr. Yaakov Toledano, dressed his wound and evacuated him to Ziv Hospital in Safed, but he died of his wound en route. The battery kept firing and didn't leapfrog from its position at Juhader, despite the Syrian artillery falling all around it.

The evening before, I had been at a "Kol Nidrei" prayer service with the men of the battery at the regular position at Tel Fares, and to this day I recall the moving moment, after which the battery moved to the Juhader position, to deploy within tank range of the line of engagement and clear the regular position to Shaul Shpitz's Bahad 9 battery.

Around 21:00-21:30 on Saturday night, October 6th, the battery noticed a number of tanks standing on the small ridge above them, 40 meters away. The XO, Lt. Nissim Sarousi, who was busy responding to the infantry outposts' pleas for artillery fire, was also engaged in unloading the ammunition, opening the packaging, and carrying the ammunition to the SPHs – arduous and exhausting work, with each shell weighing 43kg, only a little less than the weight of the warrior youths, who were collapsing with fatigue.

Sarousi called the deputy bat-com, Uri Manos. Manos told him to hail the unidentified tanks on the emergency channel 38.5, which all units were under orders to listen to, in order to prevent friendly fire incidents. Receiving no reply, and believing that the tanks in question belonged to the 188th Armored Brigade, he asked one of the officers to go up to the tank platoon commander, and demand that he refrains from driving through the battery's position. His concern was that a tank would sever the telephone cable connecting the guns to the battery command center.

The officer, Issachar Bruck, a religious man from a kibbutz in the South, took a rechargeable spotlight, approached the tank with team commander Nissim Assis, and when he shone the spotlight on it, he saw strange X shapes in green and black painted on it, and Assis even heard people speaking in Arabic.

Bruck tried to shut off the searchlight, which wouldn't switch off, slammed it on the ground, and then ran to the post and yelled "Prepare for tanks!" He managed to run a few steps, and the T-62 tanks shot a sickly green flare, and then another, unleashed hellfire from their tank guns, and concluded the performance with Goryonov machine gun fire.

Three SPH guns and the command APC were hit immediately and went up in flames. The aluminum they were made of melted in the intense conflagration, which intensified with the burning explosives and exploding shells – both of the ground piles and the chamber ammunition stored within the guns.

Sarousi, the comms sergeant, Yaakov Shragai, and comms operator Avi Siluk were first to be killed, and the SPH crews didn't survive either. Fifteen soldiers fell in the battle. Two young troopers, David Abaki and Tzachi Avinoam, who had just completed the gunners' course, fled the burning SPH eastward and fell captive the next day. The wounded were loaded onto a half-track and a truck, under the command of Hanan Anderman, who to this day is racked with guilt for remaining alive, and moved along with the rest of the troops to battery A, where deputy bat-com, Manos, and battalion medic, Toledano, awaited them. Manos sent them to the Sea of Galilee. Bruck began to run along with the battery sergeant-major, Shlomo (Sami) Elbaz, back to the position to make sure that no one was left behind, but Manos stopped them and ordered them to join the others. The group of survivors continued on its way down to the lake, but ran once again into Syrian forces, which opened fire. They scattered to the winds and later regrouped, all in the dark. Later it turned out that the wounded FDC sergeant, Moshe Zimmerman, had been left behind. A tank crew member went to bring him water but got lost in the terrain, and Zimmerman was abandoned and died of his wounds. Battery A kept firing until it ran out of ammunition, and then withdrew under cover of darkness to the lake, arriving in daylight.

The 4th Armored Brigade's tanks, which stood ready to go up the Heights through Ma'aleh Gamla, saw strange large war machines flowing down the slope toward them, and opened fire, believing them to be Syrian tanks. Luckily, they had no time to do sight adjustments and didn't hit anything, and luckily, artillery officer, Shmulik Aharon, later bat-com of the 405th during the Peace for Galilee War, was on the scene. He recognized battery A and halted the tank fire in time. The battery re-armed, was supplied with battle rations and water, and received orders to be the first back up the Heights, but Uri Manos refused, saying: "I'm willing to follow the first tank company. Thus it was, and battery A, which was the last down from the Golan Heights, was first back up, renewing its fire in support of Musa Peled's division.

The stories of the A and "Boaz" batteries can be learned from Rami Kedar's documentary film produced by Israel's Channel 1, now called the Kann Public Broadcasting Corporation, which can be viewed on YouTube, including footage of the remnants of the Boaz battery immediately following our troops' return up the Golan Heights. What happened to the cadets' battalion and the Shpitz battery, which was destroyed on Sunday at dawn, can be read in Ben-Ami Cohen's article, "Born to War Alone."

The remains of the Boaz battery.

"Looking at Each Other, Knowing We'll Stay and Fire"

Battery A was deployed on Sunday, October 14, in the area of the Jordan's diversion, and fired from there "like two battalions," in the words of Danny Avidar, commander of the 213th Artillery Division. The battery moved immediately behind the 39th Armored Battalion under Yoav Vaspi, while Koren, the battery commander, was felt not to be needed, as there were enough officers for a four-barrel battery. It was commanded successfully by XO Adi Shuman alongside recon officer, Moti Fried, and above them were Eyal Naveh, the FDO who replaced Koren, now a history professor at Tel Aviv University, and deputy bat-com Uri Manos.

Koren found a place with the 39th Battalion, ranged and fired with the battery, and later joined the lookout at Tel Fares, under Yair Koren, later a bat-com in the Peace for Galilee War. He rejoined the 405th along with battery C, with battery A consisting of five barrels, having adopted the sole surviving gun from the Boaz battery (following its repair) together with the gun's crew. Yossi Koren himself described the events in his book, *All We Cannot Leave Behind*,[20] and here below are some excerpts from it with his kind permission:

Sunday, October 7th, 1973, five in the morning

A burst of machine-gun fire shatters the early-morning silence. Bullets fly off the rocks strewn all along the side of my vehicle. Battery crew four's lookout reports seeing a tank and a personnel carrier approaching us, while firing in our direction. One of ours. We all get our blue and white flags out and wave them, but they keep firing. I grab the radio mic and yell, "Cease fire!" still waving my flags furiously in the air. Finally, realizing their error, they pull up short, and like repentant children, shuffle the rest of the way towards us before coming to an unceremonious halt just a few feet from us.

To our astonishment, it is our brigade commander, his operations chief and some other staff members who are up there with him. You can see how relieved they are that the "enemy" turned out to be us. Our brigade commander has his head buried in several maps at once and only comes up for air to whisper a few words into a radio microphone on a frequency we're not privy to. No one seems in a hurry to provide an explanation for their gunner's miscalculations, but to be quite honest, it's not an explanation I'm really looking for. What I'm really looking for are some clear-cut orders, something with a vision, something to demonstrate that what's happening right now is nothing more than the opening gambit of some ingenious master plan that the guys upstairs simply haven't shared with us yet.

The brigade commander looks up from his map for a moment and calls to me and Uri to join him up in the turret. He asks us calmly about our situation. I answer him in a calm voice of my own, tell him about our dramatic night, playing hide and seek with the enemy and itemize our remaining ammunitions – about 80 shells. "We're ready to move out," we tell him.

"I need you to fall back down towards the beach of the Sea of Galilee and

---

20   Koren, Yossi: "All We Cannot Leave Behind," Modi'in Press, 2021

head north with me around the lake towards Capernaum," he says almost whispering.

"From there, we'll be re-deploying with more fresh forces to launch a new attack to the south."

That's it? That's the master plan? I wonder. And what about cover fire for our forces if we descend off the Heights? What's going to happen here after we pull out?

Uri and I look at each other, and without saying a word, nod in agreement.

"We're not moving from here, sir." Uri dares to confront the colonel. "We still have some ammunition left and we're waiting for some more to arrive here soon... we need to block..."

The commander raises his hand. "Fine" he says. Then he talks to some tired voices over the radio to verify their exact locations and situation.

"Okay," he says finally, "we have a few teams along the Petroleum Road, just inside the Syrian lines. Just give them cover fire, everything you have." He takes out a map and writes down their radio frequencies. "Just fire wherever you can to cover them, and then go down the road to join me." And that was it.

I nod and climb back down off the tank, trying to think of how I'm going to sell this story to my men, how to dress it up, how much to tell them and how much to leave out.

Adi gives our men the new orders, and I see them running back towards the cannons, fast but not too fast, loading up the shells, this time with an extra dose of anger and indignation, and yes, even a little enthusiasm mixed in. The past night has turned them into real soldiers, that much is clear. Each and every one of them growing up overnight.

Sunday, October 7th, 1973, eleven o'clock in the morning

Ronnie's personnel carrier and mine are parked one after the other, his is carrying all of battery B's wounded. Now he comes over with some food thrown together by one of the drivers – coffee and a few crackers with jam. His eyelids are so heavy with fatigue his eyes appear as tiny slits below his forehead. One of my soldiers, Amir, is listening to a transistor radio.

"Hey, d'you guys hear that? It's a real war!" he informs us.

"A real war, huh! I never would have guessed," I say to him sarcastically, realizing at that moment that I knew it every bit exactly when he did.

"Yeah," Amir continues innocently," they're fighting on the Egyptian border too.

I just heard them say that we're supposed to keep it secret, like we did at the start of the Six-Day War." The proverbial 'Fog of War,' I think to myself, but now the only ones in the fog are us.

"Turn that damn thing off!" I shout at him, who looks at me like a child who's been scolded for wanting to be helpful. Ronnie quickly comes to his defense.

"He was just a kid back then," he says to me.

"Which means what exactly?"

"It means that for him, war is taping up the windows so they won't shatter when the bombs start falling. It means painting the car's headlights blue so they won't shine after dark. It means that for him, hearing on the radio about 'The Fog of War' means just that. It's a war..."

"Thanks for the clarification, Ronnie," I turn on him sharply. "Now just go and ask your 'pupils' what it means when a division of Syrian tanks runs roughshod over your battery and fifteen of your best friends are lying on the ground with their whole bodies covered in woolen blankets. Go on, ask them what that means!"

"Ah, well," Ronnie replies, stroking an invisible beard as if he were a Talmudic scholar, "that means that our friends Amir and Mozes and the rest of your crew haven't gotten to that section of scriptures yet, Sir. But do not despair, Sir, by the time the next war rolls around, they will all be enlightened, Sir, in evidence of the extreme fatigue, Sir, and the intense fear of dying, Sir, and the stench of the dried-up blood on their comrades' shirtsleeves, if you get my meaning, Sir!"

"Thank you, most honorable Rebbe Ronnie," I say with a playful mock-reverence intended to lower the tension. "Now tell me, what's going on with the half-track, and the wounded from battery B?"

"Not that bad," Ronnie tells me. "Our munitions man, Palty, even went back to get the firing trigger from one of the Battery B cannons to replace the one from ours that isn't working."

"What?!" I scream. "Doesn't that idiot know the area is swarming with Syrian tanks? Listen, nobody leaves the battery without my permission, and I mean nobody! Is that clear?" Just what I need, another schmuck who doesn't know what war means. Or an incidental hero, either way...

"In the evacuation half-track, there are quite a few wounded who were shy about asking for first aid," Ronnie continues, "Just bandaged themselves up and kept quiet. They're all with you now, they're getting help cleaning and loading their weapons."

"It might be a good idea to assign a crew from battery B to be part of our battery," I say thinking out loud, "Maybe that'll help them get back on their feet. I'll talk it over with the deputy battalion commander when he gets back from trying to get us more ammunition... By the way, what the hell is taking him so long?"

I decide to do a quick inspection of our crews. In the bright light of day, the cannon barrels look even blacker with soot than I'd imagined, and after twenty hours of combat, the soldiers all look like they're beginning to take the war in stride.

"How did all this happen to us?" I ask Ronnie, almost rhetorically.

"All what?" he answers with another question, while handing me a piece of halva he's sliced with the lid from one of our ration cans.

"I just don't understand what's happened to this army," I say somewhat discouraged. "'The People's Army,' isn't that what Ben Gurion called it? Destroying the whole Egyptian air force before it could get off the ground, beating three Arab armies in six days, paratroopers at the Wailing Wall..."

"Yeah," Ronnie says through a mouth full of halva, "what about it?"

"What about it?!" I say, my voice rising together with my frustration. "Listen, what have they been telling us all along, from Joshua at the battle of Jericho through Yehuda Maccabi, from the War of Independence to the Six Day War? They all came out fighting and it was all over, in a flash, then everybody packed up their weapons and went back home to the comfort of family and friends, to tell tales of their heroic deeds... Well, where the hell are they now? Here we are, stuck in the middle of the Heights with only four stinking cannons and nobody even answers our radio calls! I'm telling you Ronnie, if it keeps up like this, soon we'll see the Syrian tanks holding a victory parade, rolling by on their way to the Sea of Galilee..."

"Want some more halva?" Ronnie asks me, holding out what's left.

"You haven't been listening to a word I've been saying, have you?"

"Of course I have," he tells me, finishing the last piece of halva and wiping his mouth with the back of his hand. "You asked me what was happening, so now I'll tell you. We have to stop firing altogether because we only *have a few shells left and we have to get ready to move down towards the Sea of Galilee because we're out of ammunition too. But if you decide you want to stay here and commit suicide, well, that's fine with me, I'll even stay with you 'cause that's what friends are for. But if we are going to move out then I suggest..."* and he inclines his head in the direction of the valley to indicate that time is of the essence.

I brush away the halva crumbs from my trousers, along with all my thoughts about the depressing nature of our situation, and give the order for all the crews to get ready to move out. "And no more firing without my orders," I tell them with considerable emphasis. "Leave one loaded shell in the barrel just in case..." and I look for a delicate way to say, in case our friends the Syrians, the ones who pounded battery B last night, decide to pay us another visit, but I decide to keep it simple and say, "... only in case of real emergency. Over and out."

"Over and out," I repeat quietly, this time with the microphone off. "How very fitting," I say to myself.

This thing is far from over, but at least we're moving out.

The Battle for Ma'aleh Gamla

Or Pialkov studied the Ma'aleh Gamla battle and the role of battery A in stopping the Syrians who were trying to go down to the Sea of Galilee on October 7th, and he published his study within the framework of the "Yom Kippur War Center," which is a "non-profit organization whose goal is to impart the history and legacy of the Yom Kippur War to coming generations, to pay honor and esteem to its warriors, to commemorate the fallen, to pay respect and appreciation to the bereaved families, and to serve as a venue for the continued study of the war and its lessons."

And this is what Pialkov wrote:

A little before 11:00, Koren still refused to come down to the lake, asking that the ammunition come up to him. He concealed his guns meanwhile a few hundred meters from the Daliot Junction, down the bluff overlooking the stream. Around 12:00, Syrian tanks opened fire on his APC from Bezeq Hill to the north, just where the battery had deployed only half an hour prior. One half-track nearby was hit.

Uri Manos, in the elevated fire direction command center, exposed himself on the Picardo Route, trying to draw the fire to himself. The Syrians didn't fire, and the two assumed they were chasing them and begin descending toward the Gamla Junction, to refill at Kursi Beach, wait for the rest of the force, and advance behind it.

Around 13:00, halfway through, near the location of Moshav Gamla today, battery A met a force under the deputy bat-com of the 51st, Zion Zluf (Ziv). This force consisted of Company C, plus an auxiliary company acting as mech. Infantry, which included four recoilless cannons (or RC). Koren explained to the deputy bat-com of the 51st that a Syrian tank force, that had been on Bezeq Hill, may come down Ma'aleh Gamla and encounter his recoilless rifles. Koren left Zluf his radio network data, and suggested that he ask him for fire support after he restocked on ammunition near the quarry at the junction.

At 13:45, Zion Zaluf saw a dust cloud generated by armored movement along the Picardo Route. The network wasn't able to tell him whose forces they were, and he sent a squad on foot eastward, commanded by the intel officer. While the recoilless cannons were in motion, three enemy tanks appeared at a range of 200 meters. The RC in the rear, by the deputy bat-com, fired two shells at the tanks, hitting the track of the tank on the right and stopping all three, with the two tanks not hit were sliding down the rear slope.

Coming down the Ma'aleh Gamla route, an advance force from the 39th Battalion accidentally fired at the 405th. Luckily for the gunners, the 39th Battalion hadn't undergone sight adjustment, and so missed them. For his performance as commander, from the start of the retreat until reaching the shores of the lake, deputy bat-com, Major Uri Manos, received a citation of commendation.

At this point, the 405th Battalion's battery A, which had finished restocking its ammunitions supply, was employed on the Syrians, creating a fire screen which enabled the 51st Battalion force to come back down Ma'aleh Gamla.

Avi Dietschi, Yoel Porat, and Herzl Cohen – Heroes Deserving of Decoration

Over the years that have passed since the Yom Kippur War, I have been castigating myself over the matter of decorations. Upon the war's end, I was sucked into a whirlwind of activity, a tough war of attrition, moving bodies from field burial sites to military cemeteries, and reforming the battalion, which left me with no mind for commendations. I regret that, and it is my opinion that the entire 405th deserves a citation of commendation – both for the fighting and the lessons drawn from it, which guided the formulation of the Artillery Corps' new battle doctrine, the one that truly made it "Queen of the battlefield." Not long ago I was invited to a conference on the adjutancy in the Yom Kippur War, organized by (res.) Brig-Gen. Shlomo Cohen, who was the adjutant of the 7th Armored Brigade during the war. I asked the audience – full of adjutancy service members – whether they knew of a battalion adjutant who was killed in the war in the course of a combat mission. Yoni Noked, deputy chairman of the Yom Kippur War Center, and adjutant of an armored battalion in the Sinai during the war, raised his hand and said: "Yoel Porat, adjutant of the 405th Battalion."

And indeed, so it was. On Saturday night, October 6th, Yoel Porat and the battalion's sergeant-major, Avi Dietschi, who were at the battalion's rear HQ at Qatsabieh, wished to reach the fighting batteries and take part in the battle. Just then, a need arose to lead an ammunition convoy to the firing batteries, and there was no artillery officer present to do it. Porat, a former Shaked Ranger, and Dietschi, a former crew commander and a battery sergeant-major, jumped at the opportunity, hopped into a jeep, and lead the convoy.

Near Qatsabieh, at the water junction, they saw headlights approaching on the road. As the vehicles approached, they realized these were Syrian tanks moving. The two jumped from the jeep, warned the truck drivers, and in so doing saved their lives. Porat and Dietschi were killed with the ammunition trucks that exploded, and the jeep that turned into metal slag. Their names were commemorated when we named the 405th Battalion's home base at Qala'a after them – "Camp Yoav."

Herzl Cohen, my ops officer, volunteered to go up Mt. Hermon on the last day of the war, despite me forbidding it and Yanush ordering him to stay. He insisted on going as FSO with Golani's 51st Battalion, under Yehuda Peled, to retake the Hermon outpost, which had fallen to the Syrians on the war's first day, and which the IDF had failed until then to retake.

The operation was successful, but Herzl Cohen was killed while employing the artillery. I wrote about it under the headline "Captain Herzl Cohen, z"l,[21] My Hero at the Taking of the Hermon," in the war's 50th-anniversary edition of "Tamid Totchan" ("Always A Gunner):

Herzl Cohen climbed the Hermon alongside the bat-com of the Golani Brigade's 51st Battalion, Yud'ke Peled. Together they ranged the registration targets for the rolling barrage planned by Herzl. The Golani Brigade launched Operation "Kinuach" ("Just "Desserts), the taking of the Hermon on the night of October 21-22, 1973, a day before the ceasefire is announced.

Several hours prior, Herzl was by my side in his duty as ops officer of the 405th Battalion, in the Artillery commander APC of the 7th Armored Brigade, deep in the Syrian enclave. The battles of containment and penetration into Syria had taken a heavy toll on the battalion. Twenty of its troops had fallen in battle, joined by two reservists, ammunition truck drivers with battery C, and Captain Elhanan Korach, who had been killed as Yossi Ben-Hanan's FSO in the penetration at Jubta al-Hashab. The battalion was finally reunited, and then came a request: An FSO is needed for the taking of the Hermon. Herzl received the news on the wireless, jumped up and announced, without asking me: "I'm on my way."

"Negative," I told him. "You're not going." Yanush the brigadier, listening to the conversation, told him: "Herzl, you're not moving. You've been through hard battles and survived by a miracle. Sit

---

21   Hebrew acronym for "may [their] memory be a blessing."

tight." We couldn't keep track of him, and Herzl took a jeep from Uri the deputy bat-com, and rushed to Golani's command group, where he was received with joy by Ben-Ami Cohen, the artillery commander, and Yud'ke the bat-com of the 51st, who didn't expect to get such an experienced and veteran FSO. Herzl had been drafted in November of 1969, a STEM major at his native Nes Ziona high school. He was certified as a command post NCO, and later as an artillery officer, was assigned to battery A under Baruch Benbenishti, and not long thereafter was appointed XO. In October 1972, Herzl was appointed commander of battery A, signed up for the career military, and handed his beloved battery to Yossi Koren when he was appointed ops officer of the 405th – shortly before the war and before I received command of the battalion.

Herzl knew the Golan Heights well, and helped me, the Sinai man, to quickly fit in the nooks and crannies of the Heights in the Valley of Tears sector. In his meticulous and orderly way, he organized the brigade artillery APC, given to us two hours prior to the war, and thanks to him, we went to battle properly outfitted, with added radios, including a ground to air radio, and all the maps. We operated together – Herzl, Alex Redlus, who was the intel officer, and I – throughout the war in that APC. We were together in the heroic containment battle, in which we managed to concentrate seven battalions and stop the Syrians on the third day at the Valley of Tears. Each of us ranged, ordered fire for effect, and was in contact with the armored bat-coms, the FSOs and the FOs. On Sunday, ahead of the penetration, Herzl prepared the command group for the fire units, the FSOs and the FOs, and also our part in the brigade orders, and transmitted the order carefully and successfully. We penetrated into Syria with great success, managing the battle together until October 21st, with our body odors mixing together and with us eating, catnapping, and living together for fifteen days. Herzl climbed up the Hermon with Yud'ke, employing the rolling barrage, and on the way, they came across the corpses of Syrians killed by the artillery cover fire (thus according to Moshe Givati, in his book "The Campaign for the Hermon"). As they approached the summit, Syrians came out with their hands in the air, *due to the horrific fire, and were shot for fear of a trap. Their friends continued to fight, and Herzl drew the fire closer till the shrapnel was flying over the troops' heads, as Yud'ke Peled described it in the film "Esh-Ness." By the morning, the brigadier had been wounded, Yud'ke had been wounded, and Herzl, who had been lying right beside him and raising his binoculars, to draw the fire even closer, got shot in the forehead by a Syrian sniper and was killed. To this day, I agonize over the dearth of decorations we gave out in the battalion, and in the corps in general. Herzl deserves the highest decoration for bravery, courage, volunteerism, and sacrifice.*

Blessed be your memory, valiant hero.

Countless men among the battalion's fighters deserve to be decorated, among them Israel Kigel, a 2nd Lt. who commanded a battery throughout the battles, fought bravely, and brought all his men back safely; Yossi Koren, the last man down from the Heights, who immediately went back up, volunteering as a FSO, or the battery A ordnance specialist, Paltiel Hochman, who hurried in mid-battle, with Syrian tanks on the ground, to the remnants of the damaged "Boaz" battery, to bring a firing mechanism from one of the disabled SPHs in order to keep a gun in his own battery operational. The wheel of decorations cannot be turned backward, and the little we can do is to tell their stories wherever we may, including in these humble pages.

THE ARTILLERY CORPS BEGINS TO TAKE OFF

The Yom Kippur War changed the attitude toward the Artillery Corps from one extreme to the other. The change was led by Raful and Yanush, who had experienced the importance of the artillery in the flesh, and knew that it had a major part in defeating the Syrian army – Raful as commander of the 36th Division and later as the Northern Command General, and Yanush as commander of the 7th Armored Brigade during the war, and Raful's successor as commander of the 36th Division.

After two IDF chiefs who came from the Armored Corps – Bar-Lev and Dado – who were brought up in an atmosphere of contempt for the artillery, the appointment of Mota Gur as the IDF Chief of Staff in April '74 then accelerated the process. The Artillery Corps, under Nati Sharoni and with the backing of a new Chief of Staff and new Defense Minister – Gur and Shimon Peres – led a far-reaching change in the ground forces. The ground firepower was at long last based upon the Artillery Corps, which is designed just for that – producing firepower – and invested in the corps accordingly.

The opening salvo was the purchase of 200 long-barrel M-109 SPHs. Bahad 9 came down from Tzrifin to Shivta, transitioned from the status of a subletting tenant to the homeowner of the artillery combat doctrine, and began to stand tall. We in the Golan Heights also keenly felt the change in attitude and atmosphere. The war of attrition in the Heights was in effect a continuation of the Yom Kippur War, and the 405th Battalion, which was the most veteran and experienced in the use of the most advanced self-propelled cannon of its kind, bore the brunt of the fighting.

The battalion, with its three batteries, was deployed near the Ma'atz Junction, some five km east of the borderline, and in addition to the daily firing routine, was also called in for any special operation or need – the southern Golan, north to the Hermon, and even Biranit, on the Lebanese border, whenever Raful decided to initiate a day of battle. We didn't have a moment's rest.

Uri Manos left the battalion immediately following the war, and was appointed the staff ops officer at the Central Command artillery HQ – a theater which at the time was calm and quiet. I spent my first Saturday off at Tzrifin, trying to convince Sharoni to allow me to appoint Dudi Haramati as deputy bat-com on permanent commission. Haramati, the commander of the "Boaz" battery, was "only" a captain, but had been the 82nd Battalion's FSO during the war – and he was a friend.

Sharoni, who was usually all for promoting younger officers, suddenly dug his heels in and ruled, after half a day of lobbying on my part, in favor of Shmil Golan for the post. This was an assignment I could easily live with. Golan, a converted paratrooper who had been the Bahad 9 Battalion's deputy commander during the war, had fought like a lion and afterward performed selflessly in the harsh conditions of the winter of 1974 and the northern war of attrition, until a separation of forces agreement was signed in May.

"The Coats Did All the Work"

The attrition period began immediately following the war. I held several positions at the time, with immense responsibility and not a minute's leisure – bat-com of the 405th, artillery commander of the 7th Armored Brigade, and artillery commander of the infantry brigades that alternated at holding the line – the Golani and the Paratroopers.

Within the battalion, I focused on physical and mental rehabilitation, after an entire battery had been obliterated and 26 men had fallen. I had to learn lessons immediately – both for daily combat purposes and for tactical and strategic lessons, such as deploying by terrain, use of direct fire, creation of large fire concentrations, use of artillery rockets to stop large numbers of tanks, and improving the integration with the maneuvering forces. I am happy to say that these lessons became fundamental elements of the Artillery Corps' doctrine.

We took in three new SPHs, replaced the existing nine with long-barrels, and in addition, I visited the families of the fallen. I personally handled each family, attended every funeral, and read a eulogy at the grave of each fallen warrior. I decided to undertake the mission of consoling the families and facing their grief as I was the commander. I had experienced the loss of soldiers in the Six-Day War and the War of Attrition in the Sinai, and I knew that bereaved families require delicate handling, that they inquire and investigate and wish to know every last detail about their loved ones, and yearn for stories from their commanders and comrades regarding the circumstances of their deaths and their last moments.

The questions and doubts came mostly from the families of the "Boaz" casualties. Why were they ordered to deploy so close to the Syrians? Who treated them after they were wounded? Who announced their deaths? The Zimmerman family, whose son Moshe, the Boaz battery's command post sergeant, was abandoned wounded in the retreat, demanded and received a commission of inquiry to look into the matter.

The commission focused on the performance of the commander and troops on the scene. In light of the harsh conditions of the battery's loss, the movement of its surviving members under Syrian fire, and the fact that it was after dark, the commission concluded that no fault was to be found with anyone's performance.

From day to day, the fighting intensified, and I found myself once again in the eye of the storm – with the Paratroopers and Golani Brigades on one hand, and my own batteries on the other, firing and called up on a moment's notice from one combat site to another, in the harshest winter the Golan Heights had seen in years. The frequent demand and the way the gunners were suddenly looked at sometimes bordered on worship, and a belief that we had magical abilities.

In February 1974, Raful, as division commander, planned a raid on one of the outposts in the Lega. The execution was tasked to the 35th Brigade, which held the line of outposts in the enclave under Tzimmel the Brigadier (Aryeh Tzidon to his mother), and the force chosen to carry out the mission in practice was the Paratroopers' Rangers, under Shaul Mofaz.

The idea, in typical Raful fashion, was based on surprise, and I planned the ranging of a registration target, meaning the ranging of a target located about a mile from the actual goal, with the same survey grid, and using the ranging data for the new target, so that there would be no need to range it as well. The method was based on the fact that we fired incessantly, and so the Syrians didn't notice a few shells landing far from the outposts.

I picked a clear registration target, whose coordinates could be calculated with great precision. It appeared on the map as a prominent stone structure named Khirbet Maqrusa, northwest of Tel Shams. Tzimmel tried to explain the idea at a plan approval meeting, but tripped over his words a bit, and the impatient Raful cut him off. "Keep it simple," he told him. "Mizrachi, what do you suggest?"

It's possible that I explained the idea better. Raful had no interest in the technical details. His eyes sparkled. "Let's go," he said. "Make it so!"

The 411th Battalion, newly established, was picked as the mission's artillery support. This was its baptism by fire, but the battalion's FDO was Hanan Anderman, who rescued the remnants of the "Boaz" battery from the inferno in the war, so I was unworried. The registration target was ranged. The FSO was the experienced Yoav Agmon, who was attached to Sayeret Matkal ever since Eitan Kauli, the bat-com of the 75th who hadn't dropped the Armored Corps' pose, "fired him," after catching him urinating on his trailer.

Agmon, with a "25" radio and reception problems, employed the fire right before the force entered the target, and 40 shells came out from eight precision barrels, fresh from the plastic wrapping, and bombarded the target for a minute and a half. Mofaz entered the outpost immediately afterward, took it without casualties, and didn't wrap himself in undeserved valor. "The coats did all the work," he announced on the radio. "Coats" in the IDF radio code is the Artillery Corps.

"Deployment by Terrain"

The first exercise I visited following my appointment as Chief Artillery Officer, in my very first week in the post, was a 215th Division Artillery exercise at Nabi Musa, north of the Dead Sea, where I also gave my first CAO's order: No more traditional deployment, which means deploying over a hundred meters at the gradation at which the fire falls on the target, as that was an outdated approach, which accounts for a broad scatter, and views every target as an area target. My object was the opposite: Maximum accuracy, lethal strikes, and destroying the enemy. "Deploy according to terrain," I told Oppo, Eliyahu Barak, the division artillery commander, the battery deployment space can reach up to 500 meters.

"Every crew commander," I said, "will pick their own location – a dugout, a ravine, a dirt dike – to protect them from counter-battery fire and conceal themselves from observation as much as possible." This has a double effect – both in terms of fighting from the gunner positions, and in a significant increase in lethality.

I made it a goal to give the crew commanders freedom and improve their navigation and orientation skills, and have them view themselves as independent commanders. This sense would be reinforced later thanks to the direct fire order. The doctrine and staff-and-command personnel surrounding me translated my field-talk into the language of "CAO directives."

On a principle and doctrinal level, I saw it as necessary to detach from an outdated combat doctrine that was unsuited to the new technological age. You cannot employ innovative means and cannot utilize the advantages of sophisticated devices with a combat doctrine lagging a generation behind them.

On a practical level, the use of means such as the firing computer and the laser range finder obviated traditional deployment, making the artillery fire fare more precise and deadly, as it accounted for the unique characteristics of each gun and each target.

And now let me return to 1974, and explain where all this came from: The three batteries of the 405th Battalion, which were deployed at Ma'atz Junction since the end of the war, were completely exposed to Syrian observation from the slopes of Mt. Hermon. We were called on to fire ceaselessly, despite the counter-battery fire raining down on us, when leapfrogging to alternate positions as per procedure was impossible. The Syrian fire tracked you in motion, and met you at the alternate position as well. To overcome the problem, I decided to enter existing Syrian dugouts with the SPHs, with only the top of the turret and the barrel sticking out. Each SPH held 70 shells, and the resupply of ammunition was done by one of the guns and not by an M-548 "protected" by tarp. The fighters wore helmets regularly and wore the flack vests of the time – heavy and cumbersome "Vietnam vests" – and so we were able to continue firing continuously despite the heavy counter-battery fire landing around us. The Syrian shells hit all over the area, but failed to hit the SPHs.

During one of the bombardments, a piece of shrapnel from a 122mm shell that exploded on the edge of the dugout penetrated into the cabin. The driver, a new immigrant from Russia, sat in the cabin with the SPH's engine running for swiveling and firing. The shrapnel passed through the aluminum and stopped inside his flack vest, less than an inch from the back. I took him on a tour of all the batteries, and after all the troops and commanders heard how the vest saved his life – I gave him a "regular" one-week leave.

"Banishment from Heaven"

One of the most obvious lessons at the end of the war was that we're not going back to Camp Bilu, the 405th's home base near Rehovot, and our new abode would be in the Golan Heights. It was only natural for the artillery base to be located near Nafah – at Camp "Keren," named after a battery commander from the 55th Battalion, Lt. Benny Keren, who was killed in a car accident prior to the war. The small camp, designed for a standing battery of the line which rotated periodically, contained several prefab structures. I arrived there at the head of the battalion, only to discover that the 36th Division's medic battalion had occupied the camp.

I explained to the doctor that this was my camp, and upon his refusal to evacuate, I had the SPHs line up in a row, ordered to point the cannons at the camp at point-blank range, and told him: "Buddy, buddy, we're animals. We've been through a horrible war. Get out or I'll open fire."

The guy went pale as chalk and left with his men. We began to live in some comfort.

Not for long, though. Toward the year's end, as I mentioned, the 411th Battalion was established, the second standing battalion of long-barreled M-109 guns. I was part of the 282nd Division Artillery – the artillery unit of the 36th Armored Division, now commanded by Moshe Levi. He dropped an order on me: Camp Keren is passed to the 411th. You keep wandering.

This was an unpleasant hit. I had grown used to complete independence, and even during the war, where I was officially under Benny Arad, commander of the 212th Artillery Division, he refrained from ordering me around. But all arguments were to no avail. I knew that Moshe Levi was not the type to be impressed by SPHs in direct fire, and we were exiled to Camp Yoav. At Qala'a, north of the Waset Junction, there was an empty field, where we used to set up the battalion's camp for training. We now had to turn this compound into a home camp, and my deputy bat-com Shmil Golan, along with HQ company commander, Eliezer "Lazar" Ben-Mordechai, and Kopler who replaced him, began wandering all over the Golan. Every train car they found was tied to a half-track's winch, loaded onto a truck, and repurposed at Camp Yoav as a kitchen or a shower, in an effort to provide the soldiers with reasonable conditions in the harsh winter.

One day they were wandering around Yos Eldar's battalion, and while they were dragging a shower car along the muddy ground, two naked soldiers jumped out frightened in their birthday suits, covered in nothing but soap. Shmil took it in stride: "On orders of the Northern Command General, I'm taking the shower to Qala'a," he informed them. "You can finish your shower quickly and get out of the car, or come with us."

Yanush, who was meanwhile appointed as Division Commander, accompanied by Rami Dotan, the man who left me with the 404th's

SPHs in the field when I was a battery commander, arrived of course to tour the renovated camp. "Rami," Yanush said following the tour, "the 405th is the 7th Brigade's fourth battalion."

In their internal language, this sufficed. While the visit was still in process and immediately following, we began to receive trucks full of goodies: three pairs of work fatigues per soldier, overalls, train cars and movable structures. Everything we asked for – and everything we didn't ask for.

Winter on the Golan Heights

It was horribly cold in the enclave in the winter of '74. The snow piled up seven feet high in some places, and we had to find a response, for during the daytime while the batteries were in the field, the crews would sit in the SPHs with their helmets and vests on, and the men would freeze.

Before I came to the 405th, I delved deep into the study of the SPH. I had diligently read the manual in English, poured over the drawings, and now I recalled that the SPH had built-in heating. When the guns "made Aliyah" from the United States, the Chief Ordnance Officer decided to disconnect these heating furnaces, for fear of malfunctions, but in the situation we found ourselves in that winter, they suited us to a tee.

I ordered Nehemiah Arody, my Ordnance officer, to connect the furnaces. He understood the situation and didn't even think to ask the COO's permission, and not only did the fighters get to warm up, even the command post personnel would crowd into the guns to thaw.

Meanwhile a winter coat panic broke out in Israel. Someone – perhaps a concerned mother – asked why the combat troops don't have "dubonim" ("teddy bears") – the IDF's trademark winter coat – and headline-seeking politicians latched on to the issue. On one of those days, there was a visit of soldiers commended for excellence at the Knesset. Avi Yardeni, a leading crew commander with battery C, represented the 405th Battalion... wearing a dubon.

"How come you have a dubon," Knesset Member Shulamit Aloni asked him sarcastically, "What, are you an officer?"

"In our battalion," Yardeni answered her, "the fighters get them first."

As I mentioned, from time to time, we were required to send a battery to Biranit, on the Lebanese border. The battery would deploy within the camp, fire at terrorist targets, and provide cover fire for raids into Lebanon.

The commander of the regional brigade was Shai Tamari, and one winter day, in the midst of the attrition period, I received awful news from his HQ: An SPH blew up and troopers were killed.

I drove to Biranit quickly and was appalled at what I saw: The SPH was blown up. Its breech block was blown some twenty meters backward and lodged in one of the structures, and worst of all – two men had been killed: Nissim Vashdi, a veteran crew commander and a bold fighter, who had been through the entire war with us, and a young recruit, Shalom Vidal. Luckily for us, they were operating as a two-man team: A crew commander aiming, along with a fighter loading and firing.

What happened was that Moshe Levi, who still hadn't been weaned of the Corps' veteran officers' frugality when it came to the artillery fighters, ordered to collect abandoned or scattered ammunition from all over the Golan Heights, and bring it to the battalions without sending it, as was customary, to a munitions base for testing and preparation for use. This was how a charge of propellant explosives for the 203mm shells, which look identical to short-range charges for the 155mm shells, arrived at the battalion. This was American ammunition, still without IDF markings, and the crew members mistook them as intended for the 155mm gun they were operating. These propellants were designed to launch 200-lb shells, twice the weight of the 155mm shells, and the frugality exacted a heavy and painful price: The lives of two troopers and the destruction of the cannon.

"Arie, Where Are You Going?"

The war of attrition in the Golan continued, as mentioned above, from the end of the Yom Kippur War, on October 22nd, 1973, until the signing of the separation of forces agreement, on May 31st, 1974. Over seven straight months of fighting, with many losses and in harsh conditions, had the artillery burden falling mostly on the shoulders of the 405th Battalion. The 334th, which began the attrition with a short range of under 10 km with 160mm mortars, took part in the fighting within the constraints of their range, and then underwent a retraining to a 175mm battalion, and was off the fighting troop count for the duration of their retraining. The newly formed 411th Battalion only joined the fighting in February 1974.

I almost always stayed on call for the weekend with Yos Eldar, the deputy brigadier, and went on leave on the weekends when the brigadier stayed behind. But Yanush would allow me to go on leave only following an exhaustive debriefing – even when it was unnecessary, as the brigade sat at Nafah, served as a divisional reserve force, and had no role beyond this or that day battle. A countdown chart to the next, imminent war hung on the wall of his office, clearly indicating the commander's spirit. When I left home late one Friday evening, because the fire wouldn't stop along the line, Yanush demanded a replacement artillery commander. The line wasn't under the 7th Brigade's responsibility, but he called me first thing Saturday morning, saying "They sent me some reservist… I ask him who's firing and where, and he tells me 'Red 1234.' Who is this moron replacing you? I don't understand a word he says." This repeated itself time and again, I kept leaving late on Friday night and getting phone calls from Yanush the next morning – until I decided to switch weekends and simply stay with him on brigadier weekends. Toward the end of '74, Yanush was promoted to brigadier general and appointed commander of the 36th Division, the "Ga'ash" Division, as it was officially known. Ori Or, who had excelled during the war as commander of the 679th Reserve Brigade, and had effectively saved Camp Nafah, was appointed as Brigadier of the 7th. I knew Ori from back when he was a company commander with the 82nd Battalion, but parting with Yanush was not just parting with a brave fighter and an admired commander, but parting with a colleague with whom I had shared dark hours, and a close friend.

As I already mentioned, I filled three roles concurrently – bat-com of the 405th, artillery commander of the 7th Armored Brigade, and artillery commander for the Golani and Paratroopers' Brigades – all this with the battalion in need of rebuilding, the Boaz battery in need of reforming, intake of new long-barreled SPHs, to get settled at Qala'a, to interview officers, and also carry out missions on the line, in a period of continuous fire and incidents. Added to all this was an assignment that kept me up at night – meeting with bereaved families and the eulogies I gave at the ceremonies marking the transfer of the fallen soldiers' bodies to permanent burial sites.

Yanush knew all this, and helped me as much as he could, but always wanted me close to him. Even when fatigue overtook him and he was napping, if I wanted to tiptoe out of his room, he would open his eyes and ask, "Arie, where are you going?" So it was in the attrition and all the other roles I filled beside him – from the Northern Command Chief Artillery Officer, through corps fire support commander during the Peace for Galilee War, right up until just before his death. Even then, late at night, when I would want to leave his room after a long talk, he would suddenly open his eyes like always and ask: "Arie, where are you going?"

From Yanush to Ori Or

The farewell meeting for Yanush was scheduled for Friday at noon, and there for the first time I saw him sunk in melancholy, feeling like parting with the brigade was like severing one of his limbs. He refused to speak, parted with us wordlessly, choking, and when he left, before anyone caught him shedding a tear, heaven forbid, we were left facing the new brigadier. We very quickly learned that Ori Or was the complete opposite of Yanush.

"What's planned for Sunday?" he asked deputy brigadier Eldar.

"A day battle at Umm Butna, in the south of the enclave, under brigade purview," Eldar replied.

"Is everyone ready?"

"Yes."

"Fine," said Ori, "I'm going home. I'll come straight to the command post on Sunday morning. If I'm late, start the battle without me."

He got in his car and drove off – and the brigade HQ was left in shock. Yanush used to go over the orders with each tank commander four times before a day battle, debrief everyone to the last detail, and recon the area. In short, Yanush used to prepare for battle even when it was only the destruction of a small number of targets. Ori nonchalantly delegated, displaying complete confidence in those under his command. However, there is also a flipside to this, a laxity which may invite malfunctions.

Sunday morning arrived, we went off to the day battle, and Ori arrived at the last moment to take command. We stood with the APCs at the command post – myself a bit to the side, apart, on a higher vantage point to observe the artillery fire, when suddenly I saw a "flock" of Malyutka missiles approaching, with one of them headed straight for me.

Malyutka missiles move slowly, 115 meters per second. I saw it approaching and kept observing the targets, telling myself as I always did while at war: Before it arrives, I'll tell the driver to back up down the rear slope.

The Malyutka indeed arrived. I ordered the driver to "back up," but no response. The internal comms were cut off for some reason. I tried in vain to reach the driver, and only by luck did the missile explode a meter before the APC.

Ceasefire – and an End

On May 31st, Israel and Syria signed a separation of forces agreement. In addition to prisoner exchanges, it included Israel's withdrawal from the enclave, the size of which was some 400 sq. km, and the edge of which was only 40 km from Damascus, concession of another small area near Quneitra, and creation of a UN-controlled buffer zone, on the Syrian side of the new border line. Each side was allowed to keep 75 tanks and 6,000 troops in the ten km adjacent to the separation line.

There wasn't a single undamaged artillery piece in the battalion after eight straight months of fighting, and there was no escape from refurbishing the pieces. The entire Kurdani ordnance workshop was deployed next to us at Qala'a, and its men began to repair and refit each piece for service.

This was also the time to look back. The battalion had performed wondrously during the attrition period, with enormous output, with courage and devotion of all fighters and commanders. My demands for professionalism, my insistence on the smallest of details, my perfectionism to the last iota, and my striving for perfection, which all are part of my nature, often made it difficult for the officers and especially the battery commanders, but I have no doubt that it was for the best.

Battery commanders Nadav Amir, Yossi Koren, and Israel Kigel, HQ company commander Lazar and Kopler after him, and even deputy bat-com Golan – they all cursed me silently, or in conversations with one another, and so it happened that the battery commanders asked to speak with me one day. Amir, professional and eloquent, said: "Bat-com, try to be less rigid and more open to talking with us. We believe that it will make it easier for us to do our jobs – which is hard as it is."

I took their words to heart – after all, I love them like a father loves his children – and began acting differently, but it was artificial and alien to my nature. After two weeks, Amir approached me again on behalf of his colleagues, and said: "Bat-com, it's just not you. Go back to your normal behavior."

Either way, shortly afterward I was informed that my time in the post was over. After less than a year, most of which was spent in nonstop fighting, I was sent to command the basic course at Shivta, which is in effect the artillery officers' course.

The war and the attrition period following it were a true test for the abilities of the battalion's fighters. The difficulties we faced even during the prolonged attrition, still outnumbered by the Syrian artillery and in rough living conditions, in the harsh winter of 1974, along with the grief for fallen friends, the funerals, the visits by the bereaved families, bringing them to the Golan Heights to see where their loved ones fell – all these created a pressure cooker. I decided to throw a party to mark the end of the war, combined with my farewell to the battalion I loved so.

The spot chosen was the Lido restaurant in Tiberias, and Kopler received instructions from me: A party for the entire battalion, save for a few sentries who would remain at Qala'a, and a royal feast, with five different meat entrees. This was the heyday of Israel's beloved pop/rock group Kaveret. I asked the Education Corps to get me Kaveret, only Kaveret... and Kaveret showed up. Some of the band members forgot that they had come up in the military entertainment troupes, and pouted upon realizing that they were going to perform in the open on the lake shore, but within two songs, they caught the excitement of the troops, felt the energy flow, and wouldn't come off the stage. When they got through their entire repertoire – they started over. (Most prominent among them in his good cheer was virtuoso guitarist Yitzhak Klepter, who had become a friend even beforehand, performing for us often during the attrition period). The young ladies of Tiberias joined the party with gusto. One of them even made quite forward advances at Moshe Levi, commander of the division artillery, and he was quite embarrassed, but no further incident occurred.

The 7th Armored Brigade bid me farewell in a ceremony at the brigade HQ. Ori, the brigadier, waxed in detail, in warm and moving terms, on the part played by "the brigade's fourth battalion" in the fighting, spoke of our part, the men of the artillery HQ, in the activities of the brigade during the war and attrition, and in honor of all these, I received the brigade shield, created by Shlomo Cohen, the devoted brigade adjutant.

"We'll Hang It"

In addition to the procedure, whereby on IDF Memorial Day, each fallen soldier's grave is visited by a fighter filling the same role, I also initiated visits to the homes of all the fallen men of the 405th. We gave each family a shield with the name of the fallen soldier and the battalion's logo, to be placed alongside the plaque of rank and decoration insignia given by the IDF.

Eighteen years had passed since I had left the battalion, and in the course of my intensive activity as field operations coordinator for Yitzhak Rabin in the 1992 elections, I went with a group of leaders and influencers from home to home in Likud strongholds, in an attempt to display the abilities and leadership of the IDF's leader in the Six-Day War, and get them to switch their votes from Likud to Labor.

One day, we knocked on a door in an apartment building in Ramla, in one of the most hardcore Likud neighborhoods – the ones I loved visiting the most. When the door opened, we were greeted by an older woman with a younger woman beside her. I introduced myself as being there on behalf of the Labor party, and from the other room came an angry voice: "Throw them out."

Usually we were invited to sit down, given something to drink, and were heard out. This time we encountered unusual treatment, but the apartment seemed familiar.

I noticed the 405th's shield out of the corner of my eye, just as the older woman embraced me. "Bat-com," she said excitedly. The man who had been angry a moment before emerged from the room. His brother had fallen in the War of Attrition as a fighter in the 405th, and the older woman was their mother. He too now greeted us with hugs and kisses. All three listened to what we had come to say, and to my surprise the brother said: "Bat-com, tell us what you want – and we'll do it."

I asked my companions to bring a large poster with Rabin's image, and said: "How about hanging this from your porch?"

The guy looked at me like I had sprouted antennae from my head, but said "We'll hang it."

SHIVTA – CAPITAL OF THE ARTILLERY CORPS

Commanding the Basic Course in Venice

"Shivta is like Venice," Dr. Meir Rakutz, the dentist at Nafah, said to me when I came to him for a final treatment before leaving the Golan Heights.

"Why Venice?" I asked, "I don't remember Shivta like that at all from the squad commanders' course I did there in '61."

"Very similar," Meir'ke replied, "Sewage canals with a few structures in between."

It's hard to recall today, but Rakutz's description was not far from the truth. Bahad 9 had gone down to Shivta following a brave decision by Amos Baram, its commander, and Nati Sharoni, the Chief Artillery Officer, when the base only hosted the Armored Corps' officers' course. The Nahal's squad commanders' course had long since moved to Mt. Hazon, near the city of Karmiel in the Lower Galilee. The Armored Corps' officers' course was shut down upon the outbreak of the Yom Kippur War, and Shivta only contained a few structures from the 1950s, with pitiful infrastructure and minuscule capacity. Sharoni wanted me to deliver the basic corps specialization course to cadets with platoon commander pins, who had just graduated the basic officers' course, but would not be awarded an officer's rank until they completed the corps specialization.

It was a long course, lasting six months, and was challenging and grueling to the extreme, with people dropping out or being dismissed despite graduating Bahad 1. It included math and trigonometry studies, and required superb orientation skills for long nighttime navigations, and leading cannon batteries in mountainous or desert terrain, familiarity with the infantry and armored forces, specializing in operating and ranging, long treks on foot, in APCs, in tanks, ranging from choppers and light aircraft, all before we even get to leadership and people skills. The cadets were tested every day for six months. The course produced business magnates – from the late Eli Horowitz, founder of Teva, Dan and Gad Propper from Israeli food conglomerate Osem, hi-tech entrepreneur, businessman, and philanthropist Moshe Yannai, to Elbit CEO Bezalel "Butzi" Machlis, Rafael Advanced Weapons System CEO Yoav Har-Even, and the list goes on and on.

Usually a class of the basic course numbered from thirty to fifty cadets, but when I arrived at Shivta, in August of 1974, I found an exceedingly crowded class. In addition to a platoon of Artillery Corps cadets, who came for the regular course, I got three platoons of reserve infantry officers, lieutenants and captains, who came to undergo conversion to the Artillery Corps, platoons of squad commanders and command post sergeants, also reservists, who volunteered to undergo an officers' course following the Yom Kippur War, and a platoon of ROTC graduates of Bahad 1, intended to serve in technical roles in the Air Force, Navy, and Maintenance Corps, and were trained by us for a secondary posting with the Artillery Corps. Each platoon received its own tailor-made training program. The shortest one – for the reservists – lasted three months, and regular training lasted for six months.

The instructors were volunteers – reservists such as Ofer Rabinowitz, who was an FSO at Hermon, was badly wounded, and barely survived, and Aviel Ron, a revered battery commander at the 402nd Battalion in the Attrition and Yom Kippur wars in the Sinai, who became a revered instructor at the course (Aviel, who designed the Israeli SPH known as "Sholef," and who later became the director of the Israel Mapping Center, was killed in 2002 in the terror attack at the Matza restaurant in Haifa, along with his two children). Instructing alongside the reservists were career military battery commanders, who had just recently fought in the Sinai or the Golan, such as Yossi Koren from the 405th, Yossi Zuta from the 402nd, Yossi Goral from the 55th, and Gidi Lefever from the 334th.

This was certainly an unusual mission. The infrastructures on the base were rickety, as mentioned above, as were the Bahad 9 logistics infrastructures. The career military men were used to being home every evening, there was a glaring shortage of maintenance men for the M-50 and M-109 guns, the vehicles were old, and many of the trucks and command cars were broken down.

On the other hand, the Artillery Corps entered a dramatic makeover. Two hundred advanced M-109 cannons were purchased, and they gradually began to arrive in Israel. Their number later grew to 350, eventually reaching 600, and it became necessary to convert all the 120mm battalions and the battalions of various captured weapons, and establish new 155mm battalions. The officer corps were the cream of the crop, and it was clear to me that if we trained professional and determined leaders, they were bound to lead the newly converted units optimally, and prove themselves equal to the massive task.

A Live Fire Exercise With ... Fire

As a final exercise for the basic course, I initiated a large-scale live fire exercise, in which the cadets played the FSO and FO roles, and the instructors played Armored Corps' bat-coms and company commanders. To that end, I bartered for a platoon of tanks from a standing battalion that practiced in the Shivta fire zones. I gave them fire support for their exercise, and in exchange they gave me tanks for the FSOs and FOs for my exercise.

In addition, we also enlisted the Artillery Corps' equivalent of the squad leaders' course, the designated support battery for ranging and fire exercises and the artillery professions branch, and allocated 600 shells for the exercise.

The exercise was a masterclass. It taught and practiced the cadets in integrating in the maneuvering force and using sense combined with fire and movement. The entire exercise was mounted on tanks, APCs, and half-tracks, and all the cadets listened to all the channels. The motto was to practice a rolling barrage, in accordance with a procedure developed at the Chief Artillery Officer's HQ as a solution for the problem of short- and long-range anti-tank missiles.

Suddenly, in the dead of night, Nati Sharoni showed up. He came to see what we were doing, because they told him Shivta was a mess. With him came Amos Baram, the base commander, and they watched the exercise at dawn, with Sharoni – as he himself told me later – unable to figure out how we managed to produce a large-scale exercise with tanks, hundreds of shells, dozens of vehicles, including an armored fighting vehicle, all with the meager means available at Shivta – and how everything went like clockwork. He was overjoyed, and Baram was happy that first-hand evidence refuted the malicious rumors.

As always, I combined "country knowledge" in the basic course too. I planned a series of observations and navigations, which included identifying distant targets in daytime and night, nighttime navigations, and quick orientation in the field. The series was in effect a week on command cars along the western border – Mt. Lotz, Cave Mount, Mt. Sagi – and from there to Mitzpe Ramon and back to Shivta.

The series cost a lot of broken and scarred command cars, and every time we went on a similar series afterward, maintenance officer Yossi Dvora would wake from his nap during the commanders' meeting to bitterly protest. In 2023, during a large meeting on Zoom, initiated by Yoav Avneon, about the Yom Kippur War, one of the cadets at the course and later a travel guide and historian, one of the participants, Tzvika Tzuk, who during the course was the "country knowledge" instructor at Bahad 1, told how he helped me construct the navigations and observations series, and even sent me a document titled "Instructing command car navigation at Mt. Negev."

This document included dozens of points to which the cadets navigated, such as Nitzana Stream, Hursha Stream, Mt. Hursha, Mt. Harif, Ma'aleh Arod, the Oded Wells, Ardon Stream, Nekarot Stream, Nekarot Fort, Ein Yahav, Ein Hatzeva, Zion Stream, Hor Hahar, Sde Boker, Zin Stream, Hatzerot Israel, Ruth Stream, Borot Kedem, the rock drawings on the way to Kadesh Barnea, the "carpentry shop," Ein Rachel, and on and on.

Following was a detailed bibliography and notes such as:

— At coordinate 10480178 there is a large compound marked on the map, which Dr. Aharoni believes to be Hor Hahar (See "Hor Hahar," pp 104-106.)
— At coordinate 10480143 there is a fortress with a casemate wall from the Israelite period, directly tied to Borot Kedem (Photo No. XX.)
— At coordinate 10370097 we turn south from the Matnan Stream and travel along the IDF pre-1967 patrol road, along the border set in 1906. Southwest of the junction, in the wadi bed, we'll find a varied garden, growing on an agricultural terrace that was built hundreds of years ago, and worked on up until recently.
— A visit to the water pool, 250 meters south of Nekarot Fort, is not to be missed.

And there were some amusing incidents. In one class, in the cold Shivta winter, a platoon of reserve infantry officers went on an SPH crew practice in the training yard at the center of the base. The orders were to have ammunition vests, weapons, and steel helmets. The infantry officers didn't understand where they found themselves – first of all because of "Shivta shock," added to being torn from civilian life, work, wives, families, and studies – on top of having served for six months on an emergency callup, during and after the war. So what are these track-mounted moving houses, with us accustomed to the open spaces and fighting on foot? And then they want us to come to practice in the middle of the base like we're going into battle? In short, they decided to express their discontent by going out into the yard in thermal underwear, with ammunition vests, weapons, and helmets, but without uniforms. Someone called me to the yard, and I was already thinking up appropriate reprimands, court-martials, and brig sentences, but the platoon instructor, Ron Aviel, motioned me to keep quiet. He went through the drills as though he hadn't noticed the odd attire. The base personnel gathered to watch the strange display, and base commander Bar-David was called to the scene. The base was bitterly cold, the sky had clouded over and a drizzle had begun to fall; and Aviel practiced with them like nothing was out of the ordinary, until the big heroes approached him diffidently and asked to put on uniforms. He pretended to be surprised and refused, and only following some begging, and seeing their lips turn blue and their hands shake, did he relent and allow them to run back to quarters and get dressed.

Fire Discipline Through a Linguistics Lab

The basic course's command group was very creative, and the addition of reserve platoon instructors like Aviel and Ofer Rabinowitz added civilian smarts to the mix. An example of this was the fire discipline, meaning the amalgam of complex orders on the radio, which are supposed to briefly describe a changing operational situation, as well as matching orders, translated into artillery operational lingo. For instance, the type of ammunition, fire rate, and targets. Needless to say, clear and lucid radio discipline is the basis of communication between the firing and forward echelons, and a precondition for fast and precise execution of any mission. At one of the discussions, I suggested that we use the linguistics laboratory at Ben Gurion University, in light of my own experience at such a lab during my studies at Tel Aviv University. The lab consisted of acoustically isolated stations, with partitions between each user, which allowed self-practice on one hand, and class-wide activities on the other. We contacted the university president's chambers, and they were thrilled to cooperate with us in this experiment. We drove the cadets to several fire discipline lessons in Beersheba, and practicing at the linguistics lab saved a lot of time, and resulted in a better understanding of the processing procedure of an operational situation for an order – and of giving the order in a clear and understandable way. The ability of the instructors to enter each cadet's audio input and output system, to listen, comment, and correct, significantly advanced the fire discipline practices and operational understanding, and the creation of a reliable common language between the firing and forward echelon. During the time allocated for self-practice, each cadet could listen to the recorded orders they gave, identify their errors, and correct what was needed by the next order. In time, as commander of Shivta, I institutionalized the fire discipline coach, and we purchased a linguistics lab for the new officers' instruction branch. It was part of an array of coaches, and cadets from all branches could practice on their own there in their free time or when studying for tests.

What Can Be Learned From the Cavalry's Indian Wars

In a sharp shift, immediately after completing my term as commander of the artillery officers, I was sent thousands of miles west of Shivta to an advanced artillery course, at the United States Army Field Artillery School, at Fort Sill, Oklahoma. I flew there with the family, and I'll devote a separate chapter to that year and its lessons.

The study method there included a significant amount of self-study and practice, which was done in their great library. Aside from thousands of books, it had many video tapes, which illustrated clearly how to carry out each action, and the logic behind the processes.

I spent much time on learning the training methods and their simulation, and when I returned to Israel, I brought many tapes with me, which served as the nucleus of the Shivta TV library. I also founded the CCTV section, and we created our own films – for self-study and as an introduction to lessons.

We still weren't rich enough for individual VCR machines, but the CCTV section created original instruction films, which were shown in classes, as were recordings from Fort Sill, and instructors could come to the section and prepare for lessons with the tapes.

One of the examples was a tape that explained how to pinpoint enemy batteries by examining the craters of shells they fired, what's known in the artillery lingo as "crater analysis." The tape begins like a Western: A cavalry unit is attacked by Indians. One of the cavalrymen is miraculously saved from an arrow shot, which misses his eye and lodges in a nearby tree, and by the stuck arrow, the rider identifies where it was fired from. He draws his pistol, looks down the sights like Clint Eastwood in the direction from which the arrow was shot, and hits the Indian.

Then the tape continues, showing a crater created by an enemy shell, and explains how to calculate the azimuth from which the shell was fired. Crosschecking the azimuth with the estimated location of the enemy battery, with the aid of the target list, which is a must-have in any artillery command center, allows the observation post to seek the enemy battery by the resulting direction, or to fire without observation of the location.

The attitude of Israeli cadets to courses abroad, and the U.S. in particular, varies by the individual. Some see the course as an interlude of rest, spending time with the family, and travel, while others try to get the most out of the course and derive professional benefit from it. I tried to combine the two, but always made sure to keep the studies and success at the course as the top priority, and I'm not ashamed to say that I cracked the books till late at night. Before exams, I would show up at the base on weekends as well, to practice what we had studied over and over.

The effort invested definitely paid off. I graduated with honors, and was asked to lecture about the Artillery Corps' role in the Yom Kippur War. I believe that I contributed to improving the reputation of Israelis at Fort Sill, and most importantly – as commander of Shivta, I immediately applied much of what I learned.

How I Didn't Get the 282nd Division Artillery

Toward the end of the course, Nati Sharoni arrived at Fort Sill, at the head of a delegation of chief corps officers, along with the Armored Corps' Commander, Musa Peled, Infantry Corps Commander, Dan Shomron, and others. Sharoni stayed at my house, and asked to bring the officer who accompanied him on previous visits. Tamar made the finest Israeli delicacies, and at the end of the evening came dessert: Sharoni informed me that upon completion of the course, I would be appointed commander of the 282nd Division Artillery, the 36th Division's artillery unit, and my heart's desire.

I returned to Israel happy as a clam, but reality shattered my dreams. I learned that Aldo Zohar, my longtime friend, had been appointed commander of the 282nd Division Artillery.

"What's the meaning of this?" I asked Sharoni, "You sat in my house in Fort Sill and said that I'm getting the division."

Sharoni squirmed and said, "Arie'le, I want you next to me as corps staff ops officer. Don't worry, your day will come." He added words of encouragement that were mostly apologetics, but I turned a deaf ear. I resolved to leave the career military. I walked around the Chief Artillery Officer's HQ in flipflops, successfully passed the GMAT exam, with a view toward entering the Recanati School of Business Administration at Tel Aviv University, and decided to study for my master's degree during the three years I still owed the IDF.

But fate intervened, my brother-in-arms, Yanush Ben-Gal, who was assistant Chief Ops Officer at IDF HQ at the time, suffered deeply from the fact that he was in the "Kirya" compound in Tel Aviv, and not in the field, although he had been deeply involved in impressive operations such as the Entebbe hostage rescue. He fell ill, was hospitalized for lengthy tests at Tel Hashomer Hospital with fear of heart problems, and Sharoni was summoned to take his place as assistant chief ops officer. Avraham Bar-David was quickly appointed chief artillery officer, and I was appointed as commander of Shivta in his stead. This scrambled my academic plans and put an end to my flipflop staycation, but I got to fulfill one of the most fascinating roles of my career.

Saving Captain Zuta

Yossi Zuta, my beloved since he was an instructor under me at the artillery officers' course, had saved the life of Emannuel Sakel, batcom of the 52nd, in the Yom Kippur War. Zuta was the battalion's FSO, moving in a half-track behind Sakel's tank, when he noticed Egyptian commando fighters climbing on the tank from behind. He didn't hesitate, fired the 0.5 machine gun, took out the commando fighters and saved Sakel. Zuta was a leading platoon instructor at the officers' course I commanded. His professional requirements were strict, and he didn't hesitate to dismiss cadets despite the shortage in officers, and I often had to save cadets from his clutches who later became good commanders and even attained high rank.

He was appointed deputy bat-com of the 405th, but flipped over in the jeep he was driving along the oil route during a nighttime drill, and was rushed to Rambam Hospital in Haifa with a mortal head wound. There was fear of irrevocable damage.

I rushed to Rambam as though pursued by demons. Zuta was lying there motionless with his family beside him. A quick check revealed that the foremost expert in Israel on such injuries was Prof. Aaron Beller from Hadassa Hospital in Jerusalem, and despite the well-known resistance of doctors at any hospital to bring in an expert from a "competing" hospital, the Rambam physicians, who had already given up and pronounced Zuta a vegetable, agreed to let Beller come and examine him. But all this was on Saturday, and Beller refused to drive to Haifa. As the time element was critical, I called Nati Sharoni and asked for a chopper. I knew that Nati could requisition a chopper due to his position at IDF HQ, and he acquiesced instantly. Prof. Beller was airlifted from Jerusalem to Haifa and arrived at Zuta's bedside. He pricked Yossi's toe with a pin, and ruled: "He'll live and stand on his feet," and left the room. The sigh of relief could be heard throughout the medical center.

Eventually, after many long one-sided conversations with him by his bedside, Yossi opened his eyes. Family members told him what was new with his loved ones, I told him what we were up to at Shivta and how much we miss him, and following a long stay at the Beit Loewenstein rehabilitation hospital, he returned to normal functioning. I was already chief artillery officer by then, and I appointed Yossi Zuta as commander of the one-day training facility at Tzrifin. As expected, and with no allowances, he performed his duty in the best possible manner.

On Thin Ice With the Disappointed

I didn't have the necessary time served for the rank of colonel, and began my command of Shivta as a lieutenant colonel. I discovered that not much had changed in the past year in terms of the base infrastructures, while the tasks had doubled and tripled.

The unit training branch, which had been located at the Ovdat Rectangle, had also moved to Shivta. It set up in tents across the old access road, and it was determined that the branch commander would bear the rank of colonel, as he was in command of division artillery units, which were commanded by colonels as well. And so I found myself commanding Rami Ziv, who was older than me and outranked me, while he enjoyed the colonel's status symbol – a Volvo or an American-made personal car.

If that weren't enough, concurrent with the appointment as commander of Shivta, I was appointed commander of the 286th Reserve Division Artillery. The unit had just begun training, first battalion-wide exercises followed by a division-wide drill. I was tested as commander of the division artillery with Rami Ziv and Shimon Rom – two men disappointed by my appointment. I didn't let these background noises and status games divert me. Like all challenges I faced in the IDF, I was mission-focused – and the goal was to prepare the division artillery for war as I saw it. The intermediate goal was to pass the division-wide exercise with flying colors. In the intervals between the battalions training, in the scant free time I had left after nighttime drills, I began upgrading the corps' main instruction base according to my own lights and vision.

The 286th Division Artillery had not undergone a division-wide exercise until then, and this exercise was in fact a founding exercise. I decided to waste no time, and made sure to impart all components of the idea of artillery concentration, meaning firing in battalion and division-size concentrations, and other tactics, such as firing only salvos, from a single battery to multiple division artilleries, who fire with minimal registration fire in complete surprise. This has major significance in terms of initial shock and awe, with the enemy unprepared and sustaining massive casualties in the opening strike. We also imparted hasty movement in day or night, utilizing the improved abilities of the new SPHs, which were faster and more traversable than their predecessors, in order to make it to position in time, to quickly reach range for distant targets, and to create the ability to dominate broad sectors with fire, as well as position defense and direct fire.

The division artillery belonged to the 440th Armored Division, known as the "Tirans," and consisted of captured Soviet T-62 tanks, which had been upgraded and customized for the IDF with 105mm guns. The commander of the division, who was located in Rafah, was Baruch "Pinko" Harel. My deputy at the division artillery was Hersche'le – Yaakov Herschfinkel, nee Reshef, my good friend from the 404th and Bahad 9. The five bat-coms were excellent reservists. One of them, Chaim Adar, became a close friend, and the other officers were talented gunners, brimming with motivation.

A KGB Spy Driving the SPH

To Bar David's credit, he did an excellent job in assigning officers in the 286th Division Artillery, and I got excellent staff officers like intel officer Yossi Fruchtman, now a law professor, and staff ops officer, Menachem Fisch, who went on to a glorious career as a mathematician. And yet, since this was the unit's founding exercise, we were short on manpower. Particularly scarce were tank drivers, as they were specifically trained on the 155mm SPH. The driving course at Shivta turned out to be unjustifiably long, and indeed I changed it following the exercise, but at the time we suffered from a short headcount. Adar's battalion, for instance, had eighteen SPHs and only sixteen tank drivers. One of these, Shabtai Kalmanowitz, would much later turn out to be a KGB spy, but would remain a celebrity thanks to his connections, and the fortune he'd amassed somehow or other.

At the start of the exercise, the chief artillery officer called me to release Kalmanowitz from duty. I reported directly to Bar-David. he was a Brig.-Gen. while I was a Lt. Col. and on probation, but I wasn't quick to comply with the order. I explained to him that doing so would leave Adar's battalion with only fifteen SPHs, instead of the eighteen called for by the corps' new formation, which he himself had initiated. He realized that I was right, and backed down from the demand.

Or not. Minutes later an urgent phone call came at the base commander's office for Chaim Adar. He came running, and an authoritative voice ordered him: "Release Shabtai Kalmanowitz from reserve service."

"Who are you?" Chaim asked.

"Major General Moshe Nativ, Chief Personnel Officer," the voice replied.

Adar was not overly impressed. His senior role at the Defense Ministry had left him indifferent to rank and seniority, so he replied: "Major General Nativ, can you drive a tank?"

Nativ, who took pride in his Armored Corps past, prior to becoming an adjutant, answered: "Of course, I was a tank driver,"

"If so," said Chaim, "please come down and replace Kalmanowitz, and if you could, bring two more tank drivers with you, to ring us to full strength."

Nativ broke down too. Kalmanowitz remained in Shivta until the end of his allotted reserve service.

"Team Yoel"

The need to fix the weaknesses revealed in the war spurred an incessant desire to come up with tactical solutions to strategic problems. One of these stemmed from the fact that the enemy's artillery outnumbered us tenfold in number of barrels, critically harming the ability of the maneuvering forces to carry out their missions. Furthermore, according to a study conducted after the war among the IDF's wounded, it turned out that 50% of the wounded among the maneuvering forces were hit by enemy artillery.

Our leapfrogging procedures were improved following the Sinai War of Attrition, we lived and breathed counter-battery fire, but the maneuvering forces were mortally hit by enemy artillery. The Air Force, which was supposed to handle the problem, utterly failed and was busy licking its wounds, and the bottom line was that we were required to solve the problem within the corps' rebuilding process.

I tried to find a creative solution to the problem, and the solution I came up with along with Fisch and Fruchtman was trailblazing: To build an independent force, which not only all existing location devices be subject to it, but firing units would also be allocated to it. These units would be under separate command at all times, with the force commander authorized to act independently. The moment he located an enemy battery, he would engage it immediately and wouldn't have to await an order or confirmation. In short – you see it, you shoot it.

The force we built was called "Team Yoel," after its commander, Yoel Arditi, who was concurrently commander of the division's 160mm M-66 heavy self-propelled mortars. He was assigned all location means available – from the "juggler" (a British Cymbeline mortar-locating radar) through the "flyer," (a doppler radar, used both for ranging and detecting launches), long-range observations by the division's location battalion, aerial observations when possible, and of course, the reports of the FSOs and FOs. He received one of the four 155mm battalions, with the hope that the battalion of 175 SPGs, should we get one, would also become an integral part of "Team Yoel."

Later on, as a reservist, serving as the artillery commander of the 446th Corps, I developed the "Manog" – an acronym standing for "Corps targets and counter-battery fire center," to which the long-range 175mm battalions were subjected, along with a battalion of "Haviv" rockets, which proved their monumental capabilities in destroying the Syrian 130mm battalion on the shore of Lake Qaraoun in the Peace for Galilee War. In a large IDF-wide exercise, this mechanism received full and independent authorization to engage and destroy enemy artillery.

But there was a fly in the ointment. I forgot that the new IDF Chief of Staff was Moshe Levy, who viewed Yanush, the Corpus Commander, and myself, the Corpus Artillery Commander, the way a bull views a waving red cloth. He rained fire and brimstone down on me, declared that it was the height of folly to deploy artillery like that, and ruled that division commanders should decide how, why, and when to employ guns. Immediately upon the end of his term, operational logic prevailed once again, and the idea of the "Fire Dome" and fire centers is fully implemented in today's IDF.

Forming a staff

Back again to 1974: The division artillery exercise ended with great success. Chief of Staff Motta Gur came for a visit and made it clear that he was pleased with Bar-David's recommendation to appoint me commander of Shivta. At the conclusion of my talk with him, before my appointment, The Chief of Staff's chief of staff Haggai Regev, my friend from the 7th Armored Brigade and a man with a keen sense of humor, wrote a summary of the meeting which read as follows: "Will receive a division artillery and be principal of the Shivta school."

I don't know what exactly brought about my appointment, bypassing other, more veteran and higher-ranking candidates. Was it Nati Sharoni's commitment? Was it the glowing letter of recommendation, gushing with superlatives, sent by our military attaché in Washington, Major General Avraham 'Bren' Adan, after I had finished the course at Fort Sill with flying colors? And perhaps the longstanding acquaintance with Avraham Bar-David, who appointed me artillery commander of the 7th in the war and never regretted it? Either way, I had received a fascinating and challenging position, which provided me with endless opportunities to show creativity and initiative.

There was much work to be done, and immediately upon conclusion of the exercise, I began manning the staff. My deputy was Uppo, Eli Barak, now my good friend. But our relationship got off to a poor start. In typical fashion, I showered him with a barrage of orders and instructions, and Uppo quickly brought me up short. "Listen," he told me, "I'm not your slave. You want to work [together] properly? Treat me accordingly."

His direct response, delivered in rough language, appealed to me. From that moment, we bonded in true friendship, which peaked during the Peace for Galilee War, when Uppo was commander of the 215th Division Artillery, a warrior and commander and in effect, a linchpin at the heart of the 162nd Division's command.

The second most senior person in any instructional base is the CI – the Chief Instructor. I decided to appoint a new CI, and chose Lieutenant Eliezer Hemeli, an industry and management engineer by trade, who was a platoon instructor at the basic course when I commanded it, then was discharged and became the Eilot Regional Council's engineer in Israel's southeastern prairie, aka the "Arava." I approached him, and he was persuaded to join the career military as Chief Instructor at Shivta – with the rank of lieutenant but a Lt. Colonel's pay. Hemeli, a veteran of the 334th Battalion, was the man I had turned to in desperate pleas for light at the Valley of Tears – and now he came through for me a second time.

I informed the serving CI, Alex Buchs, a very smart kibbutznik who had instructed me at the basic course, but who had poor people skills, that he was ending his term in the post, and told him who was replacing him. He was outraged. "How does a young lieutenant replace a Lt. Colonel in such an important post?" he asked. I explained the best I could, but Alex took offense and stormed out.

As Maintenance Officer, I appointed the supremely capable Chaim Maimon. We had butted heads more than once in the past, but I knew that Maimon was the man best suited to Shivta. I knew his total loyalty to any assignment, and was convinced of his ability to run the logistics of a multi-headed monster like Shivta.

The new Ordnance Officer was Haim Schneiderman, now a professor at Bar-Ilan University. The branch commanders were determined by the Chief Artillery Officer, and we received an excellent basic course commander, in David Oron, a veteran of the 405th who came to Shivta following a term as bat-com of the 411th. Rami Ziv, the bat-com of the 403rd and Dan Shomron's artillery commander in the Yom Kippur War, was the unit training branch commander. Despite the problematic situation, with Ziv having aspired to be appointed commander of

Shivta and was disappointed that I had leaped in front of him, I knew that he was professional, strict, and a responsible officer.

The Crime ("Throw Them Out,") and Punishment (a Hearing With Raful)

Shivta was in pandemonium at the end of the division's artillery exercise, which was in effect my first day as commander of Shivta. The reservists vanished with the wind, the pieces had to be repaired, cleaned, and prepared for the next exercise – and just then, on Sunday morning, there landed in my office a group of some twenty officers and NCOs, all in spotless dress uniforms. "We're here for an HQ ordnance inspection."

"HQ ordnance inspection" was the horror of the IDF and its commanders. Bat-coms and brigadiers were deposed following such inspections, and it seemed cruel to me, to put it mildly, to carry out such an inspection on my first day in command of Shivta, with its vast amounts of equipment and the constant lack of professional personnel and career military staff, following the move from Tzrifin.

I called Bar-David. He, with his characteristic rolling r's, said: "Throw them out." I told the head of the delegation of doom: "You are not authorized to enter the base." But the officer in front of me was not impressed. He asked permission to use the phone, and within ten minutes, I received a phone call from the IDF's Chief Staff Ops Officer, Major General Yekutiel "Kuti" Adam. "Mizrachi," he said without preamble, "Have you lost your mind?"

Out of loyalty to my direct commander, I didn't hide behind Bar-David's "throw them out," and in any event, I couldn't get a word in edgewise. The inspection inspected on, and as was only to be expected under the circumstances, found countless faults. As a result of the morning incident, we received a nice round grade: 0. As a bonus, I was called along with Bar-David for a hearing and reprimand from Raful, the new IDF Deputy Chief of Staff, with Aryeh Levy, the former Chief Artillery Officer and now the Chief Logistics Officer, also present.

The meeting opened with an argument on a matter of principle between Raful and Levy, as to why the tank sheds at the emergency depots cost so much money. "I just built such a shed on my farm in Tel Adashim," said the deputy commander of the IDF. "Cost me 100 liras."

Levi tried to explain the difference to him, in vain. The debate between them went on and on, until they recalled that two others were in the room with them. Bar-David explained the situation of that Sunday, not quite owning up to his responsibility for "throw them out," but passionately pleading my case regarding the fact that the inspection was carried out the very day after a division-wide exercise, when obviously the equipment, and inventories alike would be in no shape to pass inspection. Then Raful turned to me. "What do you have to say?"

I said: "I plead guilty. I ask only one thing – another HQ ordnance inspection in three months, with a week's advance notice, if possible." Raful liked the response. He sent us packing and carried on his pointless argument with Levy.

Get 90 or Over, Get a "Regular"

On the way back south, having set myself up for another inspection, I recalled Yossi Peled. He told me that he once wanted, as commander of the immense training base Tze'elim, to construct a model of a Syrian embankment, and as he lacked the means, he recruited the entire base personnel to dig and build a model fortified Syrian embankment – after the fashion of seasonal roundups of hands for urgent farm tasks at Kibbutz Negba, where he was brought up. I said to myself, there are 3,000 people in Shivta on any given day. I'll shut down training for a week, and round up all the cadets and instructors for ordnance week to prepare for the inspection.

And so it was. When I received the inspection date, I divided responsibilities: the basic branch was in charge of the cannons, the command post sergeants branch got the armory, and so on. Each branch was assigned professionals from the relevant departments, and there was a carrot to balance the stick: I announced that whoever got a grade of 90 or better in the inspection would earn a "regular" (week-long) leave for their entire branch. Get 80-90 – receive an extended weekend. The method proved itself, and we received a rare grade of 90 overall.

That gave me an appetite, and the seminal event gave birth to another idea: We'll hold a week-long roundup like that once a quarter, and mix in maintenance of the living quarters, painting, whitewashing, creating a little garden next to each structure, and in-depth repairs of the bathrooms.

During one of these ordnance and maintenance weeks, a mess sergeant major arrived at Shivta, to serve as deputy to the camp's legendary mess 1st sergeant major, Jule. At that time, we still needed NCO support from career military men from the center of the country. And when the fellow walked into the kitchen, he saw someone standing on a ladder and priming the wall. "Where's the mess 1st sergeant major?" he asked, and Jule, from atop the ladder, replied: "That'd be me."

"What?" he asked, astonished. "The mess 1st sergeant major whitewashing a wall?"

"Yup," Jule replied. "This is Shivta."

From there we went on to a gardening and forestation project throughout the base, led by Chief Instructor Hemeli, after receiving saplings from the Jewish National Fund (which owns and runs many of the forests in Israel), as well as from a Kfar Saba classmate of mine, who now owned a large plant nursery in Beersheba. The operation kicked up a notch with a donation of drip irrigation systems from the Netafim factory in Kibbutz Hatzerim (and this little forest is verdant to this day.) But it was clear that whitewashing, painting, and planting trees wouldn't suffice, and that the base had to be cleaned, maintained, and groomed regularly as well. We prepared a binder of basecom (base commander) orders, and therein we detailed the regulations of life on work on base in short and succinct language.

Every Friday, we held a commander's review, and only that morning did I decide which branch I would visit. It was known in advance that the unlucky branch would have a bunch of soldiers restricted to base, missing out on their weekend leave a moment before heading out.

Protecting the Career Military Families

The method of bringing in NCOs from the center of the country broke down fairly quickly, and in order to meet the shortage, there was no alternative to recruiting career military men – mechanics, ordnance specialists, cooks, and so on. I decided to locate them among the conscripts nearing completion of their term of service, who knew the base well – and this was the right approach. We managed to sign up many of them, created a reliable and skilled maintenance cadre, and the massive recruiting required the instituting of leave procedures. I realized that it was important to provide the married career military men with a solid family foundation, and ensure a routine that wouldn't wear them down. To that end, and with the aid of the Chief Artillery Officer's HQ and the Southern Command HQ, we managed to get them free housing close to the base in Yeruham, Dimona, or Beersheba. The same thinking led me to require the career military men to leave the base at 17:00, save for Thursday, when we prepared all afternoon and evening for the next morning's commander's review. Even guys who until then preferred to linger on base and court the young female soldiers were forced to change their ways.

Stopping the Runs

Professor Joseph ("Yossi ") Klausner, one of Israel's premiere surgeons, served for many years as Chief of Surgery at Ichilov Hospital. Long before that, he was the resident physician and commander of the sick bay at Shivta, and married Daniella, the paramedic. With him at the sick bay were another doctor, a dentist who came from time to time, and a host of paramedics.

Like everyone who arrived at Shivta back then, the first thing I got was a terrible case of diarrhea, replete with stomach pain and vomiting. It happened to me at the divisional exercise, and upon returning to base, I called Yossi and his aide, who were always seen together. I asked Yossi why everyone has the runs here, and he explained with a veteran's grin that that's the way it is: All the newbies undergo a baptism by shit.

I had served in Shivta for a year before this, when I commanded the basic course, and as it wasn't like that back then, so I said: "It all stems from poor hygiene conditions and the lack of preventive medicine. From now on, the sick bay staff deals with this, first and foremost. Reviews of the latrines, reviews of the kitchens, daily inspections by the cooks, instilling personal hygiene habits among the staff and cadets, and instruction days for anyone coming to serve on base."

Then I added. "You have a week. If I have the runs for more than a week, you're both going to the brig for 35 days."

Yossi didn't lose his cool, although his aide blanched. "Sir," he said, "what happens if you get a runny nose?" We both smiled. My threat didn't scare him, but he knew what had to be done. It's just that until then, he didn't see it as part of his job. And that put an end to the Shivta diarrhea epidemic. Not completely, but it was no longer unavoidable doom either.

And to another anecdote, almost on the same topic.

"Air conditioners arrived!" Maimon, the maintenance officer, was the one to give me the news, and also announced proudly that technicians would come to install an air conditioner in the ramshackle old shack, a remnant from the Nahal 906 days, which housed my office. Every shell fired in the area would drop a plume of dust from the ceiling upon the occupants, and this led to short meetings and more time spent in the field. Now Maimon promised that at least it would be cool inside this historic relic.

The staff officers already imagined themselves soothed in cool streams of air, but I burst their bubble and told Maimon: "We're last in line. First of all, install air-conditioning in the classrooms and lecture halls, then the kitchen and mess halls, and only last in the offices of branch commanders and staff officers."

Maimon understood me, and the scorching summer of 1976 featured the possibility of studying under (relatively) comfortable conditions even at Shivta.

A Test of Leadership

"Scattering gravel," was how my deputy Uppo termed the manner in which Rami Ziv attempted time and again to undermine my authority. I have already mentioned that Ziv was a serious and talented officer, and that he was already a full-bird colonel when I was appointed commander of Shivta as a mere lieutenant colonel. Even when I got my colonel rank and the attendant status symbol, an American Plymouth Valiant car, his attitude remained unchanged.

At first, I walked on eggshells. I didn't want to hurt him and didn't want to make a fuss, but one Friday, Ziv didn't report to the commander's review. I usually didn't make a big deal about it, because he sometimes decided to go home on Thursday evenings. But it was the turn for my review of the unit training branch.

I found the branch officers' quarters dirty and disorderly. "Where are the officers?" I asked, and Uppo said: "Rami let them go home last night."

I ordered them brought back to base for the commander's review, even if it wouldn't be held till the evening, and only then would they be free to go home for Shabbat. Then I called Ziv. I told him: "Don't come to the base on Sunday. Go to CAO HQ for reassignment."

Immediately afterward, I informed Bar-David of my decision. He saw the problem and informed Ziv that as far as he was concerned, he was sacked. After a long hard talk, Ziv promised Bar-David to show loyalty and support, and in a conversation with me – still not back at Shivta – he admitted the error of his ways. He may have tried to excuse his conduct by claiming the officers' heavy workload during the week, but he was intelligent enough to admit his error and apologize.

BAHAD-TO-IMAGINATION MISSILE

Instruction, teaching, choosing learning methods, using coaches and simulators, training instructors, assessing instructors' quality, and choosing suitable instructors from a database – all these are particles of a whole training doctrine, which no one had taught me or the men around me. We had to reinvent the wheel, and just like with a startup – the higher your imagination soars, the better the results.

Furthermore, what you conceive of in your brain and create yourself charges you with energy, enthusiasm, and the joy of creation. And what was better than inventing instructions suited to Shivta, to the desert, to reservists, to Artillery Corps cadets, and to advanced courses.

The team that carried out the work in practice included Chief Instructor, Eliezer Hemeli, the creative Amos Avidan, Ron Krumer, and a few other officers, all ROTC men who had continued to the career military. We began by constructing a one-month instruction course, which every new instructor would be required to undergo. We followed up by setting strict standards for acceptance as instructors, decided to hold constant inspections in the classrooms, and decided that once every three months, we would announce who were the best-performing instructors. They would receive a red aiguillette and preferred service conditions, such as more leave, an instruction series at the Wingate Institute for physical fitness, better living quarters, and other perks.

All this was but the beginning. We created, as I mentioned earlier, a CCTV department, and after using it at first to show American instructional films, over time the CCTV crew and the "Good Instruction" team began making instructional films on their own. A section producing training aids and simulators was also established, under Eyal Zinyuk, who began constructing M-577s and M-113 out of plywood, demo AFVs with all the comms and fire computers which had begun entering the corps, and also fake command posts with real equipment installed in them. Later on, we installed lecture halls with firing computers, so that each cadet had a firing computer for full practice, and we prepared cross-sections of shells, bombs, and detonators, so that the cadets would have a better understanding of the munitions they were employing.

Additionally, we did full practices of all the systems within the air-conditioned lecture hall, without using the real pieces, which were in training. Only the "Inventron" ranging module, purchased from a foreign vendor before my time, turned out to be outdated, and unsuited to the new methods, which used laser range finders.

"The Adler Effect" Proves Ineffective

We displayed all the training aids and modules at the IDF exhibit, held at the Tel Aviv Convention Center on the initiative of Chief of Staff Motta Gur. Famous advertising exec, Reuven Adler, an Artillery Corps reservist, enlisted to design the corps' booth, and as he tended to go big, he decided that the "Adler effect" this time would be the covering of the entire roof of the vast booth in camouflage nets. From the nets we'd hang black and red strips of cloth, in the colors of the corps, and when the wind blew, he promised, the strips would sway, creating an impressive effect.

Only Adler forgot one tiny detail: This was an indoor venue, with no wind blowing. For lack of choice, in order not to give up the "Adler effect," we brought in industrial-sized fans, and won first place. We came in ahead of the other corps' booths, chiefly the elaborate Air Force and Navy's booths. Motta, impressed with our efforts, decided to give me and another officer of my choice a visit to the Idar-Oberstein Artillery School in Germany.

The man I chose to take with me was Hemeli the CI, who was already a captain on a colonel's pay, and awaiting us with open arms was military attaché Maxi Avigad, an Armored Corps veteran whose daughter was a clerk at Shivta. He had just entered the post, we were his first guests, and Maxi tried to impress us. He did so, among other things, by having a brand-new Mercedes Benz awaiting us. It tempted me to floor the gas pedal on the autobahn, the German freeways famous for their lack of speed limits, but despite all my best efforts, Porsches and Ferraris kept passing us by and leaving us in the dust.

The visit to the German base, situated on a high hill overlooking a bend of the Moselle River, was professionally enriching. We stayed at a training facility with air-conditioning according to the season, where the cadets watch through a giant glass window overlooking the area where the artillery deployment, target identification, ranging, and orders to mobilize troops take place – only there's no fire zone there, and everything takes place without actual fire.

I applied the idea at Shivta, when we designed the structure of the officers' training branch. We cut out a giant window in the building wall, facing the fire zones, and the cadets sat in an air-conditioned auditorium, studying firing data with a firing computer, and experienced improved performance in accordance with the science of artillery: They fired one projectile according to map figures, and it hit far off-target, then added datum after datum – coordinate in the national grid, shell weight, charge temperature, and meteorological data – and saw how the addition of each datum brings the next shell closer to its target.

Another improvement introduced following the visit was called a "cadet ranging switchboard." Prior to that, it was usually a single cadet ranging during the ranging exercises, while the others caught catnaps or skimmed the newspaper. With the switchboard, the instructor stood by the window with a two-way radio, all the cadets were connected to him through the switchboard, and the instructor would decide, like an ancient telephone switchboard, which button to press and which cadet would hear him.

He would see all those seated in the auditorium, would order them all to give a fire order at once – each on their own headset – and then would determine which order would be relayed to the battery, launching live fire. This required each cadet to be alert, because it could be their order sent out, and their calculations tested with live fire. Thus all cadets practiced simultaneously, rather than one at a time, and all were forced to maintain alertness and focus.

An Israeli Doesn't Count as a Jew

The meeting with the German school officers at the officers' club, lubricated with excellent Moselle wine, loosened the tongues. Some of the officers were older, men who had still served in the Wehrmacht in WW2 as enlisted men or young officers, and it was important to them to point out that they had served in coastal artillery or air-defense units on the Atlantic Wall, and not, heaven forbid, in more problematic roles.

Later, as more toasts were raised to the glorious artillery, they began to voice disappointment with the "overly democratic" new regime, and waxed nostalgic for strong, absolute rule, which would act with force against the Soviets – contrary to the prevalent slogan of the day: "Better red than dead."

They admired us as the heroes of the Six-Day and Yom Kippur wars, as we defeated the Soviets' allies and destroyed Russian equipment, and here we encountered a dissonance, which I had noticed back when I lived in an upscale neighborhood in Fort Sill. It took me a while to realize that Jews and Blacks were not allowed – not explicitly, of course – and that they viewed us as Israelis, rather than Jews.

The same thing happened to me as Chief Artillery Officer, when I was invited over the weekend to an exclusive golf club in Florida while my liaison, a marketing professional who was the only Jew serving as a senior executive at Martin Marietta (now Lockheed Martin), didn't come with me, as he did everywhere else. Only later – when I related this at the embassy in Washington – did I realize that the club was closed to Jews and Blacks, only it didn't apply to me, as I was an Israeli officer.

At a brief follow-up vacation in Paris, as Hemeli and I strolled down the Champs Elysee, we entered a giant Citroen and Peugeot showroom. Luxury cars were on display, and the visitors could also see cross-sections of engine blocks, showing how the pistons and other parts moved, and how the engine's multifaceted operation comes into being, including the transmission.

Upon return, we tasked Eyal Zinyuk with creating cross-sections of engines, of shells, of mortar bombs, and of detonators, so that the fighters and trainees could better understand how it all worked. In addition, we showed the barrel rifling on a large placard, to explain the rotation of the shell, and the meaning of internal and external ballistics. I have no doubt that a good fighter is a fighter well-versed in the systems he operates, and has full confidence in the weapons entrusted to him, which entails being familiar with all the effects of the weapon he deploys on the battlefield, and understanding the source of a malfunction when it occurs.

Pass the test, Go Home

The next stage was the purchase of our own linguistics lab, in the style of the lab in which we once had practiced in Beersheba, and in effect, we established an instructional compound. This was the kingdom of the CI and his team, and it churned out learning aids and instruction programs for each specialty – from comms operator through meteorology to location, and at all levels – from the gunner's course, through the artillery officers' course to advanced courses such as the FSO course, the brigade artillery commanders' course, and the advanced course for the firing echelon. This upgrade, across the board, resulted in quality instruction, motivated instructors, improved facilities, and shorter training periods.

The tank and APC driver course, for instance, was overly long until then, wasting the time of the reservists (who were the majority of the cadets.) We built a program that focused solely on field requirements, under the assumption that they all had civilian drivers' licenses. The trainees received driving lessons in all types of terrain, at day and night, and underwent written and practical driving tests on an SPH chassis, taken from an M-109 battery which had belonged to the Libyan Expedition Army, and captured in the Yom Kippur War.

At the end of the course, each trainee had to pass a daytime and nighttime driving test, in all types of terrain, including entering positions, hasty leapfrogging, and expedited movements in the dark. Anyone who passed the test received the rest of their reserve service term as a paid vacation – which created enormous motivation. Everyone wanted to pass the test as quickly as possible, get their behinds back home, and do the rest of their reserve service in the living room, the classroom, or at work – on the IDF's dime.

Shorter is Better

One of the biggest problems in the field of human resource management in the IDF is the long term of training, which leaves only a short term of actual service following, so that fighters reach the peak of their abilities only toward the end of their service – or never reach their full potential at all. The way to overcome this acute problem, which sometimes requires the signing of non-officers to the career military, was to shorten the training period.

The eureka moment came when we realized that courses at Shivta had been extended by the course commanders or the base commander, due to personal experience, and at times on sheer whim. The question was how to shorten the training without compromising quality, and the person who helped me prepare a formula for "courses according to role component" was organizational psychologist, Avivit Spayzaisen.

The course we used as a test case was the SPH commanders' course. We built it with a broad crew, including personnel from the battalions and from the CAO HQ, along with Shivta personnel, and with everyone's concurrence, we constructed a program that would directly cover all the role's components. The final exam also covered all the role's components, and those who passed it received their sergeant's stripes and were sent to the battalions.

Thanks to this direct approach, the course was shortened by over 20 percent – from fourteen weeks to eleven. Several weeks later we ran a poll in the battalions, and checked how the crews rated the crew commanders who graduated through the new method compared to those who went through the old course, and the results were unequivocal: The new graduates significantly outperformed the old ones.

We continued the long process until the end of my term as CAO, and still I didn't have time to apply the method to the basic course, which lasted six months. The work was continued by my successors, and today the course lasts four months.

Raful, who was deeply impressed by the change and was open to any idea that resulted in streamlining and increased professionalism, called a meeting on the subject among the joint chiefs of staff. Avivit presented the method, its results, and the feedback from the field, and the Chief of Staff instructed the head of the IDF's Instruction Division, Uri Simchoni, and the Chief of Personnel, Moshe Nativ, to apply the method throughout the IDF, so as to maximize the human resources output.

Thanks to the Coffee Anat Spilled

The approved complement of instructors at Shivta was 120, but when I arrived at the base, I found this complement severely depleted, and had about half that number. Not only that, but the conscripts sent to Shivta as instructors usually arrived following struggles with their commanders, and most were the type whose bat-coms wanted to get rid of, or people nearing the end of their service term. Both types were what is known in the IDF as "Shvuzim" – burnouts, who saw nothing in front of them but their coveted discharge leave. In contrast, the officers were handpicked by the CAO, and most of them, especially at the prestigious basic branch, were the cream of the crop.

So what to do? Bar-David had no time to give me an orderly handover, because he had been appointed CAO on a moment's notice. He did leave me a handover page, but it took time until I got around to reading it. Among the things he wrote in his orderly, pearly hand was: girl instructors.

Enter Anat, the new and opinionated secretary sent from CAO HQ to my office upon my arrival. On my first day there, she brought me coffee first thing in the morning, with just the two of us in the dusty office, and half the black beverage pooled in the coaster. I thought it was a coincidence. Perhaps she was scared of the incessant firing, or was apprehensive of meeting the unfamiliar base commander, and I let it pass without comment.

The next day was the same story, as was the day after. "Anat," I asked, "What's with you?" With full confidence and no hesitation, she said: "I graduated as a STEM major from a top high school in Rehovot, my matriculation scores are all As and higher, and what am I asked to do? Make coffee?"

"And what would you like to do?" I asked.

"Instructor," she said. "Impossible," I said, and after a few seconds, I added: "OK. There's a new course beginning now on German "Improver" firing computers for the 175mm guns. Join the course. If you graduate it with honors, you'll be an instructor."

And so it was. Anat graduated the course with honors, turned from a secretary to an instructor, and the rest is history. The idea caught the fancy of Amira Dotan, the Southern Command's Women's Corps' officer. She got Daliah Raz, Commander of the Women's Corps and wife of artillery officer Gideon Raz, excited as well, and a delegation from Shivta showed up at the female squad leaders' school, which was part of Bahad 12 in Tzrifin, where female officers were trained. They asked for volunteers, STEM majors with B averages and up in STEM subjects, adding that experience as a troop leader or at least a guide in the scouts or a comparable youth movement would also be a plus.

No one knew what the response would be. In practice, some 800 girls showed up, all meeting the criteria, including some from the rookie class of August. We conducted a screening process, at the end of which twenty instructors arrived at Shivta – five as comms instructors and fifteen as FDC NCO course instructors – the ones who make the calculations and, in effect, command the battery's mobile command post.

We received them like royalty – with separate barracks, of course, improved quarters, and even a large tanning area – to make them see that we wanted them, that it was important to us that they feel at home, and that they take an integral part in the work. And the experiment worked. The Artillery Corps was the first to take on female soldiers as instructors of male recruits, and then everyone else emulated us.

As the experiment succeeded, we took another step forward after the first class, and three female instructors – Michal Weissman, Leah Stein, and Nirit Zilberman – went off to an officers' course with their male colleagues. They endured the six grueling months of the completion course alongside the boys, and at the end received their officer's insignia. Leah remained at Shivta as commander of the FDC NCOs section, Michal advanced to the role of ops officer at the 91st Division, and Nirit became an instruction officer at the Central Command artillery HQ.

Artillery officer Nirit Zilberman (graduate of the first female instructors' class) with IDF Chief of Staff Motta Gur at the IDF Expo. (Photo: IDF Spokesperson / Government Press Bureau)

This earthquake had subsequent tremors: Crew commanders, TS and comms sergeants suddenly wanted to come from the battalions and instruct. Shivta became attractive due to the female instructors and thanks to the stories that spread throughout the corps about the improved conditions and leaves. We filled all our vacancies, and the Personnel Division even tasked us with carrying the girls thing too far by treating the matter as an experiment and not as filling vacancies.

This was the opportunity we waited for: To do screenings and select only the best. At a recent visit to Shivta, at a reunion of the first class of cadets I'd instructed as course commander, I saw that many procedures we set back in the day remain in effect, although the color of the aiguillette awarded to the excellent instructors is now a deep purple.

The Twice-Opened Window

I was very proud of the window of the building of the officers' training branch building, which as mentioned above, overlooked the firing zone. Therefore I was astonished when I arrived at Shivta as CAO immediately after my appointment, and discovered that the wall had been sealed with bricks.

Shivta had no commander at the time. Shraga Ben-Zvi, who had replaced me when I left the base upon appointment as Northern Command Artillery Commander, had left the corps in protest upon not being appointed CAO, despite being older and more veteran than me, and flew – with my intercession – to serve as military attaché in Kenya.

"Gimme a five-kay sledgehammer," I said, mangling proper syntax in the original Hebrew as well, and broke the wall down with my own two hands, with much umbrage and agitation. The auditorium and the window were back in business.

Lt. General Rafael (Raful) Eitan at the window auditorium. (Photo: IDF Spokesperson / Government Press Bureau)

When the new base HQ was planned, I sought to have the structure built on the "dugout" – the hill overlooking the entire base and the firing zone – and to open a large window in it, so that the base commander wouldn't be cut off from the field during deliberations and interviews, and with a good pair of binoculars, he could see anything taking place on base and in the training grounds.

As support, I enlisted Dudi Zarhi, Shivta's base architect, who thought as I did, but it wasn't enough. I was told that modesty required the structure to be down below. Commanders shouldn't reside on high. This supposed modesty – which was truly the subservience typical of the old Artillery Corps – won out.

I left for the Northern Command, and when I returned as CAO, I found the base HQ mired in the same location, by the ramshackle shack.

By then it was too late to change.

Burning IDF Gear

The "David" firing computers entered use in the corps in 1977, and were far easier to operate than the American FADAC, on which I'd trained at Fort Sill, and which was cumbersome, gigantic, and decidedly not user-friendly.

It was also a leap forward compared to the British FACE firing computer, which the 405th Battalion operated during the war. The FACE was mounted on a Land Rover. It was operated during the war by an officer named Daniel Appleberg, and it transmitted data directly to the eight barrels of the A and "Boaz" batteries, until "Boaz" was no more. After the breakthrough into Syria the FACE served batteries A and C, and as Danny Avidar, commander of the 213th Division Artillery put it, "The 405th fired like two battalions." But that was the first generation of firing computers – luckily for us, the IDF didn't purchase them, and Rafael developed the excellent "David" computer.

The new allocation standard spoke of four "David" computers per battalion – one for each battery, and an extra one at the battalion fire direction center, as backup. However, some refused to relinquish the reins of the horse even as the automobile was already running, and we were forced to continue training by the manual methods that predated the firing computer – with wooden artillery boards, logarithmic tables, and firing charge books, which took tenfold the time and opened the possibility of risky errors.

Deciding to obviate the dilemma, I ordered the collection all the artillery boards, piled them up in the middle of the base, had fuel poured on them, and we celebrated Lag Ba'Omer (the Jewish bonfire festival) out of season. Thus ended the day of the artillery board at the Artillery Corps.

Alone in the Desert

I loved Shivta's desert landscape and the immense firing zone at our disposal – from Ramat Matred and the Ovdat Rectangle to Ruth Stream, Laban Stream, the Goral Hills, and Mt. Keren. The area was strewn with waterholes, green corners with little springs, dunes, and many animals you don't see anywhere else in the country, such as the chlamydotis bird, various foxes, birds of prey, and antelopes.

Every season at Shivta was different, and I loved the winter in particular. We enjoyed amazing blooms, which lasted no more than two or three days following the rainfall, but during those days the desert filled with glorious colors. I used to go out alone in my jeep and reach hidden nooks and crannies along trails that, for hundreds and thousands of years, saw the coming and going of camel convoys to the abandoned locales of Ktziot and the Nitzana archeological site.

There was another reason for these wanderings: To find new sites for day and nighttime training and also to surprise training units, in order to assess the quality of training, camouflage, and position defenses. I knew how to appear without warning, from unexpected directions, and these surprise visits produced an official "base-com alert," which was, in effect, a duty to remain alert at all times.

Shivta back then – before Israel's cross-country Rte. 6 and other new highways – was stuck at the end of the world, and not many relished the long drive from the country's center. This gave me freedom. I enjoyed the sense of independence and managed to realize all the ideas and initiatives I thought up – both as lessons from the war, and as part of my great vision as to the meaning and place of the Artillery Corps in the military and on the battlefield.

Mayor of Shivta

I left the base in 1978 with mixed feelings. For two years of my life, I'd served as commander of Shivta, which is a city unto itself, and as mayor, I had to see to the welfare of the residents in terms of food and drink, medicine, infrastructure, construction, employment, entertainment, welfare, morale, security, environmental protection, relations with the semi-nomadic local Bedouins, fighting road accidents, as well as preventing vandalism and mischief. The entire responsibility was on my shoulders, although I had excellent staff, headed by two devoted, efficient, and loyal deputies. The close friendship forged between us lasted until their passing. The rest of the staff officers were all excellent men, but responsibility is indivisible and rests upon the commander's shoulders.

Following nighttime training, in the wee hours, I would tour the base with my indefatigable secretary, Nili, who in time married the eventual head of the IDF's command and staff, Brig.-Gen. Yaakov Zigdon. We pinpointed problems, made sure all was in order, that no one was acting out, and made sure that the Bedouins' donkeys didn't overturn the trash bins. I am happy to report that many acquaintances made at Shivta led to happy marriages.

What helped me later on my path in the IDF was the acquaintance with an entire generation of fighters and officers, for the entire corps, standing army, and reservists, who had trained at Shivta. Each of the corps' division artilleries had time for two training cycles within my term at Shivta, on top of converting and establishing battalions and divisions, as part of the abrupt change from a corps of 25 battalions to a corps of 87 battalions, intaking artillery pieces and advanced means, and training the troops to operate them optimally.

I was personally involved in every practice and every lecture class, became acquainted with the future officers, worked diligently to fully identify all potential officers, and even fought with instructors to pass cadets I knew personally, whom I had given officers' ranks despite their instructors' opinions. This mutual acquaintance caused the corps' officers and fighters to trust me during the battles of the Peace for Galilee War. After all this, my emotions were conflicted. For on one hand, I found it hard to leave the base which had become a home to me and where I felt a personal connection to each and every last person – and even to the training facilities, the gardens, the swimming pool, the wide-open firing ranges, and in short, to my city. On the other hand, the incessant responsibility and effort, day and night, and the aspiration of doing everything perfectly took a toll on me and my family, and also the time had come to move on toward the goal I had marked out for myself.

But first, let me return to a unique and significant stop along my route.

FORT SILL – FAR MORE THAN AN ARTILLERY COURSE

I arrived at Fort Sill in late 1974, and Lt. Col. Patton, who was in charge of the foreign cadets, prepared a package of Israeli newspapers for me, which he received from our embassy. The headline in all of them announced that Israel would be receiving Pershing missiles from the United States.

The Pershing was a long-range ballistic missile with a nuclear warhead. Obviously, no one in America had even dreamed of selling such missiles to the IDF, but the headline indicated the frenzy that had seized Israelis upon hearing the initial details of the military aid package promised by the U.S. following the Yom Kippur War. What was in fact purchased was a battalion of MGM-52 Lance missiles, which in the American version carried a tactical nuclear warhead. The version that "made Aliyah" had a warhead of 623 high-explosive submunitions.

What Makes a Housing Complex "Clean"

During our stay in Oklahoma, my family and I had a wonderful opportunity to get to know Americans – or more precisely, Midwesterners – up close. Legend has it that the wagons heading west to the California gold rush in the 19th century passed through here, and those that fell off the trail – the less motivated, the disillusioned, the sick, and the tired – remained in the Indian Territory of Oklahoma.

The military men and women at Fort Sill and the residents of the nearby town of Lawton were friendly, quick to say hello to anyone on the street, lived at a terribly languid pace, and the fashion, as my wife Tamar put it, was 1930s Petah Tikva. Behind all these, the southern states in the 1970s were characterized by a covert form of racism.

I was a Lt. Colonel at the time, and when I arrived for the course, I was assigned a sponsor – someone who, along with his family, was supposed to take care of me and my family, ease my integration in the course and help us all settle in the nearby town of Lawton, where we resided. Our sponsor, Lt. Col. Richard Biondi, a Texan by birth, was an artillery instructor. When I looked for an apartment in a housing complex, and wanted to make sure that there was a swimming pool there, Biondi explained to me during the tour that we shouldn't live where I had looked for an apartment. He took me to a new complex – Pecan Valley – where we did indeed set up house.

Biondi didn't explain why he endeavored to change our decision, but we quickly understood: At this apartment complex, there were no African Americans, no Mexicans... and no Jews. We were considered Israeli, which was different than being Jews. Biondi directed us to a "clean" complex.

An Israeli is Not a Jew (Take 2)

Fort Sill had no synagogue, and the church served as a mosque on Friday, a synagogue on Saturday, and a church on Sunday. During Christmas, when we took a trip with my friends, Govinda Rasu of Singapore, and Luis Bustamente of Peru, we arrived at Colorado Springs, at the USAF academy. This was a magnificent base, and the VIP quarters we stayed in were among the best in the U.S. – one step below Miramar Naval Airbase in San Diego. I searched for the Jewish chaplain in the base, which was fairly deserted due to the holiday, hoping that there was a Hanukkah candle lighting, and someone gave me the telephone number of a Lieutenant Shapiro. He invited us, along with my Gentile friends and their families, to his apartment, to partake in the lighting of the first candle and some jelly-filled fried pastries.

We found a nice man, we met Jewish soldiers serving on the base, we lit candles, and sang Hanukkah songs. The rabbi's partner made the signature holiday pastries, and when we asked where she was from, it turned out that she was a Gentile Texan, hadn't the first clue about Judaism, had no plans to acquire one – nor to convert if and when they got married. Pluralism at its best.

Mission: Fundraising

Two years prior, when I arrived in the U.S. for the first time in 1972, on my own, as part of a fundraising campaign for the United Jewish Appeal, us Sabras had an image of diaspora Jews similar to that of the refugees that arrived in Israel after the Holocaust – pale, skinny, and short, speaking in a Polish, Russian, or Romanian accent.

In Beverly Hills, I suddenly met proud and very wealthy Jews, taller than me, speaking fluent English, flanked by women dressed in the latest fashions, meticulously groomed, proud of bearing and bedecked in jewels. People who lived in giant villas, with private pools and servants. A very far cry from Fiddler on the Roof.

These American Jews, whose forefathers had come to America in the 19th century with the massive migration waves from Europe, become Americans within a generation – Ivy League graduates, wielding influence in the halls of government. There were lawyers among them, judges, physicians, businessmen, politicians, and their influence – born of the Jewish genius – was tenfold greater than their share in the general population.

I was dressed up in my IDF-issued suit and the red socks I'd found in the drawer, and was astonished. Each meeting featured Jews from a particular industry, at each meeting the host gave a speech, and he always said: "This was a pretty rough year for business, but after hearing the words of this brave officer, and the UJA review of the difficult situation in Israel, the cost of absorbing Aliyah, economic difficulties, the need to maintain a large army of fearless young men, my wife Betty and I have decided to double our contribution from last year, and this year we're giving a million dollars."

"Well Bill," he would turn to the man next to him, "What do you think about it?"

Bill, or was it John, or Henry, would repeat the ritual step for step, starting with things not being easy, on to "I consulted my wife," Donna or Margaret as the case may be, concluding with the bravery of the fighter and a doubling of his donation. Anything but have people whisper that his business was struggling.

To the side sat the UJA representative with checks ready, wrote each donor's name and amount on each check, and passed it immediately to be signed.

How to Talk an American Traffic Cop Out of Writing You a Ticket

Under the influence of the novel, Battle Cry, by Leon Uris, and the romantic scene that takes place in Yosemite Park, when asked what I wanted to do for my first weekend, I replied: "Yosemite and Sequoia Park." I received a brand new Ford Pinto, and "took off" to the two majestic parks, to acquire a modicum of humility, contrary to the ways of most Israelis abroad.

The following weekend, I said "Las Vegas," and when asked "fly or drive?" I replied "drive" like any gear head, particularly one stunned by the giant cars filling the roads. This time I received a Chevy Impala, also brand new, and as might be expected, tried to reach its speed limit on the road bisecting the Mojave Desert.

I crossed the California-Nevada state line at the same speed, and suddenly a cruiser popped up behind me, and a state trooper motioned me to pull over. Out of the cruiser came a burly man in uniform and all the accessories – sunglasses, a magnum handgun, boots, and a Stetson hat. He asked for my license and registration, and as I handed them to him, I explained to him in English that I was a tourist. He was not impressed. "Our signs are very clear," he said, "and they're in numbers."

I tried a different approach. "I'm a Major in the Israeli Defense Forces." Israelis in America still enjoyed remnants of the admiration following the incredible victory in '67, and the fame of the Middle Eastern juggernaut, which quadrupled its territory in just six days of war, had spread as far as Nevada. The policeman stood up straight and saluted. He handed my papers back and wished me "a good weekend in Las Vegas."

I came back to the gambling Mecca three years later with my family, driving from Oklahoma. We stayed at the VIP quarters at the nearby Nellis Air Force Base. We went in the morning to the officers' mess hall to dine on a sumptuous breakfast (costing 50 cents), and the two rowdy rugrats rushed ahead of us as usual, racing each other into the dining room.

Seated by one of the tables were future Major General Chaim Erez and my friend Yom-Tov Tamir. "When we heard and saw the children," they laughed, "We knew right away that Israelis were coming."

The Family

I've mentioned Sagi and Yaron, our older sons, more than once, who were with Tamar and me in Oklahoma during my studies. Sagi, who served in the Paratroopers with the "Oketz" canine unit and as a sergeant-major with an intel and observation unit in the reserves, studied business administration at Wharton School in Philadelphia after his discharge from the army. Yaron was discharged with the rank of captain, after commanding battery C of the 405th Battalion, the same battalion I commanded in the Yom Kippur War. He advanced to Lt. Col. in the reserves and studied tourism economics. They both currently run the constantly expanding family company that makes training modules and simulators.

Sagi and Dana gave us our grandchildren Noa, Guy, Ben, and Alma. Yaron and Tal blessed us with Itay, and Yaron and Gal added Yohai, Tamari, and Uri to our lives.

Ori, our third son, served as a deputy company commander in the precise long-range "Meitar" and advanced to the rank of major in the reserves. He studied civil engineering and is a company engineer at a large construction company. Along with Liora, the puppeteer, they are parents to Ariel, Laila, and Arya.

Tom, my only daughter and the love of my life – a good soul, bereft of a single evil thought, optimistic and loving – works as a rhythmic therapist with special needs people. Tom is married to Micky, who is a photographer on many of Israeli TV reality shows, and they are the parents of our grandchildren Eli, Ari, and Adam.

The powerful emotional bond between me and Tom began at the moment of her birth. She was born in the midst of the Peace for Galilee War. I arrived at the maternity ward in Kfar Saba by helicopter, straight from the battlefield, and the doctor, who used to be a battalion medic under me in Sinai, offered to let me into the maternity room. This wasn't quite done back then, but I'm a hero, so I went in.

What I saw made my knees shake. The color drained from my cheeks, and I felt faint. Tamar noticed my distress and told the doctors: "Get him out of here! Here's the last thing I need on my mind right now." The odd tableau, of the hero who had just seen dead and wounded men on the battlefield, now turned helpless when faced with the wonder of creation, must have made the nurses laugh.

God Bless America

For sixteen hours, we sat by the lavatory until finally landing in New York, and if the previous time I was greeted outside the terminal by a limousine and a driver, after a first-class flight, and was driven in great pomp to one of New York's finest hotels, this time no one was waiting. With a suitcase in each hand and the sleeping children on our shoulders, we continued straight to language school at the Lackland Air Force Base in San Antonio, Texas, and from there to Oklahoma.

"This is the America you raved about?" Tamar laughed. I chose to keep my mouth shut.

Sagi and Yaron were seven and five, respectively. Sagi went to school and Yaron to kindergarten – within walking distance of home – and both quickly learned to speak fluent English, in the slow, thick Okie accent.

I arranged another trip to the West Coast, this time as an experienced traveler to the area – to the gorgeous Highway 1, which twists and turns along the coast, to Yosemite and Sequoia national parks, and to cap it off – Disneyland. There, along the route from ride to ride, we came across the wishing well too. Sagi and Yaron received coins, threw them in the pool, closed their eyes and made a wish.

I asked: "What did you wish for?" And they both replied in unison: "God Bless America," and here we reach the point: Every morning, in every school and kindergarten in America, the Stars and Stripes are flown, the national anthem is sung with a hand on the heart, and the children recite: God Bless America.

America is a republic of immigrants, and the most sacred thing is the constitution. It is home to people from every corner of the globe, of every type and color, every faith and nationality, and what unites them and makes them one nation is the constitution and "God bless America." Even today, I am fully convinced that this nation is undefeatable.

The United States with its vast expanses, its pluralism, its inventiveness, and most of all the mixing of the races, which creates stronger and richer genes than seclusion and reclusion – all these, along with the sanctification of liberty, freedom of speech, the credo of unlimited opportunities, the mobility, the openness, and also a deep faith in democracy, are combined with draconian law enforcement. It's hard to comprehend how the founding fathers of the American nation managed to invent and institute their special democracy some 250 years ago, and to establish a nation whose citizens are bound by freedom, enterprise, and creative imagination.

In the course of my businesses, following my discharge from the IDF, I learned more and more about the greatness of the United States, whose values were predicated upon liberty and democracy in 1776, and which are standing and binding to this day.

It is hard to draw direct conclusions from that to the State of Israel, which is the state of the Jewish people, which is to say a nation state, but I believe that the mixture of origins in Israel creates a new Israeli character. The march of progress and the realization that we must overcome the forces of darkness that constantly pop up, move me to optimism.

On the day we apply the principles of liberty, justice, and democracy, give our national symbols – the flag and the anthem – their due respect, and all Israeli children, will wave the flag and sing the anthem each morning, then we can be both the state of the Jewish people and at the same time, an advanced democratic country.

The solution lies in passing a constitution. The world is galloping ahead, and if we wish to live, we must do so soon. GBA (God Bless America) is etched on the hearts of American children since early childhood, and the lessons of childhood are learned for life.

SOUTHERN LEBANON IN FLAMES

I found myself in sympathetic surroundings when I was appointed, in mid-1978, as Northern Command Artillery commander, once again serving under my friend Yanush. I left Shivta with sadness, but with great satisfaction, drove up to Nazareth, where the Northern Command HQ was located, and entered the post of Artillery Commander, replacing Shraga Ben-Zvi. Yanush, in his typical manner and based on our deep acquaintance since October of '73, immediately left me to my own devices.

These were stormy times in the North, the period of ties forged between the IDF and the South Lebanon Army (SLA) under the command of Major Saad Haddad. The liaison with Haddad was journalist Yoram Hamizrachi – a corporal with an acting rank of Lt. Colonel, an invention of Raful's, who was somehow appointed as the IDF's representative with the SLA. The idea was for the SLA to serve as a buffer between the northern Israeli locales and the terrorists, who operated under Syrian auspices.

The IDF had remained, in effect, in the areas captured during the Litani Operation, through the auspices of a new creature – the Army of Free Lebanon, controlled in the eastern sector by Major Saad Haddad, and in the west by Major Sami Shidyaq, until Haddad took over the entire South Lebanon Army. He operated against Fatah and the smaller terrorist organizations, which were at the height of their power at the time, and also to some degree against the Syrians, who had a physical military presence in the area beyond their support of the terrorists.

The tasks facing me were the building of an artillery force and the planning of independent artillery action, against an enemy that didn't hesitate to murder innocent civilians – in Ma'alot, in Kiryat Shmona, in Nahariya and elsewhere – and had no problem with firing rockets on our towns and villages, turning the lives of innocent civilians and little children into hell.

The Northern Command was still under the influence of the Litani Operation, which the IDF embarked upon following the kidnapping of the "bloody bus" near Kibbutz Ma'agan Michael, stopping it at the Country Club Junction at the entrance to Tel Aviv, and the cold-blooded murder of 35 citizens. But occupying the territory between the border line and the Litani River, staying in it for three months and destroying terrorist infrastructures, all failed to stop both the launching of rockets with a range of over 20km and the terrorist infiltrations. These peaked with the horrific attack in Nahariya, in which a heinous terrorist shattered the skull of four-year-old Einat Haran, after murdering her father before her eyes, and after her sister Yael was smothered to death by her mother, in a failed attempt to calm her.

Yanush, as I mentioned, gave me free rein in planning and carrying out artillery action in response to terrorist activities, allowing me to fire up to 40 shells with no need for authorization, if and when I saw fit.

"Write It Down, Write It Down"

I placed a location and observation array in the eastern sector of the theater commanded by Lieutenant Tal Asraf, a talented professional who also spoke French, and positioned it in a villa in the valley of Marjayoun, which served as the observation and command post at the northern end of the SLA's enclave. I placed a second array at Shaqif al-Hardun, in the western sector.

I received instructions to rely in part on the SLA artillery, under the command of Fares Fakheili, which operated captured 130mm guns, that had been made obsolete in the IDF, as well as towed 155mm guns, IDF surplus, and 120mm mortars fired from the crew commander's back yard. But from the very first visit, I realized that our salvation would not be forthcoming from their direction. The guns were rusted, filthy, and neglected, and when I asked why, Fares replied: "We have no oil, rags, or cleaning equipment."

I turned to look at my staff ops officer, Avi Nimni, and Fakheili told him in Hebrew: "Write it down, write it down."

I realized that this was the drill: You say, "write it down" and then you go home. I told Nimni loudly, so that Fakheili would hear: "Get the trucks and take all the guns and mortars away from here."

The Lebanese realized who he was dealing with now. "Why?" he asked. "Why?"

"Because," I said.

He understood me and said: "We don't need anything. Come tomorrow and everything will be clean, in order, and ready for battle."

And so it was, including a target registry, observations, and establishing a direct line to Major Haddad and Asraf's villa. And still, with all due respect to the SLA, it was clear to me that we must build an IDF artillery framework, based on the standing artillery divisions.

The Pamphlet Shell

My first specific mission was a pamphlet bombardment. A battalion of the official Lebanese army began moving south, aiming to wipe the SLA out and return the south of Lebanon to the control of the Lebanese army. The question was how to chase this force away without attacking it, so as not to turn the Lebanese military into an active belligerent party. The idea was to fire shells filled with pamphlets, that would persuade the troops and officers of the battalion to go back the way they came from. We woke up the good people of the IMI central lab, and in joint consultation we decided to use scattershot shells, which were armed with metal strips to disrupt enemy radar. We filled these with pamphlets and ordered Haddad's gunners to drop them on the approaching battalion.

The pamphlets, written in flawless Lebanese Arabic by Haddad and his men, read as follows:

> Oh, my brothers and countrymen, the glorious fighters of the brave Lebanese army, how can you fight us? We are your brothers, and will welcome you with open arms. Join us in the Army of Free Lebanon. Know this, our brothers, that while you move south to fight your brothers, the evil Syrians are fucking your wives in Beirut.

I don't know if the pamphlets did the trick, but the Lebanese battalion turned around and went back to Beirut.

Sometimes You Need Smoke and Mirrors

In one of the earliest fire incidents, the terrorists fired Katyusha rockets into Kiryat Shmona. There were casualties, wounded and dead among the civilian population, but I had already prepared a response. The 282nd Division Artillery was deployed in the Finger of Galilee. All its standing battalions, along with reserve battalions and other battalions, eleven artillery battalions in all, were deployed according to the combat doctrine, ready for precise fire, with the registration targets ranged and the guns able to land fire by surprise in a precise barrage.

We went up – Yanush, Major Haddad, me, and other commanders – to the Booster, near the village of Taybeh in the SLA enclave, and Yanush, hot for revenge, chose the village of Qaaqiat al-Jisr. Some of the Katyushas had been fired from there, there was a terrorist concentration known to be located there, and Yanush said to Haddad: "Destroy the village."

A long while passed before Fares Fakheili could be located, and until he could man a 122mm cannon. Eventually, he fired a shell, which fell somewhere in the village and only caused the terrorists to take cover. Yanush saw it just as I did, and ordered: "Fire!"

I had prepared Shmil Golan, the deputy commander of the division artillery, in advance for a barrage of some 200 barrels, and instructed him to fire air burst bombs, streaming smoke, and phosphorous. I didn't want to destroy a village with all its inhabitants. The memory of the razing of the Czech village of Lidice in response to the assassination of the SS leader Reinhard Heydrich came to my mind. We are no Nazis. A massive barrage hit Qaaqiat al-Jisr. The entire village seemed to rise in the air and slam back down to earth.

The SLA men jumped up and clapped, jubilant and elated. We got into the grey jeep, with me driving and Yanush beside me. "Arie, what have we done?" he said. "We killed civilians." I saw a tear in the corner of his eye.

"Yanush," I told him, "Don't worry. It was just smoke and mirrors. We didn't kill any civilians. At worst, people are shocked, and perhaps there are some wounded. I fired air burst bombs and smoke, assuming that everyone was shut inside. I gave relief to the desire for vengeance, and it was a pretty good demonstration – for the terrorists and the SLA guys alike."

Yanush grinned, and that was the end of it. The intelligence report noted that 33 terrorists were killed in open outposts and observation posts. Three civilians were wounded. As I promised Yanush, no civilians were killed.

Yoram Hamizrachi Fans the Flames

One day, I was called urgently to the Northern Command General's chambers. "What's going on?" Yanush asked, "I'm receiving reports about an inferno of fire in Marjayoun, the terrorists are firing Katyushas, and the SLA and the terrorists are exchanging fire. Why aren't you reacting?"

I checked with Asraf to see what's going on in his sector, and his response was astonishing. "There's nothing going on," he said. "You can hear the birds chirping. No rockets and no gunfire."

I asked Yanush where the report was coming from, and he pointed at the telephone receiver he was holding. "Yoram Hamizrachi is hysterical."

I said: "Peace and quiet reign in southern Lebanon."

Yanush explained to Yoram that Asraf reports that there's no fire and all is quiet, but this apparently didn't suit the "Lt. Col." "He's a liar," Hamizrachi said, "He's a fraud."

I suggested that Yanush check where Yoram was calling from at this early hour. This was usually the time of his morning bath in his Metula home – and indeed that turned out to be the case. This incident expedited the unceremonious removal of Yoram Hamizrachi from his peculiar role, and the establishment of an orderly IDF HQ within the SLA.

Who Destroyed My House?

"Let's put on a demonstration," Yanush said to me when David Ivri, commander of the Air Force, came to visit the SLA enclave in the spring of 1979. We had deployed eight-inch guns at the time, and this required us to remove the 175mm barrels and replace them with the 203mm, or eight-inch barrels, which we called "Hatchet." The range of this cannon was 16.8km, and my experience in the Sinai had taught me that this was the most accurate cannon in the world. Later, during the attrition period immediately following the Yom Kippur War, we used the 203mm to fire at the command post on Tel Khara, in the Syrian enclave on the Golan Heights, and the 334th Battalion, under Aldo Zohar, carried out the mission with precision.

I chose a target for Ivri – a farmhouse with a Syrian intelligence and observation post on the roof, manned by several officers and soldiers. For the benefit of gunners reading the book, I'll note that the method was to line up the target with the sights, then elevate according to the range table to the range measured by the laser range finder. We fired a long shell first, a second shell short, and the third shell went straight into the house, blowing it up and leaving nothing of it but a pile of rubble.

It was a 99kg shell with a concrete-piercing M-78 fuse, and a delay which exploded inside. Ivri was amazed, and what he had to say in our praise was: "You're just like the Air Force! What precision!"

But the story doesn't end there. In the late 1980s, I arrived as a civilian for a meeting at the Dan Carmel Hotel in Haifa. As usual, I was very early, and meanwhile I went to swim in the pool. A pretty young blond sat on the seat by the water, reading a book in English. We got into a conversation, and she told me that she and her husband, both Lebanese originally, live in the ski resort village of Villars-Sur-Ollon by Lake Geneva.

"What are you both doing here?" I asked, and she replied: "We have a large farm in southern Lebanon. We grow organic vegetables there, and fly them to Geneva with the approval of Northern Command General Yossi Peled, who is a friend of ours."

"Isn't that wonderful," I said. "Peaceful coexistence."

"But before the war," she went on, "the IDF destroyed the house we had in the middle of the farm."

She named the farm. I didn't want to tell her who destroyed her house and why, nor did I mention my military past. When her husband joined us, we exchanged memories of Beirut and Junia, and of skiing at Verbier, not far from their Swiss home.

The Nahariya Cannon

The city of Nahariya took a lot of fire in the summer of '79 from a 130mm cannon that was hidden deep in the orchards around Tyre. The terrorists would fire at night, and immediately move the cannon to a new position somewhere else deep in the citrus groves. During one of my wanderings in southern Lebanon, I joined the Intelligence Corps' 869th Observation Unit, which was conducting long-range electro-optical observations with advanced 20X120 telescopic binoculars (aka LREEOOD, the final "D" standing for "device.") The binoculars were connected to a television screen, and displayed a large, accurate image of the battlefield in real time, as well as a recording video for later use.

The observation post was located in Shaqif a-Hardun, overlooking Tyre and its environs, and the observers knew the sector well. We placed a battery for their benefit from the 404th Battalion, under batcom Tzachi Ganor, behind the lookout. The battery was on immediate alert with all six barrels, and as the entire area was ranged and registered with fire – there was nothing left to do but wait. The moment the observer noticed movement, he put an X on the target, read out a coordinate to the battery, and the moment the first 130mm shell was fired from the Fatah cannon, our battery fired a volley. The hidden cannon was caught in the act and got blasted sky-high – and all caught on camera for a TV movie.

The observer was wounded two days later and hospitalized, and when I went to visit him, I brought him a bottle of fine whisky. He earned it and then some. The enemy cannon, by the way, which was not only disabled but later captured, is on display to this day at a city square in Nahariya.

A French-Style Encounter

"Drive to Ras a-Naqoura," was what Amos Baram, Chief of Staff of the Northern Command, asked of me one morning. He called me on the radio, and explained that the French paratroopers at the UN HQ are bristling, after one of their officers was killed the previous day in an encounter with SLA soldiers.

One of the traditional roles of the command Chief of Staff was to act as liaison with the UN forces in the Golan Heights and Lebanon. I was in the SLA enclave as usual, this time with Tzvika Yosef, the SLA's maintenance officer (apart from Major Haddad and a few other senior locals, most of the officers' cadre of the SLA consisted of IDF personnel assigned to the task). We traveled in a grey jeep with the emblem of Free Lebanon on the dashboard, with Tzvika driving and me beside him.

The UN camp was quiet as we approached, with no movement to be seen. The gate was locked, and when we approached with the jeep, a platoon of French paratroopers suddenly emerged from the dugouts behind the gate. All barrels were trained on us, and I heard the rifle bolts clacking. I recalled that we were driving in a jeep that appeared to belong to the SLA, and I knew that the vengeful French would be trigger happy. I ordered Tzvika to stop the jeep and said: "Don't move and don't say a word."

After ten motionless minutes, I stepped out of the jeep, so that the French could see that I was an IDF officer.

Their commander, watching me through binoculars, identified the colonel insignia on my shoulders and allowed me to approach. We exchanged a few words in English, and he relented, ordering his men to lower their weapons.

Within the camp, we received the respect due to Israeli officers, and I explained how we intend to solve the problem. Tzvika Yosef, still shivering, enjoyed a sip of white wine, as a true son of Zichron Yaakov, and once the atmosphere had thawed sufficiently, I informed Baram that the mission had been accomplished. I left out the part of how we were a hair's breadth from execution by a firing squad.

"Your Slip Is Showing"

Bruce Williams was one of the aides of the American military attaché in Israel. He was a charming and easygoing man, who spoke Hebrew and understood every word spoken around him, and those who didn't know that got burned.

Williams was familiar with the IDF brass, eagerly drank up every bit of gossip, and later would be the first to inform me that I was being appointed as CAO, as we happened to cross paths in the VIP room at the Sde Dov Airport, each headed to a different destination.

"Arie," he told me on one of his visits to the north, "You're bringing American arms into the enclave." At that time, there was a strict prohibition on introducing American weapons to the SLA enclave. The cover story was that while the SLA was using weapons supplied by us, it was mostly weapons captured in battle. We ostensibly never crossed the border, and we always entered the SLA enclave in vehicles painted in SLA grey. When we violated the prohibition and brought SPHs into the enclave, we did so at night or for very short periods, at hours when the American satellite wasn't passing over our area.

This was an open white lie, but as long as we didn't violate it blatantly, there were no problems. And here comes Williams and says: "You fired."

I said, "maybe we fired from our territory, in response to rockets," but he was no sucker, and only spoke of what he knew.

"No," he said, "the range of the 8-inch guns is 16.8 km. To hit the targets you fired at, you had to go inside. I saw the shrapnel from American shells with my own eyes. Watch it, my friend."

He contented himself with a wink – one that carried a clear warning.

FOs as Rangers

Yanush proposed incursion operations into Lebanon on a nearly weekly basis. Some of the operations were canceled by Raful, then Chief of Staff, although he too almost always relished a fight, and more cancelations came from Defense Minister Ezer Weizmann. He didn't want to inflame the sector, and conducted a moderate policy.

Despite all the cancelations, many operations were still carried out. This was our bread and butter, and thanks to these, I forged friendly ties with officers such as Moshe "Bogie" Yaalon and Israel Ziv, who commanded the Paratroopers' Rangers ("Sayeret Tzanhanim") unit in succession, Giora Inbar, commander of the Golani Rangers, Shaul Mofaz, bat-com of the 202nd, Amnon Lipkin-Shahak, Brigadier of the 35th, and Ilan Biran, Brigadier of Golani. I participated in all the planning sessions, command groups, and approval of plans with Raful, and could see precisely who he valued and who he couldn't stand.[22]

He was particularly partial to those who served under his command in the Yom Kippur War – the men of the 7th Armored Brigade and Golani. The paratroopers were almost always among his favorites as well, except for Lipkin, whom Raful viewed as a wiseass and a doubting Thomas. Amram Mitzna from the Armored Corps, an opinionated officer who was Yanush's favorite, was viewed by Raful as all talk and no action, despite the fact that he was awarded the Medal of

---

[22] Lipkin-Shahak, Mofaz, and Yaalon all became IDF Chiefs of Staff later in life, and government ministers after that. Inbar left the IDF as a brigadier general and became a successful businessman, activist, and philanthropist. Since 2021, he has been serving as chairman of the referees' union at the Israeli Football (soccer) Association.

Distinguished Service and the Chief of Staff's Commendation for courageous combat performance in the Six-Day and Yom Kippur wars, respectively.

One day, Giora Inbar complained to me that every time he gets a new FO, they're usually lacking in physical shape, and unsuited to perform as FO in a Golani Rangers operation. I decided to assign regular FOs to both ranger units, to take part in all the rangers' training, belong to them organically, and become rangers.

The first was a young man named Ilan Cohen, in time Director of the Prime Minister's Office under Ariel Sharon. He reported to my office immediately following his completion of the basic course. "I want to transfer to the Paratroopers," he told me candidly, "I don't want to stay in the Artillery Corps." I replied instantly: "No such thing," and just then I recalled Inbar's complaint. "You'll be permanent FO with the Golani Rangers."

Cohen jumped at the offer. Rangers FO, and later Rangers FSO, became a regular thing, and was formally standardized when I was appointed CAO.

The Kukri Knife – and the Sleeping Soldier

My good friend from the university, Shlomo Ilya, was the Northern Command Intelligence Officer when I was the command CAO. Ahead of a long-range mission by the 35th Brigade, under the legendary Yoram "Ya-Ya" Yair, Ilya invited me to come with him to the headquarters of the Nepalese Gurkha battalion, which was part of the UN force. We wanted to make sure that their outposts wouldn't fire on Ya-Ya, who moved below them en route to Kaukaba.

The Nepalese, who were very fond of us and hated the terrorists, cooperated willingly. We ate dinner with them, at the end of which I received a gift – a kukri knife, the traditional Gurkha machete-style chopper blade, razor sharp and curved, the better to lop off heads with. I kept it for many long years, but it got lost when we moved from Kfar Saba.

Operation Kaukaba was cut short due to a gap that formed in the raiding column, after one of the soldiers fell asleep by the side of the road during a momentary halt. The forward part continued to walk, and when the gap was discovered, the search for the missing soldier began. The search was led by the brigade's staff ops officer, Amal Asad (later a brigadier general, and commander of the IDF's coordination and liaison unit in the West Bank). To aid his search, I fired 175mm guns at the terrorist villages of Suhmur and Yahmur. The soldier was eventually found, unharmed.

Sometimes You Need to Dismiss

Alongside the operations of other units, I decided to initiate operations based solely on artillery fire. One of these operations was entering a battery from the 282nd Division Artillery into Tel Dibin in the enclave. The object was to destroy a terrorist outpost which we couldn't reach from our territory. The operation was set at command level, and the mission was assigned to the 282nd Division Artillery, the standing artillery of the 36th Division.

Tel Dibin is eight kilometers north of the Fatma Gate, beyond the towns of Marjayoun and Al-Hiam. Usually, a reserve battalion was deployed there with 160mm self-propelled heavy mortars, which had a range of only 9.5km, and I preferred a 155mm battery from the 405th Battalion. The idea was to fire some 40 shells and get out immediately, so as not to be discovered in broad daylight.

It was a dark winter's night. A torrential rain poured down incessantly. The movement, which was supposed to take half an hour, got longer and longer, until after four hours, I decided to intervene. I saw that the division artillery commander and the bat-com weren't responding, and ordered: "Fire on location," meaning stop where you are, deploy hastily, and open fire.

The deployment, which in practice took 40 seconds, was delayed as well, and not a shell was fired. With a heavy heart, I decided to call the operation off, and to bring the men and the guns back to Israeli territory before daybreak, but just then I received notice that the battery's M-577 was stuck in the mud and couldn't be extracted. I ordered the vehicle's crew out of the enclave, and ordered them to leave the mired M-577 under guard and well-camouflaged.

In the inquiry, it turned out that the division artillery commander and the bat-com of the 405th sat jeep by jeep, by the border fence, and communicated with each other by radio. Rather than go with the battery, the bat-com chose to stay in Israel, and left the complex operation on the shoulders of an unexperienced XO with the rank of Lt.

With the concurrence and blessing of Ori Or, the division commander who was also disappointed by the failed execution, I deposed the negligent bat-com and the division artillery commander, who approved his staying back, far from the executing force. The M577 was extracted by a Lebanese tractor and brought back to Israel the next night.

The Dark Side of "Commander Independence"

In another command-level operation, I sent a light aircraft up for aerial observation. Yanush and I sat on the Booster, in the enclave, and a 175mm battery from the 334th Battalion fired and missed, and the aerial observer, an officer who had been dismissed from flight school in the late stages of the course, reported that the battery wasn't responding to corrections.

The operation, planned for a brief window of time due to the constraints of the American satellite, and approved by Defense Minister Weizmann, had failed. I went down to question the men of the battery and the bat-com, Yossi Dagan, my darling since the Valley of Tears, and I once again discovered the "junior commanders independence syndrome."

"Why weren't you or the deputy bat-com with the battery?" I asked, and Dagan replied: "Commanders' independence."

I viewed both these incidents as a personal failure, since I'd failed to explain to those under my command the limits and limitations of delegating and granting independence to juniors, which are most important, but also entail downsides. In special surgical operations, when top fighters – bat-coms, company commanders, and select troops – penetrate deep into enemy territory, the same standards should apply to the choosing of our own artillery personnel. The experienced commanders must personally command the forces supporting the raiding force, regardless of its size. Dagan left the IDF following his term as bat-com. Since that night, I made sure to brief and investigate personally at any command-level operation involving an artillery force.

Yanush Is Reprimanded for Arms Trading With the Enemy

For many long months, Major Haddad pestered Yanush about 160mm mortars. He wanted a weapon with a range of almost 10km, and monstrous payloads. At some point, Yanush apparently got tired of it. He asked me to come to his house in Caesarea, and took me in his car to the Soltam plant in Yokne'am. After closeting himself on the top floor with Shlomo Zabdolovich, the owner of the factory, who happened to hail from Yanush's birth town of Lodz, they came down to the boardroom, and Zabdolovich instructed the CEO, Yaakov Lior, to give me two towed 160mm mortars.

Lior, a recipient of the Israel Security Prize for his part in developing the "Galil" assault rifle, quibbled: "Where? What for? Who approved this? After all, doesn't removing weaponry from the plant require permits?"

But Zabdolovich waved him off.

I summoned Yusuf, the command artillery HQ's legendary maintenance 1st Sgt. Major, and his men took the mortars, painted them grey, and we took them under cover of darkness into the SLA enclave.

Haddad received them with great ceremony. We instructed Fares Fakheili and his men how to look after the mortars and how to fire them, and two days later, they already opened fire on a forward Syrian post at Aisheia, causing an international incident. Yanush was summoned before the joint chiefs of staff, and reprimanded by the Deputy Chief of Staff, Kuti Adam, based on a complaint filed by Assistant Defense Minister, Mordechai Zipori. He was a member of the Talik-Gorodish clique, which sought every opportunity to besmirch Yanush.

It is infuriating, and perhaps ludicrous, to have to report that Yanush, the revered commander, was reprimanded for "trading arms to the enemy," but that's what happens when personal intrigue outweighs relevant considerations.

In any event, Yanush came back and told me that he received an order to bring the mortars back. I racked my brain trying to come up with an excuse for Haddad, and eventually explained to him that cracks in the barrel had been discovered in this production run, and firing them might blow up the mortars and their operators, including the home of the crew commanders from whose back yard the mortars are being fired. I promised him, by all that is holy, that we would give the mortars back as soon as they were repaired.

LIGHT RIPPLES
Taming of the Shrew

Major General Israel Tal, aka Talik, was appointed in 1979 as commander of the 446th Corps, the corps of the Northern Command, and some time thereafter, he arrived for approval of plans at the HQ of Yanush Ben-Gal, the Command General. The same Yanush whose promotion Talik had halted before the Six-Day War, following a severe clash with Gorodish (in which Yanush was undoubtedly in the right.)

Along with the general at the plans' approval came the corps artillery commander, Oded Boneh, a man of the old school of the Artillery Corps. Talik, who resigned from the IDF and came back and resigned again several times during those years, presented an operational plan for breaking through the Syrian lines in the southern Golan Heights, and said right off the bat: "The plan cannot be carried out, unless every Syrian "pita" outpost is hit with 3,000 shells." This was an astronomical figure, which requires amounts of ordnance and firing units comparable to the bombardment of Berlin at the end of WW2. And this was the same Talik, Deputy Chief of Staff in '73, who three weeks prior to the outbreak of the Yom Kippur War, dismissed the artillery with that infamous statement: "I have 120 105mm barrels in an armored brigade. I have no need for another twelve 155mm barrels."

A brisk debate ensued, at the end of which Talik persisted in his position. They agreed to hold another discussion, and I set up an ambush ahead of it: As Northern Command Artillery Commander, I ordered Israel Lebell, my staff-ops officer, and Rami Yavin, the intel officer, to hang a giant aerial photo showing all the Syrian outposts along the penetration routes behind the map board. I asked them to note on the map which outposts have weaponry that could impact the penetration route with fire, and when it would begin to have such an impact according to the Corps' schedule, based on the range of the weapons in each outpost.

In light of this data we prepared a detailed fire plan, beginning with artillery preparation and ending with close accompaniment of the troops by fire using cluster shells, with each target hit by only eighteen cluster shells, compared with 324 air burst shells and double the amount of explosive shells in Boneh and Talik's plan. I relied on a performance study presented by Shmulik Keren, head of the Artillery Corps' research branch, who used every last bit of intelligence regarding the Syrian "pita" outposts along the penetration route. His performance study proved the feasibility of the fire plan we presented, and even received the stamp of approval from the staff ops division.

In the re-run of the plan approval session, after Talik repeated the old tune about 3,000 shells on each outpost, regardless of its location of firepower, I asked that the map board be rolled aside. The giant aerial photo was revealed to all those present, with the outposts marked, along with arrows denoting their impact on the routes, and the amount of ammunition needed to destroy them.

Talik was stunned. "Where is the data from?" he asked in his authoritative voice, which once shook the foundations of IDF HQ and caused many a commander to lose sleep. I presented the document composed by Keren and Talik, the foremost technology expert in his own mind, couldn't handle the detailed performance study. He ran out of objections.

Eventually, Israel was not forced to invade Syria, and the penetration plan was not carried out, but the important lesson was learned: The old Artillery was gone. The IDF now had a new Artillery Corps.

"Empty Guns, Huh?!"

Prime Minister and Defense Minister Menachem Begin, Chief of Staff Raful, and Northern Command General Yanush sat with us in a crowded command post at Misgav Am on the night between the 18th and 19th of August, 1980. Golani and Paratrooper forces were operating beyond the Litani – at Ramat Nabatiyeh and Ramat Arnon – as part of Operation Movil ("Leader"). Ezer Weizmann had resigned as Defense Minister three months previously. Ariel Sharon wouldn't succeed him until after the 1981 elections, and meanwhile, an ambulance stood at the ready below us in case, heaven forbid, something happened to Begin.

One of the objectives tasked to Golani was to capture the Beaufort Castle. The brigade's soldiers moved forward under the command of Ilan Biran, later to become Central Command General, when suddenly word came of wounded soldiers and later of two "poppies" – dead soldiers. Begin shook his head morosely. Raful pressured him to deploy the Air Force, because that was his M.O. – to escalate. Deputy Defense Minister Motke Zipori, a nemesis of Raful and Yanush, quickly voiced his opposition. Begin accepted his position, and Raful ordered me – in protest – to stop the artillery fire. Out of the corner of my eye, I saw Yanush signaling me to continue, and I didn't stop the fire.

Eleven battalions were concentrated for the operation. They rained thousands of shells, and when Raful left the command post to answer a call of nature, he saw the entire valley below us spitting hellfire toward Lebanon. He was hard of hearing but had the eyes of a hawk, and he said to me angrily: "Arie, I told you to stop."

"I stopped," I told him, "but we can't leave shells in the barrel. The explosives cook in the heat, and barrels turn red hot and sometimes blow up, so I gave the 'empty cannons' order."

Raful bought the explanation, but just then a 175mm battery began to fire from Margaliot at distant targets, aiming to silence the enemy's artillery. Each shell flew directly over our heads with a deafening roar, and Raful realized what was going on. His anger at Zipori and Begin had already cooled off, so he just looked at me sideways and said: "Empty cannons, huh!?"

We Don't Do Dry Runs

The artillery battalions of standing Division Artilleries 215 and 209 – the division artilleries of the Central and Southern commands, respectively – would arrive from time to time for operational deployment at the Northern Command during the years 1978-1980, and I would always send them directly to deploy operationally in the SLA enclave. And here came the turn of the 403rd Battalion, under the command of Shimon "Shema" Shacham, who had been a logistics officer at the 282nd Division Artillery when Yanush commanded the division.

Shema, a talented and proactive officer, had undergone retraining as an artillery fighter, and quickly advanced to the role of bat-com. His battalion deployed in the Marjayoun area, and sometime later, I came to visit with Command General Yanush. The deployment was excellent, the battalion was orderly and properly outfitted, except their camouflage nets were desert yellow, whereas in the Northern Command, we used camo nets in the hues of the local landscape – brown and green.

Shema came running, halted, and saluted, and Yanush told him: You look superbly prepared. Target number this and that – battalion barrage."

Shema ran around frantically, shouting: "Battery target, battery target!" The camo nets were removed, and several minutes later Shema came back to us, although we heard no launches. He said: "Last volley fired."

"But nobody fired," Yanush said, "I saw and heard no fire."

"What," Shema asked, "Do it wet?"

"In the Northern Command we fire at targets and destroy them," Yanush replied. "We don't do dry runs."

How I didn't Command an Armored Brigade

One morning in late 1979, following a nighttime exercise at Tel Shiban in the Golan Heights, where the command group for the penetration into Syria in the Yom Kippur War was held six years earlier, Yanush and I laid out on the lawn for a short rest before the next stage of the divisional exercise.

I was frustrated by then with waiting to be appointed CAO. I wanted it very much, viewed it as the peak of my military career, and I was ready for it with every fiber of my body. Avraham Bar-David was about to complete his term in the post, I didn't know if I would be chosen, and as my doubts increased, I told Yanush: "I want to retrain for the Armored Corps and receive a reserve armored brigade. I've done the tank company commanders' course. I'll have no problem fitting in as Brigadier and continuing from there."

Yanush understood me. "No," he said. "You're gunner number one. We can't do without you. You're staying in the corps." This may have been a catalyst for my appointment as CAO. I think Yanush spoke with Raful before he sent me a week later for an interview with the Chief of Staff.

Chief of Staff Interview

The Chief of Staff interview was set for 07:00. I arrived right on time as usual and found Raful alone in his chambers, making coffee. He used to sleep in a shack at IDF HQ when he worked until late, and was in the office before the secretaries and the aides.

"Good morning," I said.

"Good morning," he replied. "Want coffee?"

"Sure."

Raful made two cups of muddy black coffee, entered the office, and I followed. He perused the papers on his desk, and after about ten minutes raised his eyes and asked: "Arie, what are you doing here?"

I replied: "I was sent for…"

"I didn't send for you," he said, and after a glance at the page before him, he added: "You were sent. What do you want?"

"To be CAO," I answered.

"Fine."

That's the same way Raful would talk on the radio, even in the most difficult times. "Fine," he repeated, and after a few seconds said: "Within two weeks you'll be CAO. Let Bar-David know you're replacing me."

He did it for shock effect, and that was his cynical, at times macabre sense of humor. We continued the conversation; I laid out my vision before him and received his blessing. On the other side of the door, I could hear the staff filling the office.

I still had to go through a bureaucratic process of an assignments hearing, at which Bar-David recommended me for CAO. I'm certain that he did so wholeheartedly, both due to our shared history in the Yom Kippur War and his selecting me as commander of Shivta, and because he himself went through a similar process when appointed as CAO by Motta Gur, bypassing more veteran colonels and brigadier generals, who were not supportive, to say the least.

And Raful also produced a comic moment. He was fond of large townhall-style meetings, at which he would present a topic and await the audience's reactions, and he convened all the colonels of the Artillery Corps, some 20 men or so, to voice their opinions on who should be CAO. The three veteran brigadier generals – Amos Baram, Benny Arad, and Haim Granit – who at that point in time were serving in posts outside the corps, did not participate in this discussion, as they viewed themselves as ideal candidates for the role. All the others, save for colonels I had removed from a post and one other veteran, voted for me.

I was the youngest of them all. The southern and central command generals pushed for the appointment of their command artillery commanders, and the atmosphere became so tense that Amnon Ofek, commander of the Northern Command's heavy division artillery, whispered in my ear: "Let them do like in the rabbinate – a Sephardic Chief Rabbi and an Ashkenazi one." I decided to repeat the advice out loud, and told Raful and his deputy, Kuti: "I see that you're having a hard time deciding, so Amnon has a suggestion – Appoint a Sephardic CAO and an Ashkenazi CAO." Everyone laughed out loud, and the meeting ended amiably.

And now it was time to get to work.

CAO IN THE PEACE FOR GALILEE WAR

Telling Yanka'le That Eyal Has Been killed

Eyal Zur, son of Colonel Yanka'le Zur, commander of the division artillery of the 96th Paratroopers' Division, was killed on April 21st, 1982. He was en route to an observation post near the Litani, when his jeep triggered a landmine placed by terrorists.

Eyal was a talented artillery officer and an instructor in the basic course – a role that only went to the best of the best. He went up north as part of a reinforcement detachment from Shivta, ahead of a heating up of the sector whose signs could be seen in the intel reports, and he was scheduled to observe south of the town of Nabatiyeh. I had found this observation point during one of my tours of the area. The place was called Peqa'ani, north of the town of Taybeh in the SLA enclave, in a relatively open spot, but covered with growth.

It was an ideal spot, right on the bank of the Litani, and you could see all of the Nabatiyeh Heights, which was spread out below like the palm of your hand. Apparently, the terrorists identified movement to or from the observation post, and laid the mine.

Word reached me at one of the command groups held at the Northern Command ahead of "Operation Oranim" ("Pines"[23]). Yanka'le participated as commander of the 96th's Division Artillery, and I as CAO. I took him out of the meeting, and along with friends informed him of the tragedy. Yanka'le was beside himself.

---

23   Operation Oranim was an IDF contingency plan, entailing the entry of the IDF into Lebanon, removing the PLO and Syrian military forces from the country, and installing a Christian regime in Beirut. It was the basis of Operation Peace for Galilee.

South Lebanon on Fire

July 1981 saw another severe deterioration on the Lebanese front. Fatah and other terror organizations frequently opened fire at the north of Israel. Fatah had taken over southern Lebanon almost completely, and Yasser Arafat sent out terror attacks into Israeli territory and launched Katyusha rockets as he pleased. Israel responded with aerial attacks and targeted reprisal operations. The SLA did what it could, and this ping-pong continued to no end. During the escalation initiated by the terrorists, there were two division artillery units deployed in the north – one in the western sector, and one in the east. I decided to use all the observation and location means at our disposal to provide precise targets: The "Fulton" ("Emitter") system developed by the Israeli Aerospace Industries, which could identify the location of enemy batteries by the exit sound, using microphones deployed over a broad sector; The "Lahatutar," ("Juggler") the Cymbeline mortar-locating radar which I mentioned above; The "Meofef" ("Flyer"), a doppler radar used both for ranging and location; and also LREOOD (Long rang electro-optical observation device.) We also made use of the Military Intelligence Directorate's unit 869, which was equipped with advanced day and night observation means, and was skilled at using them, with observation officers who knew the sector well. We placed an FO at every 869 outpost, and I gave the division artillery commanders free reign to stop anyone trying to cross the 20km mark and approach Israel. Truck, car, donkey-drawn buggy, motorcycle – no one passes. Real time reaction with no need for further authorization. Concurrently, I ordered proactive fire on select targets, such as terrorist outposts and artillery concentrations, and any target detected, without thought to saving ammunition.

American envoy, Philip Habib, was rushed to the region, and managed to achieve a ceasefire. It saved Arafat and his cohorts from a mortal blow, but the blows it took until then provided proof that a campaign can be won with firepower alone – if there are no constraints upon us, and no one holding us back, and with Arik Sharon as Defense Minister and Raful as Chief of Staff, the two key words were – no restraints. In his book "1982 – Lebanon: The Road to War," historian Yigal Kipnis describes the furious reaction of the Chief of Staff and the head of MID, Yehoshua Sagi, at a discussion with Prime Minister Menachem Begin, who leaned toward acquiescing to the demands of the Americans to halt the fire, on pains of the Americans halting delivery of F-16 aircraft to Israel. Raful and Sagi, along with Yanush, still the Northern Command General, demanded to keep up the artillery pressure until the PLO surrendered unconditionally. But Begin yielded to pressure from Washington. The Americans, as always, made sure to save our enemies at a critical moment, and the terrorists, battered and bruised, adhered strictly to the terms of the agreement.

But nothing stays the same for long in the Middle East. Less than two months after the incident that took Eyal Zur's life, the situation deteriorated further, reaching a head with the assassination of Israel's ambassador to the UK, Shlomo Argov, following which Israel launched Operation Peace for Galilee on June 6th, 1982.

Eleven months had elapsed since then, but the events of July 1981 served as the prelude to the war. They provided us with the opportunity to examine whether what we'd been doing at the Artillery Corps since the Yom Kippur War, and mostly since January 1980, in preparation for inevitable war in Lebanon, was indeed working. My answer was and is clear: The entire Artillery Corps – standing and reserves – had proved its abilities and was ready for war. The fighters knew what was required of them, were trained and skilled, and the preliminary campaign had given us confidence to boot.

Raful and Sharon had also been convinced that they had serious and professional fire power at their disposal, even if they didn't realize to what extent. "The Artillery Corps surprised with its fire, speed, and precision," said Raful. "We were surprised – and the enemy was surprised."

How the "CAO's Target" Went Down in History

Without artillery it wouldn't have happened. The artillery fired on both sides, and I recalled an illustration from a book we had in my parents' house, where you see the Children of Israel crossing through the Red Sea, crossing over dry land. That's what I felt like at those moments of extraction: Walls of steel, fire, and smoke on either side of us. An incredible feeling, really moving.

— Ami Zagagi, ops officer of the 362nd armored battalion at the Battle of Sultan Yacoub, about the extraction of the force in an operation gone awry.[24]

In the field of artillery, there are definitions and names for different sizes of artillery forces and fire concentrations. A battalion-size fire concentration is called a "David Target." The fire concentration of an entire division of artillery is called a "Statue Target." The fire concentrations, which we taught and practiced prior to the Peace for Galilee War, with several artillery divisions raining concentrated fire on a single target, were not named. In the operation to extract the armored battalion which had been ambushed and surrounded at Sultan Yacoub, such an immense fire concentration was dubbed a "CAO's Target," both because I was directing the fire, and due to the power of 18.5 battalions, over half the entire artillery force of 32 battalions deployed throughout the war.

It happened on Friday, June 11th, 1982, and lasted for 22 minutes – from 08:45 to 09:07. Seconds after I ordered: "Fire!" a tremendous barrage fell down on the valley where the 362nd Battalion was stuck, and for 22 minutes, 320 cannon and rocket launchers rained an enor-

---

[24] In writing this chapter, I availed myself of the following works: Shimshi, Elyashiv: "Nua Kvar Lekhol Haruhot" ("Move Already, Damn It"), Ben Shemen Press, Ch. 8; "Hamehirim Beyoter Lehashpia Be'esh| ("The Quickest to Impact by Fire") Maarachot Press; Zigdon, Yaakov, and Siman-Tov, Sagi: "Artillery in the Battle of Sultan Yacoub" in "Totchanim BeShele"g: Sipur Milchama" ("Gunners in the PFG: A War Story") Modi'in Press, 2016.

mous amount of some 8.000 shells in precision fire. They managed to extract Ira Efron's armored battalion from the inferno in which he found himself in the "little Mitleh,"[25] as the valley was called in the 90th Division's planning charts.

My command was passed on through all networks. Ehud Becher, commander of the 90th Division's artillery force, employed the eleven battalions at his disposal, and the other battalions were operated by the deputy division artillery commanders and the bat-coms of independent units, who listened in on the countdown.

The barrage included all types of weapons – 155mm SPHs, 175mm SPGs, and also six 290mm Haviv rockets (a rocket developed by the IMI, with warheads that contained 1,100 cluster bomblets, which deployed in the air over the target, hitting anything in a 150-meter radius.) The barrage was planned by Yaakov Zigdon, Ehud Barak's artillery commander, who served in effect as staff-ops officer at the corps command post, and Ehud Aviran, the former commander of the 209th Division Artillery, whom I called up from his post as deputy head of staff and command at IDF HQ, and appointed as corps artillery commander, and in effect as my deputy.

The 155mm cannons fired cluster bombs and explosives at the slopes of the valley, to the sides of the surrounded battalion, and in front of the force, the Haviv rockets and 175mm shells hammered the Syrian armored reinforcements. As usual in battle, I felt no emotion but concentration to the point of pain on the mission. I strained all my knowledge, experience, practice, and improvisation to complete the mission, which was executed to perfection, and in time became an exemplar of fire deployment in war, and became the Artillery Corps' calling card throughout the Peace for Galilee War.

But I must go back in time.

---

25 The Mitleh is a strategic passage through the rough terrain of the western Sinai Desert, and the site of one of the IDF's most storied and hallowed battles. However, subsequent and even real-time analysis concluded that the battle – along with its 38 heroic casualties – was, in fact, operationally needless. The commander who initiated it – none other than future PM Ariel Sharon – was heavily criticized by his superiors for the action, which has remained a byword for both a heroic battle and a particularly bloody one

"We'll Go In, Lay Down 400, and Come Back"

About a week before the war, when everyone knew that we were only waiting for an opportunity to enter Lebanon for "Operation Big Pines," with incessant planning sessions and plans being approved at all levels, Yanush came back from Harvard University to take command of the 446th Corps. There were four officers he considered his loyalists – intel officer Shlomo Ilya, Chief Maintenance Officer Rami Dotan, the Chief of Staff's chief of staff Arik Arad, and myself – and we met him at the Country Club Hotel outside Tel Aviv, where he was staying. He made a strident statement as to the impending war: "We'll go in, lay down 400, and come back." A sort of repeat of Operation Litani.

It was obvious that Raful would prefer Yanush over Moshe "Bril" Bar-Kochva, who indeed had to content himself with the 479th Corps, in charge of the Golan Heights, and also over Ehud Barak, who was by then head of the IDF's Planning Directorate. While Barak aspired to command the corps in the impending war, in the end he had to accept a position as deputy to Yanush, who was undoubtedly the most experienced and suitable of them all. Barak's desire to command the corps was so great that when he sat next to me at a meeting of the Joint Chiefs of Staff, a few days before the Peace for Galilee War broke out, he slipped me a note that read as follows: "Ariusha, talk to your friend, so he doesn't take the pauper's ewe." I grinned and said nothing. Barak always had an uncanny talent to identify who influenced whom, and he was the pauper in this biblical allegory. During the four years Yanush served as the Northern Command General, the 446th Corps was commanded by Talik and Bril. This was a marginalized command, deliberately atrophied, as Yanush wanted no organizational framework to impede his direct command over his divisions and brigades. Now, with Amir Drori serving as the Northern Command General, the neglect of the corps could come back to bite Yanush in the ass. And so, on Tuesday afternoon, the third day of the war (to the beginning of which I will get back shortly), with me occupied with my missions on the coastal and central routes, Yanush calls me on the radio. "Arie, come save me," he said, guilt-tripping me in the finest Polish tradition, as though he simply couldn't live without me. He knew that he didn't need to say a word beyond "come" and I would be there, but he wrapped the order as an emotional appeal not to be denied.

Early the next morning, Rami Dotan and I drove to the Corps HQ at Kibbutz Misgav Am. Rami drove in his Volvo, but going up on one of the mountains, the car stopped. The IDF Chief Maintenance Officer's personal vehicle had run out of gas. I told him: "Let's push up to the top, make our way down to the jeep parking lot I saw down there, and take fuel from them." We got out of the Volvo, pushed it up the slope, and somehow I managed to jump into the driver's seat as it began to accelerate downhill, and stopped to wait for Rami. Ten minutes later, we reached Yanush. I appointed myself "Corps Artillery Super-Commander," a title which didn't exist until that moment, and I urgently called in Ehud Aviran, who was deputy head of the IDF's R&D Directorate, and appointed him Corps Artillery Commander instead of Yossi Shaya, an officer with a glowing past, but now a reservist who didn't fit in the new model of the Artillery Corps.

Haviv Ya Habib

The sector of Lebanon, in all its routes, from the coastal road up to Beirut and the mountain routes to the east, does not allow for the deployment of tanks and a mad dash forward as do the expanses of the Sinai. It was clear that the unarmored infantry would have a key role in the penetration, and that significant firepower would be needed to breathe reality into our slogan: "Don't bang your heads against the wall – we'll blow the wall up before you get to it."

Put simply, to allow the maneuvering forces to carry out their missions with minimum casualties. I planned to fire all types of weapons, employ all systems, and fully exhaust the technological capabilities we had worked on so hard over the past few years. One of these advanced means was the aforementioned "Haviv" rocket, which was designed to be what the U.S. military calls an "assault breaker." They themselves were concurrently developing the MLRS as a lesson from the Yom Kippur War, when the 240mm rockets stopped the Syrian tanks in the Valley of Tears on October 9th, 1973.

Immediately following that war, the U.S. Armed Forces established TRADOC – the Training and Doctrine Command, entrusted with setting fighting doctrines, outlining directions for development, and instruction. It became a sort of super-HQ of the ground forces, which took on powers in the field of force construction pursuant to the fighting doctrine. The first commander of TRADOC, General William E. DePuy, sent teams to study the Yom Kippur War, and one of their conclusions was to provide the ground army with a powerful weapon, capable of stopping an assault of tanks, as done by my personal command in the heroic containment battle of the Valley of Tears, as mentioned above.

We, as I said, concurrently developed the Haviv – a 290mm rocket launcher, the warhead of each rocket containing 1,100 anti-tank and anti-personnel bomblets. These were designed to penetrate tanks through their upper, less protected parts, using a hollow charge. The shell of the bomblet was slit, so the explosion would also yield a shrapnel cloud.

Finding a Coordinate Without a Ruler

On Wednesday afternoon, the Air Force received the go-ahead to destroy the Syrian AD missiles in the eastern sector, and Operation Artzav ("Slug") was a major success. It was the signal for the start of the campaign against the Syrians in the Beqaa Valley – a campaign we all awaited, ready for action and hungry for battle. I wanted to operate the Haviv missiles. After deploying two batteries, comprising of four Sherman tanks each, in the eastern part of the corps' sector, I mounted four Haviv launchers on each of the Shermans, with rockets equipped with the aforementioned warhead. The operation was under my complete authority. This is how I viewed it throughout the war – and that is how I acted. I needed no authorization and expected no direction. I fired and updated. But that evening, seeing no masses of Syrian tanks charging down on us with fire and fury, I decided instead to operate my beloved Haviv[26] against our traditional enemy – the Syrian artillery. The target I chose was a battalion of 130mm cannons, which according to the aerial photos was deployed along the banks of Lake Qaraoun, and fired at a range of 27 km.

The intel officer pulled out a square ruler and tried to extract coordinates from the map as though we were in a previous generation, but I had no time for niceties and the fellow was sent packing for reposting. I called Uri Manos, my deputy bat-com back in '73, and now the Northern Command Artillery Commander, and asked him to get me the coordinates from the digital target bank in the command artillery HQ's computers, according to an updated aerial photo from that same day, and I passed the coordinates on to the Haviv battalion.

I had a "private" Bell-206 helicopter at my disposal during the war, and it went everywhere I went. Thus I was able to skip between the units and be anywhere I found it vital to be at any given moment, according to my reading of the battle.

This was how I arrived at the command post in the village of Meshki in order to watch the Air Force planes attack the Syrian surface-to-air missile batteries, and what I remember most are the clouds of red dirt raised by the bombardment. This was the opening note of the campaign against the Syrians in the eastern sector – a confrontation we had thus far avoided by orders from the political echelon. This was also an extraordinary opportunity to employ the Haviv.

At one in the morning on Thursday, I ordered Yair Koren, commander of the Haviv battalion, to fire 22 rockets at the Syrian 130mm battalion. Koren, a Kibbutznik form Ashdot Yaakov Meuchad, an introverted, taciturn, consummately professional converted paratrooper, served in the attrition period as a regular aerial observer – a role requiring professionalism, courage, and an even keel. He ordered "Fire," and 24 thousand bomblets landed on the twelve barrels of two stunned Syrian batteries. Unfortunately, a third battery leapfrogged

---

26 The Hebrew word Haviv, like its Arabic counterpart Habib, both mean "liked, beloved."

elsewhere that evening, unwittingly saving itself from annihilation. The IDF's armored and infantry forces, which reached Lake Qaraoun at dawn, discovered a horror scene: Every single piece of equipment, down to the ammunition trucks, had been hit and burned. The area was strewn with bomblets, and those who hadn't been killed in hellfire from above had fled for their lives.

Haviv rockets firing

A month later, Israel received a visit from the Chief of the South African Defense Force, General Constand Viljoen – who had become Raful's bosom buddy, the two taking to each other as only a pair of farm boys could. Viljoen had begun his military career as a gunner, before retraining as a paratrooper and commando fighter. Raful asked me to demonstrate the wonders of the Haviv to the distinguished guest, and when I toured the smoking remains of the Syrian battalion with him, I suddenly saw that he was about to step on a dud. I leaped at him and pushed him away. The shaken Viljoen couldn't stop thanking me, and in my subsequent visits to South Africa, I was treated like a prince.

At the start of the first visit, he asked me what I would like to see, beyond the official itinerary. I said: "The new cannon that Dr. Bull has built for you."

Canadian engineer, Gerald Bull, became famous when he tried to build a long-range cannon for Saddam Hussein, capable of carrying a nuclear warhead from Iraq to Israel. He was found dead under mysterious circumstances in his home in Belgium, but prior to that, he had managed to design a cannon with a range of 40 km for the South Africans.

Dr. Bull, who was considered a ballistics genius, hoped to reach outer space with a cannon shell, as indicated by the name of the company he founded: The Space Research Company. Politics were of no interest to him, and as he was in constant search for funding to realize his dream, he was willing to design cannons to anyone willing to pay, including long-range cannons for China and South Africa. He also helped Israel design a shell with a 46km range, a subcaliber of a 175mm shell, which is to say a 130mm shell with a lower weight, encircled by lock rings. The shell was launched with the blast required for the heavier 175mm shell, resulting in a range extended by fourteen kilometers.

I met Bull twice, and found him to be a fascinating man of immense knowledge. He ended his life after allying himself with Saddam Hussein, once again in the hope of reaching space with a shell fired from a cannon barrel.

I asked to see the cannon in action, view the impacts, and drive its self-propelled version, which was mounted on an APC with monster truck wheels. I witnessed a large impact scatter, reaching 400m in radius at the end of the range.

My second request was to cross into Angola, which was a battleground then – out of curiosity and to study the methods of another army. We visited a forward operating base of the South African commandos, some 200 km within Angolan territory, and received a briefing from the unit commander on the infiltration of groups of ten fighters into the bush for two weeks at a time, returning with proof, best left undetailed, regarding the success of their mission. Beyond the military aspect, it was fascinating to observe the wild herds of animals from a low-flying helicopter (keeping to low altitude for fear of shoulder-mounted AD missiles), with my feet dangling from the chopper.

Throw Aside Whoever's in the Way. Rush Ahead!

At dawn on Thursday, June 11th, 1982, a tank battle broke out between the 262nd and 90th Divisions of the 446th Corps, and the Syrian 1st Division. This would be the last tank battle of such magnitude in the IDF's history, and those who have watched any Hollywood battlefield epics, from "Waterloo" to "Pearl Harbor," can imagine the visual portrayal of a battle of massive forces. Yanush deployed the two divisions as a field marshal, not through screens and computers.

When the 90th Division, under Giora Lev, battled the Syrian force in front of it to a stalemate, Yanush brought the 7th Armored Brigade, under Eitan Kauli (nee Keinan) from the flank, with the new Merkava Mark 1 tanks. The firepower, precision, and surprise provided by the first battalion of Merkava tanks, coming from a new direction, proved too much for the Syrian tanks, and they began catching fire and going up in flames, one by one in rapid succession.

The 1st Syrian Division was defeated and retreated, and our aim as evening fell was to reach the Beirut-Damascus road and seize control of it. After a consultation at the command post, Yanush chose to move there along the central route – the Sultan Yacoub route. I opposed this proposal and suggested that we move along the farming area, east of Jabel Baruch and west of Jabel Arabeh, which was bisected by irrigation canals – starting with infantry movement by the 623rd Reserve Paratroopers Brigade, and followed by clearing the path for tanks.

Yanush feared he would get mired in the irrigation canals of the farming area, and so preferred the Sultan Yacoub route. The mission before me now was to advance the artillery along the eastern sector, in order to get within range of the Beirut-Damascus road – and do it before dawn, when the assault on the road would commence. I gave a clear order to all artillery units: Our mission is to advance at all costs.

The routes are narrow and mountainous, I stressed. Throw aside whatever is in the way: Truck, tanker, tank, car. Rush ahead!

Ehud Aviran took command of the mission and came down from Meshki Village. He began mobilizing the artillery battalions, clearing their way, and rushing them on like General Patton in the epic blockbuster film.

The battalion fighters, commanders, and enlisted men alike, labored on the mission. I decided to send the 449th Division Artillery, under Franco Gonen, along a parallel route. Oded Kaplan, the division artillery's deputy commander, was in effective charge of the unit's four battalions. He entered Lebanon through the Fatma Gate, moved full steam ahead past Lake Qaraoun, with no armored forces ahead of him, and instructed the lead bat-com, Shimon Shatsmiller, to take the lead in an M-109 which was ready for direct fire.

At dawn, Kaplan deployed the division artillery in the space east of Lake Qaraoun and south of the village of Al-Qaraoun. He came within range of the Beirut-Damascus road without getting stuck in the traffic jam of the central route, but was amidst significant risk, as he moved in uncleared territory as a vanguard Israeli force. By the Friday, this entire artillery armada stood armed, within range, ready for battle.

How the Haviv Battalion Was Not Destroyed by Friendly Fire

The Air Force is supposed to operate independently. The skies opened on Thursday morning, but later that day, disaster struck as two of our Phantoms accidentally attacked the 931st Nahal battalion, under Yom-Tov Samia, killing 28 soldiers and wounding around 100. This is a well-known tragedy, but its roots are less so.

In the Yom Kippur War, the Artillery Corps was in charge of tactical coordination with the Air Force. Each FSO and brigade artillery commander had a surface-to-air radio, and we were trained and proficient in directing, leading by map, and leading by terrain. But we were playing chess with ourselves. The Air Force, despite sending a pilot to the air-ground support department at Bahad 9, did not practice cooperation with us. Furthermore, its commanders, unable to face their resounding failure in the Yom Kippur War, searched for alternative scapegoats and tried in vain to lay the blame on us.

In the Peace for Galilee War, the Air Force took the issue of close air support under its own wing, assigned air coordination officers (AOs) to the brigades and divisions, and considered the problem solved. Many in the ground forces also believed this to be the solution. I understood it to be a grave mistake. I, and everyone who in 1973 had experienced the Syrian aircraft firing on us freely, even killing Avraham Snir, Kahalani's FSO, with Kahalani himself saved only by miracle, and with our own Air Force not rushing to our aid – we knew that this erroneous attitude could cost us dearly. The Air Force did not really take part in the ground war, although it took the matter upon itself, and the cooperation was neglected.

Yanush and the corps' chief of staff, Amram Mitzna, flew that night to the "palace" – the Northern Command's command post at Mt. Canaan. Ehud Barak, Yanush's 2nd in command, toured the forces. I collapsed from fatigue after a week of intensive action around the clock, in the field most of the time, skipping from sector to sector, present at every place where combat was ongoing, providing operational and logistical solutions for the firing units, and also slapping backs. After all, even battle-hardened veterans are human beings, and they too were glad to see their efforts noticed and appreciated.

Now I found myself a spot on the ground, within the Corps artillery mobile command post's side tent, and fell into a deep slumber. Ehud Aviran accelerated the movement of the firing units to new positions at the time. Yaakov Zigdon, called up from command and staff, updated the deployment on the maps, the status of our troops and the positions of the enemy. At 01:30, he woke me up and said: "There's a problem with Ehud Becher." Becher was in command of the 454th Division Artillery, in the 90th Division. I made contact with him, and heard that a tank battalion had gotten stuck in a Wadi in the Sultan Yacoub area, with Syrian anti-tank missile squads, taking heavy fire. They could neither move forward nor retreat, Becher said. Stuck in the craw.

I ordered Zigdon to transfer all units already deployed in the new positions and get ready to fire to Becher's command, and by morning eleven battalions had gathered on the 454th's network. I concurrently also logged on to the Ira Efron's network, the commander of the entrapped battalion, and followed developments.

Becher operated from the division command post with the deputy division commander, Ran Sarig, by his side. But they had no line of sight to the area, the battalion's FSO disappeared early in the movement, after his tank malfunctioned and he didn't switch tanks. So the artillery commander of the brigade to which the entrapped battalion belonged, the 399th, a reserve armored brigade under the command of Micky "Swet" Shachar, suffered shell shock and was out of commission. For lack of choice, Becher ran the cover fire for the tank battalion while dialoguing with the surrounded battalion's intel officer, Iron Ben-Porat, who became an ad-hoc FSO.

In short, what happened is that the 362nd armored battalion received orders to move along the "Micha" route – the main route in the small valley at the foot of Sultan Yacoub, and to set up a blockade in the area known in the IDF code lingo as the "Toblano Triangle." The 399th Brigade, to which the battalion belonged, relied on information received by the corps intelligence from Nachman Rivkin, brigadier of the 943rd. Rivkin held Jabel Arabeh, but mistakenly believed that he was holding the ridge above the Toblano Triangle. He reported that the area in front of him was clear of enemy forces, and according to the location he reported, the conclusion was that it would be possible to enter the Toblano Triangle. This was also the report received by Ehud Aviran from the corps staff-ops department, and according to this intel, I ordered the deployment of the Haviv rockets as northward as possible, to achieve range to the Beirut-Damascus road.

Brave, taciturn Yair Koren moved ahead of the Haviv battalion. He saw a soldier walking toward him, approached him, and identified him as a Syrian commando fighter, armed with a folding-butt AK47. Koren took his weapon and loaded him on the jeep. He didn't know yet that he had, in fact, deployed the battalion in the middle of an uncleared Syrian compound, and that Syrian troops who had missed the fallback order were still milling around. When the battalion deployed, Koren also learned that he had become cut off from the battalion's ordnance officer, who was moving behind him with the cranes used to load the rockets. Just then, Ira Efron arrived with the 362nd and reached the rear Haviv battery, the Haviv battalion being in fact the first IDF force to move along the route. Efron saw the giant slabs of the Haviv launchers mounted on their Sherman chassis, didn't identify them in the dark, and hailed them on the emergency network, for the unknown force to identify itself. No one answered him and Efron was about to open fire, but luckily for us, he sent the battalion's recon platoon ahead. Some of the scouts reported hearing talk in Arabic, some reported hearing Hebrew, and Efron decided to err on the side of caution, and try yet another means of identification, and fired a green flare. Concurrently, and in a miraculous coincidence, Koren took out the flare gun from its flannel wrapping from the jeep's security chest. He saw the green flare, was certain it was his lost ordnance officer, and fired a green flare in response. And so the Haviv battalion was saved from certain annihilation by friendly fire.

"You Sent Us to Die"

Parenthetically: The Haviv battalion was composed of fighters selected from the CAO HQ personnel. This was not a homogenous battalion but an amalgam of men, some of a low combat profile, some only children, who all shared high levels of education and "kaba" – the IDF's personnel quality grading scale. They weren't "standard issue" combat troops. Some had only gone through the most basic of basic training, and most had not served in combat battalions.

I came later to have a talk with them, while the fighting was still ongoing. I complimented them on their performance in destroying the Syrian 130mm battalion at Lake Qaraoun, their part in extracting the armored battalion at Sultan Yacoub, and the destruction of the Syrian SA-6 surface-to-air missiles. They sat in front of me frozen, without the trace of a smile on their faces. One of them, a chubby, pale FDC sergeant with John Lennon glasses, cried out from a wounded heart: "You sent us to die."

I expressed regret for what had happened, described and explained the situation at length, and then sang their praises some more, until the atmosphere thawed.

You're in the Little Mitleh

Efron's armored battalion kept moving according to plan despite coming under fire. Unfortunately, it was friendly fire, opened by a company commander in the 573rd Battalion, another battalion in Rivkin's brigade, which had slid forward and taken up positions.

The tank driving before Efron's was hit and caught fire, as did the one behind him. Five fighters were killed. Efron was certain it was enemy fire and extracted forward with two companies, leaving the two damaged tanks to be handled by the rearguard company. That company, moving with the battalion aid station, was delayed by ten minutes in order to treat the wounded, and then ran into a Syrian force and couldn't advance.

Efron moved forward quickly in the meanwhile, stopping far beyond the Toblano Triangle, where the blockade was to take place. It shortly turned out that he had entered an anti-tank compound of the Syrian 58th Brigade. An orderly, organized compound, known as the "Little Mitleh" in the IDF's 90th Division's plans. But he himself, as I said, believed himself to be in the Toblano Triangle, directly below Sultan Yacoub. He also failed to recognize the shells Becher had fired to help him. Only after Herzl Gedge fired a surface-burst illumination shell at Sultan Yacoub, did Efron finally identify his location.

Ira Efron, incidentally, claims to this day that he wound up where he did under the order of one, Ehud Barak. And so the Rashomon-like effect goes on.

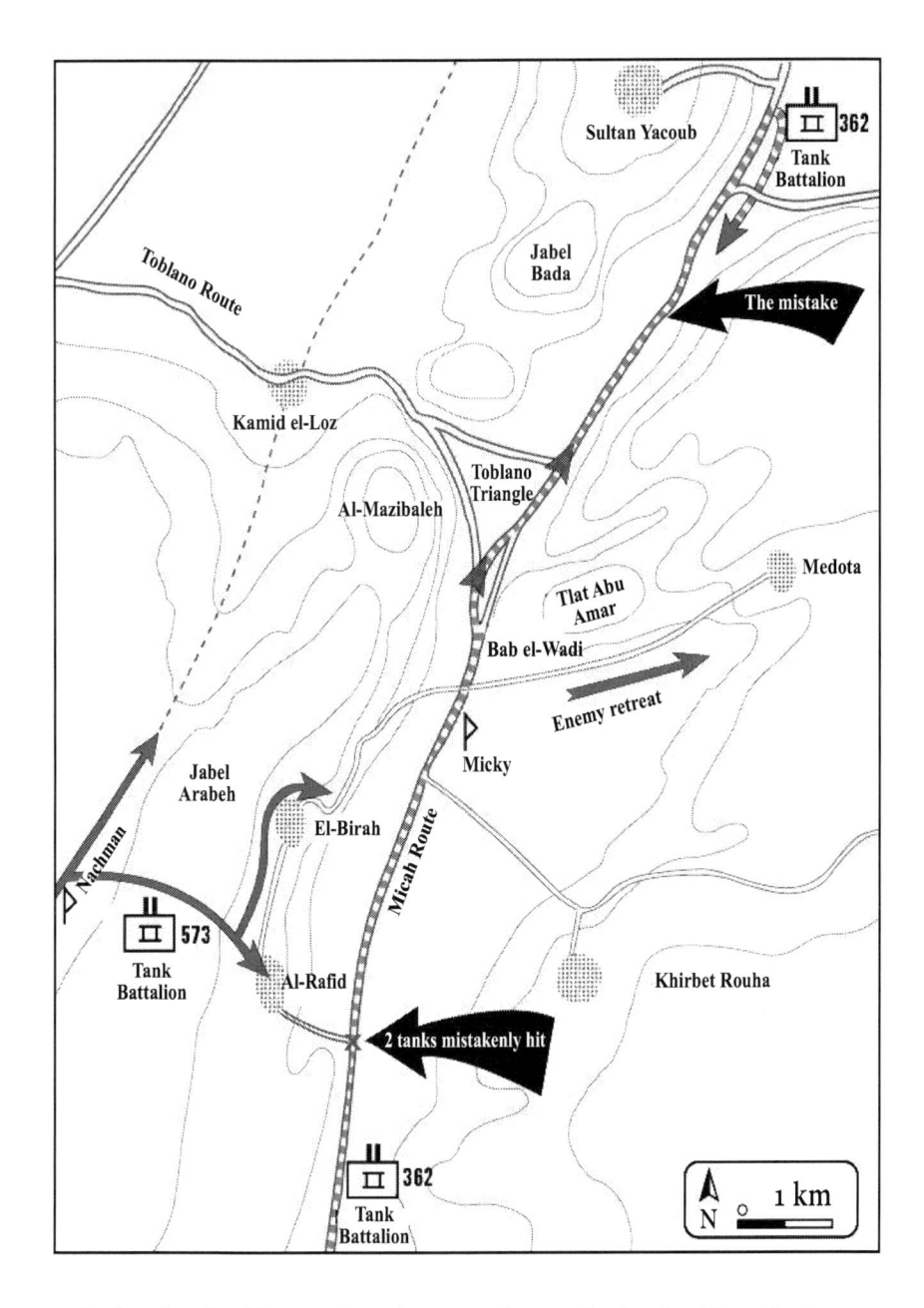

The battle of Toblano Triangle, 1982 (From the book Eifo Ani Nimtza Laazazel ("Where the Hell Am I") by Elyashiv Shimshi, Maarachot Press, pp 33 (Heb.).

Yanush didn't know exactly where the 362nd Battalion was, and wanted Efron to move faster. He feared a delay in taking up position at the blockade, and got on the battalion radio network to spur Efron on. "With a jeep, I'd have been at the blockade by now," he told him. Where did this statement come from? Three years before, Yanush and I had entered Lebanon in two grey jeeps near Biranit, passed the UN checkpoint staffed by Irish Catholics not free of antisemitism, and drove unimpeded all the way to Aqia Bridge. This drive gave birth to the "Ben-Tovim"[27] plan. The Northern Command staff-ops officer, Moshe Kafri, named it after me, "Arie Ben-Tovim," because I was the one who proposed to cross the Litani through the Aqia Bridge and not through the booby-trapped and fire-ranged Hardaleh. In my tours of the area, I saw from the Peqa'ani lookout, that the Aqia Bridge was thronged with local vehicles, and was quickly and conveniently accessible. During the war, the 36th and 162nd Divisions indeed crossed it.

Salvation Will Come From Neither the Air Nor the Infantry

Ehud Becher, who as mentioned above, was positioned with Ran Sarig at the 90th Division's command post, protected the 362nd Battalion with artillery fire on the positions controlling the routes along which the battalion moved. Each battalion reaching the planned deployment area was placed under his command, and so eleven battalions had gathered under him.

Even before that, I realized that the mission of extracting the trapped armored battalion was an independent Artillery Corps mission, and I did not await orders. I commanded Zigdon to prepare a "fire box" to extract the entrapped battalion. Yanush, too, quickly realized what was going on, and decided to throw the 880th Division

---

[27] "Ben-Tovim" is an existing surname in Hebrew, and means "well-born," "of good birth."

into battle, under Yom-Tov Tamir, my friend since back when he was ops officer with the 79th Battalion before the Six-Day War, and I was their FSO.

"You'll get all the artillery," Yanush told Tamir on the radio. I ignored, or possibly failed to hear his words. I was focusing on transferring every possible unit to Becher. This required me to overcome the resistance of the division commanders, and particularly Emannuel Sakel, commander of the 252nd Division, and expedite the mobilization of the firing units forward. The planning of the "fire box" remained Zigdon's exclusive domain. The purpose of the "fire box" was to prevent the enemy from reaching the besieged unit, by erecting walls of fire around it. I knew I could count on Zigdon without a second's thought.

Yom-Tov Tamir mobilized the 645th Brigade from the east, under Amatzia Atlas. But Atlas took nine casualties almost instantly and withdrew. Efron's Battalion was hastily put under Tamir, and we continued as we were.

Toward dawn, with the stormfront of a horrible disaster darkening over our heads, we deliberated as a short corps planning group. The question was sharp and plain: How to extract the 362nd Battalion? Present was Yanush, Barak, Mitzna, and me, and with us, Ran Pecker, as the Air Force representative. He too was summoned by Yanush.

The idea of executing the extraction by using a force of paratroopers was deliberated. Yair "Gutzi" Ogen from Kibbutz Yagur, was the brigadier of the 939th, a reserve paratroopers' brigade, and he was called up to arms. He arrived at the command post in Meshki with his command staff, all in battle vests, ready to fight, and when he heard what was afoot, he said: "I can carry it out this evening." His troops were still on the way, in buses, and it was clear that they would want to go on reconnaissance afterward, would need aerial photos, and time to study the mission. In short, by the time they were ready, there would be no one left to extract.

The eyes turned to the Air Force. Pecker shifted uneasily in the command post canvas chair, and finally delivered an odd statement: "Hot MSA." This meant "A hot missile-saturated area." But the Air Force had supposedly taken out all the missiles a day and a half beforehand, so what MSA and what was so hot? I knew the answer, and it was a hard one: Following the terrible tragedy of the bombing of the 931st Battalion, the mistaken attack on the 401st Battalion, and the attack on a reserve force's HQ on the Meshki Ridge, the Air Force had decided to stop providing close cover to our forces, especially in a narrow ravine like the Little Mitleh, in which the IDF and enemy forces mixed with each other.

Ehud Barak understood how Yanush and I thought, and he knew our history, so he said: "Artillery!" And indeed, at 04:00, Yanush informed Yom-Tov Tamir: "You'll get all the coats."

A Tremendous "Fire Box" Saves the Surrounded Battalion at Sultan Yacoub

I presented the plan to extract the entrapped force through a "fire box" to be created simultaneously by all eighteen and a half artillery battalions present in the eastern sector. I explained that the 175mm and "Haviv" battalions would operate on the tanks attacking Ira from the north, as well as reinforcements expected to flow from the direction of the Beirut-Damascus road, since we already knew of tanks moving in that direction. Concurrently, we would concentrate the precise M-109 battalions, to fire cluster and explosive ammunition from both sides of the besieged battalion, and both sides of the route through which they would retreat. When we were ready to create this fire box – we would order Efron to extract backward. Yanush approved the plan. I ordered Yair Koren to fire three Haviv rockets in succession for ranging, and moved the Haviv firepower three times southward along the route of the road, toward the beleaguered armored battalion. The Havivs advanced 500 meters at a time. After the three leaps, when the 362nd heard the cluster bombs exploding, I realized that we were ready, and at 08:45, a monstrous artillery barrage was fired. It lasted until 09:07, when the 362nd Battalion extracted backward and was saved from annihilation.

Eyal Zagagi, deputy commander at one of the 109mm battalions, fired all night to extract the battalion where his brother, Ami Zagagi, was serving as ops officer. Talk about brothers-in-arms.

And another anecdote, incidental to the battle. Several weeks following the battle, I visited the corps' wounded at Tel Hashomer Hospital. Ehud Becher, an old friend to this day, joined me. "That's Mizrachi, the CAO, who saved us," some of them muttered, and approached me as though to kiss the hem of my cloak. These were the survivors of the Sultan Yacoub battle, most of them yeshiva boys, who were moved to follow the ancient custom and kiss the hand of a benefactor. The sentiment was authentic, and for all my toughness, I felt a tremor in my heart at the heartfelt gesture.

The impressive professional coup, the echoes of which within the IDF were strategic, took place despite the fact that the "CAO's target" wasn't carried out in strict accordance with procedures and doctrine, due to the special circumstances. The demand for support and the employment thereof should be in the hands of the FSO moving with the battalion, but the forward chain of command didn't function, what with an FO who went missing and an FSO who likewise vanished. The artillery commander also went into shell shock and was of no use.

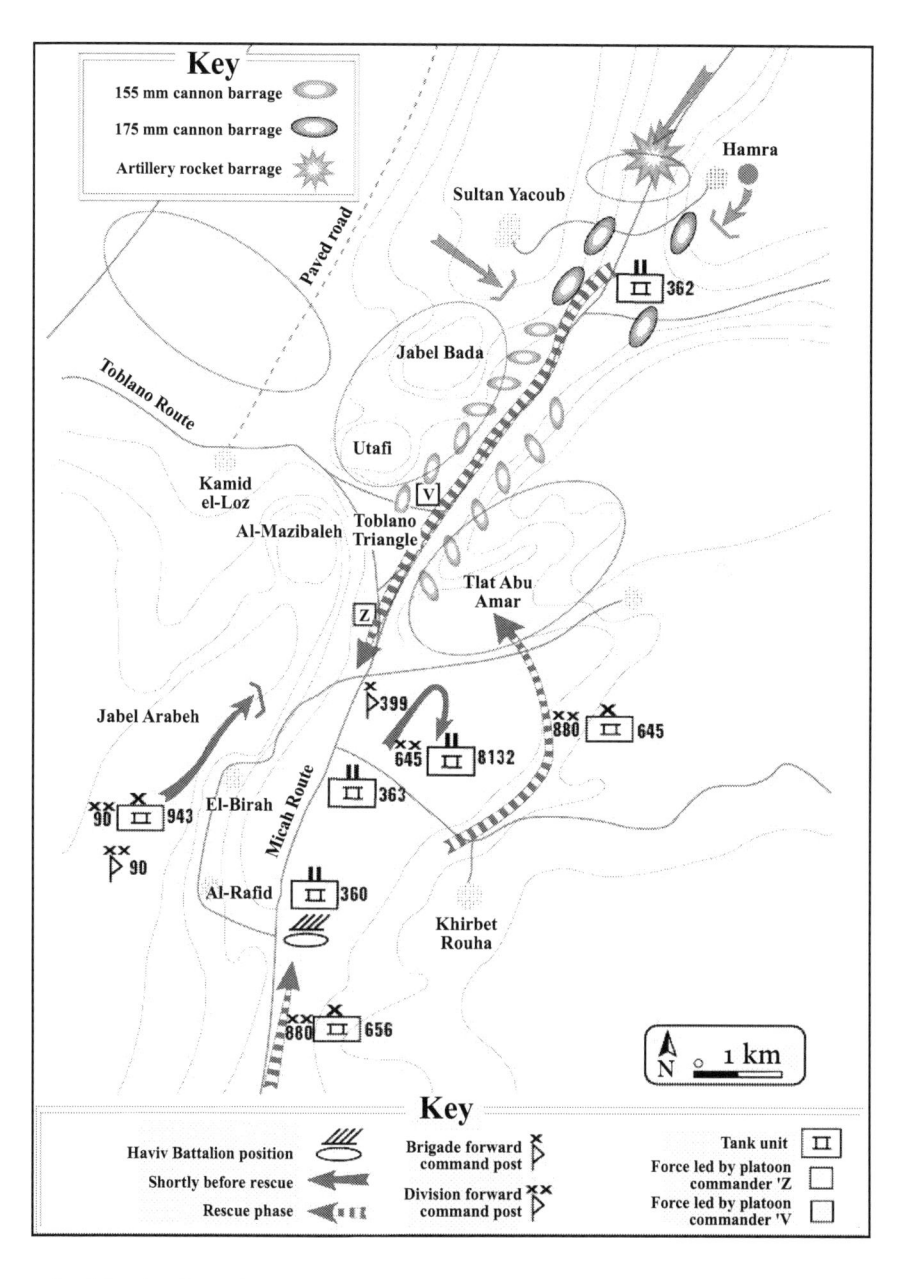

The "fire box" at the Battle of Sultan Yacoub (From the book "Of Speed on the Battlefield" by Elyashiv Shimshi, Modan Press, 2011, pp 159.

Years of practice and the professionalism of the young bat-coms, who were deeply familiar with the secrets of the new ways of the gunner, learned well what their tools and men could do, and displayed initiative and ingenuity, along with the immense knowledge and consummate professionalism of the corps' brass – Ehud Becher the leader, Yaakov Zigdon, whose name became legend, Ehud Aviran who wrote the Artillery Corps' doctrine – and with all due humility, me as well, as Chief Artillery Officer, after appointing myself artillery commander in the sector – all these combined to yield the historic result.

And after all that, I dare say that anyone who held those senior positions would have reached the same amazing results, thanks to long years of practice in all arenas, conditions, seasons, hours, and situations, and thanks to the initiative, professionalism, talent, and motivation of the human factor in the corps.

THE ART OF POSTING, SIGNING, AND GROWING

As I said, at the heart of the corps' success in the Peace for Galilee War were the fighters, and chief among them the commanders, notably the young officers, who formed the foundation of the corps' chain of command. I allow myself some of the credit for this change, because I made sure, since entering the position of CAO, to replace most of the bat-coms of the reserve battalions with young bat-coms, graduates of the standing M-109 battalions, who knew the gun and the new Artillery Corps' doctrine, were full of belief in their own abilities, were proud of their unit and didn't bow down to other corps.

While I was facing a bare cupboard early on, the words of the legendary Yanka'le Aknin continually echoed in my mind: "It's all about posting," and during the first year, I signed 83 officers to the career military. For instance, the late Herzl Gedge was an XO at the 411th Battalion, and began commanding a battery while still completing the six-month contract he'd signed with the career military, which was a condition for participation in the officers' course. When I was artillery commander of the Northern Command, he for some reason wrote to my secretary (who had later gone on to an officers' course and came back as the CAO's chief of staff) as follows: "If Northern Command artillery commander Arie Mizrachi is appointed CAO, I'll sign with the career military."

When I was appointed CAO, I called him in for an interview. He told me that he was about to be discharged, was taking a long post-service trip, and then intended to come back to his family's farm in Neve Yamin.

I tried to entice him into signing on with the career military, and when nothing availed, I said to him: "Gedge, your word is your bond, right?"

He looked at me and said: "No one breaks my word."

Those who knew Gedge, his decisions, and the honesty and integrity he unfailingly displayed, knew this to be true. I pulled out the note. "Is this your handwriting?"

He turned pale, but said, "My word is my word," then signed on, and ended his military career as a brigadier general.

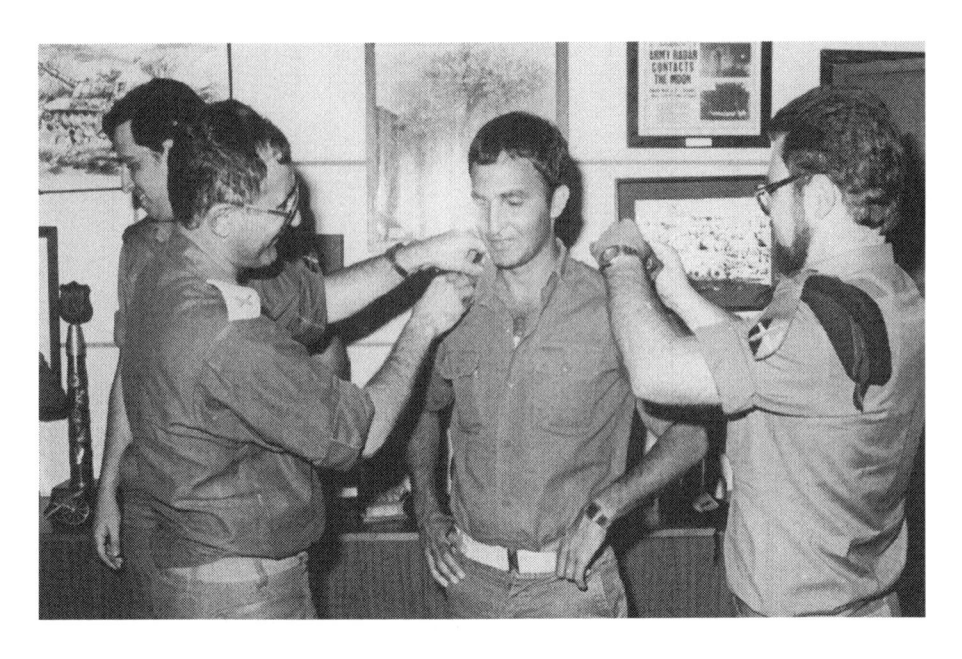

Herzl Gedge awarded the rank of major.

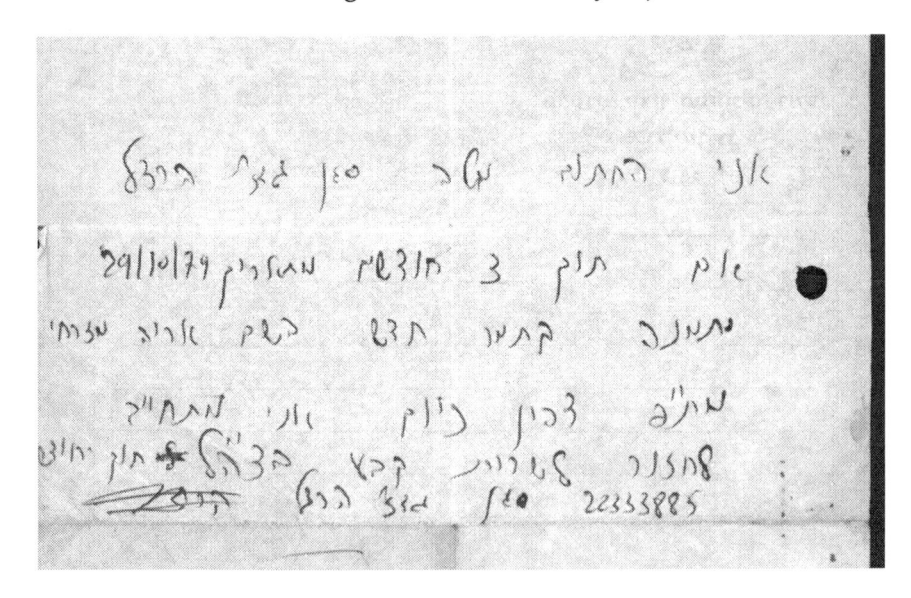

The note

On that dark and sudden day in Lebanon, it was Herzl Gedge, the 25-year-old bat-com of a reserve M-109 battalion in Ehud Becher's division artillery, who discovered Ira Efron's error. He was the one who fired a ground surface illumination bomb at Sultan Yacoub, and who said "Ira, look back," when Efron failed to identify the signal.

CAO Neri Horowitz, Major Hofit Golan (Herzl Gedge's daughter) and me.

How Ofer Nimrodi Didn't Jump From the Balcony

Ron Prosor, later Director of Israel's Foreign Affairs Ministry and its Ambassador to the UN, describes in his book "Undiplomatically," how he was signed to the career military for five months, over the objections of his girlfriend, and how the five months turned into a year, so that they gave up on a post-service trip to the United States, only striking it off their bucket list twenty-five years later. It happened at a meeting I held with a fine group of officers at the home of Captain Moshe Shibber in Ramat Hasharon. It was attended, in addition to Prosor, by Tzvika Fuchs and Eitan Dangot, and I signed up all three to the career military.

Shibber was killed several months later, and Prosor later chose a diplomat's life over that of a soldier, but Fuchs commanded the 215th Fire Division (the new name for a "division artillery") and was later head of the ground forces' doctrine, instruction, and training division, with the rank of brigadier general. Dangot commanded Shivta in his last posting in the Artillery Corps, and was later appointed Coordinator of the Government's Activities in the Territories (aka COGAT) with the rank of major general.

When the subject comes up, my wife Tamar always likes to recall the scene with Ofer Nimrodi, later a scandal-plagued newspaper magnate and businessman, who arrived at our home in Kfar Saba – a small, 3rd-floor apartment, no elevator, as far as possible from the Nimrodi family's stately mansion in Savyon (Israel's equivalent of Beverly Hills).

We sat down in the small living room. Nimrodi was approaching his discharge at the time, and I tried to get him to sign on, but he held firm: "I'm already enrolled for MBA studies at Harvard. My father won't let me sign."

"You're not leaving unless you sign," I told him.

He ran to the balcony and said: "I'll jump."

I had wanted him very much since being the commander of Shivta and the Northern Command artillery, but from the first moment, it wasn't easy. I already mentioned the agreement I had with Matan Vilnai, when he was commander of Bahad 1, that when a cadet from the Artillery Corps was facing dismissal, he would call me. I would cross the area through the Ovdat Triangle and Mitzpe Ramon, participate in the dismissal hearing, and if I thought the man was worth keeping, he would be sent to do a basic course.

When the person who came up – not for dismissal, but for transfer to another corps – was Ofer Nimrodi, he tried to use his family connections to get a transfer to the Intelligence Corps, due to his father being a senior intelligence officer, and later an IDF military attaché in Iran – anything but go back to the Artillery Corps. I crossed over, and following a long conversation persuaded him to stay with the corps.

I met him again when I was the Northern Command artillery commander and he was an FO with the Golani Rangers, during an operation to test the traversability of the Hardaleh Bridge over the Litani. A Rangers officer stepped on a landmine and lost his foot. A rainstorm raged that night, precluding the possibility of landing a chopper, and who if not Nimrodi arrived at the villa, sending the coded report to the firing units with one hand, holding the wounded man he was carrying on his back with the other. The same Nimrodi who used to leave the BMW his father bought him in Tiberias, and take a bus the rest of the way, so as not to flaunt his privilege to his mates and subordinates.

When he said, "My father won't allow," I invited myself to a meeting with Nimrodi Pere. It was held beside their enormous pool in Savyon, and began in discord. As usual, I put no rein on my tongue, and we parted at the end of the day with mutual appreciation, but most importantly with the father's blessing for Ofer to sign on for one year as a battery commander in the 334th Battalion. As expected, he did stellar work.

The same happened with Michael Stieglitz, brother of Avital Sharansky (wife of Anatoly, the famous Soviet dissident imprisoned for wishing to make Aliyah). Michael, who had served as an officer in the Soviet army, refused to undergo a reserve officers' course, insisting on undergoing the full six-month course with the conscripts. In order to sign him up, I constructed a shortened track for him, in which he indeed went to do his basic course with the conscripts, and became a model officer.

I also built a similar shortened track for Shuka Dorfman, who arrived as a sergeant in the 50th Battalion out of the desire to serve in the corps, and climbed the ladder over the years, all the way to being appointed CAO.

The Boat Method

My "Laser" sailboat was drydocked at Beit Yanai beach. Almost every Saturday, I would take it down into the water, and often invited officers approaching their discharge, to talk to them about signing on. I would sail with such a recalcitrant or undecided candidate, and when we reached the open sea, I would "plant," meaning that I would slacken the sail, causing the boat to list and sway – usually in the middle of a swarm of jellyfish – just the spot to say: "You won't sign? Get off the boat, then."

I don't think anyone actually thought they were about to be tossed overboard the Laser, but the talks that developed in such intimate settings at sea led to quite a few signings.

At the officers' course in Shivta, there was also a company of ROTC officers – 30-40 Technion or university graduates, who were meant to practice what they'd studied in the professional corps – Comms, Ordnance, Air Force, and Navy – and to serve concurrently as officers in Artillery Corps reserve units as secondary postings. Throughout the course, we promoted artillery, and how important and interesting it is to serve with us, and by the end of the course, it always turned out that a large number of graduates wished to sign up with the Artillery Corps.

The commanders of the original corps from where these men had come from, who were counting heavily on the ROTC officers in the pipeline, were furious, but Nati Sharoni as CAO withstood all pressures. Guy Brill, head of the corps' research branch, a bat-com, and in time commander of the 454th Division Artillery, was one of these "turncoats," but in his case, the main objection came from his wife, Anat, in time a senior Defense Ministry executive, who conducted the negotiations with us about Guy staying in the corps.

This was a repeating pattern: We were required in many cases to speak with both spouses, in order to persuade the wives or girlfriends, and as they say, deception is the way of war. When I realized that I had to deal not only with the officer, but also and mainly with their better half, I often came armed with my wife Tamar. So it was, for instance, in the case of Eshel Pashti, and when I handled him, Tamar softened up his partner. Pashti's girlfriend persisted for a while, but eventually Tamar succeeded. Pashti left the military with the rank of colonel, after commanding Fire Division 214, which operated Rafael's precise Tammuz missile.

Thus, brick by brick, layer after layer, and with the aid of Moti Laniado, the corps' staffing officer, I built an extraordinary human infrastructure, which proved itself in the most difficult tests and also in the day-to-day grind, and this grew exponentially for years to come.

And myths arose surrounding this subject. One held that the door to my office in Tzrifin had a low lintel, and that anyone entering for an interview banged their head on it, sat down, and signed on. Upon leaving they'd bang their heads again and say "Oy, what have I done."

Nurturing Officers

The officer shortage was critical, but it was clear to me that we didn't just need any officers. The corps was desperate for crack officers, excellent navigators, with broad vision, leadership, and the ability to fit in with the human tapestry of the Artillery Corps, so that they would constitute a quality command cadre for many years ahead.

To that end, we had to outline an attractive course of posting and a service outlook for those we wanted to sign, and provide them with stability, without fear of shifts and surprise moves to unplanned roles. Subject to these rules, I incorporated academic studies at the IDF's expense into the advancement track of each officer who signed on for long periods of time. Such a period of study constitutes a stop of rest and recharging for the officer and their family as well, beyond the expanded horizons and the acquisition of deeper analysis and critical skills.

In light of my personal experience, when I was given no respite during my studies and spent half the period in reserve service, I decided that officers in academic studies would not receive secondary postings, but would spend all their time – including the vacations – on study.

All well and good, but the study quota for the Artillery Corps was small. I sought to increase it. The head of the staffing administration, David Maimon, who later became a major general, understood the matter and wanted to help, but his hands were tied. At one meeting, I asked him if the other field corps use their full quotas. He grinned and said: "Got it. You'll get whatever the others don't use."

It was quite a bit, and I acted similarly when it came to sending officers to continued education at military academies abroad, and even academic studies abroad.

The Chief of Staff didn't like to "waste time" on school issues, and at one Joint Chiefs of Staff meeting, Raful was particularly grumpy when the Navy Commander brought up the idea of shipbuilding design studies in California. He wanted to send a naval officer there, and Raful bit his head off: "Do you build ships? Negative. No go!" Then he rejected a proposal by the Air Force Commander. I had one candidate for approval for study abroad that day, Yoni Shimshoni, who conditioned his signing on to the career military on IDF funding his studies at Princeton University. I had the head of personnel, Moshe Nativ, on board – but the Raful barrier loomed high. I said to Raful: "Look, all the candidates are blues and whites. I finally found a greenie fit to study abroad. What, we're not going to send him? Raful finally smiled, and said: "Approved." Shimshoni served in the corps for years, commanded the 215th Division Artillery, and was later deputy head of the IDF's planning division.

Despite the desire to outline the officers' future years ahead, an army is not a 'self-serve buffet,' and often immediate needs arise to fill positions, and then there is no choice but to break the news to an officer that the plan has gone awry. It happened to me with Dan Harel, later Deputy Chief of Staff, who was commander of the commanders' course at Shivta. Harel was scheduled to go on study leave in August of 1982, but I had to appoint a new commander for the 402nd Battalion. Fighting in Lebanon was ongoing, the battalion was carrying out direct fire missions, and it needed a brave and capable officer. I had to inform Harel that the plan had crashed due to the circumstances, and despite understanding me, I feel that he never forgave me. In any event, his performance in the war brought his skills to light and in the end led him to the senior positions he filled – CAO, Southern Command General during the Disengagement from Gaza, Deputy Chief of Staff, and very nearly the first gunner Chief of Staff. After taking off his uniform, he served as Director-General of the Defense Ministry.

Promoting Youngsters

As CAO, I had almost unlimited possibilities to put the policy of rapid advancement for talented young officers, which had been my guiding principle throughout my career in the IDF, into practice. But assignments and promotions to colonel roles required approval by the Joint Chiefs of Staff, and I almost always faced pressure, especially from command generals, to promote the men they knew, even if they weren't suited to those roles.

The man who stood in my way more than all was Moshe Levy – as Central Command General, Deputy Chief of Staff, and Chief of Staff. I've already mentioned the bad blood between Levy and myself, undeserved by me, and at one of the appointments hearings with the Chief of Staff, when he was Central Command General, he nominated an administrator who served as an administrative deputy at the command's division artillery, in charge of the fitness of the emergency depot of the division artillery, which is a reserve unit.

In plainer language, Levy proposed to promote to colonel, and appoint as commander of a division artillery, an officer who had been a first sergeant major for many years, and was a non-combat administrator, without having gone through an officers' course, or having served in any command post whatsoever. The very nomination was an insult to the corps. Haim Erez, Southern Command General, sat beside me and said to me: "Arie, what do you care, he just sits at the emergency depot anyway." I got angry and replied: "You take him, let him command an armored brigade."

Raful, with his selective hearing, heard what he wanted, as usual. He turned to the head of personnel, Nativ, who confirmed my position. The proposal fell through, and Moshe Levy jotted down another open grudge against me in his notebook.

A few months passed, and in late 1982, the matter of appointing a commander for Shivta came up on the agenda. I wished to appoint Lt. Col. Moshe Rauch (nee Ronen,) deputy commander of the standing 282nd Division Artillery, who was an experienced and highly esteemed officer. Ronen performed admirably in the Peace for Galilee War, was praised and appreciated by his commanders and subordinates alike, and was the best candidate in the eyes of most of the corps' officers as well.

Moshe Levy was already Deputy Chief of Staff at this point. He strenuously opposed the appointment and tried to propose a candidate I had ruled out. The man had commanded a reserve division artillery, and I had explained to him why he was unsuited to the position in a long personal interview.

Raful deliberated and harked back to the "village hall" method. I reported with all the corps' colonels, some 25 in number, at the IDF HQ boardroom, Raful polled them one by one, asking who was suited to command Shivta, and after they unanimously said: "Ronen," Raful, suspicious peasant that he was, turned to me and said: "You scared them, huh?"

I swore up and down that I had spoken to none of them, but Raful, perhaps reluctant to completely humiliate his second in command, said: "Commander of Shivta is the number two role in the corps." He checked to see who the most senior and most veteran officer was, and told Rami Ziv, my deputy: "You'll be commander of Shivta." Ziv was beside himself. He had already filled three colonel positions, saw himself as a candidate to replace me when the time came, and now he was being moved to another post. But he said not a word, and the deed was done.

Raful summoned Ronen for an interview. He knew him well from the war, and said to him: "Would it be terrible if you got a colonel's rank and command of a reserve division artillery in the first-line division in the north?" Ronen allayed his concerns, told him that he was a suitable posting, and that he could wait.

That Was Then, This Is Now

And on the same subject, but going back a bit earlier: After the CAO replacement ceremony, the past CAOs gathered in my new office, and Israel Ban-Amitai came up to me and said: "I have one piece of advice for you – pick your replacement now, and build him up as CAO."

I took Ben-Amitai's advice to heart. I decided to go back to the formula set by Bar-David, when he marked me as his successor, and asked myself who the most promising young colonel was, whom I could build up as CAO. But I made a rookie mistake and chose an officer who enjoyed an excellent reputation around the corps – even though I personally felt otherwise. He had been under my command when I was the Northern Command artillery commander, and disappointed me when he was the bat-com at a live-fire mission exercise at Shivta.

It began at dawn when I showed him the trail coming down from Mt. Safoun, and said: "Tanks coming down from the Safoun. Direct fire!"

"No such thing with a 175mm," he said, forgetting that I was the establishing bat-com of the 412th, which did wonders in the Yom Kippur War with 175mm cannons. I told him: "There is now. The tanks are coming your way, and you have to stop them. Running is not an option." For lack of choice, he ordered his men to mount sights, and suddenly there was such a thing as direct fire with 175mm cannons. They fired and hit the center of the trail descending from the Safoun. In late 1982, under pressure from above, the man was appointed artillery commander of a corps – and disappointed again. It happened when we initiated a day battle at Sultan Yacoub, which had become the lair of Syrian HQs and was free of civilians. Tanks began firing on targets, while the artillery was hardly to be heard. I quickly entered the artillery HQ and asked why. The commander explained that he had decided to fire "barrel on target," meaning surgical, slow, and far less effective fire. He also marked the enemy batteries with pins in different colors, by type, as though we were on the eve of the Yom Kippur War, with eleven batteries to 154.

I got angry, as though there had been no war and as though the artillery wasn't the queen of the battlefield, but had returned to its wretched status from before the war. "I see," I said, and turned directly to the deputy division artillery commanders: "Target Sultan Yacoub, cluster barrage – fire."

Within minutes, a tremendous roar thundered, as the 150-artillery barrels fired a cluster barrage. IDF brass, which came to observe the day battle, once again witnessed the artillery's might. Sultan Yacoub burned. Vehicles caught fire one by one, spewing black smoke.

When I left the IDF, Raful chose another officer to replace me as CAO – and rightly so. It was Oded Tira, a veteran officer, who had performed well as the staff-ops officer of the 209th Division Artillery during the Yom Kippur War, later commanded the same unit, which is the heart of the corps, as a brigadier general.

FOUR STORIES FROM LEBANON ON THE EVE OF THE WAR

Beirut, Hometown of the Shkuri (nee Mizrachi) Family

In the early 1980s, Israel's cooperation with the Christians in Lebanon took the form of assistance in means and weapons systems, and of professional trust toward a friendly army. The Mossad was responsible for the ties with the Maronite Christians, who constituted some one fifth of Lebanon's population. IDF representatives stayed regularly, almost openly, in Junia and even in Beirut, to train the Falange fighters, collect intelligence, and help arm them. The Artillery Corps' staff-ops officer, Noam David, also spent long stretches of time there, establishing excellent relations with the Falange gunners.

I had no doubt that war would break out before too long, and I was convinced that it would be carried out according to the "Large Oranim" plan, which among other things entailed the landing of forces north of Beirut and the folding of Lebanon from north to south, with the object being the elimination of the terrorist state and the removal of the PLO from Lebanon. I decided to fly to Junia on my own, in order to familiarize myself with the sector and the Falange, to seek observation posts and locate deployment areas. I arrived by chopper, in civvies, armed with a handgun, and with a sealed packet of cash to be used in an emergency. We landed on the beach, a few meters from the Beirut-Junia coastal road. We got into the famous Mercedes sedans used by Mossad personnel, and drove toward Junia as though we were on the French Riviera road from Cannes to Nice. Luxury cars, "Casino du Liban" in shimmering neon letters, restaurants, and bars appeared everywhere. No signs of war could be seen, but only the good life.

I made my plan, and when I met with Bashir Gemayel and he asked if I had any special requests, I replied that I had two: To reach the summit of Mt. Lebanon, and to visit Wadi Abu Jamil, Beirut's Jewish quarter, the abode of my large family, the Shkuris. The only reason I'm not named Arie Shkuri today is because my father, who made Aliyah illegally at seventeen, slipping through Metula, had to adopt a name that was common in the Mandatory British "Palestina-Eretz Israel," and someone recommended the name Mizrachi.

Beirut was divided between the Christians on the one hand, and the terrorists and their Syrian allies on the other. Bashir explained to me that the former Jewish quarter is in the PLO's hands, and offered to take me to a wall separating the Christian and Muslim neighborhoods, so that I could peek through a hole at Wadi Abu Jamil, protected from sniper fire. And indeed, that very day I got to look at what in the distant past had been the Jewish neighborhood of Beirut, and was now a slum inhabited by Palestinian refugees. The next day, we ascended Mt. Lebanon, through a ski resort that could easily have been in the Swiss Alps, of the sort I would later become acquainted with following my discharge from the IDF, when I would work as a consultant to the Swiss military.

The road up the mountain wound its way between gorgeous chalet cabins. We stopped to eat at a restaurant with a stage in the center. It resembled a huge bathtub full of burning charcoal, covered in a giant tent that looked like a circus tent, with a large opening at the top to release the smoke. We were served fresh tabbouleh salad, choice cuts of meat roasted on hot coals, kubbeh nayeh and regular kubbeh – all in the finest traditions of Lebanese cuisine, just as my aunt Jamila would make with her own hands. An orchestra was playing, guests got up to belly dance between courses, and all said joie de vivre and carpe diem. Lebanon's rich preferred to hide their heads in the sand, and not see the darkening skies.

The Falange's northern command HQ was in the Tripoli sector. There I met with the "command general," Samir Geagea. When he took me on a tour of the no-man's land between the Falange forces and the Syrians, he proposed that we take a shortcut along the conflict line. The Mossad representative warned me that this road has not been used in a long while, as it was dangerous, but courage/stupidity won out. I said: "An Israeli general is not afraid of the Syrians."

The Mossad liaison got off the jeep. Geagea also looked frightened, as he was certain that I would decline the offer like everyone else, but I persisted, and he, for fear of losing face, said, "OK, but we'll drive west."

He left me the right-hand seat, facing the Syrians, and sat in the middle, between the driver and me. The driver stepped on the gas, and the Syrians, not expecting anyone to pass there, didn't have time to react. When we made it to safety, Geagea's fear evaporated. He jumped off the jeep, whooping triumphantly, yelling "We opened the road!" and favoring me with a warm embrace and a Levantine oath of brotherhood-in-arms.

I spent two days with the man, who was a pediatrician by trade, a graduate of Sorbonne University in Paris, spoke fluent English and French, and also excellent Hebrew, having undergone a command and staff course in Israel. You could discuss any topic with him – from film, through philosophy, to military doctrine, and he was highly familiar with the IDF brass, from the Chief of Staff on down, including Chief Military Rabbi Gad Navon, also a Sorbonne graduate. His outward appearance was impressive as well, a tall man, with an imposing forehead, and the look of a Franciscan monk.

Upon returning to Israel, I reported my disappointment with the Falange – with their general preparedness, the amateurish approach, the sense that these were militias big on talk and low on action, and the fact that I saw no real preparation, nor willingness for an independent fight. I also noted that the exception to this rule were the gunners, who were exceptionally well organized. I also expanded on my impression of Samir Geagea, who in the name of Bashir Gemayel had led the massacre of the family of Lebanese president Suleiman Frangieh in 1978 – a massacre that claimed the lives of his firstborn son, Tony, his wife, and his daughter, along with some 30 bodyguards, in the course of the struggle for the leadership of the Maronite community. A bespoke suit and Western mannerisms on the outside, and on the inside a heartless murderer, capable of extinguishing the life of a three-year-old infant.

Against the backdrop of all of the above, the tour of Falange artillery units in Beirut and Junia actually impressed me. Noam David and his men had done a crack job, and female Maronite ops NCOs, after the model of the Shivta instructors, young girls who spoke fluent English and were driven by patriotism, professionally executed the fire direction missions, and were entrusted with communications between the observers, the firing, and the maneuvering units.

I was convinced that this artillery force would stand up well to an eventual wartime test, within the constraints of a small force. What concerned me, as I said, was the Falange leadership, which projected bravado and determination, but wrapped it in empty slogans and hollow boasting.

Deep down, I was skeptical as to what the Christians would do in the moment of truth – would they fight by our side, or stay on the side.

Dinner with Bashir

I found myself at a fancy seafood restaurant for the first time in my life in Junia, by explicit invitation of Bashir Gemayel to have dinner with him. I had never had shellfish and other delicacies of the sea before that, but as usual, wanted to try everything. The restaurant belonged to a French couple, and their flagship dish was squid in its own ink: a bowl of black liquid, in which the squid was floating, all topped by a layer of grated white garlic. A royal delicacy.

To end the visit, I asked to buy baklawa. When I was five years old, on the eve of the War of Independence, we received a visit from my uncle Daniel Shkuri, my father's older brother and the leader of the family, who owned a glassware factory. He came with his wife Victoria, who kept her nose turned up throughout the visit at our poor Kfar Saba home, despite my father having treated Daniel like an emperor and his wife like a queen.

Despite her sourpuss demeanor, the visit left a sweet taste in my mouth, thanks to the baklawa they brought with them from Beirut. The flavor or the baklawa remained on my tongue and in my memory, and that's what I asked for. To this day, Tamar and my children recall the thin, round wooden box of baklawa I brought back with me from Beirut.

"Black Cluster, White Cluster"

At one of the planning approval meetings, headed by the Chief of Staff, I explained that the opening artillery salvo of the "Large Oranim" plan is scheduled to be executed via "black cluster." This meant American 483 shells, each carrying 88 anti-tank and personnel bomblets, with a hollow charge and improved shrapnel spray, allowing upper penetration of tanks and other armored fighting vehicles, causing massive casualties to unprotected troops due to the excellent shrapnel effect. I was listened to attentively and received unanimous concurrence, with those in attendance clearly viewing me as the unassailable authority on artillery. No one asked questions, and I motioned to Ze'ev Zacharin, the Chief of Staff's head of chambers, to write down the summary, so that my words would receive the official stamp of approval, and I wouldn't need further clearances once the operation began. "White cluster" was a 449 shell with 60 winged bomblets, designed to land and then explode. It was an outdated shell, with a huge rate of duds, which created a sort of anti-personnel minefield. We discovered it during training at Shivta, when we set Mt. Safoun as an anti-personnel cluster area, where there were several injuries of soldiers, and mostly of local Bedouins. Later, in the war too, the use of "white cluster" caused minor injuries among our own infantry troops. The efficacy of these two types of munitions, particularly the "black cluster," were more lethal by several orders of magnitude than standard ordnance such as explosive, or airburst explosive shells.

War Games

The head of the IDF's instruction department, Major-General Uri Simchoni, was asked by Raful, several months prior to the war, to prepare a "war game" in which a PCA (possible course of action) of conquering Lebanon from south to north would be looked into. He did so out of the assumption that "Large Oranim," which was a much smarter plan and better expressed the IDF's spirit, would not be approved of due to political reasons.

Simchoni – formerly the commander of the Egoz Rangers unit, which often operated in Lebanon, commander of the Golani Brigade, and a division commander during the Litani Operation – prepared the exercise, codenamed "Shoshanim" (Lilies), along with Yossi Ben-Hannan, and its conclusions were presented at a senior brass meeting at the "pit" deep under the IDF's HQ compound in Tel Aviv. Its conclusions were clear: It would be difficult to deploy tanks along the mountain routes, and movement would be possible only in avenues, meaning in narrow columns, in a manner most helpful to the defending force. Along the coastal route, which crosses constructed areas and cultivated land, and is crisscrossed by water canals, the limitations would be even more difficult. Firepower would have a key role, Simchoni made it clear, because the maneuvering forces will be forced to base their operations on infantry forces, and movement will be slow.

The only possible brainstorm came from Raful and Ben-Hannan, who proposed a flanking motion through the sea by the 96th Division, headed by the 35th Brigade, landing it at the Awali River estuary, north of Sidon.

The Armored Corps' men refused to understand the difficulties, and kept thinking "tanks," until the Chief Medical Officer, Eran Dolev, stood up and said that according to estimates of professionals at the CMO's HQ, some 400 fatalities were to be expected in a PCA of conquest from south to north.

Raful got angry. "Doc-tor," he said, "You treat the wounded and don't estimate fatalities, you're the Chief Medical Officer, not the Chief Rabbi."

Dolev said nothing. This was the only doubt raised regarding the plan to move from south to north, and it too was silenced.

In all the plan approvals and debates, not once did anyone doubt the need to drive the PLO out of Lebanon, which had become an enemy country, openly threatening Israel, and sending out bombing and shooting attacks. No one was willing to accept a situation where Israel might be attacked simultaneously by the Palestinian population of the Gaza Strip and the West Bank, and by the PLO from Lebanon.

The danger was clear and present. No intelligence or strategic experts were needed to realize that the reality of a terror state, backed by Syria, might ignite a regional war, with no one knowing how Egypt, Jordan, and Iraq might react. At no hearing was the least doubt voiced as to the just cause of the war. All commanders, at all levels, sounded and looked filled with ambition, each with a knife between their teeth, seeking to eliminate the threat – and along the way to prove the mettle of their units, and their own personal prowess as well, of course.

Senior commanders, including major generals, said in retrospect that they had opposed the war. I heard none of them say so in real time. They may have confided in their pillows at night, but outwardly the IDF was one unit, sure of its power. Anyone telling stories later apparently did so to justify themselves politically, or to excuse a personal failure. I didn't believe any of them, and I find their behavior hypocritical. I make a complete distinction between my camaraderie and friendship with these men and my fact-based feeling regarding their immaterial motives and their self-righteousness regarding the war. My own political position is clear and well-known: I was one of Rabin's men and a man of the Labor Party, when it still existed as such, and I am free of any ulterior motive or interest when I say what I do. The Peace for Galilee War ended in a great victory, which led to the removal of the PLO from Lebanon. The mission, as dictated by the political echelon, was completed to the fullest. I was well familiar with the political arena of the late 1980s and early '90s. I also knew the spiteful lefties, who turned the Peace for Galilee War into the First Lebanon War, seeing it as a golden opportunity to replace the government, and to take revenge on their nemesis, Arik Sharon. In this political campaign, all means were deemed kosher, including the cynical political exploitation of the IDF's fallen, and the turning of a victorious war into a resounding failure.

Let me make it clear: it was the decision of the next defense minister, Moshe Arens, and the next Chief of Staff, Moshe Levy, not to leave Lebanon. The same approach was copied by each successive Israeli government, until Ehud Barak's 1999 electoral victory. That was what led us into a quandary and saddled the war with the image of a failed wallowing in the Lebanese mud. Contrary to the narrative cemented in the memory of most Israelis, Sharon and Raful wanted to leave immediately following the completion of the mission.

A VICTORY, NOT A FAILURE

"Muster the Entire Corps on Silent Call-Up"

I had a standing agreement with my friend Ze'ev Zacharin, also a Kfar Saba resident, that the moment he realizes that it's beginning for real (which he would know before me, as the Chief of Staff's top aide) – he would call me right away. On Thursday, June 3rd, 1982, Israel's ambassador to the UK, Shlomo Argov, was gunned down, and the next afternoon I got a phone call from Zacharin: "Come!"

"Can I join the chopper from Tel Aviv to Nazareth," I asked.

"No," he said. "Drive up north, and you'll make it before us."

I got into my Valiant and drove north like mad, reaching the gates of the Northern Command HQ just as the Chief of Staff's chopper was landing.

Joining the Northern Command General, Amir Drori, were Raful, Air Force Commander David Ivri, MID head Yehoshua Sagi, IDF HQ head of ops Uri Sagi, myself, and our respective chiefs of staff. Raful said: "We have the go-ahead from Begin. I'm flying to Jerusalem right now to present the "Small Oranim" plan to him. But it's a surprise operation. It has to be kept secret."

"Small Oranim" was the plan to conquer Lebanon from south to north – from the Israeli border northward. The heart of the plan was a concurrent advance along three routes – the coastal route, the central mountain route, the eastern route through the Beqaa, without clashing with the Syrians unless they opened fire. Concurrently, a landing was planned at the estuary of the Awali, north of Sidon, some 60 km from the Israeli border. No end line of 40 km was set, and an intermediate goal was defined: To reach the Beirut-Damascus road without clashing with the Syrians. No goal was set to capture Beirut, nor a political objective of setting up a regime convenient to Israel. The objectives were military, per se.

And Raful, like Raful, was talking about surprise and secrecy. Some surprise, when you're talking about mobilizing and moving five divisions, artillery preparation, and the aerial strike having already landed on the Beirut stadium, where Fatah stored its arms and ammunition, in retaliation for the ambassador's assassination.

It was late Friday afternoon. Zero hour was set for 11:00, Sunday morning. Drori, known as a man of few words, asked if it would be right to bring Golani back from weekend leave. A debate ensued, at the end of which Raful said: We start with only standing forces. Four of the five divisions are standing.

He meant the 252nd Division under Emannuel Sakel, scheduled to penetrate through the Beqaa, the 36th Division under Avigdor Kahalani, whose targets were Nabatiyeh and Sidon, the 162nd Division under Menachem Einan, intended to penetrate through the mountain route, the 91st Division under Itzik Mordechai, intended to penetrate up the coastal route, through Tyre to Sidon, and the 96th Division under Amos Yaron, based on the standing 35th Paratroopers' Brigade, which was meant to land by sea at the Awali estuary and advance on Beirut.

Two reserve divisions were supposed to join the effort on the eastern front – the 90th Division under Giora Lev, and the 880th Division under Yom-Tov Tamir, as part of the 446th Corps under Yanush Ben-Gal, and his deputy Ehud Barak. The Golan Heights were to be secured by the 49th and 131st Reserve Divisions, under Moshe Bar-Kochva and the 479th Corps. The fact that reserve reinforcements would be needed was kept silent until I burst into the conversation. I knew well who I was dealing with, and knew that in order to get what I wanted, I needed to demand an immediate call-up of all my reserve battalions.

Raful was outraged. "Mizrachi," he said, "You'll screw up my operation. I know you." I insisted that I needed time for commanders' recon, to erect munitions piles, check and prepare the position, deploy observation posts, measurements, and commanders' briefings. Raful realized that I was right, but was unwilling to renounce the silent op idea, so he told me: "Fine, but not today. Tomorrow evening," meaning Saturday evening.

I nodded at Zacharin and he nodded approvingly back at me. I left the room before Raful could renege, and went up to see the Northern

Command's artillery commander, Manos. From his office I called my deputy Rami Ziv, who was already with the entire staff in Tzrifin, and told him: "Muster the entire corps on silent call-up."

Final Field Test

My plan was to employ 50 artillery battalions in the first phase: 32 battalions in Lebanon, mostly M-109 cannon and some 175mm guns and 160mm self-propelled heavy mortars, as well as the Haviv and American Lance missiles (precision missiles with a 70km range, with a warhead containing 623 bomblets); and in the Golan Heights, to protect the flank against Syrian intervention, eighteen M-50 battalions, from the artillery divisions still equipped with that heavy and cumbersome weapon.

The orders went down through the Artillery Corps channels and through the divisional channels; and the preparations, all rehearsed and practiced countless times, were launched. Of course there were mishaps and misunderstandings, and some remnants of resistance to my status and orders still simmered, particularly among old-timers still clinging to methods that were by now prehistoric. But these were small pockets. The corps was quickly wound up as tight as a spring for war. We viewed it as a one-time chance to prove its capabilities, and turn it into positive proof of its status as "queen of the battlefield." If anyone had concerns, they were kept quiet.

I made clear that everything was on the move, and cleared my schedule on Saturday morning to join my bosom friend Uppo, Eli Barak, commander of the 215th Division Artillery, whose standing units were already deployed along the line and within the SLA enclave, and had been firing for a few days. We went up to the villa in Marjayoun together, and chose a narrow point on the road to Nabatiyeh as a target. It was a route used exclusively by terrorist vehicles, so we decided to block it with an artillery ambush using "black cluster" munitions, and the result was excellent. Terrorist vehicles were lit up one by one, and the cluster's efficacy was proven live and in color.

On Saturday night, upon my return to catch a nap at the "palace" on Mt. Canaan, ahead of a senior brass meeting with Defense Minister Arik Sharon at the Northern Command HQ, I saw the reserve battalions moving before my eyes, on their tracks – from Camp Yiftach, south of Rosh Pina, north toward the SLA enclave and their positions. They moved along the road in full nighttime discipline, with orderly accompaniment and direction by the Military Police.

It was a good feeling. *There, the orders are being carried out.*

Arik Speaks for the Record

Sunday, June 6th, 1982. At 05:00, we gathered – the Command General and his senior staff, the division commanders, and several brigadiers – for a final briefing by the Defense Minister ahead of the operation. Sharon embarked on a long monologue, and we couldn't believe our ears. This is Arik the Terrible? "This is not a second Litani," he thundered. "You will not destroy homes. You will not harm civilians. You will only harm the enemy, and the enemy is the PLO. We have no intention of fighting the Syrians, unless they open fire first – and even then, only with permission."

Everyone's eyes were torn wide open. Out of the corner of my eye, I noticed the IDF HQ secretary and her stenographers, and the rolling tape recorder, and I realized: Arik is speaking for the record.

We took off from Mt. Canaan to Ras Biyada, to observe Tyre and the coastal route. Present were Itzik Mordechai, Uri Sagi, and David Ivri. When Mordechai explained the movements of the division to take Tyre and advance on Sidon, Arik stepped back a little and crooked his finger at me to join him. He stood alone, overlooking the terrain. "Arie," he said, "You and the Air Force," and he made a sweeping motion with his hand, repeating it several times, to make sure I got his meaning.

Of course I got it. I understood this language since I was five years old, when Arik and Rechavia Vardi were regular visitors to our home at night, and my father would take them on tours of the neighboring Arab villages.

At the same time, Sharon decided to move zero hour back to 10:00 AM, to prevent the possibility of the operation being canceled at the last minute, due to American pressure or political struggles. At 10:00 AM, the Peace for Galilee War was indeed launched, with a tremendous artillery cluster barrage all along the sector.

Nino Levi Is Surprised

The operation plan, as noted above, entailed a landing by the 96th Division, headed by the standing 35th Paratrooper Brigade under Ya-Ya at the Awai estuary. Dangot, who had been a battery commander in the 402nd Battalion, was chosen in advance to command the vanguard artillery unit that would land with them – with two SPHs, an M-577 command vehicle, and an M-548 tracked ammo carrier. He had practiced it for a long time at Nitzanim Beach with the division forces, and was well-prepared. The two SPHs were supposed to be joined by the 35th Brigade's battalion of towed 120mm mortars, landed by chopper. First, half the battalion, under the command of the deputy bat-com Hillel Ahrman, and then the other half, under bat-com Haki Porat.

The need to provide preliminary artillery cover for the landing forces before the landing and also when they are still unable to fire themselves, was solved by deploying 175mm guns from the 55th battalion at their maximum range, 32.5 km, on Jabel Ballat.

The question, asked by the bat-com Yair Zinner and his deputy Eli Yaffe, was how to range and hit the terrorist outposts controlling the landing area at night, with the Air Force not operating yet and therefore no aerial photos being available. The idea we came up with at my HQ was to range with the "Shillem" – an advanced ranging radar, unique in the world at the time, developed at Elta Systems.[28] The Shillem was planned for a range of 70 km, and was among the finest newly developed radars, most of which were intended for the Air Force.

The modus operandi was novel: The ranging cannon fires three shells, the radar intersects the shells in flight at 69 points, in a sort

---

28 A subsidiary of Israel Aerospace Industries.

of window through which the shells fly. Then it predicts the point of impact, measures the difference between the target's coordinates as ordered and the result, and relays the difference as a correction command to the entire battalion or division artillery firing with that type of barrel. But there was a fly in the ointment. The Shillem was a single prototype, which had only finished several months of exercises in the Sinai, the Jordan Valley, and the Golan Heights, and was returned to the factory for restoration and the beginning of mass production of such radars. To be precise, the "Shillem" was completely dismantled at that moment. I called Dr. Nino Levi, CEO of Elta, catching him on a Friday night dinner with his family in Ashdod. Nino, a calm and polite man who came from Jewish-Italian origins, with classic European mannerisms, was considered a world-class expert on radar. He answered the phone with his soft, familiar tone, and following a few words of apology I said: "Nino, I need the 'Shillem' deployed in Manara by tomorrow night, ready for action."

Silence ensued on the other side of the line for long seconds. Nino didn't ask why or what, and in his amazing serenity, simply said: "Understood. Consider it done." The next day, the "Shillem" was deployed in Manara. Under the M.O. described above, the ranging shells didn't need to explode on the ground. The "Shillem" located them in the air and measured their location, and then we could detonate them with a time fuse far from the target, so that the enemy wouldn't know what was in our sights. The 55th Battalion did indeed range in real time with the "Shillem," and it hit all the terrorist targets overlooking the Awali estuary prior to the landing.

Me and My "Saifan"

Lebanon's modest size greatly eases moving from place to place, and the relative proximity to Israel's central Gush Dan metropolitan area enables quick access to any point. But such movement is possible only by air and not on the ground, due to the topography. Narrow and gridlocked mountain routes in the country's center and east, and a narrower and even more jammed coastal route in the west turn any ground-based movement in Lebanon into a nightmare.

To my great fortune, thanks to my friends at the Staff-Ops Division and the Chief of Staff's chambers, and thanks to Rami Yehoshua, my superb chief of staff (and now a co-owner of the Yehoshua-TBWA advertising firm), a "Saifan" helicopter (aka Bell 206) was placed at my disposal whenever I wanted. Throughout the war, from day one until the terrorists were deported from Beirut, I had the ability to visit all units and reach all critical locations requiring my intervention. My reading of the battle on the ground level, augmented by up-to-the-minute intel at the Defense Ministry and Chief of Staff's level, allowed me to be where I needed to be, and to have an impact.

One of my regular pilots, Ran Hanegbi, recently met my son Sagi, and told him of our adventures in Lebanon, with my eyes constantly sweeping for high-voltage power lines. One of the Air Force's choppers crashed after hitting such power lines on Friday, following the ceasefire. As I was later told, Yanush and his chief of staff, Arik Arad, got worried, because I had taken off at the very same time to the central sector, to deal with a matter that required my intervention as CAO, and they thought I had been on the chopper that crashed.

As in the previous wars and operations in which I had taken part, this time, too, I was focused on the goals I set for myself: To place the Artillery Corps at the forefront so that it would fulfill its purpose and allow the ground and air forces to complete their missions successfully, and without casualties. In the book "Totchanim BeShele"g,"[29] by Yaakov Zigdon and Simantov Sagi, fighters and commanders describe my personal involvement in almost every significant incident in the war – here are three examples:

Yossi Zinger tells how he was the platoon instructor at a basic course, and at the end of the course – still in the midst of war, as we began to discharge reserve forces, I appointed him artillery command-

---

[29] "Gunners in PFG" – Peace for Galilee. The name is a pun, playing on the fact that the acronym for "Peace for Galilee" spells "snow" in Hebrew. Lebanon, with its celebrated ski resorts, is associated with snow in Israel, where the white precipitation is mostly limited to the northern border. So the book's name can also be read as "Gunners in the Snow."

er with the 35th Brigade. In July, when I arrived at Beirut International Airport, he told me that the paratroopers were in desperate need of artillery cover, but he was identifying the targets at ranges beyond the reach of direct fire.

Out of the depths of my memory, I dredged an ancient method predating the Six-Day War, of a hasty deployment called "position controlled." It was used back then mostly by 120mm mortars mounted on half-tracks within tank battalions, and was later adopted by the 404th Artillery Battalion – the first self-propelled Priest cannons – but was decommissioned when the 120mm mortars began to go out of use.

The method required getting a theodolite up on the XO's ridge, behind which the battery was deployed for concealment and protection. The XO directed the aiming device at the target, and relayed aiming data to the SPHs. The difference was that now we could measure the range with a laser range finder, which we didn't have in the '60s, and along with the theodolite, we achieved direct hits on the targets by the entire battery (or entire battalion) – straight with fire for effect, with no need for ranging fire.

Zinger, as I said, was trying to figure out how to employ his fire rapidly, efficiently, and with maximal precision in the airport area. We dredged up the old method in an updated version, and it was successful. The terrorists' mortars were silenced, and the fire on our forces at the airport ceased.

The second example told of an incident with the 403rd Battalion, which was left alone on the second day of the war along the central route. I flew above them and asked the excellent bat-com, Yaakov Ben-Kiki, what he needed. Ben-Kiki replied, "Ammunition and water."

From the chopper I contacted the maintenance people at the Northern Command, and within minutes a CH-53 was offloading a platform loaded with cases of shells and water packs in the battalion's staging area. They kept on fighting, and in fact saved the 500th Brigade in the Battle of Ein Zahlateh, which began immediately thereafter.

A third case happened when I employed the "Haviv" missiles, deployed in an area codenamed "August 60" under Shema, Shimon Shacham, who had concentrated many battalions within his deployment area. When I came to visit them, I was concurrently in contact with Brigadier General Amos Amir, who coordinated the Air Force's activity at the Northern Command. Amir asked us to destroy a battery of Syrian SA-6 surface-to-air missiles. The fire was ranged and employed via a "stabilized mirror," meaning a Dornier DO-28 aircraft carrying an artillery officer, who was equipped with an LREOOD (Long-Rang Electro-Optical Device), and moved along the coast with a sight range of up to 60 km.

I went up high in the air with the chopper, to make sure that the target had been destroyed, and that no further rockets were needed. We were running out of them, and needed to be frugal. As I expected, the missile battery had indeed been destroyed.

Lifting the 411th Battalion

On Sunday and Monday, I learned in real time of the falling of two beloved officers, whom I'd personally signed up to the career military: Gidi Rosh and Barak Roshgold, of the 411th Battalion. Both were the cream of the crop of the Artillery Corps, and Gidi had even won a commendation for his actions.

Barak was a battery commander and the battalion's FDO, and Gidi a battery commander as well as a recon and survey officer. The absence of two officers filling such major roles, right at the start of the war, could have hampered the battalion's performance, even without accounting for the fact that both men – as well as Avi Bar-Ze'ev, a squad leader shot by a sniper – were beloved figures. I decided to take preventive action and urgently called up two talented instructors from the basic course – Sharon Amir, now Adv. Amir, senior managing partner at Nashitz Brandeis Amir, and Boaz Raviv, now CEO at a hi-tech firm. I loaded them on my Wagoneer and went looking for the 411th.

The battalion was moving along the Sidon perimeter, within the column of the 211th Brigade under Eli Geva. Eli, my friend from the Valley of Tears, who in '73 had been the "Ampa" company commander in the 82nd Battalion, acquiesced to my request and went with his tanks to save the 334th Battalion from a commando attack.

We reached the outskirts of Sidon, where Haggai Regev, another friend from the Valley of Tears, was preparing to enter the city at the head of a force from the Armored Forces School Brigade.

I got in Haggai's tank and asked him for a tank to accompany me along the Sidon perimeter road till I reached the 411th Battalion. Haggai mumbled something and declined. I decided to go without an escort, and with me the two future battery commanders, Amir and Raviv, and two hitchhikers – Major-General Jacky Even, commander of the military colleges, and Rami Dotan, the Chief Maintenance Officer.

"Well, what did he say?" Amir asked. Even and Dotan listened in.

I said: "The road is open, no problem."

I tasked Amir and Raviv, who were sitting in the back, with the navigation, and while they were arguing between themselves, I noticed that we had missed the turn north, which was a stroke of luck. A jeep belonging to one of the ranger units, which had driven ahead of us and continued another 400 meters, was ambushed by terrorists, and extracted only following a battle that left two soldiers wounded.

Cannons roared on all sides, but within minutes, we reached the 411th. We were received with open arms by the bat-com Yoram Raviv, his deputy Shmulik Weiss, and the XO Shuli Levi. The three of them knew Amir and Raviv, and the fact that they were chosen to replace Gidi Rosh and Barak Roshgold allayed their concerns.

Moshe Ronen, deputy commander of the 282nd Division Artillery, with Shmulik Weiss, deputy bat-com of the 411th.

Saving the 939th Brigade

Listening to the radio networks alerted me about a difficult battle between the 939th Brigade and terrorists who were barricaded in Sidon. I ordered Yoram Raviv to divert one of the batteries of the 411th Battalion, and aid the reserve paratroopers with direct fire from the flank. The battery began firing after establishing contact with the 939th's artillery commander Itay Admon, son of the IDF's first CAO, Shmuel Admon.

The task of taking Sidon was entrusted to the 36th Division, under Avigdor Kahalani. It reached the gates of the city after entering Lebanon through the "Finger of Galilee," and after the Golani fighters had captured the Beaufort and the town of Nabatiyeh. I heard Raful on the radio urging Kahalani to hurry and open the Sidon traffic blockage, in order to rendezvous with the 96th Division, which had landed from the sea at the Awali estuary, beyond Sidon.

Concurrently, another traffic jam had formed, precluding the 36th from linking up with the 96th from the east. It was formed along the narrow mountainous route, from the Aqia Bridge northward, with the tanks of the 162nd Division not allowing ammunition trucks and gasoline tankers to pass them, creating endless convoys.

I hurried to the 36th Division's main HQ, spread out under camouflage nets halfway from the Beaufort to Sidon, to inform Itzik Gazit, commander of the 282nd Division Artillery, that I had commandeered one of his batteries for direct fire. I met his staff-ops officer, Shimon Mizrachi, who was in control of the situation and was full of initiative, and Moshe Ronen, Gazit's energetic and creative deputy, who led the 282nd Division Artillery in combat.

Two Syrian Migs attacked the division HQ just then. Total pandemonium broke out, and my attempt to reach Kahalani in the war room was in vain. The place was crawling with reporters and TV cameras. Kahalani sat in an executive armchair and gave interviews on and off the record.

The surreal scene was cut short a minute later when Raful, who had also returned from Sidon and had realized that the 939th Brigade was in trouble, entered the war room and angrily asked Kahalani: "Why aren't you in Sidon?" He looked around, became annoyed at the sight of the reporters and the cameras, and said: "Stay here. Command of capturing Sidon is transferred to Itzik Mordechai," meaning the 211th Brigade, the 939th Brigade, and the 411th Battalion were transferred to Itzik Mordechai's command, joining his own organic forces. The missions of taking control of Sidon and joining with the 96th Division were tasked to him, while Kahalani and the 36th Division stayed put.

Genius and Shuach Cross the Uncleared City of Sidon

In my view of the battle, I was greatly concerned with the large traffic jam along the central route, and the fact that only the 403rd Battalion could blaze the way for the 162nd Division and the 500th Brigade along the crowded mountain route. I sought a creative solution of how to beef up their supporting firepower, and I decided to transfer the two reserve battalions of the 215th Division Artillery through Sidon, and deploy them north of the city, to support the fire effort on the central route from there. The two bat-coms were known as "Shuach" and "Genius," both highly experienced officers, with well-trained battalions. They belonged to a standing division artillery, but enjoyed the great advantage of a command that had prevailed through the War of Attrition and the Yom Kippur War.

I looked for someone to command and lead them and approached a colonel from the corps, but he mumbled something about not having a jeep, and I decided to forego his services. Shuach, (Pinchas Shavit, as he was known to the population registry), and Genius (none other than the famous Elhanan Tannenbaum), had fought together in the Sinai in the War of Attrition and in Yom Kippur, knew each other well, and had become friends. I called them both and told Genius, the more experienced of the two: "You're the commander. You're going to cross Sidon along the main street with increased hull ammunition and M-548 tracked ammunition carriers– with a squad leader with a machine gun in the turret of each SPH and another fighter atop the sighter's seat with an M-16. Fire at the top floor, and get the hell out quickly. When you're on the other side of town – deploy."

The operation was executed to perfection. No surprise to me. The two battalions crossed Sidon quickly, deployed on its north end, and then joined the division artillery's deployment. Thanks to the rapid crossing, the firepower at the 500th Brigade increased three-fold, and it successfully blazed the way to the Beirut-Damascus road.

THANKS TO DIRECT FIRE

In the Peace for Galilee War, direct fire was employed extensively – in all phases of combat and in different techniques, according to the terrain and the enemy.

Direct fire was employed first and foremost by the M-109, which looked like a tank, enjoyed excellent traversability, and was equipped with lethal ammunition, highly suited to urban environments. Thanks to the elevation angle that the M-109 has and which the tank doesn't, almost 90 degrees, aka a "Howitzer," its impact is more devastating. The 155mm shell explodes within the structure it hits and doesn't go through it like a tank's shell, which has a higher muzzle velocity, in order to be able to penetrate armor.

We employed 203mm SPH cannons after replacing their barrels from 175mm caliber on the same chassis, and direct fire was also employed beyond telescope range, which is 3,200 meters, using the firing computer. In addition, as I related above, I dredged the "position controlled" fire technique out of the attic of my memory. The self-propelled Howitzers became tanks, and in some cases, moved at the head of the maneuvering forces, despite being made of aluminum. Our infantry troops were convinced this was just another tank – with a bigger barrel – which could clear the way in an urban environment with great success.

Above all, direct fire expressed my character as a fighter: I always viewed myself as fighting at the head of the charging force and using my command, navigation, and combat skills, to contribute as much as I could to the success of the entire mission. In my various roles, I always felt satisfaction when charging and firing – be it with my sidearm and my tank's gun, or when employing firepower.

Direct fire can be traced back to the fifteenth century and the earliest cannons. The Russians bombarded Berlin in World War Two with towed guns in direct fire, but the more sophisticated cannons became and the longer their range grew, the more direct fire was abandoned in favor of indirect fire.

I had initiated direct fire late in the Six-Day War, when we wanted to take out the "monkeys" – the Egyptian FOs mounted on the antenna that loomed over the exit from the Mitleh route to the Canal – with a 105mm Priest cannon. In the Sinai, when I was staff-ops officer of the 209th Division Artillery, we used direct fire from 203mm guns on a mockup of an IDF outpost along the Bar-Lev line, fortified with steel mesh cages filed with rocks, in order to test the durability of the IDF fortifications against large caliber, heavy shells, and equipped with concrete-piercing fuses. The precision of the 203mm guns remained etched in my memory. Like any experience and lesson, I made use of it when I was under pressure, and my mind was racing like mad trying to pull a solution out of the endless battles, practices, plannings, books, and lessons I had accumulated and retained.

In time, I regretted the short amount of time I had with the 405th Battalion before the Yom Kippur War, because I only had time to advance basic practices, like the change to firing in 360 degrees. As the reader may recall, two batteries were fatally hit in the southern sector of the Golan Heights – the Bahad 9 battery, which took fatal hits from Syrian T-62 tanks, and the 405th's "Boaz" battery, which for ten straight hours fired some 1,000 shells from four barrels, and was hit by Syrian tanks misidentified as ours. I mention it here again, because I felt a fire burn within me: Why didn't they defend themselves? Why didn't they employ the horrific weapon they possessed? Why didn't they fire directly at the Syrian tanks?

Never, and I take full blame for this, did we conduct a true, in-depth debriefing of that battle, and I carry the blame because it happened in my battalion, and these were my troops. There were extenuating circumstances: A major surprise, they weren't trained in direct fire and in infantry fighting, nobody bothered with defense positions and the fighters were exhausted following incessant firing, with the officers busy with refilling ammunition stocks – but I take no comfort in that.

Despite the lack of an in-depth investigation, I applied my conclusions even before we returned to the enclave and the attrition campaign: I gathered the entire battalion for a demonstration, including

HQ, the adjutancy, and the female personnel. We placed the chassis of a Syrian tank, filled it with propellant explosives and fuel, and with the leader of battery C's squad 3 leader, Avi Yardeni, standing in the turret and me driving the SPH, we drove fast, stopped on a dime, swiveled the barrel, and fired – with the first shell blowing the Syrian tank up from 600 meters away.

The object of the exercise was to make it clear to all battalion soldiers: There's nobody out there to protect us. Or as the Sages put it: If I am not for me, who will be for me? The shell of a 155mm self-propelled howitzer, even if it hits the target before the fuse is primed, which happens 70 meters after the shell exits the muzzle, destroys a tank by the sheer kinetic steel-on-steel impact.

Since then, direct fire has become a core value of the Artillery Corps, and has constituted a part of the training of any standing or reserve unit operating 155mm, 175mm, and 203mm artillery pieces.

"I Shall Insist on Including Gunners in the Front Line"

Our finest hour in the Peace of Galilee War began in Tyre, continued in Sidon, and reached Beirut, as proven by the comments of Major General Noam Tibon, as quoted in the book "Totchanim BeSheleg":[30]

> Even to this day, I insist and shall insist on including gunners in the front line – whether for direct fire in urban areas or to achieve maximal range in front of the troops.

Tibon was relying on his lessons as a Sayeret Matkal commando soldier in Beirut, going on to say:

> The procedure was that the tanks blast the way open for the rangers. It quickly turned out that the tanks may be efficient,

---

[30] Zigdon, Yaakov and Simantov, Sagi, "Totchanim BeShele"g – Sipur Milchama" ("Gunners in the Peace for Galilee – A War Story"), Kinneret Zmora Bitan Press, pp 446.

but only up to three floors in height. The fighting was difficult, the sniper fire was incessant, and anyone poking their head out of a building or setting foot on the sidewalk was immediately shot by a sniper nested on a high floor. Non-stop RPG fire also rained down on the force.

The crew leaders in the SPHs stood exposed in the turret with their flack vests. We instructed the SPH to target and fire from any house we thought someone was firing from. The gunners' platoon enabled us to carry out our mission and clear the street within half an hour.

When I asked former Chief of Staff Gadi Eisenkott what he recalls of the artillery in the Peace for Galilee War, he made similar comments.

Ahead of the storming of the Al-Uzay neighborhood [in Beirut], I wanted to be a point company commander. Gabi Ashkenazi gave me a mission to pin down enemy forces, and I was displeased, to say the least – until he gave me a battery of 155mm SPHs for direct fire as compensation, and then I smiled.

Indeed, Eisenkott figured out the targets and blazed the way open for the charging force with surgical precision, with monstrous firepower tenfold more decisive than the machine guns and light arms of his own troops.

Ya-Ya put it in playground terms: "When someone bigger beats me up, I call my big brother with his 155."

Three Little Tales of Direct Fire

1) Two fourteen-floor buildings, full of terrorists, stood at the eastern end of the Lailaka neighborhood, impeding the troops of the 35th Brigade from moving about on their missions. Arnon Ben-Ami, commander of the 96th Division's artillery, and Yossi Zinger, the brigade artillery commander, decided to topple the twin towers by direct fire at their support columns, using Dangot's battery and a 203mm battery from the 334th Battalion.

The guns were ranged and fired – each battery at its own building, to prevent squabbles over credit – and both buildings crumbled to the ground in unison.

Much later, Ben-Ami told me that he had read a report stating that this sight inspired Osama bin Laden to destroy the Twin Towers of the World Trade Center in New York, but this is likely a modern fable.

2) At the entrance to the Al-Uzay neighborhood, one of the forces was led by the commander of the 17th Battalion, with Golani's squad leaders' course cadets. Dori Sapir, a battery commander with the 402nd Battalion, was second in the convoy, with a shell in the barrel, including propellant, which is the explosive charge that launches the shell, the firing safety was off and the barrel lock (the platform on which the gun rests during travel, locked to prevent the barrel shaking and eroding the stabilizing mechanism) was released. All he had to do was swivel the firing mechanism and pull the cable.

The movement was done at night, and RPG fire was shot at the lead of the column from 100 meters away at the entrance to the neighborhood. Sapir showed no hesitation. From his position in the turret of the SPH, he ordered the driver to stop, swiveled the barrel, fired, and blew up the house in which the anti-tank squad was hiding.

The bat-com of the 17th was not privy to this decision. An RPG whistled by his head, and an instant later, the 155mm SPH emitted a massive exit blast. The house to his right took a monstrous hit, and the bat-com found himself between two smoking flames from hell – one from the shell's exit and one from its impact. Anyone who has been within 100 meters of a 155mm shell's impact can attest – it turns your innards to jelly.

3) The AA bat-com Israel Sar-El commanded the 947th Battalion in Beirut – a battalion of 30mm anti-aircraft "Vulcan" guns. The Vulcan is known for its hellish fire rate, intended to create a screen of shells in front of low-flying enemy aircraft, and Sar-El invented a modus operandi of working in tandem – a Vulcan on an APC along with a 155mm cannon, where the Vulcan cleared the top floors of snipers, and then the SPH climbed into position and destroyed the building.

Bringing down Beirut's twin towers.

A 155mm SPH in direct fire mode.

Dangot's Battery Cracks a Brigade HQ

I arrived in my chopper at the Monte Verde Ridge, overlooking Beirut on one side and the Alei Ridge on the other, with neither Beirut nor the ridge yet in IDF hands. Uri Simchoni, the deputy command general, came to meet me with a Lebanese customs official, who pointed at a building on the ridge above me, explaining that the HQ of a Syrian armored brigade was based there. I scanned the structure with binoculars, and indeed saw antennae towering from the roof, and brisk traffic of military vehicles.

I called up Eitan Dangot with his battery. He identified the HQ, moved the six SPHs up to position, placed the telescopic crosshairs on the target, elevating in accordance with range and load, for what is known as firing beyond telescope range. The third shell cracked the building like an egg, and the other SPHs joined in on the "fun," completely demolishing the headquarters and its surroundings. After Alei was captured, I arrived on the scene. The corpses of Syrian officers and troops lay among the ruins, and buried under them, shattered radios were strewn all over, together with battle maps still spread out on the splintered tables.

Dangot's battery after the landing, and me in conversation with David Ashraf, leader of squad 3.

Arnon Ben-Ami, commander of Division 96's division artillery, briefing me (to the left, on the radio: Eitan Dangot).

On the way back I told the pilots, "I got a recommendation from the Lebanese guy for a great restaurant on Monte Verde. Let's have lunch." A gorgeous view spread out below those windows of the restaurant not overlooking the smoking city of Beirut, and within minutes, six Lebanese men sat next to us.

"Hello General Mizrachi," said the most senior among them, who was the leader of "Al-Arz," one of the Maronite Christian militias. "We remember your visit to Beirut a year ago and the enormous help we received from you, and we'd like to buy you lunch." Out of the corner of my eye, I saw Mossad operative Shmulik Evyatar, signaling to me not to disclose that I knew him, or that he was an Israeli. We dined on the finest Lebanese cuisine, helped down with repeated toasts of Arak Zahlawi, Lebanon's famous anise liquor, and at some point, I noticed that one of the Christians was much fairer of complexion than his comrades. I said in Hebrew to the pilots and to Rami, my chief of staff, "Lebanon has always been a thoroughfare, and here's the proof. An Englishman passed through here, left his mark, and there's the result."

Four years passed and I flew to Switzerland, this time as a civilian, with the head of the Artillery Corps' doctrine and research branch Aharon Amoyal, to attend a joint military exercise. We were asked to give our opinion of the Swiss artillery, which included some 400 M-109 SPHs, as well as an Israeli-made aerial drone, and I also scheduled a meeting with the IDF attaché in Switzerland, Mordechai "Leibaleh" Alon. I had been told that Alon had once been Sayeret Matkal's intel officer, and when he entered the hotel lobby, we were both thunderstruck – he was the blondie from the restaurant on the Monte Verde, and he did not forget my erroneous surmise about his mother.

Ofer Mashraki RIP

From the Monte Verde Ridge, Dangot's battery continued to the ridge directly overlooking Beirut. From there it fired on targets at ranges of 600-800 meters – mostly buildings where snipers sat in the top floors and shot at our infantry troops. Dangot's job was to locate them – directly or with the aid of FOs, who were joinable to the infantry forces and noted precisely from which window on which floor the fire was coming from. An SPH would immediately aim at that window, and take out the entire floor.

I arrived for a visit at the battery with Raful. He had just finished an emotionally charged discussion with members of a paratroopers' unit, who gave him a hard time about the civilians present in the fighting zone, and suddenly Ofer Mashraki stood up and said: "Chief of Staff, we understand the object of the war and understand our role, but when I fire at the fourth floor to hit terrorists, and suddenly I see children running out of the building covered in blood, I have a problem."

Raful listened very carefully, and answered him at length about the need to allow the infantry to pass through the city, and the meaning of war. "He who rises to kill you, rise first to kill him," he said, quoting the Sages. "There is no intent to harm civilians and children, heaven forbid. But when shots are fired to kill our fighters, we must rise first to strike at the enemy." Contrary to the impatience and intolerance attributed to him, particularly regarding any attempt to undermine the model of the warrior with a blade between his teeth and battle lust in the eyes, Raful was attentive and patient at that meeting.

On the way back we heard on the radio that the position we had just left was under fire, and that the battery was leapfrogging. After a few minutes, Dangot reported to me that he had several wounded and one killed: Ofer Mashraki, who had gone up to the SPH's turret following the meeting with Raful, to carry on with his mission.

I parted with Raful, returned to the battery, and gathered the troops. I was convinced that they knew of Ofer's falling in battle, and that I needed to comfort them and get them back in action. I said: "I'm hurt as you and with you over Ofer's falling," and to my surprise I saw some of those in front of me clutch their head and burst out in tears. They didn't know yet that Ofer had been killed.

We sat for a few more minutes, and then I ordered Dangot to deploy at another position and employ direct fire.

Pride and Prejudice

I had two flak vests in my Wagoneer – one for the driver and one for the ops officer – and as usual I left the vehicle without a vest while visiting the direct fire position of a 203mm battery from the 334th Battalion. I walked toward the M-577 command vehicle, and just then 60mm mortar shells began to fall – the kind I remembered from the War of Attrition in the Sinai: You hear no exit noise, and the bomb just drops on your head.

I found myself in a silly position: The crews were standing exposed on the SPHs, with only personal armor, because it's a cannon mounted on an armored chassis. So how can I, the idiot who didn't bother to put on a flak vest, run in front of their eyes to the command vehicle (which may be made of nothing except aluminum, but still gives a sense of safety)? The troops would see me, and they must not see a frightened CAO running for cover when they themselves are exposed, without so much as a turret.

I cursed under my breath, kept walking at a slightly accelerated pace, passing through the crews as I smiled and waved at them, and with a sigh of relief I entered the M-577.

Dangot moved at the head of the 35th Brigade's maneuvering forces all the way from the landing. Dan Harel joined him after receiving command of the 402nd Battalion and moved along with the Paratroopers Brigade's 450th Battalion, and each of them experienced the same oddity: Paratroopers were clinging to the SPHs to find cover during the march to contact, and refused to understand, despite warnings, that they were clinging to a barrel of dynamite. An aluminum SPH, loaded to capacity with 70 shells, double the recommended standard, had its crewmembers literally standing on explosive shells. One direct hit could blow it all sky-high, turning it and everyone on and around it into fine ash.

A 203mm SPH in direct fire.

Shells (Don't) Collide in Mid-Air

During the tedious crawl toward the Beirut-Damascus road, I came by chopper to visit Uppo at the 162nd Division's HQ. He was running the artillery fire with a firm hand in all directions, along with his staff-ops officer, Meir Ran. Furthermore, Uppo and the division's intel officer, Doron Tamir, were running the battle in effect, with Uppo becoming the darling of the division commander, Menachem Einan. Or as Einan put it: Uppo needed to be kept in mothballs during peacetime and brought out at war, because that's when he shows his true abilities.

We were on a hill we called "Hamesulaat" ("The Rocky,") across from the town of Ansariyeh, which was taken in the attempt to reach the Beirut-Damascus road along the central mountain route. On the side of the road sat a dead Syrian commando fighter in a dugout. He was still clutching an RPG launcher, with a large cluster bomb hole that had torn through his metal helmet and gaped his cranium. A chilling sight.

Raful arrived on the scene in his chopper. We advanced to watch the artillery fire raining down on the targets, and suddenly Raful discovered a radar antenna. He drew his pistol and said: "That's a ZTSU radar." ZTSU was a Russian-made anti-aircraft cannon. I stopped him from shooting at the very last moment, explaining that the radar, which looks sort of like a square satellite TV antenna and does indeed resemble the Russian antenna, is our own "Meofef" ("Flier") radar, ranging the fire.

We watched countless cluster shells flying through the air, on their way to release their bomblets on the target, and Raful was pleased with the massive fire. He was not shy in voicing his admiration, saying: "Arie, you're firing so much that the shells are colliding in the air." That is indeed what it looked like to the non-gunner's eye, seeing hundreds of explosions in mid-air. I explained to him that what he was seeing were the explosions of the time fuses, opening the cluster shells and releasing a trail of 88 little bomblets which land on the target.

Just then a salvo from a Syrian 130mm battery landed on us. Raful dropped instantly to the ground while I remained standing. I was an old hand in counter-battery fire from back in the War of Attrition, and I knew that these shells had already exploded.

Raful got up, all furious at having dived for cover while the gunner stayed on his feet, but by then I was awaiting incoming fire. I pitched my ears, heard six exits in the salvo and hit the ground. Raful remained standing, till Zacharin and I grabbed his ankles and dragged him down. He didn't say a word about the double incident, and found solace in some Syrian bully beef found in the dugouts. After he ate some, he said, "Poor bastards, this is what they're fed."

Chief of Staff Raful under fire. (Photo: Memi Peer / Government Press Bureau)

"Stepping Out for a Sandwich? Toss Twenty Rockets"

During the advance north, our forces captured ten brand new Korean 122mm rocket launchers, hidden deep in the terrorists' bunkers. Captured along with the launchers, each equipped with twenty launching tubes, were 3,000 rockets. Raful, who had acquired a reputation as an "eye for an eye" kind of guy, met with me by chance on the Kafr Sil Ridge, overlooking the coastal route at the southern entrance to Beirut. "We captured rocket launchers and ammunition," he said, "Take them and fire at Beirut."

I tried to avoid the unplanned chore, which seemed like potential trouble. We weren't familiar with the weapon, didn't know whether the launchers were in good order and could possibly blow up, taking their operators with them. And the rockets – were they serviceable? I sought an excuse and said, "Everyone is busy with the battles. I don't have a free unit to start the intake, training, and firing." But Raful insisted. "Look," he told me, "The entire valley is full of firing SPHs." Indeed, there were tens of our battalions, deployed and spitting fire. "Put a launcher next to every SPH," he said. "Should a crew leader step out for a sandwich? Let him pull the cable and toss twenty rockets at Beirut." I saw that I couldn't shake him and called my friend Dr. Mordechai Pearl, aka Gingi Pearl. He had commanded the battalion of 240mm rockets shortly beforehand, and ordered him to quickly put together a battalion of launchers, get the pieces ready for action and join in the firing on Beirut. The great advantage of the captured Soviet launchers was their range – 20km – and Pearl carried out the mission in his customary precision. He opened the safe of his office at the Technion and pulled out a fire table of 122mm launchers which he had found at some point and kept. The launchers were painted in the IDF's khaki, the adjutancy provided personnel to complete the basic lineup he had composed from among the 240mm veterans, and they even held a short practice.

The battalion deployed just three days after Raful's "sandwich" quip right next to the 240mm battalion, and participated for three weeks in the battle for the outskirts of Beirut – and Beirut itself following the murder of Bashir – until the rockets ran out.

An FO in a Submarine, an FSO on a Missile Boat, and SPHs in the Hull of a Ship

The personal connection between the staff-ops officers of the CAO's HQ – Noam David, formerly bat-com of the 403rd, and the ops officer Yigal Barzilai – and their colleagues at IDF HQ was excellent The cooperation with the Air Force and its head of ops, Ran Goren, and with Ze'ev Yehezkeli from the Navy, was continuous and fruitful.

In the course of this cooperation, we decided to place an FO on a submarine which was cruising below the surface of the sea off Beirut, so that he could range through the periscope, and for the mission we chose Elhanan Zuta. His job was to locate and range 122mm and 130mm, deployed in Ras Beirut, and he indeed scoped and ranged the Lebanese capital. The location HQ, under the command of Herzl Gedj, employed fire on his orders and destroyed a battery of D-30 122mm cannons. We used Yoav David as an FSO on a missile boat, and he provided us with another pair of eyes on the coastal route and Beirut.

And staying at sea: The 96th Division's landing operation at the Awali estuary included Dangot's battery too, as mentioned above – two outfitted and armed SPHs, with an M-577 as a command post and two M-548s loaded with ammunition. They all landed safely on the beach, and immediately deployed and were ready to fire in order to clear the road for the 35th Brigade.

Then, at the change of guard on Monday morning, six 175mm SPHs were loaded onto a landing craft, under the command of Ami Shiloh, bat-com of the 412th. They too landed at the Awali estuary, and their long range reinforced the artillery in the central and western sectors. They also operated in the eastern sector in a few cases, participating in the "CAO target" fire concentration at the Battle of Sultan Yacoub.

But the capstone in terms of amphibious landings was the transporting of an entire artillery division to the Port of Beirut aboard a civilian ship. This operation entailed the sailing of the 216th Division Artillery, which included two "Ro'em"[31] battalions with 36 155mm SPHs, along with the unit's HQ, the vehicles, the ammunition trucks, the fuel, and all the rest of the logistics. This was in early August. The roll-on, roll-off ship that had pressed into service for the operation was the "Jasmine," which was normally used for importing automobiles to Israel.

The plan was for two additional battalions to enter Lebanon by land. One of them, the 8202nd under Rubi Rockney, was already deployed in the area of Kafr Sil by early August. The other, the 8141st under Alex Kroskin, was supposed to join with it in motion. The two battalions of the 216th Division Artillery were transported by sea to the Port of Beirut as mentioned above, and the four battalions were supposed to move toward the deployment area in Junia.

The division artillery was commanded by Yaakov Yaffe, who was FSO in the legendary Battle of Umm-Qatef in the Six-Day War. His deputy was "Zatz" – Yitzhak Zarnitzki, who in the Yom Kippur War commanded the 829th Priests battalion, and had employed direct fire in aid of Ya-Ya, then the bat-com of the airborne Nahal, in the recapturing of Tel Saki. The two bat-coms were Yossi Frum and Eli Baram.

This fleet of vehicles and armaments reversed into the hull of the ship along with some 500 troops. The captain sailed them toward Cyprus, and then turned sharply toward the Port of Beirut, as only the northern part, the one further from the Israeli border, was in our hands, while the southern part was held by the terrorists.

The 216th Division Artillery made a successful nighttime landing, and joined the other two battalions that had already moved northward toward Junia. I escorted them up until a moment before they sailed from Ashdod and then received them in Beirut, to make sure that all was running smoothly at both ports. Happily, there was no need for intervention. Everything went like clockwork. Also present at the landing was Amnon Lipkin-Shachak, commander of the 194th Division, and Bashir Gemayel, who himself had come to receive us as well.

---

31 The Ro'em was an Israeli innovation: a 155mm cannon manufactured by Soltam, mounted on a Sherman tank's chassis with a metal enclosure – like a house on tracks with a cannon barrel protruding from it.

SOUL-SEARCHING

The foreign TV networks broadcast our massive artillery fire almost non-stop as the siege on the terrorists in Beirut was tightened, and the echoes of the cannons were heard around the world. The same, of course, can be said of Israel's Channel One, the only TV channel in the country back in 1982, and during one of the days of the battle for the Lebanese capital, the channel's reporter, Dan Semama, interviewed troops under fire.

Semama did not content himself with playing spokesman for the troops and voicing his admiration of the brave soldiers, but asked hard questions and described situations and phenomena unfamiliar to civilians. The TV screen suddenly brought sights, previously known only to those who had fought, into every living room, dilemmas faced only by those who had experienced such situations, and incidents of horror, of fleeing civilians and of cruelty. In questioning me, Semama pressed me hard regarding harm to civilians, and what now goes by the euphemism "collateral damage."

We were less than a decade removed from the horrible war, in which our enemies sought to destroy us on Yom Kippur, and Israeli TV brought the war into every Israeli's home, just like what happened in America with the Vietnam War. In my humble opinion, this was the reason why public protests broke out even before the fire had stopped, in addition to the political motive, which surely was the driving force behind many of the protesters and was dominant in the scheme of things.

Semama was unrelenting, and in his solid way, drove to the heart of the problem. "How do you ensure that you're not harming civilians when you fire at a target in Beirut?" he asked.

The truth had to be told, that we did all we could to precisely hit each target, but at the end of the day, artillery is a statistical weapon. Four men ran this battle – Arnon Ben-Ami, Herzl Gedj, Yossi Zinger, and Herschko (Yitzhak Ben-Zvi), head of the target acquisition branch at Shivta, who was appointed target acquisition commander of the 96th Division – and not once did they carry out "vengeance strikes."

I didn't duck the question, and said: "Listen, if I discover a terrorists' 122mm cannon, placed on purpose next to a hospital, and I see that this cannon is hitting a platoon of paratroopers and causing casualties, of course I command to concentrate fire on it. My duty is to create a protective wall for the IDF's fighters, and however much it may cause sorrow and pain – we're at war. My mission is to destroy an enemy harming our troops."

This was no theoretical example, and I was surprised by the amount of responses I received. All were in my favor, and none were defiant or abusive, as is customary on today's social media. One interesting response I received was from Gideon Mahanaimi. I didn't know him personally; I only knew that he had demanded that Moshe Dayan resign at a general command conference at Hazor Airbase in 1974. I had yet to attain the seniority required to attend, and Col. Mahanaimi was a famous figure in the IDF. What some call "The good old land of Israel," and "salt of the earth."

"It's been a long time since I have seen a convincing and courageous performance such as yours," he told me on the phone. "This is the first time I've seen an officer speak sense, explain the situation, and give a quiet, pointed, and non-hyperbolic response."

The Twenty-Minute Window

Twenty minutes. That was the precise amount of time from the moment we began to fire on targets in Beirut until we received an order to halt. The critical hours were the daytime hours in the US, during which we were forbidden to initiate fire, but only to respond.

During these twenty minutes, the rotation went as follows: You fire at a target, always by surprise, one barrage in a short burst. The entire target area was ranged and registered for fire, including meteorological data, and the force firing at the target was always a concentration of a division artillery and up. The proactive fire was usually based on intelligence reports regarding Syrian military movements endangering our troops, preparations for artillery fire against our troops, or what is now known as a "ticking bomb" situation. Philip Habib and his men would immediately report the bombardment to the White House, Washington would quickly phone the embassy in Tel Aviv, the embassy would make an urgent call to Prime Minister Begin, and from him the order would be relayed station by station till it reached us.

Twenty minutes. Oddly reminiscent of Paolo Coelho's "Eleven Minutes."

Cluster Bombs at Ein Hilweh

Itzik Mordechai's command room was on the outskirts of Sidon on the roof of a building overlooking the Ein Hilweh refugee camp, the largest refugee camp in Lebanon. Most of the civilian population had long since abandoned the camp, and it was the scene of heavy fighting – from alley to alley, as well as in the surrounding orchards.

Itzik Mordechai commanded the 91st Division, also known as the Galilee division, and also on the roof, of course, was the division's artillery commander, Amos Tor. He was a man of high values and learning, who knew the country like the back of his hand, and was the one who hit a T-34 tank with direct fire from a Priest cannon. He had since left the military, but in my mad pursuit of brave, quality officers, I persuaded him to return to service and take command of the 282nd Division Artillery. In Ein Hilweh that turned out to be a mistake. Your childhood heroes don't always stay heroes. Sometimes they freeze in time – life moves on, and they get stuck behind with their heroics.

The most effective method of clearing Ein Hilweh required artillery fire using cluster shells. The camp was already empty of civilians, who had all fled. The access routes to the camp cut through orchards, which were used by the terrorists as ambush sites, and there is no operational ammunition fit for such a situation, save the cluster. On the other hand, the cluster bomblet duds create a sort of minefield, and Tor found it hard to live with the thought of civilians who may return to the camp and get wounded or killed.

This type of ammunition was banned in 2010 in the Oslo Convention, signed by over a hundred countries, but not by Israel, the U.S., Russia, China, India, Pakistan, and Brazil. But Amos Tor, a leftist kibbutznik raised on peace and fraternity in Kibbutz Negba, began to pace the roof from corner to corner.

I told him: "Amos, fire clusters."

He didn't answer, and wandered off to the other corner.

I decided to take over and ordered Reuven Levy, deputy commander of the Northern Command Division Artillery, to have the 8193rd Battalion, under David Boaz, fire clusters. This was a battalion of brand new Soltam-manufactured M-71 155mm towed cannons. Reuven, also a kibbutznik, from Ramat Hacovesh, and a soulmate of mine till his death, commanded the division artillery's battalions which were assigned to the 91st Division. He gave the fire command, the battalion's cannons fired clusters, and the bomblets penetrated every hiding place, hitting the terrorists. Following the massive fire, our forces managed to capture the Ein Hilweh camp almost unopposed.

Following this incident, I realized that Tor was buckling under the load, and heavy-heartedly but decisively, I replaced him with Pini Doron, deputy commander of the 209th Division Artillery. He did a great job in the eastern sector battles in the first week of the war including the Battle of Sultan Yacoub, and I decided to promote him in wartime. It was a professional decision that practically begged itself, and it incidentally gave me the opportunity to recognize Doron for the excellent work he had done.

How Sharon Was Persuaded Not to Take Beirut With Ground Forces

I have already mentioned the soul searching of crew leaders who successfully employed direct fire, preventing many casualties among our troops. One person who did it particularly well, for example, was Yossi Zinger, the young artillery commander of the 35th Brigade, who was strict in firing only at targets where, as best as he could ascertain, there was no civilian population.

Even Raful surprised me in the conversations which I related above with the paratroopers and the Dangot battery, with his patient and understanding attitude, as he tried to explain why in some cases, direct fire in urban environments was unavoidable – this in complete contrast to the intolerance he displayed toward commanders and fighters who hesitated in battle and didn't seek to engage the enemy.

And here's comes the commanders' convention in Beirut, following which Eli Geva, commander of the 211th Brigade, resigned his commission. The temperatures in the debate over entering Beirut kept rising, but at the same time, Arafat and his besieged cohorts received encouragement from Philip Habib and the Americans, and refused to surrender. It was obvious that a ground incursion would take a heavy toll. When they did the calculations, they found that the clearing of each building would require a platoon of men. The clearing of three buildings requires a company, and the clearing of a block would occupy a battalion, so that the entire IDF infantry, standing and reserve, would have to be deployed in taking Beirut in house-to-house combat. It was supposed to be a briefing with the Defense Minister, but Raful called me over beforehand and said: "I want significant fire concentration the moment Arik steps off the chopper."

I got his drift: Raful doesn't want to send ground forces into Beirut, and wants to show Sharon that the terrorists can be subdued with firepower alone. He asked me to create a corridor of fire from the beach to Beirut, in an open area free of civilians, dotted with a few terrorist outposts.

I ordered Uri Manos and Shimon Rom to allocate eleven battalions – six from the command and five from the 96th Division – and ordered Moshe Ronen, deputy commander of the 282nd Division Artillery, to concentrate them in his sphere. The moment Sharon stepped off the helicopter, Raful gave me a hand signal, and I ordered: "Fire!" Once again, a CAO's target, and once again, a group of commanders standing on a hill, surprised by the force despite being no novices to fire, to the point where some of those present looked for cover.

The exit roar from the large amalgam of cannons deployed in front of us and behind, and shortly thereafter, the concentrated fire of eleven battalions landing on target before our eyes, were terrifying. Arik saw this and took it to heart.

"Give Me Beirut for Three Days"

After this resounding demonstration, the command post hosted that famous commanders' debate, which got out into the media and caused an uproar due to Eli Geva's resignation from command of his armored brigade. The discussion was brisk and professional and the commanders, as was our custom then, spoke directly, without hesitation, unafraid to speak their minds. This is the greatness of the IDF: At no discussion and no operational briefing of those I witnessed, was a commander precluded from speaking their mind. We listened patiently even to those who spoke nonsense at great length and in an all-knowing tone.

Two men voiced the greatest opposition to a ground incursion into Beirut: Shai Avital, commander of Sayeret Matkal, and Geva, who stood out as boldly critical back in the Yom Kippur War. They both pointed out the irrationality of a ground incursion of a large and dense city, partly prepared for defense, let alone a capital. Their words carried no political undertones, contrary to the later claims of self-interested politicians, and their reasons were professional – theirs and those who did support a ground incursion.

I too, stood up and spoke my mind: "Give me Beirut for three days," I said. "You, the Defense Minister and the Chief of Staff, be a barrier and stave off the repeated ceasefires, and I promise you that after three days, the terrorists – those of them still alive – will come out with their hands up."

I had reasons for saying what I did, which I will elaborate below. "We know Arie and his methods," said Eli Geva, and I realized that his position, while professional, had a conscientious element as well.

Raful didn't cut off anyone. At the end of the discussion, he turned to the taciturn Amir Drori and asked for his opinion. The Command General turned his head in a sort of half-circle, which some interpreted as a yes, and some as a no. He was not a significant factor throughout the war, and said nothing this time as well.

THE FIRE STORM

A foreign network's reporter captured the artillery firestorm in Beirut one day, describing to his viewers a massive firing of an entire division artillery on a Syrian rocket battalion. Or as he put it: Look at the Israeli artillery. The Syrian rockets had only just been launched, and at that very second a tremendous fire concentration dropped on the firing battalion and destroyed it.

What rapid response, what accuracy, the reporter waxed enthusiastically, despite not being suspected of pro-Israeli sympathies, as he backed up his praise with real-time footage.

After watching this report, I said to myself: What an unprofessional reporter. The rockets take two minutes or more to fly to their target, and by the time you locate the target and give the fire order, and add the flight time of our own shells – even with the most efficient and rapid execution, it has to take five to ten minutes. But the compliment and the commendation were given, so why be a spoilsport.

Years later, I spoke about that TV report, and my own internal discourse about it, at preparations for an event marking 30 years to the start of the PFG War, at the Gunners' House in Zichron Yaakov. "The reporter actually got it right," I was told by Meir Ran, the 215th Brigade's staff-ops officer.

"How is that possible?" I asked, and Ran explained to me in detail how the fire center in Beirut operated. All intelligence sources were recruited for the mission, including Unit 8200 electronic surveillance, Magellan Rangers observations, field reports from FSOs and artillery commanders – and of course, the devices of the TA battalion orchestrated by Herschko, with the radars, the long-range observation, the stabilized mirror, and the 869th Observation Unit.

In that case, he said, we intercepted information on the wire of intent to launch a battalion-wide barrage of rockets. We pinpointed the location of the battalion, the area was laid out on a grid and ranged, and the moment the information was received, an entire division artillery received the target and fired a barrage. Seventy-two barrels fired for four minutes, and almost 300 shells landed on that battalion and annihilated it, the very moment the rockets emerged from their launchers.

"See-Fire"

This concept was a development of an experiment I conducted as commander of Shivta and commander of the 286th Division Artillery. This concept was enshrined in the CAO directives, and the entire corps began to practice what I call "See-Fire" during my tenure. See an enemy? Kill him! Don't wait. You have location devices and you have firing units – act in a short circle!

This concept was a continuation of my rich experience, and the experiment I'd conducted in command of Shivta and of the 286th Division Artillery, when I established "Team Yoel." I placed all means of observation and location at his disposal, as well as firing units, and gave him permission to open fire without further clearance the moment he identifies a target. This was ostensibly an organizational, tactical solution, but it had a decisive impact on the significant change in the corps' status, which until then was perceived as unable to cope with the enemy's plethora of artillery. The enemy militaries operated under the Russian "Red War God" doctrine. Using a tactical and organizational solution, backed with advanced technology, we managed to change the status of the Artillery Corps and its role in the campaign, and it became "queen of the battlefield."

The ability to deal with the counter-battery fire which we took in the War of Attrition and the Yom Kippur War and barely responded to, and the fact that artillery accounts for half the casualties among the maneuvering forces, increased the need and motivation to find a solution – and to implement it quickly.

This was how I operated as the Northern Command artillery commander, when I concentrated all the location devices at the villa in

Marjayoun, and applied the advance approval I had from Yanush, the Command General, to open fire at will. This concept was applied with great success in the Peace for Galilee War and in the firestorm in Beirut. It helps to understand how the corps developed to a position of control of the ground-based joint fire, concentrating all observation means and data in the hands of the gunner, at all levels, and concentration of all means of fire from land, air, and sea.

Thanks to Personal Contacts and Barters

Collaboration with units that possessed newer and more advanced means than ours for observation, intelligence, and target acquisition became an obsession with me. The system of personal fiefs in the IDF, which prevails to this day, mostly among the intelligence community, and the refusal to cooperate in the name of secrecy, is something I cracked through personal connections, and after creating facts on the ground, I managed to make them permanent through the barter method. Give and take.

An example of this was the collaboration with the 869th Observation Unit. Through personal contacts and smooth talking, I managed to man their superbly outfitted observation posts, for instance the post overlooking Tyre, and the entire coastal route, and I already related how we used it to destroy a terrorist 130mm cannon, which had been hidden in the orchards of Tyre and was firing at Nahariya. I was obsessed with destroying that cannon. A battery from the 404th Battalion under Tzachi Ganor was placed behind the Shaqif al-Hardun ridge on top alert, and when the observer identified an exit, he put it in the crosshairs, and the battery fired an instant salvo. The TV report shows the terrorists' cannon blown up into the air, and the sharp-eyed observer, who was later wounded in the war, got a hospital visit from me and a bottle of fine whisky.

The command group that ran the artillery fire in Beirut managed to foster a cooperative atmosphere and to forge strong ties and mutual trust with all intelligence agencies operating in the area. I myself visited them often, and also flew, as mentioned above, in a Dornir DO-28 with a "stabilized mirror," which is, in effect, an LREOOD. We used it to range 175mm cannons to fire at a battery of SA-6 missiles on the eastern front, and at artillery batteries. The footage exists somewhere, clearly showing hits and the destruction of the missiles and the cannons.

Incidentally, we adopted the airborne "LREOOD" because all the divisions, intelligence units, and commands wanted drone assistance, which provides commanders at all levels with real-time visuals. The use of drones was in its infancy then. What we see on TV screens and seems natural today, was brand new in the PFG War, and there was a long waiting list. Drone assistance was handed out sparingly, but those who received it quickly forgot about the "mirror," and it came to be used exclusively by us.

"We Were Surprised and the Enemy Was Surprised"

I was always annoyed at the long wait for artillery fire, which was the product of a professional conception on the part of the corps' founding fathers, themselves products of the British school of artillery: most of them viewed precision, deployment, and technical professionalism as the main issue. They didn't pay much attention to what was happening before their eyes, in the field, and issues such as availability, response speed, and integration in the ground campaign were not at the top of their agenda. I worked to change this approach throughout my career – by improving and expediting the firing echelon's professional processes on the one hand, and by instilling faith in the artillery among the forward line maneuvering forces on the other, to get them to see our personnel and abilities as an inseparable part of the maneuvering array.

For seven and a half weeks, from June 25th to August 18th, 1982, when the agreement on the terrorists' evacuation was signed – during the period known as the "Siege of Beirut," which was mainly a siege of Yasser Arafat and his men, the other terror organizations, and the representatives of the Syrian military – the Artillery Corps acted in the most effective manner and became world renown. This was reflected in global professional literature, as can be seen in the two examples below.

American military historian Richard Gabriel, famous for his in-depth studies of the Vietnam War, writes in his book, "The Peace for Galilee Operation":[32]

Artillery is the newest combat arm of the IDF, created out of whole cloth after the 1973 war. In 1973, the IDF had about

300 artillery guns, most of which were towed pieces. By 1982, the number of guns had increased to over 958, most of which were self-propelled, large-caliber artillery. Prior to 1973, ar. Artillery played essentially a support role, with limited mobility in support of the tank. Today IDF artillery is completely mobile to keep up with the rapid advance of tanks and armored personnel carriers; it has become a full partner in the combined arms team.

The IDF can field about fifteen artillery brigades. Its weaponry is comprised mostly of M-109's and M-107's, added to a number of locally produced Soltam M-71's and L-33's. In addition, it deploys a considerable number of 160mm mortars mounted on old Sherman chassis, as well as a number of M-50 155 mm guns mounted on Super Sherman chassis. Mobility is further augmented by the ability of the IDF to move artillery pieces to the battlefront on transporters.

Artillery proved effective in most instances during the Lebanon war, although to some extent its effectiveness was reduced by the terrain, which prevented its playing the highly mobile, fast-moving role envisioned for it in the new combined- arms doctrine developed since 1973. Operations were often slowed to a crawl by terrain and hostile fire in urban areas. In the east, artillery proved effective in counterbattery fire against Syrian positions, a fact helped considerably by the

---

[32] Richard A. Gabriel, *The Peace for Galilee operation, The Israeli-PLO War in Lebanon*, (1984) pp. 204-205.

Syrians' refusal to redeploy artillery rapidly with the changing tactical situation.

The effectiveness of artillery in the eastern zone was also increased considerably by the Israelis' complete air superiority. In the west, the effectiveness of artillery was limited by self-imposed restrictions to limit property damage and civilian casualties. However, the artillery was technically very good. It made good use of new devices such as the RPV's, which were flown over the battlefield to provide real-time intelligence through V pictures of enemy targets. It also made good use of intelligence gathered by aircraft flying over the battlefield. In addition, fused the new Rafael David fire-control computer system (made in Israel), which made it fairly effective at sheaving artillery and linking concentrated fires. It also deployed a number of new fire modes built around the new Telkoor M-131 multi-option fuse.

In Beirut, artillery played a crucial role in suppressing enemy fire and destroying PLO strongpoints within the camps and the city. Often, in responding to PLO Katyusha and mortar fire, the IDF was able to sheave its artillery rapidly and respond almost immediately by pouring scores of shells on a single area.

Effectiveness of artillery is often directly related to the ability to sheave effectively, and the Israelis, with almost no experience in this tactic before 1973, seem to have learned quickly and developed the technique to a high degree. During the siege of Beirut, the IDF seems to have discovered the technique of "sniping" with large-caliber artillery pieces by firing single rounds into PLO military targets at point-blank range.

Artillery performed well in Lebanon, with no major problems. However, battle conditions presented it with considerable advantages that it may not have on a different battlefield in the future. The conditions of battle in Lebanon did not allow for a true test of the artillery and structure envisioned in 1973. Its new role was to deploy in support of rapidly moving armored infantry forces in a closely coordinated combined-arms attack.

A test of that role will have to wait for the future [sic].

The second quote is from the book "Field Artillery and Firepower," by British General J.B.A. Bailey,[33] who gave me a copy with a personal dedication:

> *By 1982 artillery had become, in effect, the newest combat arm of the IDF. In 1973 the IDF had three hundred pieces, many of which were of 105-mm caliber, and most were towed. By 1982 it had 958 pieces, most of which were SP, and of 155 mm or larger caliber.*
>
> *Before 1973, artillery had tried to support tanks but had often lacked comparable mobility. By 1982 the Israelis could field fifteen artillery brigades to accompany tanks and armored personnel carriers.*
>
> *On 6 June 1982, Israel launched Operation Peace for Galilee. The IDF entered Lebanon to fight the PLO but became embroiled with Syrian forces. Israeli artillery proved effective against slower-moving Syrian artillery, and it was valuable in breaking down fortified positions in rough terrain and in urban areas in support of infantry-heavy [divisions]. in Beirut the M109 was sometimes used to fire directly at strong points. If tanks were isolated, they became very vulnerable, especially at night, and on occasions they were saved by bringing down defensive artillery fire.*
>
> *The targeting and speed of response of Israeli artillery was enhanced by the intelligence gathering of new RPVs and the Rafael DAVID fire control computer. The logistic system needed to be yet more flexible to feed increasingly mobile artillery, and problems were eased by resupplying forward gun positions directly by helicopter.*
>
> *Artillery firepower proved its worth, but the campaign in Lebanon was unlike those of 1967 and 1973, and it was a harbinger of the changing strategic environment in which Israel would have to operate thereafter. It was conducted within tighter political controls, which hindered efficiency in purely military terms? Even so, it attracted intense political criticism at home and abroad, which grew*

---

33 Maj. J B. A. Bailey, *Field Artillery and Firepower, Israel and Lebanon, 1982-2002*, (2003) pp. 401

more intense the longer the campaign lasted. Blitzkrieg had become a thing of the past; the Arabs had changed the rules of the game.

The onslaught of Israeli firepower in a densely populated area, where winning "hearts and minds" was necessary to achieve broader strategic objectives, showed once more that victories on the battlefield do not necessarily constitute success in more complex situations. A record of earlier military successes led the Israelis to apply oversimplified military criteria to the use of force, in a campaign in which political intricacies touched military tactics as well as strategy. Israel faced new operational predicaments.

This complexity has permeated all operations involving Israel and its neighbors since, and the use of Israeli artillery has not always taken this fact fully into account [sic].

The artillery's tremendous effect found a clear expression in Raful's simple language. In an interview with journalist Gad Lior in August 1982, he said: "We were surprised, and the enemy was surprised. It used to take them half a year to hit a target. Now if they don't hit the target on the first shot, they investigate it for half a year."[34]

This is the place to note that there had been significant technological advances in the world, in the decade preceding the PFG War. We always tried to be at the forefront of technology and to utilize innovations from around the world to improve processes, improve precision, significantly reduce response times, and update the fighting doctrine as per the innovations. Thus, for instance, the introduction of vector-based ranging through the use of the laser range finder, to mark the distance to the target and to the shell's impact, and to relay this data to the firing computer at the battery, which then calculates the correction and enables immediate fire for effect.

---

[34] Gad Lior, "Tamid Totchan," Vol. 73, September 2022.

"Non-Combatants"

It is an unavoidable fact that artillery fire is statistical. The level of precision may have improved greatly thanks to incessant development and acquisition of technological means – from firing computers, through laser range fingers and muzzle velocity radars on each barrel, to correct each one individually, to ranging radars and location radars – but all these do not make artillery fire a precision-guided weapon, the kind that costs $100,000 per projectile, as opposed to $1,000 per artillery shell. So there was no way we could completely prevent harm to non-combatants. To be precise, we emphasized speed, power, and lethal effect.

We never explicitly ordered to avoid harming civilians. It was clear – and this *was* a clearly worded CAO's directive – that we destroy enemies and enemy targets that have a clear definition: An outpost, an artillery battery, a tank, a concentration of forces, a convoy. Obviously, never once has a civilian target been defined for an IDF cannon.

We also preemptively swept away archaic notions such as "harassment fire," as we set a clear goal: We fire to destroy an enemy. Want noise? Buy a rattle. Want to harass? Key a car or use a stink bomb. We have a crystal-clear mission.

Those who were particularly conscientious about avoiding harm to civilians were the younger commanders – the generation of new batcoms, squad leaders, the officers at the observation posts and at the firing units, and the other troops who were in direct contact with the enemy and integrated into the maneuvering forces. They set the tone, out of self-awareness, broad education, and being attentive, sensitive individuals. They didn't do so for public relations or due to political persuasion. It stemmed from the way they perceived war and the way each of them applied, in their own little domain, the things they'd learned, and the values instilled in them at home. I don't think they did so because they grew up on the Meir'ke Pa'il's "Purity of Arms" sermon or the "Volokolamsk Highway," but rather due to their human quality and the education they'd received. I spoke on the matter with the commander of the 282nd Division Artillery about service in the territories. As his men are combat troops for all intents and purposes, just like infantry men, and carry out the same missions, I asked him whether, beyond the professional training, the commanders devote time to "humane" conduct. His response surprised me: "No need," he said, "Our fighters receive that education at home, and in any event, we always have a finger on the pulse."

What Brought Arafat to His Knees

It is an abundantly clear fact that firepower, mostly that of the Artillery Corps, is what brought Yasser Arafat to his knees. Facing a choice between departure and death, he chose to evacuate.

Artillery shells are fired day and night and are not weather-dependent like the Air Force, which when available comes, bombs, and leaves. Constant physical and mental artillery pressure, 24 hours a day, broke the terrorists.

Artillery was also what brought about complete quiet in the Gaza Strip following 2014's Operation Protective Edge. It wasn't precision missiles nor the Air Force that silenced the Shuja'iyya neighborhood in Gaza, but Golani's talented artillery commander, and the 405th and 411th Battalions, who fired 600 shells — as told to me by none other than Golani's brigadier at time, now Major General Ghassan Aliyan, the Coordinator of the Government's Activities in the Territories. Complete silence ensued following the massive bombardment, and the Hamas terrorists didn't dare raise their heads until the end of the operation in that sector.

And back to 1982: When Arafat and his cohorts completed the evacuation of Beirut, on August 31st, the objective of the war was achieved — to remove the PLO from Lebanon and to achieve a favorable quiet long the northern border. The goal was achieved despite the fact that some 800 terrorists still remained in Beirut, and despite the fact that they still held some key positions.

"Fly in the Phantom and Let's See You Identify Targets"

At one of the discussions during the battle for Beirut, I told Maj-Gen. David Ivri, the Air Force Commander, that the Air Force's participation in the fighting is negligible, because his pilots don't know how to identify targets, and drop their bombs again and again on the same spots.

Ivri was displeased at my comments, and replied: "Take a flight on a Phantom, and let's see you identify targets from the air."

I accepted the challenge gladly. First of all, understanding the abilities of my partners was necessary to efficient battle management in all aspects, including the aerial one. Second, I always wanted to fly in a fighter plane. As a veteran aerial observer, I was confident in my abilities, but I didn't account for 5 Gs of speed.

I drove to Hatzerim, and the pilot who flew me was Uzi Rosen, commander of the 107th Squadron. I wriggled into the pressure suit, and sat behind him in the navigator's seat, and Uzi explained to me what to do. The day was beautiful and the view magnificent. I loved the speed and saw tiny Israel as though laid across the palm of my hand.

"What's down here?" Uzi asked, just as we passed over Qala'a, aka Camp Yoav, where we were based with the 405th in the attrition period following the Yom Kippur War. "Qala'a," I said, "And there's also an Israeli AD base here right next to the artillery base, watch out."

Uzi's response came quickly. "Hold on tight," he said, opened an afterburner, and flew us straight to Mt. Hermon. At the last second, he pulled the stick, lifted the plane's nose and we soared upward like a rocket.

I didn't barf. I actually felt good, and kept on identifying targets – this time terrorist bunkers on a wadi bank. From there we flew to the Baqaa – and suddenly heard the surface-to-air missile warning signal. We were locked on.

Uzi didn't break a sweat, and opened an afterburner. Once he took us out of the danger zone, I realized why the pilots hadn't listened to the surface-to-air channel during the Yom Kippur War.

The flight was over, I got doused with a bucket of water as per Air Force ritual, and Ivri called. "You really did identify all the targets," he said, and in light of the evasive action I had just witnessed, which would leave a pilot precious little time to communicate with anyone on the ground, I replied, "Now I understand you guys better."

Caposta Sr. and Caposta Jr.

I stood next to Raful when a 120mm mortar bomb fired by the terrorists fell a few meters from us, at the Beirut airport, while we were capturing it. The bomb directly hit a "Namrash 81" (an APC with an 81mm mortar mounted on it) used by one of Golani's support companies, and troopers were still extracting their comrades' bodies from the burning APC, which is when I demonstrated the "position-controlled firing" method to Yossi Zinger and he, as I related, scored a direct hit on the terrorist position from where the fire had been launched.

It was that very same day that Raful brought a friend with him, Micha Caposta, the legendary Rangers' Company commander under Motta Gur in the capturing of the Old City of Jerusalem during the Six-Day War. There is nothing stronger than the brotherhood-in-arms of those who shared the reprisal operations in the 1950s, the parachuting at the Mitleh, and other legendary ops, and Raful said: "Micha's son is an SPH driver in the 405th, take him to see his son."

It was a request, not an order, yet in the turmoil of battle, I made the time and took Caposta to see his son, who was deployed in a direct fire mission at a forward position. Explosions sounded all around, and he didn't bat an eyelid, but when I pulled the son out of the driver's cabin and the two tough men hugged, it was a moving moment. A generational meeting of warriors.

What Now?

We thought that the battle was over on August 31st, when Yasser Arafat, along with a large host of delinquents deserted Lebanon and "their people." They wandered to Tunis, to keep declaring from there that "We'll return to Yafa and Haifa yet," while their brethren languished in refugee camps, precluded from emerging from refugee status and integrating in the countries where they had been living for decades, as members of other nationalities had done.

I felt that our part in the victory had been significant – much outweighing our share of the troop count – and that the artillery, by its own force and its personnel's initiative, had justly earned the title of "queen of the battlefield."

I could have breathed a sigh of relief, but then the same thing happened that always does after I successfully complete a mission: What now?

It quickly turned out that the battle wasn't over, and the Sabra and Shatila affair occurred – the ugly, problematic affair, which clouded the results of the war and was inflamed politically, serving as a hatchet against Begin, Sharon, and Raful.

My political inclinations are known, and I've stated them here as well. Our home was always a Labor household, and ever since I can remember myself as a child, "Davar," the labor movement's main newspaper, would be stuck in the blinds of my bedroom window. Despite this, I completely dispute the prevailing view, fostered by the left's domination of the main media organs of the time, which besmirched the war and the men who oversaw it, and disregarded its achievements. For how is the success of wars measured? By the number of years their results hold up. In this case, until 2006. Twenty-four years.

I can hear the reader protesting: "But Israel got stuck in Lebanon for eighteen years, until Ehud Barak dared take the IDF out of that quicksand in the year 2000, and those years cost the lives of hundreds of soldiers." True, the entanglement in Lebanon should have ended far sooner, but as I wrote above, neither Begin, nor Sharon, nor Raful are to blame for us getting stuck there, but rather their successors in the Likud leadership and in the Chief of Staff's chambers.

SABRA AND SHATILA:
THE DISGRACE AND THE BANDWAGON

In the three years preceding the Peace for Galilee War, the ties between us and Lebanon's Christians strengthened greatly, and mostly with Bashir Gemayel's Falange forces. I vividly recall the moment Gemayel was elected President: the Mossad had done painstaking work in gathering all his supporters for the crucial vote in the Lebanese parliament, in reversing the position of opponents through various means, and in preventing steadfast opponents from attending.

During a posting meeting at the Chief of Staff's chambers, which I attended regarding an assignment in the corps, Military Intelligence Director Yehoshua Sagi relayed the good news that Bashir had been elected, immediately followed by a phone call from Gemayel himself to Raful, thanking him for the support, and Raful wished him luck.

Despite all this, Gemayel had played a double game during the war. He refused to truly take part in the battles and bleed his men for the sake of "Liban al-Hur" – Free Lebanon – preferring to have IDF soldiers risk their lives. He explained it by wanting to be president of all of Lebanon and be part of the Arab world, and therefore he must not openly take part in the IDF's war against the terrorists and the Syrians.

Our anger kept growing, and at every hearing, discussion, or command group, wonder and disappointment were voiced at the conduct of those whom we had come to, in order to help free their country from the yoke of the terror groups.

On August 23rd, Bashir Gemayel was elected President of Lebanon "on the Israeli army's bayonets," and eight days later, Yasser Arafat went into exile, leaving behind a Lebanon in ruins and masses of deserted Palestinian refugees. "Only you can save us," refugee women in the camps told us. "The Arab leaders are liars, and our leaders are rats. Only you can."

True to his devious ways, Arafat left hundreds of terrorists in Lebanon, in all the key points in the destroyed city and the refugee camps, "to fight to the last drop of blood." Three weeks later, on September 14th, Bashir Gemayel was assassinated by a "Greater Syria" adherent, and the horrible events at the Sabra and Shatila refugee camps took place between the 16th and 18th of September.

The truth must be told: none of us, the senior commanders, ever raised concerns of vengeance by the Falange fighters against their hated enemies, the Palestinians. Anyone claiming to have spoken of such may have done so in hindsight, spoken to themselves, or said their piece in the quiet channels of the military intelligence and the Mossad. No one explicitly laid such a scenario on the decision-makers' desk.

The analysis of the Christians' capabilities and the forecast for their behavior, which were the responsibility of the Mossad and the MID, failed miserably. Even Mossad honchos Nachik Navot, Yair Ravitz, and Shmulik Evyatar, who may have voiced concerns, voiced them whisperingly in the critical hours – and out loud only after the fact.

Even on the day of the massacre, when Amos Gilad, then a young major, who was the MID representative in Amos Yaron's command post, said clearly: "There's a massacre going on," no one listened to him. He turned directly to the chief of the MID, but Moshe Hevroni, the chief's chief of staff, told him: "The chief of the MID is sleeping." Gilad persisted, relayed the news along the staff-ops channels, and was reprimanded in the morning by the Chief of the MID for relaying reports on the staff-ops network.

The 96th Division, under the command of Yaron, oversaw the capturing of Beirut, and the Falange, operating under the 96th, were sent to capture the Sabra and Shatila refugee camps. The division's command post set up at a point controlling both camps, and Amos Yaron described it in his words, in his book "Ruach Hamefaked" ("Commander's Spirit[35]): "By evening I had settled in a command post erect-

---

[35] Yaron, Amos: "Ruach Hamefaked;" Yediot Books Press, Rishon LeZion 2022, pp 122-125

ed on a rooftop overlooking Sabra and Shatila. Several hundred meters away, I could almost see the camps with a naked eye."

Employing the Falange at this stage had two motives: The one, our desire to have the Christians actually fight, and the second, the sense that the war had ended in victory with Arafat chased away, and now it was a Lebanese problem.

We were the controlling force on the ground, but this statement must be qualified in light of an incredible confluence of circumstances: The IDF was battle-weary, having seen the end of the war and celebrated its victory, a failure by the Mossad and the MID, and an insensate commander on the ground, the division commander. Yaron placed his trust in Elie Hobeika, the commander of the forces that entered the camps, and also wanted, as we all did, to see the Christians finally fighting, particularly since our own fighters were exhausted, and we feared additional casualties a moment before declaring victory and going home.

Yaron himself admitted as much at a senior command conference in late 1982. Unwittingly, and out of naivete, he placed the blame on the IDF's shoulders. The moment he said at the conference, "We didn't see," "We didn't think it would happen," "We're responsible," Sharon realized with his keen political instincts that the political echelon was getting off free.

Yaron volunteered to carry the blame on behalf of the IDF, with the naivete and integrity of a warrior reared on telling the truth – and paid the price. But Sharon didn't forget it, and gave him full backing later on in life – when Yaron served as Defense Ministry Director during Sharon's term as prime minister.

Hobeika, the senior Falange commander who was a covert Syrian agent acting on Assad's orders, one of whose own men carried out Bashir's assassination – he of all men was next to Yaron in the command post. He asked for artillery lights and bulldozers, so as to let as few of the camp residents as possible – women, children, elderly – flee the butcher's knife.

Amnon Ben-Yair, Arnon Ben-Ami's staff-ops officer, and now a reserve division artillery commander, was present. Prior to Ben-Ami leaving for Israel, to be awarded the rank of colonel at the Chief of

Staff's chambers, he ordered Ben-Yair not to fire illumination in support of the Falange except by his direct order, and with him present.

Several days before, a paratrooper had been killed by an illumination ogive, which kept on flying and hit our forces encircling the enemy on the other side. Ben-Yair obeyed Ben-Ami and didn't fire any illumination, but the Air Force picked up the task, providing the Falange with light to continue their heinous deeds.

ALWAYS SPEAK YOUR MIND

The events of Sabra and Shatila opened a pandora's box and got a snowball rolling, which grew and grew until the Kahan Commission, the firing of Sharon, the end of Raful's term, the deposition of the Chief of the MID, and the removal of Amos Yaron from any command post. But the affair gathered immense political momentum far beyond that. Senior media figures, who never got over Labor's 1977 electoral defeat, joined with the left-wing parties in order to remove the Likud from power, and thus the Peace for Galilee War, which had ended in a clear-cut IDF victory, which had achieved its objective in the last major war in our area, became a scapegoat and has been etched in the nation's memory as a shameful debacle.

Amram Mitzna didn't take part in that senior command conference, but his resignation pending the defense minister's departure became the left's banner. Mitzna, by the way, only threatened and didn't resign. He remained in uniform to receive the rank of major general, despite the fact that Sharon had not been deposed yet.

Yanush joined in on the "mutineering" and asked us to speak out against Sharon, because he already knew that he wouldn't be appointed Chief of Staff. I acceded to his request and spoke, and to this day, I regret the nonsense I blurted out there. Deep down, I didn't believe there was cause to blame Sharon for the events of Sabra and Shatila, or for deceiving Begin and the government. We were all party to the war, and the bottom line is that we won it. It should be noted that before the end, Yanush also came out in Sharon's defense, and like me, regretted his stance.

Always speak your mind. I learned that lesson then, and I carry it to this day. I'm sorry that I never got to tell Arik Sharon that I view the Peace for Galilee War as a great victory, and credit it to his foresight, stemming from his desire to cement the State of Israel as the Jewish People's nation-state for thousands of years.

ENTERING BEIRUT: THUNDER SUDDENLY ROLLING FROM ALL DIRECTIONS

Upon delivery of the order you suddenly hear rolling thunder, coming from every direction conceivable. A boom and another boom and another. These are joined by echoes caused by the city's topography. The rocket battalions' fire whistles by. A magnificent sight.

Suddenly Raful emerges from the briefing room and asks: What's going on? We calmed him down, and told him it was just our preparatory artillery fire.

So wrote Amnon Ben-Yair, staff-ops officer of the artillery support HQ at the 96th Division, in the book "Totchanim BeShele"g" (pp 460,) describing the events on the eve of our entrance into Beirut, on September 15th, following the murder of Bashir Gemayel.

This monstrous fire concentration, of 24 artillery battalions, was employed with a single command by Arnon Ben-Ami, the division's artillery commander. Ben-Ami, a fighter who always ran toward the fire, and received a commendation for the manner in which he employed fire in impossible situations in the Yom Kippur War, was entrusted both with planning the preliminary artillery strike, and with planning the fire accompanying the four brigades that entered Beirut under a canopy of fire. Herschko (Yitzhak Ben-Zvi) and Herzl Gedj were there too, and everything was operated and employed by Ben-Ami in the most professional, cool-headed, and efficient manner possible.

For nearly ten years, we had eaten, breathed, and practiced it. The technique was clear and familiar. Even in practice, the command was required to improvise how to employ artillery in all sorts of situations not previously practiced, such as coordinating fire for four brigades maneuvering at once. Now we reaped the fruit of our efforts. A perfect execution of artillery preparation and a fire plan never attempted by the IDF before, with optimal use of all the cutting-edge means at our disposal.

It is important to me to note that the firefight at the entrance to Beirut was conducted without my intervention. Everything ran smoothly, worked like a well-oiled machine, and fell into place perfectly – and all this illustrated the greatness of the Artillery Corps. The training and proficiency manifested perfectly in the test. If early in the war, I still had to intervene and dictate moves and combat tactics; at the entrance to Beirut, all was done by the excellent men on the ground.

Most of the commanders distinguished themselves in the battle. All the division artillery commanders and their deputies, who controlled the deployment space, the bat-coms and most officers beneath them – almost all performed effectively. There were a handful of mishaps, which I mentioned, but on the other hand there are far more positive examples, such as that of Ran Cohen. Ran, a dyed-in-the-wool leftist from Kibbutz Gan Shmuel, a Knesset Member, a minister, and a former leader of left-wing parties Mapam and Meretz, didn't hesitate for a moment when the time came, and as deputy commander of the 96th Division's artillery unit, he even asked me, ahead of entering Beirut, for a few artillery units, to concentrate fire on a village deserted by its residents and turned into a terror base.

He got his wish, and Cohen, an early leader of Peace Now, employed fire concentration with full force, and excelled at his duties as a fighter and commander.

Other examples were provided by Uppo (Eli Barak) and Uri Manos – two fighters who would have failed a test of eloquence, but in battle, with many heroes of the tongue and the keyboard losing their wits, they were a solid rock. Neither Uppo, the main factor in the employment of the 162nd Division, along with division intel officer Doron Tamir, who were dominant in more than employing fire, nor Manos, who acted according to professional considerations independently, without waiting for orders from the Command General, enjoyed a sympathetic reception when appointed.

It got to the point where Amir Drori tried at the beginning of the war to replace Manos with Shmulik Reshef, who was without a posting. This attempted deposition was met with a furious response from me, Drori never mentioned the matter again, and I imagine he too was grateful for it by the war's end. Manos, with his focused and matter-of-fact approach, and his devotion to duty, didn't even notice what was going on behind his back. Most of the young officers, except the artillery commander of the 399th Brigade which got stuck at Sultan Yacoub, performed well, showed initiative, and reaped success.

Briefing commanders before entering Beirut.

RUMINATIONS ON THE PEACE FOR GALILEE WAR

The First Great Fire Concentration – in the Last Great War

The Peace for Galilee War was Israel's last major war. I reemphasize that we won a decisive victory in that war, and achieved the objectives set to us by the government: To expel the PLO from Lebanon, and to remove the threat of a Palestinian terror state north of Israel.

This war also saw the last major tank battle in IDF history, when the 446th Corps – with two divisions and other forces – defeated the Syrian 3rd Division, forced it to retreat to the Beirut-Damascus, and in effect took it out of combat. This was the first time that the IDF employed a massive fire concentration of eighteen and a half artillery battalions.

The war also ended in victory in the sense that no war broke out in the North for 24 years – until the Second Lebanon War. Complete quiet also reigned on the Syrian front – both in the Golan Heights and in Lebanon.

How, Who, and Why the Success Turned to Failure

Three failures clouded the success of the war. The first was the operational failure at Sultan Yacoub, which became etched in collective memory mostly due to the captives and missing from the battle, whose memory has stayed with us long after the war.

The second cloud was the intelligence and command failure in the Sabra and Shatila affair. It was for good reason that the Kahan Commission harshly criticized both the top echelon – Prime Minister Begin, Defense Minister Sharon, MID Chief Yehoshua Sagi,

Mossad Chief Nachum Admoni, and even Foreign Affairs Minister Yitzhak Shamir – and the commanders in the field. Raful was nearing the completion of his fifth year as Chief of Staff, and only due to that was he unharmed by the inquiry commission's recommendations, and ended his term on schedule.

As I wrote, the desperate attempt by the political left to regain power at all costs, even that of harming the IDF, adversely affected the manner in which the Peace for Galilee War was cemented in Israel's history – including the fact that it is mostly referred to nowadays as the First Lebanon War, and not Peace for Galilee as it deserves. The same people also damaged the understanding of the necessity of launching the war – and worse: damaged the fighters and the memory of the fallen.

This cannot be accepted and excused by "that's politics." The very soul of Israel was harmed by a localized failure becoming the be-all and end-all, tarnishing a resounding victory as a terrible failure.

The third cloud was the decision to remain in Lebanon, a miserable decision inspired by Moshe Arens, appointed as defense minister following Sharon's removal, and Prime Minister Shamir, who succeeded Begin after the latter resigned due to exhaustion from the demands of office, and after them due to indecision by Defense Minister Rabin, who because of the incessant operations in Lebanon, like a non-stop war, became convinced that security must come first. His confidante Shimon Sheves even boasted to me that Rabin was familiar, in minute detail, with every IDF outpost, route, and commander in Lebanon.

Raful told me in plain language in early 1983, during a personal conversation in Lebanon, "Next winter we're not here. We have no business here." I can't personally vouch for such a statement by Arik Sharon, but according to Raful, he held the same position.

Eighteen bloody years passed until Ehud Barak promised it in the elections, defeated Netanyahu, and finally removed the IDF from Lebanon, in May of 2000.

However, it should be reminded that Barak joined those maliciously slandering the Peace for Galilee War, in order to magnify the achievement of leaving Lebanon. He declared that the Peace for Galilee War is what led to the creation of Hezbollah, although the truth is as far from that as could be. Studies prove that Hezbollah was established in 1979 by the Ayatollah regime, which adopted a strategy of exporting the Islamic revolution around the world, starting with Muslim countries and prioritizing those with significant Shi'ite populations, such as Iraq and Lebanon. Dr (Brig-Gen.) Shimon Shapira proves it with research in his book "Hezbollah: Between Iran and Lebanon."[36]

A Year Off for Reservists

I tried as much as possible to ease the burden of the reservists, who had done a wonderful job in the war, and not to call them up for operational service in Lebanon. Such service means leaving the family, work, studies, and everything that constitutes a normal life. Worse: it means danger to life and limb. Unlike other commanders who were eager to pile up "properties," meaning as many units under their command as possible, even without any real need, I viewed such hoarding as foolish.

Thus, for example, I managed to thwart a Northern Command decision to leave a reserve 160mm mortar battalion at Jabel Baruch, because their presence there produced no operational benefit, both due to their short range, 9.5 km, and because there was no threat on the horizon.

My influence at the Staff-Ops Division was great, and the saying "The CAO does as he pleases" was prevalent among the various theater commanders – those majors and lieutenant colonels who, like in any organization, set the tone more than the brass. And indeed, up until the time I finished my term and left the IDF, in August 1983, the Artillery Corps did not perform reserve operational duties. Only after-

---

36 Shapira, Shimon, Hezbollah: Between Iran and Lebanon, (Tel Aviv, 2021)

ward did the corps' reserve units begin to be called up for infantry duties in Judea and Samaria.

How to Prepare for the Next War

The Artillery Corps proved its diverse abilities in the Peace for Galilee War, and the tremendous force of land-based firepower. Our artillery made it easier for the maneuvering forces to complete their missions, and the fire units did not wait for requests. They were involved in the battles and fired even before the maneuvering forces realized they needed the support.

We carried out long-range independent missions, such as destroying surface-to-air missiles, as well as missions using direct fire at very short ranges – not only in support to the forces maneuvering in urban environments, but also in independent missions with which we were tasked. The full integration with intelligence units of all sorts, particularly in the battle for Beirut, and the ability to overcome the inherent aversion of intel personnel to cooperation of any sort, caused them to start viewing the gunners as brothers-in-arms, and to understand that they must join hands with us, beyond simply providing intelligence to the commander.

To the best of my knowledge and understanding, the efficient and productive combination between intelligence of all sorts, maneuvering forces, and land-based firepower, which includes control and coordination of air power – a combination that materialized in the Peace for Galilee War, particularly the Beirut firestorm – laid a solid foundation for the construction of the force and the formulation of a uniform IDF fighting doctrine.

The necessity of a powerful artillery force, proven in the Yom Kippur War, gave birth to the monumental growth in the ground forces' firepower – both quantitively and qualitatively. It was realized during the terms of Motta Gur and Raful as Chiefs of Staff, and turned out to be a force multiplier.

The Israeli Air Force is a glorious corps, and will always be the linchpin of Israel's security. There is a good reason for the vast budgets it receives, and its abilities are indeed wondrous. It operates every day and every hour, far from Israel's borders, keeping the skies above us clean, operating the Iron Dome, and neutralizing threats.

In the foreseeable array of threats, the Air Force is and will be employed as a strategic arm. Along with the Navy, both constitute a strategic arm in the deterrent aspect as well, and beyond this the Air Force will have to protect the civilian population from a threat understood only by a precious few – the threat of thousands of precise missiles and rockets, which may completely shut down life in the country.

The next major war, should it break out, will be Armageddon according to the worst forecasts, and as we mark the 50th anniversary of the Yom Kippur War, this horrific scenario must obviously be accounted for.

The Air Force will have many tasks in such a scenario, and it is doubtful whether the order of priorities will allow it to take part in the ground war. Thus, the IDF, which is mainly a land-based military, has no alternative to strengthening and enlarging the ground forces, and particularly the ground-based firepower – both in terms of force building, and in terms of uniformity of command.

There is an old book named "Popski's Private Army," which tells of a British recon unit in the Western Desert in WW2. The author, who calls himself "Popski" despite actually being named Vladimir Peniakoff, describes a visit he paid to his friend, a captain at the British forces' HQ in Cairo, prior to General Montgomery being appointed to command the allied forces in the Western Desert. He was surprised to see his friend bearing the insignia of a colonel, with a driver driving him in a brand new car to lunch at the officers' club in one of Cairo's fanciest hotels. When he wondered how the promotion came about, his friend told him how he used to share a desk at the HQ with another captain, and as he was not too busy with his work, he found time to send a meaningless memo to all staff officers, and received a deluge of responses.

The contents of the letter and the responses matter not, but the documents piled up on the friend's desk and began sliding off, and a colonel seeing the overflowing desk believed Popski's friend to be overwhelmed by work, so he promoted him to major, and gave him two captains to assist him.

The major saw that his trick worked, and repeated it. A general passed by, saw an entire department overworked, promoted its commander to colonel, gave him a few lieutenant colonels as aides, and assigned this massive entourage a separate wing – and that's how the captain became a full bird colonel, with all the perks and benefits. Until Monty came along and burst the bubble, fired people left and right, forced everyone who'd survived the purge to attend exercise hour at dawn, and sent everyone he possibly could to the combat units.

I have no doubt that the IDF's Montgomery will appear one day, and that change will come, if only because of what we learned in the flesh when the IDF became an empire in too many minds, became fat and bloated following the Six-Day War, and came to its senses in the Yom Kippur War. But even without a Montgomery, there must be fresh new thinking about the structure of the IDF, in order to drastically reduce the HQs, cut out the fatty tissue, and strengthen the muscles – the fighting units.

In light of the growing threats, and the fact that our Air Force, the best and most efficient in the world, will be forced to devote the majority of its efforts to missions critical to Israel's defense, there is no choice but to significantly increase the ground-based firepower, and essentially the Artillery Corps.

Even today, the barrel component of the corps is only some 40% of the troop count. A significant increase of counter-weapon systems, such as precision rockets, long-range rockets, and assault drones, will provide a proper response to the challenges which the IDF will face in a future Armageddon – and not only in extreme scenarios.

At the same time, we must not neglect the barrel-based component: In combat scenarios against an enemy hiding in an urban environment, where the use of precision guided weaponry is inefficient, only massive fire from artillery barrels can silence an enemy, destroy it, and decide the battle.

THE "IRON SWORDS," OR "OCTOBER 7TH" WAR

October 8, text from Arie Mizrachi to the bat-com of the 405th, Eitan Gillis

"Good week, Eitan,

This is your war now. I suggest you refresh direct fire, take out the telescopes, direct fire at a range of 3200, and practice, just in any case, from position defense to urban combat in Gaza, when all other options are exhausted.

Also – battalion-wide barrage.

Good fortune in battle,

Arie

October 9th, text from Eitan Gillis to Arie Mizrachi

"Dear Arie,

Indeed, it is a great privilege, and great responsibility, to command the 405th in battle. We have already commenced operations in accordance with the battalion's spirit, tradition, and legacy.

We reported without being called, took trailers not our own to arrive, and where there were no trailers, we came on tracks.

You should know that in many decisions I've made, I asked myself "What would Arie do?"

See you after the war and we'll report a victory!"

Since the outbreak of the October 7th War, I've been touring the units, imparting my experience, and answering pointed questions.

The most common question is what the difference is between the surprise of Yom Kippur, on October 6th, 1973, and the surprise of October 7th, 2023. Fifty years have gone by, and again we are caught by surprise.

The main difference is that on Saturday, October 7th, 2023, 872 civilians were murdered, 253 were kidnapped and taken hostage. Entire settlements, kibbutzim, moshavim, and towns were invaded, set on fire, and parts of them utterly destroyed. Hamas personnel did as they pleased in Israeli territory, murdering, raping, pillaging, and burning throughout that Saturday.

On October 6th, 1973, in the Golan Heights, the standing army fought fiercely, was on top alert, and many infantry fighters, armored crews, gunners, and pilots fell in defense of their homes.

The Syrians never crossed the River Jordan and no Israeli civilian or settlement was hurt.

The standing army fulfilled its purpose while sustaining horrific losses, preventing the enemy from reaching the locales of the Galilee and the Jordan Valley.

In the Swords of Iron War, we are fighting against a Hamas entity ruling in Gaza following democratic elections since 2006, which at the start of the war had a trained, organized, standing military force of 40,000 fighters, with advanced arms and the ability to produce rockets and munitions in the Gaza Strip. Furthermore, for almost two decades, Hamas has built a fully-fledged underground city, with tunnels stretching hundreds of kilometers long.

Hamas has a government with ministers and ministries which control Gaza fully, economically, educationally, and healthcare-wise. Hamas has full control of Gaza's economy, runs UNRWA, and receives donations and grants from around the world, mostly from Qatar.

Throughout its reign, Hamas has employed significant rocket terror against the State of Israel, occasionally causing casualties which have halted everyday life in the Gaza border area, and hitting the center of the country as well.

Hamas employed indoctrination which guides the education and consciousness of Gaza residents toward a single purpose: The destruction of Israel and establishment of a Palestinian state "from the river to the sea."

To achieve this vision, all means are acceptable.

And indeed, on October 7th, 2023, Hamas embarked on a spree of terror, murder, and rape, with 3,500 of its elite Nukhba troops crossing into Israel at dawn on a rampage of slaughter, destruction, violation, humiliation, and kidnapping. The operation was of a fanatical religious movement, akin to Al-Qaeda and ISIS.

Following these came masses of Gazan civilians, seeking to pillage, abduct, and sexually abuse the defenseless Israelis.

Israel's government decided to launch a widespread operation to eliminate Hamas and its military capabilities.

The IDF acted at first with firepower alone, and on the night of October 26th and the morning of the 27th, embarked on a broad campaign to conquer and destroy Hamas, which continues as of the time of this writing, in late March 2024.

Once again, the Artillery Corps won the esteem of all Israeli citizens, writing its name in the IDF's hall of fame. The corps employed all of its arrays, from a rolling barrage blazing the way for the maneuvering forces, through the drone array – the Zik, the Sky Rider and the Sky Galloper, the rocket arrays, and the coordination of all fire, for land and air alike, by the fire arrays in the maneuvering brigades and assault teams at the maneuvering battalion level, to direct fire.

Almost each and every M-109 SPH – the old and trusty warhorse – fired some 1,000 shells with almost no mishaps, at all ranges.

The corps' Zik unit (aka Unit 5252) was the first to destroy some 250 Hamas terrorists on the morning of October 7th, until the drone missiles ran out.

Combat tactics practiced well and long prior to the war, such as rolling barrages, mass artillery concentrations, direct fire, and "fire on our forces" were employed with great success.

The Air Force, which had adapted to cooperation with the ground forces and optimal management of the Artillery Corps' assault teams, acted for the first time with maximal efficiency and flexibility to destroy targets in tandem with the maneuvering forces.

In this book, written in August 2022 and published in July of 2023, I wrote the lesson of the Yom Kippur War surprise (pp. 115 above):

"This lesson is true today as well: We must not be complacent. We must eradicate any sign of petrification, and lance every boil, significantly cut back on headquarters, and direct the lion's share of the resources to strengthening the executing arms. They are the ones who should receive the most attention and resources – not only in lip service, but in actual practice, in budgets and quality personnel."

And to end on a personal note – two of my grandchildren are currently serving in the IDF: My granddaughter Noa is a gunnery instructor who instructed the Artillery Corps' units fighting in Gaza, and Itay is a border patrol fighter in the friction and terror zones surrounding Jerusalem.

The legacy of defending and protecting the People of Israel in the Land of Israel continues to this very day.

GLOSSARY

Artillery – A French term adopted worldwide, as a catch-all for cannons, mortars, rockets, and the systems, aides, and headquarters related to their employment. The corps that operates the artillery and is responsible for the IDF's firepower is the Artillery Corps, which unlike in the past is a sophisticated, highly technological corps, which in addition to cannons and mortars also operates rocket launchers, assault and observation drones, and confidential arrays. In battle, the corps operates through two arrays:

The forward echelon, the first array based upon battlefield geometry, is in the front with the armor and infantry troops, ranging and directing the weapons and employing them as per the needs of the charging forces, to allow them to carry out their missions and minimize the number of casualties. The firing echelon, which is the second array and where the weapons are, and which is usually located at a distance from the front battle line, operating against targets at ranges varying from contact distance to hundreds of kilometers. The Artillery Corps is composed of division artilleries. Each division artillery is composed of 4-6 battalions, as well as support units for surveying, locating targets, observations, and of course logistical units. An artillery battalion consists of three companies, which for many years were called "batteries" (the term used in the book.) Each battery, divided into two platoons, is composed of 4-6 cannons, mortars, rocket launchers, or missile launchers. As of 2022, artillery divisions became known as "fire brigades" and batteries as "companies."

CAO – Chief Artillery Officer, the commander of the corps, who is also defined as the Chief of Staff's firepower advisor. Until 1984, the CAO reported directly to the Chief of Staff, and enjoyed command and operational independence. The CAO consolidates the fighting doctrine, commands the corps' instruction base, is responsible for assigning and promoting the corps' officers, and recommends the appointment of colonels (in practice, CAOs appointed colonels with the Chief of Staff's concurrence.) Since 1984, the CAO reports to the CGF (Commander of Ground Forces.) The powers formerly held by the Chief of Staff are now held by the CGF, leading to a significant decrease in the status of the CAO, and his control of the corps depends on his strength of personality.

Division Artillery is equivalent to an armored or infantry brigade. Each division artillery is an organic component of an armored or infantry division.

Division Artillery Commander – holding the rank of colonel, commanding all the division's fire means, for coordination with its commanders and with the commanders of other forces to employ the fire. In combat, the deputy division artillery commander commands the firing echelon of the unit.

Battalion – an artillery battalion consists of three cannons, mortar, or rocket batteries. Until 1978, the bat-com, holding the rank of Lt. Col., functioned during combat as a brigade artillery commander (see term) and was part of the HQ of the brigade to which he was assigned, while the deputy bat-com commanded the firing units. Since the change, the artillery commander holds the rank of major, and is an integral part of the brigade.

Battery – equivalent to an armored or infantry company, and divided into two platoons. Each battery had four cannons up until 1976, and six in the Peace for Galilee War.

Battery commander – equivalent to an armored or infantry company commander. Until 1978, during combat, the battery commander would become an FSO (see term).

FDC – Battalion fire direction center, responsible for communications and for operating the battalion's batteries. Keeps in constant contact with the forward artillery echelon and the other assaulting forces.

Brigade artillery commander – Part of the brigade HQ, with the charging force in battle, coordinating the fire from the front line.

Command Post NCO – a member of the battery HQ crew, who operates the firing computer at the command post.

Command Artillery Commander – part of the regional command's professional staff. The title indicates the role: command of the regional command's division artillery and the one who in times of combat operates the division artilleries under purview of that command. Until the Yom Kippur War, this position carried the rank of Lt. Col, while the other division artillery commanders were colonels, which created a hierarchy problem. Today the post carries the rank of colonel, but the personality of the commander fashions the chain of command on a daily basis and in battle.

Aerial Observation Commander – An observation commander, who is an airborne artillery officer – in a light aircraft, a chopper, or a fighter plane. His duty is to observe targets from the air to locate enemies, and then to range and employ fire.

RSO – Reconnaissance and Survey Officer, conducts preliminary reconnaissance, determines the firing positions, and leads the battalion to them as a sort of battalion recon company. (A division artillery RSO surveys and prepares the unit's positions and leads the unit's battalions to them using the unit's recon company.)

XO – Artillery Post Officer, commanded the battery in battle until after the Yom Kippur War, after the battery commander pivoted to the FSO role.

FSO – Fire Support Officer, holding the rank of captain. Spends the battle next to the infantry or tank bat-com as part of the command group, observes the fire, directs the firing echelon, and employs all fire systems – from the ground, air, and sea. Today, he commands a team that also includes assault NCOs with the maneuvering companies.

ACO – Air Coordination Officer (Air Force term)

FO – Forward Observer Officer, usually a 2nd Lt., positioned on the front line with an infantry or tank company, observes and employs the fire. Today called an assault NCO.

Fire for Effect – After the ranging fire is done, the "real" fire is launched. This is the fire for effect, launched to destroy the target.

Ranging – A shell fired from a cannon flies high, passing through various atmospheric layers. To hit the target, one must make geometric calculations and account for the other factors affecting the flight of the projectile, such as weather, and the wind speed as well as its direction. The forward echelon observes where the ranging shell fell, passes on a correction through the radio network (for example: right 100, add 400.) The battery re-calculates, and the cannon fires again and re-shoots. This is continued until the observer determines the rounds will have devastating effects on the target and orders "Fire for Effect."

Deployment – The positioning of cannons and preparing for firing. The traditional deployment of a single battery used to spread out over an area of about 100 sq. meters, and was designed to hit targets according to the deployment. As CAO, I shifted to deployment by terrain, over as much as 500 sq. meters, with each cannon surveyed and receiving firing data individually from the firing computer. Such deployment increases the battery's survivability, gives the crew leaders more independence, and improves accuracy.

Missile – A canister of explosives with a warhead that homes in on the target through one of several methods – a laser beam, electro-optic matching, GPS, and others. A precise, expensive weapon.

Shell – a steel canister filled with explosives, weighing from 43 to 99 kg.

Katyusha – 122mm-240mm caliber rockets, fired in a barrage from a launcher with varying numbers of launch rails.

Rocket – A metal canister ranging from 122-290 mm, fired from a launcher at a distance of up to 40 km. The rocket is propelled in flight by an internal combustion engine. As it does not pass through a barrel when launched, it contains more explosives but is less accurate.

Propellant – gunpowder placed in the cannon's breech behind the shells. The amount of explosives depends on the range. When the cannon is fired, the blasting explosives turn from solid to gas. The extreme heat caused by the process creates an explosion, which launches the shell from the cannon.

Explosives – the material within the shells, designed to blow them up. After the shell is inserted in the barrel and the charge of propellant is inserted, the anvil of the cannon is locked, and a firing mechanism is placed in the center, which contains a blank projectile. The blank ejects a jet of fire into the propellant, igniting them. The explosive material ejects the shell from the barrel, sending it in a trajectory at the target. The firing of a cannon is done by a cable pulled by the gunner.

Artillery chaff – A shell containing metal strips, intended to imitate our aircraft and mislead the enemy's radar.

Cluster bomb – a shell or rocket with a load of bomblets, which opens in the air, spraying the bomblets on and around the target.

High explosive – a shell full of explosives, which explodes upon impact. The shrapnel from the shell increases the damage.

Air-burst explosives – A shell meant to explode above the target. The shrapnel from the shell harms mostly exposed targets

Phosphorous shell – contains phosphorous material, which ignites upon contact with oxygen. Causes severe burns as well as an instant smokescreen.

Smoke shell – Contains compartments that emit smoke for screening.

Illumination bomb – Contains a light fixture that opens over the target, descends slowly by parachute, illuminating the battlefield.

Ogive – The canister containing the smoke boxes or the light fixtures in smoke or illumination shells, which continues flying after releasing the load.

Bomblet – A grenade filled with explosives, designed to pierce armor or to explode on impact.

David – A firing computer manufactured by Rafael Advanced Defense Systems, the first used on all cannons, which in fact computerized and streamlined the corps significantly in the PFG War, compared to the corps in the Yom Kippur War.

Front bucket and back bucket – The surveyed spaces in the same survey grid in the deployment space (back bucket) and in the target space (front bucket.)

M-548 / Alpha – A tracked and armored ammunitions carrier designed to carry artillery munitions.

Direct fire – Telescope-aided fire to a range of up to 3,200 meters. Originally intended for position defense, and developed during the PFG War into a major component of urban combat.

Lahatutar / "Juggler" – a British-made Cymbeline radar, which tracks the trajectory of mortar bombs in order to locate and range the enemy.

Position-controlled – A method of deploying batteries, in which the cannons are concealed behind a hill, a mountain, or some other topographical feature. The FDO observes the target from the top of the hill or mountain with a theodolite, and directs the cannons to destroy it.

M-577 – A closed and elevated APC, large enough to stand up in.

Firing computer – a computer especially planned and programmed for artillery purposes.

Laser range finder – A device that measures the distance (range) to the target using a laser beam. Also used to determine the location and direction of artillery positions prior to the GPS era.

Shovel – a sort of bulldozer's scoop, used to stabilize a self-propelled cannon from behind. The shovel aids the gun in overcoming the multi-ton recoil created when firing a shell.

Theodolite – An optical device that measures sight angles, in order to place several cannons in the exact same direction.

Flyer / "Meofef" – A ranging radar that operates on doppler, meaning based on echo reverberation, akin to the way bats navigate. Also enables the location of enemy artillery.

Fulton – a location device which deploys microphones in an area and identifies the location of enemy batteries by the sound of the exit fire.

Basic course – Corps specialization completion course for Artillery Corps cadets, following the completion of the basic officers' course at Bahad 1, at the end of which the graduates receive the rank of 2nd Lt.

Rampart – A dirt dyke that provides protection for the tanks and allows them to climb it in order to fire.

Shillem – A ranging radar manufactured by Elta, capable of ranging up to 70km.

Vulcan – A rapid 30mm caliber air defense cannon, mounted on an APC.

Tiger – the codename of the 405th Battalion's battery D. In the Yom Kippur War, it operated cutting-edge airborne 105mm cannons at a range of some twelve km.

M-50 – A French 155mm cannon, which the Ordnance Corps mounted on a Sherman tank chassis.

Lance – A precise American missile with a range of 70 km, with an inertial navigation system, relying on gyro (not GPS yet). The Lance missile was originally designed as a tactical nuclear missile. The IDF purchased it with a warhead of 623 bomblets.

Priest – A 105mm SPH on a Sherman chassis.

Ro'em – an Israeli-made 155mm SPH manufactured by Soltam, mounted on a Sherman Chassis and enclosed by a giant fighting chamber, looking like a house on tracks.

Cantine / "Shekem" – A battalion of 240mm rocket launchers, consisting of twelve trucks, carrying twelve launchers each, and firing 144 rockets per barrage.

FDO – Fire Direction Officer. Located at the battalion ops center and coordinates the battalion firepower.

THANKS

First and foremost, thanks to two women: Vered Belzieger and Orit Tatruashvili, who have traveled a long road with me, for many years. Vered, who was tasked with deciphering my handwriting, spent many a long night on prints and corrections, in a cross-continental effort. Orit, devoted and meticulous, who collated the material and passed it on to the editor at numerous meetings, even in the wee hours of the night. I love you both.

To Yehuda Ya'ari, my wise and patient editor, who helped me greatly.

To Eran Zmora, a brother-in-arms since the Valley of Tears.

To the experienced and practical Maya Lahat Kerman, and to Noam Bitton, who collated and prepared for print.

To all my friends and family, who read the manuscript and provided wise comments.

To Rechavia Berman, for his effort and perseverance in translating this book from Hebrew to English.

To the team at eBookPro: Benny Carmi, Naveh Carmi, Corrine Hadar, Oren Klass, and everyone else who helped make this book happen.

To Lt. Gen. (Ret.) Peter M. Vangjel – a warrior, commander, and friend. A very special thanks for your time and effort in editing our "gunner's language" into plain and practical English. The observations and notes you provided throughout this book come from many years of experience on the battlefield and in command of large units.

Printed by Amazon Italia Logistica S.r.l.
Torrazza Piemonte (TO), Italy